Great coffee, like great acting is an art. Our family has been perfecting the way we roast our coffee for over 50 years. We only work with the very best – which is why we only use 100% Arabica beans from all over the world and roast them right here in Australia for freshness. The result is acclaimed in the award winning restaurants and cafés that appreciate what it takes to be the best. Because they know that we know coffee.
Vittoria Coffee - our expertise is still a family tradition.
We know coffee
Vittoria
100% ARABICA
ESPRESSO
Coffee

THE AGE

good food Guide

Edited by Janne Apelgren

Fairfax Media

facebook.com/goodfoodguide

twitter.com/@goodfoodguide

33rd edition published by Fairfax Media, 2012

Fully revised and reset for this edition

1 Darling Island Road, Pyrmont NSW 2009

General manager, Food & Wine, Fairfax Media Lisa Hudson

Managing editor Ardyn Bernoth

Production editor Robyn Carter

Copy editors Simone Egger, Cathy Gowdie, Nina Rousseau

Production team Jenny Bowman, Tony Clayton, Yvonne Colley, Roslyn Grundy, Anne Rogan

Design Peter Schofield

Cover design Dean Hastie, John Shakespeare, Peter Schofield

Restaurant photography courtesy of restaurants and *The Age* Photo Library

Hat logo design David Band

Printed and bound in Australia by McPherson's Printing Group

Fairfax edition ISBN 978-1-921486-44-9

Trade edition ISBN 978-1-921486-46-3

CURIOUS WHO HAS THE BEST WINE LIST IN TOWN?
WE'RE A CURIOUS BUNCH
BROWN BROTHERS
MILAWA · AUSTRALIA
BROWN BROTHERS
CODA.
WINNER, BROWN BROTHERS WINE LIST OF THE YEAR, 2013.
Brown Brothers - Proudly supporting The Age Good Food Guide Awards.
brownbrothers.com.au

CONTENTS

萬壽宮

Flower Drum

17 MARKET LANE MELBOURNE 3000 VIC T: 9662 3655

www.flower-drum.com

INTRODUCTION

Pull a seat up at the bar, and take a sip of sake (or perhaps a natural riesling), as we explore the year in food. *The Age Good Food Guide* team dined at more than 600 restaurants, always anonymously as paying customers, to bring you this edition. We found more than 120 new places, and along the way, our reviewers discovered a lot about the way we like to eat now. Here's how we saw it.

- Gertrude Street became the food epicentre of Melbourne. The raffish route 86 has at least nine exciting *Guide* entries in a single kilometre.
- Rabbit, roo and wallaby started to appear, and appeal, more often on menus.
- The Mexican Revolution was a bit of a fizzer, but the Italian Renaissance ruled. The taco overtook the bun as the city's favourite hand-held. A bunch of lively new Mexicans opened and were as overstuffed as a Californian burrito. Though they saw off cheese-and-beans Mexican, only a few did justice to this vivid cuisine with its countless regional variations. Italian food, on the other hand, is currently stellar, thanks to a number of small, new, big-hearted spots like Lupino and Mister Bianco, who've raised the bar for other local Italians.
- Speaking of the bar, we got used to sitting at it. Heck, we even got to prefer it to sitting at tables, whether at stalwart Cumulus Inc, or Casa Ciuccio's smart 'kitchen table'.
- Dude food matured. Not quite the 'stoner share-house food' (thanks, Dani Valent) it once was, it grew into global street food as menus hopped from Korea to the Caribbean (Circa, The Smith).
- Everyone had a nip and tuck. Many places got smaller (Red Emperor, The Deck), had a makeover (David's), or altered their offerings for the times (Comme, No35).
- Placemat menus ruled. Pages of entrees, mains, desserts were dumped for single sheets that leapt from snazzy cocktails to feel-good desserts.
- The raw menu found itself a spot, too, with oysters, carpaccio and tartare given their own room.
- Anywhere you could fit a bit of dirt (goodbye to Attica's staff parking) a vegie or herb patch popped up. Some greenovers were state of the art (Vue de Monde, we're looking at you); some were as simple as taking recycling seriously.
- The hills are alive, and so are the valleys and beaches. Victoria's vigorous country restaurant scene saw bold openings (Kazuki), little neighbourhood places (Darmagi, Dee's) and revitalisation (Paringa) that delivered Victorians what's still Australia's best regional dining.

In a tough year, we saw some big gestures from Victorian restaurants and diners, such as supporting Unicef and Fairfax's Bread for Good campaign to fight famine in Africa. Thanks to the MoVida restaurants and their customers, who raised a Victorian record of $12,637, reminding us that while others go hungry, we're eating very well.

Janne Apelgren

Vittoria Coffee Restaurant of the Year

VUE DE MONDE CITY ▲

Vue de Monde is a grand vision, Shannon Bennett's tilt at building a masterpiece that combines sublime food, polished service and a stunning setting to deliver an experience that belongs firmly in its home town while reaching for global standards. It's pricey, sure, which means it won't be for everyone, and its booking policies can be prickly. But it's also unique, combining theatre and spectacle and occasion with a phenomenal attention to detail, from the list of rare teas to the bespoke cheese trolleys. And most appealingly, it's a lot of fun, too.

Regional Restaurant of the Year

◀ **PROVENANCE** BEECHWORTH

The room is on the austere side of elegant, the service can be countrified or cosmopolitan, but, oh, the food! Whether you choose to travel degustation or a la carte, Michael Ryan's innovative dishes are, quite simply, gorgeous. Japanese influences meld seamlessly with European. And the accommodation out the back is among Beechworth's best, making Provenance *the* dining destination of the abundant north-east.

Plumm Wine Glasses
Best New Restaurant

PEI MODERN CITY ▲

It may have been a newborn, but Pei Modern bistro arrived walking, talking and perfectly attired in March 2012. It revitalised an under-utilised spot in the forecourt of the partly I.M. Pei-designed Collins Place, gave chef Matt Germanchis an outlet, and his boss, star Sydney chef Mark Best, a southern bolthole. Add the terrific service team, cracking bar, and all-day trading and you wonder how Melbourne ever did without it.

Best New Regional Restaurant

GLADIOLI INVERLEIGH ▲

Chef Matt Dempsey is a bit of a local hero in the Geelong region. Having put Waurn Ponds on the map with his cooking at Pettavel, he's gone west to Inverleigh, with a new restaurant, Gladioli, showcasing his refined food in a weatherboard cottage. Take the 20-minute drive from Geelong and you'll discover it's not only an important new country restaurant, but a casual charmer.

Samsung Diners' Choice Award

EZARD CITY ▲

Teage Ezard's elegant basement bunker feels like a great spot for a foodie assignation, and users of *The Age Good Food Guide* app and website agree. It may be a city stalwart, but Ezard remains an innovator whose rusted-on signatures – oyster shooters and caramelised pork hock – have kept diners coming back for more since 1999.

Dan Murphy's
BYO Restaurant of the Year

LADRO GREVILLE PRAHRAN ▲

Apart from producing some of Melbourne's best pizza, Ladro Greville is BYO friendly, helping to make a night out more affordable. Even better, Monday night corkage is only $5, with proceeds to charity.

Citibank Chef of the Year

MICHAEL RYAN ▶

Michael Ryan has been knocking around the north-east for some time now, but whether he was cooking at someone else's place (Wardens), a restaurant within a motel (Range) or, since 2008, his own (Provenance), he's kept food critics swooning. Little did we know he was only warming up. Ryan's obsessive fascination with things Japanese now sees him deliver uniquely beautiful dishes that exhibit a mastery of flavour, whether he's treating zucchini (zucchini!) as a hero ingredient, dishing up Milawa duck or tossing chestnut fettuccine with burnt butter, hazelnuts and sage.

Chef's Hat Young Chef of the Year

◀ MARK BRIGGS

This young Briton came to Australia as a backpacker, worked on Heron Island, landed a job at Vue de Monde, then opened the Sharing House at South Wharf in 2012. The judges noted Briggs was 'in a league of his own'. He says, 'Ever since I was about 10 I always wanted to be a chef ... I just enjoyed cooking.' Melburnians are reaping the rewards.

Champagne Louis Roederer Sommelier of the Year

TRAVIS HOWE ▶

On the Coda website there's a cheeky note that states: 'Coda's wine list is not here – it's in the restaurant!' It sums up Howe brilliantly. No matter how good a list looks on paper, it must come alive in the restaurant. With ease and without affectation or arrogance, Howe guides, suggests and enthuses about wine but never dictates, dominates or demeans. He is the epitome of a modern Melbourne sommelier. And a perpetual smile suggests Howe digs his gig.

Donlevy Fitzpatrick Award

VERNON CHALKER ▲

Melbourne would be a poorer, less colourful place without the charming Mr Chalker. From Gin Palace and Collins Quarter to Madame Brussels and Bar Ampere, he's given the city a great dose of the unique and the idiosyncratic while keeping his immense sense of old-fashioned hospitality perfectly intact.

Vittoria Legend Award

ALLA WOLF-TASKER ▲

From a bare lakeside block Alla Wolf-Tasker built one of Australia's most beautiful boutique hotels centred on a restaurant that remains its beating heart. Staff she's mentored can be found around Australia. She's a tireless advocate for local tourism, farmers and hospitality. Oh, and she opened a second place, Wombat Hill House, turning a rundown cottage in Daylesford's Botanical Gardens into a charming cafe ... now she and other local dog walkers have somewhere to pause for coffee.

Thermomix Award for Innovation

JOOST BAKKER ▲

This Dutch-born tulip farmer has inspired a legion of diners, as well as chefs who came to buy his flowers and fell for his philosophies, too. Bakker dances across disciplines as a designer, artist and environmentalist. His Greenhouse restaurants (the first was built in Federation Square in 2008) have won global attention with their appealing sustainability, jam jar glasses, mulchable wooden cutlery and urine-recycling loos. Find his work in restaurants from Hare & Grace to Vue de Monde; his 'zero waste cafe', Silo, is in Hardware Lane.

Service Excellence Award

AINSLIE LUBBOCK

She writes a great wine list, has some of Victoria's best restaurants on her résumé (from Attica to the Royal Mail), and she's assembled a crack service team for her latest gig. At Pei Modern Ainslie Lubbock is a little bit sommelier, and all restaurant manager, performing both roles with appealing aplomb.

Sustainability Award

COLIN McLAREN, VILLA GUSTO

Colin McLaren and his team at this Buckland Valley boutique hotel and restaurant take sustainability seriously, from the sophisticated (grey-water systems, LED lighting) to the simple (permaculture fruit and vegie gardens and Isa Brown chooks, which devour 25 per cent of the restaurant's food waste).

Brown Brothers Wine List of the Year CODA CITY

Straightforward, simple and easy to read, Travis Howe's French-leaning list is offset by intriguing local wines and a decent smattering of Europeans. It's almost without headings – just 'sparkling', 'white' and 'red', really – mostly grouped by variety, palate weight and texture. Think aromatic riesling and chenin blanc or palate-thrilling fiano, sylvaner and verdicchio. There's a nod to Burgundy without over-inflated prices, plus savoury, spicy reds including blaufrankisch, grenache, tempranillo and sangiovese. All complement perfectly Coda's eclectic, often Asian-inspired contemporary menu. Half bottles feature, too – surely the best way to match and taste without waste.

Citibank Best Short Wine List CASA CIUCCIO FITZROY

There are fewer than 100 bottles, mostly under the $80 mark, all perfectly pitched to the share-friendly Mediterranean fare, on this list crafted by co-owner Simon Benjamin. Eclectic choices centre on boutique producers such as Mac Forbes from the Yarra Valley, and Wines by KT from South Australia. Savoury wines such as sangiovese, grenache, pinot noir, chardonnay and friulano star, and there's a thoughtful selection of delicious wines from Italy, Portugal and Spain. And Luke Lambert makes the Ciuccio blanco and tinto (sounds much better than house white and red).

Best Regional Wine List TEN MINUTES BY TRACTOR MAIN RIDGE

You'll find two lists here, one short and sweet, the other long and lovely. The former offers wines by the glass (including flights) and enticing half bottles. There are the tremendous Ten Minutes by Tractor wines – chardonnay, pinot gris, sauvignon blanc, rosé and pinot noir. Move on to half a dozen each of whites and reds with boutique options, such as biodynamic Lark Hill gruner veltliner or Mount Majura shiraz. As to the large list, it's impressive, if sometimes pricey, and bound to win over everyone from wine geeks to aficionados. It's a paean to Burgundy, the passion of owner Martin Spedding, but there's an extraordinary selection of Mornington Peninsula chardonnay and pinot noir, too.

Honorable Mentions

THE CRIMEAN NORTH MELBOURNE

Kekfrankos. Plavac mali. Krstac. It's not every day these hard-to-find grape varieties are highlighted on a small wine list. Sommelier Lazlo Evenhuis's appealing selections fit neatly with the Eastern European cuisine at the Crimean, where there's also a focus on smaller Victorian gems, like Hurley Vineyard pinot noir and Curly Flat chardonnay.

MERRICOTE NORTHCOTE

One of the smallest wine lists in town, but ever vibrant and charming. Bronwyn Kabboord adds new and disparate styles, grape varieties and vintages often, and keeps prices affordable. And sake is a recent addition.

MOVIDA AQUI CITY

This vinous pleasure cruise takes in one of the most comprehensive and slick selections of Spanish wine around, and starts with sherry. Much-loved varieties sit alongside highly regarded producers on the medium-sized list. In the mix, too, are wonderful Portuguese, Australian, French, Italian and Austrian wines. Liz Carey's list has something for everyone, and superbly matches MoVida's Iberian dishes. Brilliant.

SPICE TEMPLE SOUTHBANK

Now it's added some of the city's best yum cha to its repertoire, Spice Temple's wine list has been finetuned accordingly by David Lawler. Still fabulous, still capped at 100 wines and with an enterprising selection of aromatic whites and reds, it's not ridiculously priced, either.

City

🎩🎩🎩

Attica, Jacques Reymond, Vue de Monde

🎩🎩

Cafe Di Stasio, Cutler & Co, Ezard, Flower Drum, Matteo's, MoVida, The Press Club, Rockpool Bar & Grill, Stokehouse

🎩

Albert St Food & Wine, Bacash, Becco, Bistro Guillaume, Bistro Vue, Cecconi's Cantina, Church St Enoteca, Circa, Coda, Cumulus Inc, Dandelion, Donovans, Easy Tiger, Embrasse, Estelle Bar & Kitchen, European, Gills Diner, Golden Fields, The Grand, Grossi Florentino, Il Bacaro, The Italian, Kenzan, Koots Salle a Manger, Longrain, Maha, Mercer's, Moon Under Water, MoVida Aqui, Paladarr, Pei Modern, P M 24, The Point Albert Park, Sarti, Shoya, Spice Temple, Steer Bar & Grill, Tempura Hajime, Town Hall Hotel, Yu-u

Regional

🎩🎩🎩

Royal Mail Hotel

🎩🎩

Lake House, Loam, Provenance, Stefano's, Tea Rooms of Yarck, Ten Minutes by Tractor

🎩

A la Grecque, Annie Smithers' Bistrot, Bella Vedere, Chris's Restaurant, Eleonore's, Gladioli, La Petanque, The Long Table, Montalto, Neilsons, The River Grill, Scorched, Sunnybrae, Teller, Terminus at Flinders Hotel, Villa Gusto

STOP PRESS

Botanical, South Yarra. Chef Cheong Liew was handing over to long-time colleague Luke Brabin at Botanical as we went to press. Owners Colonial Leisure Group restated a commitment to quality dining at the popular local, announcing Brabin's promotion to executive chef.

Cafe Di Stasio, St Kilda. Ronnie Di Stasio was transforming a shop neighbouring his eponymous Fitzroy Street eatery into a new bar, dining space and grill, due to open in November 2012.

Coda 2, City. The sibling to Coda (unnamed when we signed off this edition) will have an Indian/Malay/Sri Lankan focus, and is just around the corner.

Cucina di Esposito, Carlton. Maurice Esposito turned Esposito @ Toofey's Italian, with a char-grill, handmade pasta, sustainable seafood, his mum's recipes and produce from his parents' garden.

David's, Prahran. David's was renovated, and introduced a new menu – rustic Shanghainese cuisine with an emphasis on shared bowls.

Enoteca Vino Bar, Carlton. The Enoteca Sileno dining space was being relaunched as a more casual eatery.

The Millswyn, South Yarra. The Millswyn was undergoing a quick nip and tuck, but promising to stay on the same elegant path, at press time.

Nama Nama, City. This casual Japanese eatery from Simon Denton takes the site of his previous fine-diner, Verge. There's a Japanese-inspired bar, Hihou, upstairs.

Neapoli, City. The City Wine Shop owners' new bar, cafe and wine store opened in Russell Place.

Orto, Hawthorn. The former Chester White was remodelled as a casual Italian trattoria by owner George Sykiotis, with chef Luigi Buono, formerly of Cafe Latte.

Rosetta, Southbank. Neil Perry's eighth restaurant was due to open at Crown in September 2012. At Crown's northern entrance, it's to be a rustic Italian eatery, with a wood-fired oven and rotisserie at its heart.

Sartago, Richmond. A little Mediterranean-flavoured local with a cafe/wine bar downstairs and an elegant restaurant up is the creation of chef-owner Riccardo Messora (Enoteca Sileno, Caffe e Cucina and Tutto Bene).

Trocadero, Southbank. As part of the Hamer Hall refurbishment, Comme and Stokehouse get a sibling, this modern Mediterranean bar and brasserie.

Virginia Plain, City. New to Flinders Lane, this bar/restaurant has an interesting team behind it, including a former Vue de Monde chef and sommelier.

Goodbye for now ...

The Argo, Archies on the Creek Dining Room, Balzari, Bruin, Chester White, Duck Duck Goose, The Grange Beaumaris, The Kitchen Cat, MoMo, Pandora's Box, Pearl, Star Anise, St Jude's, Verge

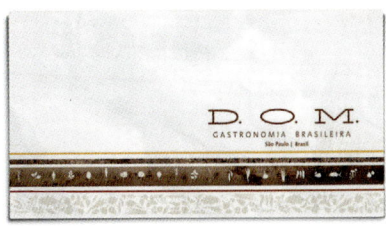

ALBERT ST FOOD & WINE

382 Sydney Road, Brunswick **8354 6600**

Handsome, accommodating, and tasty – what's not to like? Albert will cook you weekend breakfast, supply you with provisions and coffee, satiate you at lunch and dinner, and give you something good to go with a sneaky after-work wine. Good to see chef Philippa Sibley presiding over the all-day delicious menu. So, PS, don't skip dessert.

CASA CIUCCIO

15 Gertrude Street, Fitzroy **8488 8150**

Like bees to a honey pot, Melburnians have flocked to this Bar Lourinha sibling at the top end of Gertrude. Ciuccio (pronounced: choo-cho) has a buzzy, confident vibe and a share-friendly mod-Med menu. And if the words 'smoked coal-pit meats' set your heart aflutter, you've found your spot, at the shared 'chef's table'.

CIRCA

2 Acland Street, St Kilda **9536 1122**

Can a restaurant that's had more lives than a cat be new? Circa certainly feels that way. It's now overseen by Paul Wilson under new owners, same chef. Add a Scandi blondwood fitout, glimpses of St Kilda outside, and a ridiculously delicious cuisine-hopping 'Pacific rim' menu (Korean-inspired taco, for example).

ESTELLE BAR & KITCHEN

243 High Street, Northcote **9489 4609**

Some of the city's best palates (winemakers and chefs) became early adopters of Scott Pickett and Ryan Flaherty's idiosyncratic Northcote eatery, treating it as the dining room they'd have out back if they could. Tasting menus only, five to nine courses. Just do it.

LUPINO

41 Little Collins Street, City **9639 0333**

Got no nonna to call on when the urge for big-hearted Italian strikes? Here's your spot. Smart, simple, savvy, Lupino is the neighbourhood restaurant everyone deserves. It's in the CBD, so anyone in Zone 1 can claim it as their own.

MOON UNDER WATER

211 Gertrude Street, Fitzroy **9417 7700**

Andrew McConnell's bijou dining salon behind the Builders Arms is a tranquil white room that feels almost like it's from another era. The only offering is a four-course set menu, elegant and beautifully pared back, in a restaurant that breaks the McConnell no-bookings, share-plate, full day-and-night mould.

PEI MODERN

Collins Place, 45 Collins Street, City **9654 8545**

It's hard to believe there was ever anything else in the spot now occupied by star Sydney chef Mark Best's smooth all-day bistro, let alone a prosaic post office. Prop at the bar, drop in for breakfast, or come for the full three courses. Collins Place dining is once again fine.

THE SMITH

213 High Street, Prahran **9514 2444**

If your idea of eating out doesn't involve donning heels and a wee designer skirt (or the hipster boy equivalent) come at lunch 'cos the Smith's diners look like they've been sent by a casting agent. The global menu matches everyone's mood, or opt for *The Age Good Bar Guide*'s favourite cocktail, the Toorak Princess. Party time, excellent!

ABOUT THIS GUIDE

How we review
Every year we visit up to 600 restaurants for *The Age Good Food Guide*. Our team of more than 60 experienced reviewers always visit anonymously, and pay for their meals. Some restaurants are visited several times. The *Guide* accepts advertising, but this does not influence whether a restaurant is included. The editorial team's decisions are independent of commercial considerations.

New
This symbol denotes the restaurant is new to the *Guide* this year (not necessarily a new restaurant).

Opening hours
In most cases, we have listed the time the kitchen accepts last orders, rather than the restaurant's closing time.

Prices
Typical prices are listed for each course. Prices change frequently, so these are a guide only.

Rating the restaurants
Restaurants are given a score out of 20 and the best are awarded chefs' hats – from one to three. The scores are nominated by reviewers and finalised by the editor and editorial panel. The score comprises a maximum of 8 for food, 3 for wine and wine service, 4 for overall service, 3 for atmosphere, personality and comfort levels and 2 for value. If there is contention over the score, the restaurant is revisited. In finalising the score, we also consider whether the restaurant has achieved what it set out to achieve. Places that score 11 out of 20 or less are not included. The restaurants in the *Guide* are diverse, and those with a similar rating may be quite different in style. A score of 13 for a neighbourhood cafe is excellent but disappointing for a more ambitious and expensive place. In regional Victoria, places scoring below 14 are given a brief review.

Wheelchair friendly
Using information supplied by restaurants and reviewers, restaurants that offer both wheelchair access and disabled toilet facilities are listed on page 279.

Accuracy
This *Guide* undergoes a rigorous fact-checking procedure. However, we urge readers to be aware things can change after we go to press, and we apologise for any inconvenience this may cause.

Thank you
Our gratitude to Vittoria Coffee and Citibank, whose generous support ensures *The Age Good Food Guide* continues to be authoritative and independent.

Talk to us
We welcome your suggestions and feedback.

Email *goodfoodguide@theage.com.au*

Website *goodguides.com.au*

Facebook *facebook.com/goodfoodguide*

Twitter *@goodfoodguide*

Post PO Box 257, Melbourne VIC 3001

Scoring system

12 Reasonable

13 Solid and satisfactory

14 Good

15 Very good: consistently notable

16 Great: worth seeking out

17 Excellent: one of the best

18 Outstanding

19 Brilliant

20 The best of the best

Abbreviations

AE American Express

DC Diners Club

MC MasterCard

V Visa

E Entrees

M Mains

D Desserts

Accommodation available

new New to the *Guide*

Citibank dining program partner restaurant (advertisement)

THE TEAM

Editor
Janne Apelgren

Senior reviewer
Larissa Dubecki

Editorial panel
Janne Apelgren, Larissa Dubecki, Michael Harden, Dani Valent, Richard Cornish, Jane Faulkner (wine)

Reviewers
Douglas Aiton, Janne Apelgren, Gayle Austen, Peter Barrett, Ardyn Bernoth, Paul Best, Adam Carey, Nathan Chisholm, Mark Chu, Don Churchill, Pat Churchill, Leanne Clancey, Andrew Cornell, Richard Cornish, Gabriella Coslovich, Justine Costigan, Donna Coutts, Peter Cruttenden, Mary-Jane Daffy, Emiko Davies, Larissa Dubecki, David Dunstan, Kate Dunstan, Jill Dupleix, Simone Egger, Kelly Eng, Rita Erlich, Claude Forell, Stu Gaunt, Michael Gordon, Cathy Gowdie, Roslyn Grundy, Rachel Gubby, Andrew Hagger, Bob Haldane, Michael Harden, Bob Hart, Angus Holland, Barbara Humphries, Dugald Jellie, Sarah Lewis, Caitlin Mahar, Elissa McCallum, Hugh McNaughtan, Hilary McNevin, Emma Miller, Gary Munro, Kenneth Nguyen, Jane Ormond, Matt Pirrie, Michelle Potts, Annabel Ross, Nina Rousseau, Anastasia Safioleas, John Schauble, Lucinda Schmidt, Geoff Slattery, Peter Stratton, Gail Thomas, Dani Valent, Tessie Vanderwert, Sue Wallace, Kim West, Patrick Witton

Gourmet cafes
Dani Valent

Best bars
Michael Harden

Top 10
Michael Harden

Interstate
Megan Anderson, Rodney Dunn, Terry Durack, Nigel Hopkins, Natascha Mirosch, Barbara Sweeney

Judging panel, Chef's Hat Young Chef of the Year
Alla Wolf-Tasker, Guy Grossi, Philippe Mouchel (panellists abstain from judging their own staff)

CITY & SUBURBS

Moon Under Water

Abla's

109 Elgin Street, Carlton **9347 0006**

LEBANESE **14.5/20**

Abla Amad was a pioneer of Lebanese cuisine in Melbourne. Now she's a stalwart. Her humble, homely restaurant has been in every one of the *Guide*'s 33 editions and in 34 years it has changed little. For many, that's its charm. The hospitality is undeniable. Curious about the Lebanese wine? You may be offered a taste. Want to bring a gang? The place is full of convivial groups feasting on the $60 banquet. BYO? No problem. Half serves? They're volunteered. While newer Lebanese restaurants have been more fashionable, innovative (and pricier), Abla's remains as its regulars seem to like it. The food's reliable and comforting: smoky eggplant dip; neat, lemony silverbeet rolls filled with rice and chickpeas; white zucchini in tomato broth and stuffed with parsley-flecked rice. Tabbouleh accompanies skewered grilled minced lamb; rice, lentils and caramelised onion come to be dolloped with tart yoghurt. Cool, light rosewater custard beneath a pistachio crust is as sweet as the service.

Open Mon-Sat 6-11pm; Thurs-Fri noon-3pm
Typical prices E $15 **M** $27 **D** $9
Cards DC AE MC V Eftpos
Wine A compact list that includes some Lebanese wines worth sampling; BYO (corkage $5 a bottle)
Owner & chef Abla Amad
Seats 90; private room
www.ablas.com.au

And ... Prepare Abla's food at home with her cookbook, *Abla's Lebanese Kitchen*.

Aja

132 Bridport Street, Albert Park **9645 8388**

MODERN ASIAN **12/20**

Aja's menu jumps around Asia like a cashed-up package tourist, and touches down in each country for about as long. There might be soft-shell crab rice-paper rolls with Thai basil and avocado; and Shanghai pork dumplings, with a flavoursome and firm filling, rather than the boiling soup usually within. Prawns in soft strands of poached eggwhite are a delicate offering from China. Mains might include sizzling Korean beef (perhaps a little sweeter than in Seoul) with house-made kimchi. 'No-nonsense' stir-fried noodles are exactly as named; simple, silky and with fresh snowpeas, onion, red and green capsicum and beansprouts. To counter generous seasoning, follow the advice given to any traveller in Asia, and drink plenty of bottled water. Desserts like 'hazelnut delight' - deep-fried glutinous sweet-potato dumplings with a crushed hazelnut and coconut filling - may be too heavy for some, particularly those who ordered generously on the savouries. The lacquered sheen of the sleek, soft-lit room has a unifying effect, which helps make Aja a pleasant stopover.

Open Daily 6-11pm; Sun-Fri noon-3pm
Typical prices E $14 **M** $34.50 **D** $10
Cards DC AE MC V Eftpos
Wine Good range of mostly Australian wines, with some special-occasion bottles; BYO (corkage $9 a bottle)
Owners Michael Wong & Jamo Lo
Chef Michael Wong
Seats 60; private room
www.aja.net.au

citibank Privileges

And ... Try the frequently changing set menu.

Akachochin

Shed 7, 33 Dukes Walk, South Wharf, Docklands
9245 9900

JAPANESE **14/20**

Izakaya-style dining, Japanese tapas if you like, is dining for the times, and Akachochin's owner, restaurant entrepreneur Paul Mathis, has always been a la mode. So here it's about smaller sharing dishes, designed for drinking, but fun, too. Akachochin, in the newly opened South Wharf promenade warehouse strip, is large and airy. On a sunny day or balmy night especially, this simple, modern spot of clean lines and old timber, open to the Yarra, appeals for whiling away an afternoon or catching up before a show. The menu covers the raw, grilled, fried, steamed and braised. Though the precinct is still evolving and needs the buzz of an event to come alive, the fare is assured, with modern takes on Japanese bar specials from Nobu's former head chef. Japanese-style kingfish tartare with wafer-like rice crackers is a tangy delight, the sushi is deftly crafted, seared wagyu comes with crisp leeks and citrus miso, and grilled curried scallops with sea-urchin sauce simply wow.

Open Tues–Sun noon–4pm, 6pm–late
Typical prices E $12 **M** $15 **D** $12
Cards AE MC V Eftpos
Wine Excellent regional list of sakes and plum wines, most in 300ml bottles; wines are from the list of sibling restaurant the Sharing House
Owner Paul Mathis
Chef Kengo Hiromatsu
Seats 63; outdoor seating; bar
www.akachochin.com.au

And ... The sushi bar's inviting for single diners and couples, and summer will bring outdoor tables.

Albert Park Hotel Oyster Bar & Grill

83 Dundas Place, Albert Park **9690 5459**

SEAFOOD **14.5/20**

Eating ethically has never looked so good as at this sleek corner pub where the seafood on its fish-focused menu is sustainably sourced and playfully prepped as zingy street food and barbecue share-plates. Oysters are hard to beat for starters, while grab-and-gobble street-food options include Asian (yabby and prawn rice-noodle rolls) and Latino (soft corn tacos piled with coleslaw and rock flathead in a cloak of heavy smoky chipotle dressing). For mains, there are eight or so varieties of fish to choose from – whole or in fillets, wood-barbecued or grilled – and prepared one of four ways: saffron, tomato and chilli or Thai herbs, for example. Well-informed staff can help you to choose; phew. Non-seafood options could include lamb, organic chook or Angus steak. The plush, blush-colour carpeted dining space is screened from the front bar and split by a long marble table. Lobster-pot lampshades, an open kitchen and inviting courtyard complete this funky, casual scene.

Open Daily noon–3pm, 6–10pm
Typical prices E $18 **M** $36 **D** $15
Cards DC AE MC V Eftpos
Wine Lots of half bottles on offer, as well as 14 foreign-leaning offerings by the glass; vast list of full bottles, priced for the postcode
Owners Julian Gerner & Tom Walker
Chefs Paul Wilson & Stephen Burke
Seats 70; outdoor seating; private room; bar
www.thealbertpark.com.au

And ... The Fish Cafe offers quick, inexpensive meals (mostly under $20) and Friday 6pm to 7pm is oyster 'happy hour', with $1 oysters.

Albert St Food & Wine

382 Sydney Road (corner Albert Street), Brunswick **8354 6600**

EUROPEAN **15/20**

Long before Albert St opened in this swish, high-ceilinged converted bank, the food world was abuzz. This was to be a restaurant, cafe, wine bar, bottle shop and provedore rolled into one all-day-trading emporium. Big names were at play: owners Stuart Brookshaw (ex-Bondi Icebergs) and Ruth Giffney (ex-Longrain), and chef Philippa Sibley (ex-Est Est Est and Circa). Locals mobbed the large, warehouse-like timbered space. Others travelled to grab a stool at high bar tables or settle into the adjacent restaurant to share charcuterie of pistachio-crusted salami or prosciutto with tart-sweet house pickles and rough-hewn grissini. The food runs from pastas (pliant potato gnocchi with sticky, fall-apart organic veal, saffron and peas) to pizzas (mushroom and taleggio on light, thin crusts) to classic Western Plains pork coteletta. Then there's dessert: signature sauternes creme caramel; the pristine, unadorned Meyer lemon tart; or strawberries with tangy balsamic icecream, baby basil and crunchy meringue. Albert St's a hit, set to become a classic.

Open Tues–Fri 10am–late; Sat–Sun 8am–late
Typical prices E $19 **M** $32 **D** $14
Cards DC AE MC V Eftpos
Wine A savvy, monthly changing list of about 220 wines; strong on locals and Europeans with carafes and half glasses and weekend wine tastings
Owners Ruth Giffney & Stuart Brookshaw
Chef Philippa Sibley
Seats 100; outdoor seating; private rooms; bar
www.albertst.com.au

And ... Buy house preserves and Sibley's cookbook *PS Desserts* onsite or online.

Anada

197 Gertrude Street, Fitzroy **9415 6101**

SPANISH **14.5/20**

Anada's room is smart and simple: exposed brickwork and concrete floors amplify the buzz of a creative-looking crowd drinking tempranillo and grazing from glazed terracotta dishes. A landmark on hip Gertrude Street, this slender bistro stands out more for its rich Iberian flavours rather than for grand scale or lavish design. The great range of tapas and raciones runs from light and clean through to dense and complex. Start simply with oysters and lemon, move on through char-grilled quail on freekeh and pomegranate seeds. Then, to a bright cleansing gazpacho with a hint of chilli, and delectable whole beef cheek with fava-bean puree. Salads, perhaps baby beetroot with mint and smooth labna, provide lively interludes. Cheery churros with chocolate are a deserving dessert choice, but also consider the range of delicately scented sorbets and icecreams and thoughtful selection of Spanish cheeses. No-fuss staff keep the plates coming, squeezing between tables and bobbing between lively conversations.

Open Mon–Thurs 6–10.30pm; Fri 6–11pm; Sat noon–11pm; Sun noon–10.30pm
Typical prices E $4 **M** $20 **D** $12
Cards AE MC V Eftpos
Wine A good range of mid- to high-end Spanish and local wines, plus sherries
Owners Jesse & Vanessa Gerner
Chefs Jesse Gerner & Andrew Fisk
Seats 40; outdoor seating; bar
www.anada.com.au

And ... There are two sittings (6pm or 6.30pm and 8.30pm) and two tasting menus.

Arabesque

Shop 1, 1-3 Carre Street, Elsternwick **9523 1108**

MIDDLE EASTERN **12.5/20**

Comfortably seated on a striped banquette, behind a table swathed in maroon and crisp white linen, gives you a ringside seat for the heady Ottoman flavours in Arabesque's dining room. Filo pastry fingers redolent of cinnamon, lamb and pinenuts are tempered by a syrupy sweet pomegranate molasses and make a perfect start. Moist charred calamari tentacles rest on a rocket salad bright with lemon. Lengths of roast red capsicum are simply sublime between creamy feta chunks and fat slices of fiery sucuk (sausage). A tower of vibrant yellow saffron pilaf is the pièce de résistance, speckled with meaty kofta balls, a velvety tahini sauce and lashings of coriander. And while the day's fish (perhaps blue-eye) may arrive a tad dry despite a rich ratatouille topping, it's all speedily whisked to the table with affection and just enough cheek from the staff to enliven proceedings. Arabesque dishes up warmth, baklava and Turkish delights in all the right quantities.

Open Daily 6–11pm; Thurs–Sat 11.30am–3pm; Sun 8am–3pm
Typical prices E $14.50 **M** $28.50 **D** $8
Cards AE MC V Eftpos
Wine A pithy and affordable selection of mainly Australian offerings, most of which are also available by the glass; BYO (corkage $8 a bottle)
Owner Fahrettin Elmas
Chefs Fahrettin Elmas & Chris de Boer
Seats 95; outdoor seating; bar

And ... There is live music on Sunday evenings, and two good-value banquet options.

Araliya

629 Glenferrie Road, Hawthorn **9818 5120**

SRI LANKAN **14.5/20**

Culinary explorers, head to this slice of Sri Lanka. Chef Sriyan Wedande's take on the centuries-old cuisine of his birthplace, with its Indian, Portuguese, Dutch and English influences, is a sophisticated affair, and the owners' five-star hotel background gives this comfortable, well-loved, long-time local extra charm. Dishes zing with traditional flavourings such as curry leaf, black pepper, green chilli and tamarind. Resulting tastes fascinate, but don't overwhelm. Wafer-thin roti is rolled around herbed goat's cheese omelette. Traditional, sticky jaggery palm sugar makes braised wagyu brisket full-flavoured and dark, while crab is baked with green chilli and cheese. Nine non-meat side dishes are a vegetarian's nirvana: look for tangy twice-cooked pickled eggplant with dates; pumpkin with coconut and mustard seeds; or beetroot and turnip sauteed with curry leaves. Desserts leap from traditional (Dutch-inspired honey and semolina love cake) to modern (passionfruit parfait with pistachio brittle and coriander-seed tuile). Perfect with a pot of premium Sri Lankan brew.

Open Daily 6–10.30pm; Thurs–Fri noon–3pm
Typical prices E $20 **M** $36 **D** $15
Cards AE MC V Eftpos
Wine 140 wines carefully chosen to match the menu, with a reserve list and wines by the glass
Owners Sriyan & Dee Wedande
Chef Sriyan Wedande
Seats 60; private room; bar
www.araliya.com.au

And ... Araliya offers top-notch takeway.

Arcadia Gastronomique

152 Union Road, Ascot Vale **9375 2751**

SPANISH/EUROPEAN **12/20**

Starting life as a French bistro, this friendly neighbourhood place has been on a steady march over the Pyrenees and now, save the odd Gallic or North African-inspired main, the transformation seems complete. Pictures of dancing senoritas adorn the warm, wood-lined interior where locals revel in heroic portion sizes and macho flavours. Perhaps begin with vinegary white anchovies finished with a healthy dash of garlic, scallops atop roasted field mushrooms sprinkled with shaved, dried jamon, or rich, salty slices of black pudding. Paella could do with more saffron and less salt, but there's plenty of tender chicken and shellfish among al dente rice, while plump, house-made gnocchi luxuriates in a sauce of queso de Cabrales (full-flavoured blue cheese from northern Spain), walnuts and batons of crisp pear. It's rib-stickingly indulgent, and another pear, poached in red wine and arranged with artistic daubs of raspberry coulis, is a blessedly light relief. Service sometimes lacks polish but is unstintingly friendly.

Open Tues–Sat 6–11pm; Sat 9am–12.30pm
Typical prices E $16 **M** $30 **D** $12
Cards MC V Eftpos
Wine An increasing focus on Spanish wines along with reasonably priced locals; 12 by the glass
Owner & chef Andres Ruiz-Mesa
Seats 42; outdoor seating
www.arcadiadining.com.au

And … Churros are always on the dessert menu – and are delicious.

Arkibar

27 Coventry Street (St Kilda Road end), Southbank
9690 6688

ITALIAN **13.5/20**

Visually, Arkibar is based around good architectural aesthetics (one of the owners is an architect), and culinarily, around good food (another owner is the chef). Operating since 1999, it's a restaurant that still ticks so many boxes: the dining room has rich chocolate timber wall panels, white tables and modern artwork, and it serves an evolving Italian menu. There's a printed list with bruschetta and antipasti, as well as constant changes on the blackboard above the front counter, where you'll find soup and pasta, as well as a fish dish and meat. Depending on the season, there may be a spaghettini with ocean trout, salsa verde and pea puree, or a dish of roasted quail, served over a robust eggplant caponata. There may be occasional bare patches in service – with perhaps a wait to be welcomed – but compensation comes in knowledgeable recommendations, particularly of the desserts, where a classic tiramisu or lemon-curd tart come in perfect bite-sizes to round out a vibrant meal with a sweet finish.

Open Mon–Fri 7.30am–2.30pm; Thurs–Fri 6–9pm; Sat 8.30–11.45am
Typical prices E $18 **M** $33 **D** $13
Cards DC AE MC V Eftpos
Wine Lots of Australian wines plus some quirky Italian choices; 12 by the glass
Owners Raymond & Susy Esposito, Michael & Shirley Bialek
Chef Raymond Esposito
Seats 45; outdoor seating; bar

And … Book ahead for dinners; walk-ins will probably miss out.

The Atlantic

Riverside, Crown Complex, Southbank **9698 8888**

CONTEMPORARY/SEAFOOD **14/20**

The Atlantic's casino-side window displays fresh fish on crushed ice like precious (and pricey) jewels. Inside, the light but sometimes loud riverside atrium is veiled discreetly by fishing-net-inspired curtains, but the nautical themes are a subtle leitmotif throughout, from embossed fish on the leather-backed chairs to ropy light fittings. Plump prawns dominate a too-chilly seafood cocktail with lashings of dressing; a beautifully charred calamari fresh off the wood-fired grill makes a finer start. You can order whole fresh fish such as King George whiting from Port Franklin, then choose to have it roasted, steamed or grilled. The menu takes to the land for slow-roasted chicken, duck and grilled wagyu steaks. You'll need sides, like crunchy thrice-cooked russet potatoes. On the upside, there's a brilliant array of gorgeously fresh seafood. On the downside, quality control may be uneven – beans flaccid, a honey parfait delivered slouching over. Staff are as coolly efficient as a well-drilled nautical crew.

Open Daily noon–3pm, 6–11pm
Typical prices E $30 **M** $42 **D** $20
Cards AE MC V Eftpos
Wine A beautifully balanced hit list of local and international stars, strong on the pricey and prestigious
Owners Hatem Saleh & Tony Schiavello
Chef Donovan Cooke
Seats 300; outdoor seating; private rooms
www.theatlantic.com.au

And ... The Atlantic's Champagne and Oyster Bar is open till 1am daily; the Den bar, in the depths of the Atlantic, stays open till 3am daily.

Attica

74 Glen Eira Road, Ripponlea **9530 0111**

CONTEMPORARY **18.5/20**

Ben Shewry tells a great Australian story, for a Kiwi. His food is connected to its roots (literally, there's a kitchen garden out back) like few other chefs'. You might find sweet, rare wallaby; pearl meat given spark by beads of finger lime; luscious marron in a chorizo broth; the signature potato cooked in earth; one dessert of rare native fruits on sheep's milk yoghurt beneath ruby native-currant shaved ice; another that unites seasonal fruit, honey and meringue in a miniature beehive box. Staff are as polished as you'd expect. The small rooms, dramatic in black, with spotlit pools of creamy white, make the most of close-ish quarters. They are often full of food tourists and dish-snapping diners, as befits Shewry's now global profile as a proponent of nature-based cuisine, despite the suburban location of this restaurant co-owned by two doctors. By the petits fours of speckled, salted-caramel chocolate eggs, every diner should have their own tale to tell. Attica is the best it's been.

Open Tues–Sat 6.30–9pm
Typical prices Chef's table $95 (Tues); degustation $125 (5 courses Wed–Thurs), $175 (8 courses Wed–Sat)
Cards AE MC V Eftpos
Wine Old and New World gems, many well priced; wine matches to the menu are recommended
Owners David & Helen Maccora, Ben Shewry
Chef Ben Shewry
Seats 60; private room
www.attica.com.au

And ... Want to spot the chef? Visit the loos – you can peek into the kitchen en route.

Ayame

237 Glenferrie Road, Malvern **9500 9424**

JAPANESE **13/20**

With its cool, grey tones and uncluttered, typically Japanese decor, Ayame seems comfortable in its own skin. It's a fact affirmed by locals who file through its doors for platters of sushi and sashimi - available in entree and main servings - that might include salmon, tuna and kingfish, or crisp, light tempura of prawns and vegetables lifted by a tomato, basil and pinenut sauce. Kingfish also stars in tataki form, as does beef in the gyu-niku tataki, the thinly sliced seared beef making firm friends with the soy, sesame and garlic dressing. A bowl of delicate agedashidofu comes topped with a nicely contrasting crunch of soft-shell crab, which sums up Ayame well: mainly traditional fare, executed well. Smiling staff will ensure you don't over-order - handy if you want desserts that might include black-sesame icecream. If you can't decide on one of the four sweet options, the moriawase for two people allows you a taste of them all.

Open Tues–Sun 6–10pm
Typical prices E $16 **M** $30 **D** $10
Cards AE MC V Eftpos
Wine Compact mainly Australian list of 12 reds and nine whites, a dozen available by the glass; plum wine and sake also available; BYO (corkage $6 a bottle)
Owner & chef Lin Zhang
Seats 50

And ... To get close to the sushi action, request a seat at the sushi bar.

The Aylesbury

103 Lonsdale Street, City **9077 0451**

CONTEMPORARY **14/20**

Simplicity and source are the watchwords for Jesse and Vanessa Gerner's CBD debut, set in a handsomely paint-stripped space. Wagyu beef might end up cured and air-dried, then sprinkled delicately with chervil flowers and tiny clusters of morcilla, bone marrow and crisp breadcrumbs for a superb starter. Meatier still is char-grilled saddle of wild boar, its gaminess offset brightly by blood plums and a glaze of pomegranate molasses. Mains are labelled 'share' here, or there's a $65 'feasting menu' if you fancy. Bite-sized house-made buns are a fixture, maybe filled with rabbit, yabby or turkey. Though the skilled kitchen team might have the odd stumble (beignets arrived undercooked on one visit), caramelised Central Victorian peaches with a strawberry sorbet, cava poured theatrically over at the table, are perfect. The Bellini cocktail as dessert - irresistible.

Open Mon–Fri noon–3pm; Mon–Sat 6pm–1am
Typical prices E $14 **M** $32 **D** $12
Cards AE MC V Eftpos
Wine Thoughtful seven-page list organised by colour and body, going off the beaten path (and, occasionally, organic and biodynamic)
Owners Jesse & Vanessa Gerner
Chefs Jesse Gerner & Joel Hales
Seats 72; bar
www.theaylesbury.com.au

And ... Take the elevator to the fifth-floor bar for a big-city view.

Bacash

175 Domain Road, South Yarra **9866 3566**

CONTEMPORARY/SEAFOOD 🎩 **15/20**

You don't have to adore seafood to eat here; Michael Bacash cooks meat and poultry beautifully, too. But if you're looking to fall in love with fish, this narrow, white-clothed restaurant, especially its park-facing front room, is a good place to begin. Start, perhaps, with the classic coupling of scallop and pork belly, with creamy Jerusalem artichoke and crunchy pistachio 'crumb'. Spaghetti marinara is a signature and a benchmark: tender pasta with olive oil, garlic, parsley, prawns, mussels, calamari and juicy seasonal fish. Generosity is evident in another Bacash classic: whole flounder with a choice of sauces spooned on at the table, a mountain of fries and a clean, green salad. Snapper may come as a refined version of a traditional Lebanese dish: gently cooked with sumac, silverbeet and caramelised onion. Make time for a souffle – maybe chocolate or passionfruit – it's worth the 20-minute wait. Take time, too, to seek advice from floor staff: from perch to pinot, they know their stuff.

Open Mon–Fri noon–3pm; Mon–Sat 6–10pm
Typical prices E $21.50 **M** $42 **D** $16.50
Cards DC AE MC V
Wine Established and emerging producers from the New and Old Worlds; fairly priced, poured with knowledge and flair
Owners Michael Bacash & Fiona Perkins
Chef Michael Bacash
Seats 70; outdoor seating; private room; bar
www.bacash.com.au

And ... A private dining room upstairs looks across to the Botanic Gardens.

Bamboo House

47 Little Bourke Street, City **9662 1565**

CHINESE **14/20**

You won't find a spruiker outside Bamboo House, even on the quietest of days, but inside you'll regularly spot business leaders, pollies or families out for a special night. While the city's culinary tastes may have changed over the past 30-odd years, Bamboo House's hasn't – and that's part of its charm. At this classic Chinese restaurant, waiters in black hover discreetly, dishes are delivered swiftly on to starched linen tablecloths and deftly plated into individual serves. The menu's split between classic Cantonese and spicier northern Chinese. Begin with chicken soused in a superior rice wine or crunchy Beijing style. The tea-smoked duck (marinated, steamed, smoked, then fried) is a speciality, while the market fish (perhaps a fillet of ling) comes steamed in classic soy, ginger and spring onion. Lamb cutlets are dusted in five-spice and fried. The desserts – including fried bananas and red-bean cakes – are in keeping with tradition.

Open Mon–Fri noon–3pm; Mon–Sat 5.30–11pm; Sun 6–10pm
Typical prices E $11 **M** $28 **D** $14
Cards DC AE MC V Eftpos
Wine Mostly Australian, with a reasonable selection by the glass
Owners Tommy Chung, Eric Lam & Denny Wong
Chefs Tommy Chung & Eric Lam
Seats 80; private room
www.bamboohouse.com.au

And ... Consider pre-ordering the 'beggars chicken' – a fragrant whole chook enshrined in a ready-to-crack dough case.

Bar Idda

132 Lygon Street, Brunswick East **9380 5339**

SICILIAN **14/20**

Each year, Bar Idda feels more bedded down in its cosy corner digs, beloved by the neighbourhood for its genuine warmth and unfussy Sicilian authenticity. Bottles of wine land on the plastic-covered tables with chunky glassware so you can pour your own, and a tiny TV mounted in the corner plays Italian soaps (sound down). The La Spinas – chef Alfredo and wife Lisa, who runs front-of-house – visit Sicily at least once a year and inspiration shows in the fresh, produce-driven dishes, designed to share. Mulinciani (tomatoey, cheesy eggplant) is a staple, and the salumi is usually made here. Tangy house-pickled octopus might be pan-fried with potato pieces, bitey with celery leaf and fennel. Zeppole, small potato, parsley and anchovy doughnuts, come dolloped with a lemony yoghurt mayo, and a home-made barbecue is used to great effect in mains such as butterflied baby chicken with a finger lickin' cinnamon, sea salt and sugar rub. Desserts veer from traditional (cannoli and cassata) to one-offs such as super-creamy blackberry gelato. Bar Idda just keeps getting better.

Open Mon–Sat 6–10pm
Typical prices E $12 **M** $17.50 **D** $10
Cards MC V Eftpos
Wine Almost exclusively Sicilian list, including 11 by the glass
Owners Alfredo & Lisa La Spina
Chef Alfredo La Spina
Seats 55; outdoor seating; private room; bar
www.baridda.com.au

And … Feast days are celebrated as they occur in Sicily with five-course Sunday lunches.

Bar Lourinha

37 Little Collins Street, City **9663 7890**

IBERIAN/MEDITERRANEAN **14.5/20**

There's a special place in Melbourne's dining heart for this little bar with its kitschy mix of hanging frames, knick-knacks and splash of retro-style green wallpaper. Matt McConnell's fun take on Iberian food sings with bright, uncomplicated flavours. It's all made for sharing, so take a place at either the bar, communal high tables with stools, or cushioned banquette by the front window and chat to the skilled staff who know a thing or two about food and wine. Start with menu mainstays of octopus banderillas – bite-sized skewers of pickled octopus and anchovy-stuffed olive – or the sublime signature carpaccio-style yellowtail kingfish, followed by a seasonal special of heirloom carrots, plump figs and creamy labna. House-made pork sausage with white beans and parsley, and slow-cooked fleshy 'pork butt' drenched in a bright, sweet piri-piri sauce will have you crying 'perfecto' before dessert arrives: perhaps a silky sweet pomegranate crema with pistachio praline, or a sophisticated chocolate, hazelnut and espresso trifle.

Open Mon–Thurs noon–11pm; Fri noon–1am; Sat 4pm–1am; no bookings at dinner
Typical prices E $8 **M** $18 **D** $11
Cards AE MC V Eftpos
Wine Compact, considered list of mostly European labels, with a handful by the glass
Owners Matt McConnell, Jo Gamvros & Simon Benjamin
Chefs Matt McConnell & Marcus Allen
Seats 40; private room; bar
www.barlourinha.com.au

And … Private function? Try the upstairs room.

Barca Food & Wine

1007 High Street, Armadale **9822 8515**

EUROPEAN **14/20**

Gee it's nice not to have to queue for a table, rush out to make room for a second sitting or share your food. These are among the many old-school dining pleasures a night at Barca guarantees. There's also the casually handsome bistro setting (long mirrors, comfy banquettes, arresting 1930s poster art and flickering tea-lights); the discreet yet friendly staff; and the assured, unpretentious modern European food. Plump, garlicky prawns mingling with cherry tomatoes and croutons in a terracotta pot make a satisfying starter. Mains are substantial, be it a hunky veal schnitzel leavened by a salad of shallots and parsley tangy with balsamic vinegar, or skinless fillets of John Dory with pickled witlof, creamy pureed cauliflower and a sweetcorn foam. It's the sort of place that tempts you to take on a leisurely three courses, right through to a scoop of delicate white-chocolate mousse complemented by a tart passionfruit coulis and shards of honeycomb.

Open Daily noon–3pm, 6–10pm
Typical prices E $19 **M** $36 **D** $16
Cards DC AE MC V Eftpos
Wine Largely Australian list offers decent choice aound the $50 mark; 20 by the glass
Owner Charles Sedgley
Chef Mark Glenn
Seats 60; outdoor seating; private rooms
www.barca.com.au

And ... Barca does wine and tapas 3pm to 6pm daily, and $25 lunch specials.

Barrio

77 Upper Heidelberg Road, Ivanhoe **9499 9907**

MEDITERRANEAN **12.5/20**

Barrio means neighbourhood in Spanish, and it's a fitting name for a place that's become a popular gathering spot for locals. Housed in a century-old former fire station, the dining room's grand proportions and moody coffee-coloured interior, complete with glossy wood tables and sparkling glassware, are paired with a flexible, Mediterranean menu. Start by grazing on tapas including bomba – Spanish croquettes filled with soft potato and pork belly paired with sweetish tomato sauce – or a simple dish of perfect crisp-fried calamari with salsa verde. Four pastas and risottos are available as entrees or mains. A substantial main of seared salmon fillet appealed with a jammy tomato sauce and glistening fried eggplant spears. The lamb tagine tended towards dryness, but was lifted by fluffy cous cous and a creamy pot of yoghurt. Desserts stick to the familiar, although a rich, orange-infused crema Catalana was a standout. Brisk service sometimes lacks a little warmth, but you'll rarely be kept waiting.

Open Tues–Sat noon–3pm, 5.30–11pm
Typical prices E $16.50 **M** $34 **D** $14
Cards AE MC V Eftpos
Wine Australian and Old World list with a focus on Italy, France and Spain; 10 mostly Australian by the glass
Owners Paul Rae & Henry Honner
Chef Ricky Holt
Seats 65; outdoor seating; private room
www.barriorestaurant.com.au

And ... Barrio stays open between lunch and dinner so drop in for cake and coffee or pre-dinner drinks and tapas.

The Baths

251 The Esplanade, Brighton **9539 7000**

CONTEMPORARY **13.5/20**

If first impressions count, then the Baths flies out of the gate, courtesy of a stunning view over the bay from the light-filled, elegant dining room. Once you've finished admiring the sunset, you can focus on the smart, modern fare coming out of the kitchen. Start down a hearty path with the twice-cooked Otway pork belly on a smooth ginger-and-apple puree with calvados jus, or opt for lighter fare such as zucchini flowers filled with Persian feta, thinly veiled in batter and fried, supported by almond gazpacho and a tumble of finely diced tomato and olive. Big appetites are catered for on the mains front with saddle of rabbit, Cape Grim beef or a chunky pork cutlet heaped with young coconut, beanshoots and papaya, surrounded by a sweet moat of chilli sauce, a knowing wink to Asia. If you can resist the impressively presented desserts – and who doesn't love a crisp-shelled pavlova? – there's a French-dominated cheese selection.

Open Daily noon–3pm, 6–10pm
Typical prices E $20 **M** $37 **D** $15
Cards AE MC V Eftpos
Wine Globe-spanning, 250-plus bottle list for most budgets; plenty by the glass
Owner Paul Raynor
Chefs Paul Raynor & Darren Mercaldi
Seats 120; outdoor seating; private room
www.middlebrightonbaths.com.au

And ... Sunday is corkage-free BYO, and there's a $15 kids' menu.

Becco

11–25 Crossley Street, City **9663 3000**

ITALIAN **15/20**

Where Chinatown collides with little Italy in once notoriously brothel-dotted Crossley Street, warm-hearted Becco has been a 15-year fixture, casting an inviting glow across the bluestone gutters from its big streetside windows. Here, a respect for produce and traditional Italian cooking is teamed with an enchanting generosity (hefty chunks of bread; brisk, friendly service) and the crisp, linen-dressed dining room makes for a delightfully cosseting rather than cutting-edge meal. The buzzy conviviality appeals to both date-night diners and big-end-of-towners. Starters arrive pronto, as in a tooth-stickingly good slab of pork belly with apple and radish. For mains, comfort comes in fall-apart duck confit with pan-fried potatoes and a grappa-spiked jus, tempting to pair with a side of chilli-kissed spinach, or ossobuco and parmesan gnocchi with gremolata that delivers plenty of bang. Then, a playful chocolate brownie, cherry granita and coconut foam dessert comes at a quick clip. Traditional tiramisu is a menu fixture.

Open Tues–Sat noon–3pm, 6–11pm
Typical prices E $22 **M** $41 **D** $17.50
Cards AE MC V
Wine A list worth lingering over, with a focus on stellar Italian and Australian wines, including 16 by the glass and 500ml, digestifs and grappas
Owner Simon Hartley
Chefs Corin Sutton & Steven Ward
Seats 82; outdoor seating; private room; bar
www.becco.com.au

And ... Tuck into stuffed olives or prosciutto and grissini in the moodily lit bar.

Benito's

445 Little Collins Street, City **9670 5347**

ITALIAN **13/20**

Benito's regulars love this unpretentious spot for its comfortable, worn patina, and assured southern-Italian cooking. They come for hearty breakfasts like baked eggs with sausage and tomato; grab booths for lunch, or sit cheek by jowl with the legal/banking crowd tucking into shared assaggini (small tastes) and antipasti. (There's little chance of keeping that deal confidential on the close-set centre tables.) Regularly changing arrays of morsels include salumi, salt-cod fritters and marinated octopus. Expect daily specials like char-grilled salmon on a pea mash or a succulent roasted spatchcock on caponata. The house lasagne with pork ragu is famously popular, as are daily pastas, maybe oil-rich spaghetti marinara or a fricelli with pork-and-fennel sausage, peas and chilli. And there's always bloke-friendly steak to pair with a red. The hearty, good-quality well-priced food more than makes up for the close quarters and occasionally missing service. In the evenings the pace is more subdued, making it a great place for an aperitivo or casual dinner.

Open Mon–Fri 7am–10pm
Typical prices E $15 **M** $29 **D** $13
Cards DC AE MC V Eftpos
Wine Interesting, well-priced collection of Australian and particularly Italian, blackboard specials and good range by the glass
Owner Quang Nguyen
Chef Anthony Catania
Seats 50; bar
www.benitoscafewinebar.com.au

And ... It's also a bottle shop.

Bess

105 Swan Street, Richmond **9428 5999**

EUROPEAN **14/20**

The team previously behind Prahran's the Max is back – at this brasserie-handsome old bank that's all high ceilings, wicker chairs, big bar and checkerboard floor. Katie Krauss-Mitchell's modern comfort food is less Slanket, more Hermes throw – time and again tried formulas are given new life. The steak tartare is among the city's most beautifully plated: think hand-chopped meat, decorated with a spotted, opened quail's eggshell and mandoline-sliced radishes presented in almost floral fashion. Even hoary veal schnitzel is elevated, dusted with fragrant cinnamon and accompanied by purple slaw and taramasalata (creamed roe, though an inconsistent front-of-house team might not know as much). Among the sophistication, there's some simpler please-all-comers appeal, with a knackwurst dog, Bess burger and fish and chips. But the best is left for last. Eton Mess is re-imagined with perfect house-made honeycomb in place of meringue, the strawberries topped with shredded mint, and the cream folded into organic yoghurt with vanilla and honey; Bess's Mess gets our blessing.

Open Daily noon–10pm
Typical prices E $14 **M** $30 **D** $16
Cards MC V Eftpos
Wine A mostly southern hemisphere list, displaying both sub-$50 affordability and eminent drinkability
Owners Brendon Mitchell & Katie Krauss-Mitchell
Chef Katie Krauss-Mitchell
Seats 85; outdoor seating; bar
www.bessrichmond.com.au

And ... Enjoy the fireplace in winter.

Bistro Flor

555 Nicholson Street, Carlton North **9381 4443**

EUROPEAN **13.5/20**

Cosy Bistro Flor exemplifies the great little local, with terrific food, attentive service, good value and that feeling of being let into a club of happy, well-fed and cared-for customers, even if only for one night. Original terrazzo floors, modern art and small wooden tables may evoke a Paris bistro, but this was once a typical corner store and its creeper-entwined exterior with iron lacework is quintessential Carlton. Starters include wafer-thin house-cured salmon with croutons, creamy wasabi and avocado, and a special of delicate gazpacho, speckled with crab and a hint of chilli. Subtlety is replaced by full-on flavour in the main plates – think soft gnocchi paired with rich braised rabbit, spiked with black olives and rosemary and the tang of salted ricotta, or tender pork neck, its richness offset by smoky eggplant and pickled crabapple. House-made cannoli, the crunchy pastry encasing smooth banana and mascarpone, will have you feeling the love till the last.

Open Tues–Fri 6–9.30pm; Sat 8am–9.30pm; Sun 8am–3pm
Typical prices E $15 **M** $26 **D** $12
Cards AE MC V Eftpos
Wine A French and Victorian-dominated list, with many good choices under $50, plus a wide range of digestifs, including fig and quince liquors
Owner Matthew Palmer
Chef Matthew Kennedy
Seats 40; outdoor seating
www.bistroflor.com

And ... There are breakfasts, brunches and $35 lunch specials at weekends; and a $55 four-course feasting menu.

Bistro Gitan

52 Toorak Road West, South Yarra **9867 5853**

FRENCH **14.5/20**

The aim, so they say, is to 'create a dinner table just as it would be for a family in France'. Happily, the family behind this bistro call Jacques Reymond 'dad'. The ground floor of a Victorian-era former hotel, with long windows looking across to Fawkner Park, has been reborn as this casual, airy space with worn parquetry, white-clothed tables, young, assured service and a sense of having been here forever. Expect well-judged twists on classics: a prawn cocktail with house-made tomato sauce, pink citrus and bitter leaves; a vivid steak tartare delivered in little lettuce canoes; a lush entree of chicken livers and pappardelle, rich but not cloying. A main of garfish may come boned and lightly crumbed, while quartered young chicken is mustard-crusted and juicy, served on savoy cabbage and bacon. It's all billed as French and 'gypsy', but comes with oriental appreciation of balance and umami. Chocolate mousse continues the theme: rich and airy, with cinnamon-scented pineapple and a puddle of anglaise.

Open Mon–Sat 5–10.30pm; Tues–Fri noon–3pm
Typical prices E $19 **M** $32 **D** $15
Cards AE MC V Eftpos
Wine Australian and French dominated, mostly under $100; 15 by the glass, 250ml or 500ml pour
Owners Nathalie, Edouard, Antoine & Jacques Reymond
Chef Steven Nelson
Seats 65; outdoor seating; bar
www.bistrogitan.com.au

And ... Enjoy smart, light bites at the bar between 3pm and 5pm.

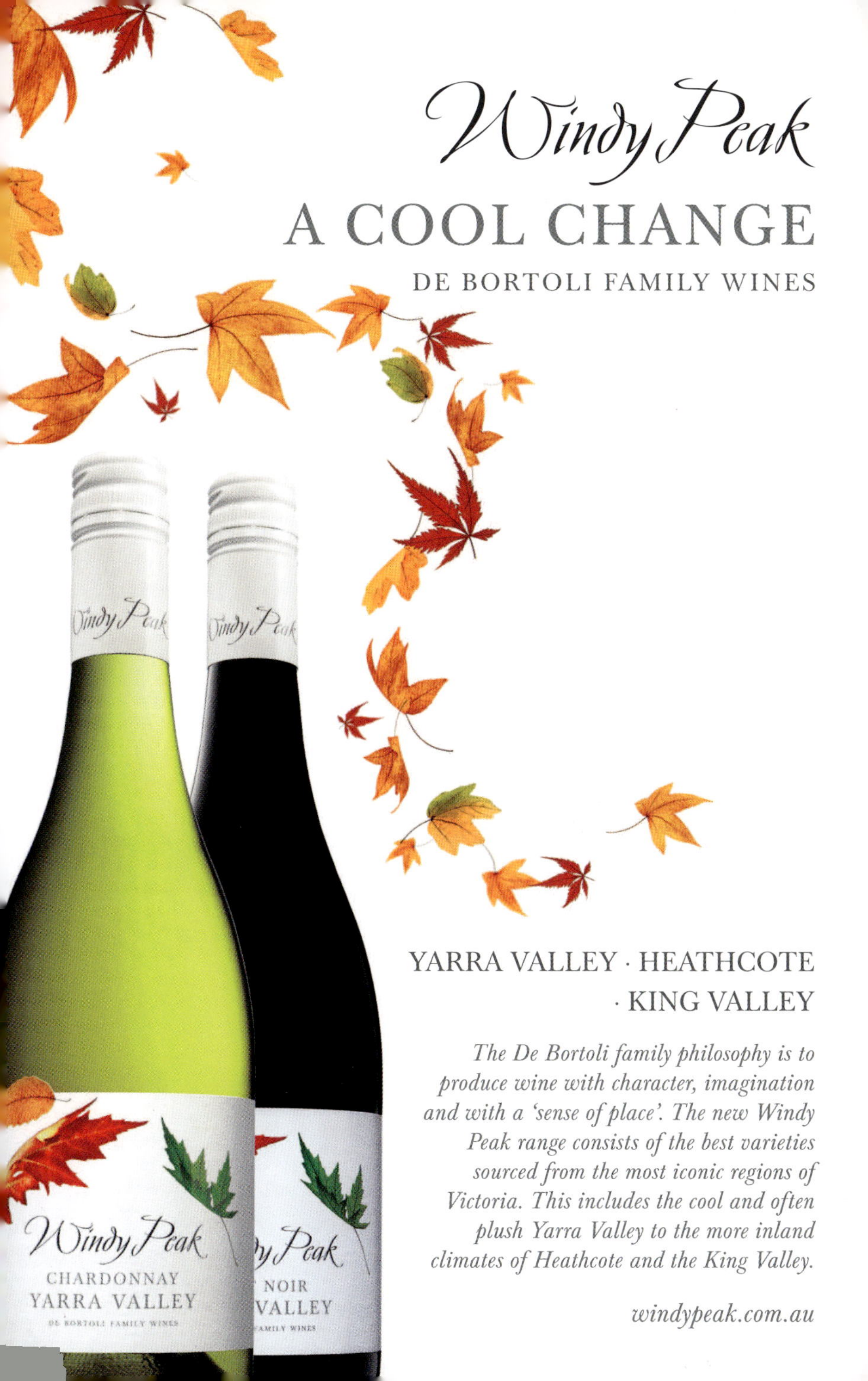
Windy Peak
A COOL CHANGE
DE BORTOLI FAMILY WINES
YARRA VALLEY · HEATHCOTE
· KING VALLEY
The De Bortoli family philosophy is to produce wine with character, imagination and with a 'sense of place'. The new Windy Peak range consists of the best varieties sourced from the most iconic regions of Victoria. This includes the cool and often plush Yarra Valley to the more inland climates of Heathcote and the King Valley.
windypeak.com.au
Windy Peak
CHARDONNAY
YARRA VALLEY

Bistro Guillaume

Riverside, Crown Complex, Southbank **9292 4751**

FRENCH **15/20**

Francophiles be warned - Bistro Guillaume will make you giddy with glee. French accents swirl around the elegant dining room, with its signature light fittings that resemble blousy pantalons, and there's champagne by the glass, steak frites and Guillaume's silky Paris mash on the menu. Jaunty green highlights and a one-page placemat menu hint at a sense of fun. There are simple classics - oysters shucked to order, charcuterie - prepared and delivered with care. Rustic pork and chicken liver terrine is lively with thyme, neatly wrapped in a prosciutto ribbon and served atop a lick of dijon mustard. French onion soup warms the heart, sweet and thick and crowned with a slice of gruyere-topped grilled baguette. Mains might break from tradition somewhat, with dishes like barramundi fillet balanced by spirited carrot and ginger puree and coriander butter. *Enfin*, three plump profiteroles, house-made vanilla-bean icecream sandwiched in their mouths and covered with a warm, velvety chocolate sauce, poured at the table, prove the pièce de résistance.

Open Daily noon-late; Sat-Sun 8am-11am
Typical prices E $24 **M** $34 **D** $18
Cards DC AE MC V
Wine Succinct, no-nonsense selection; reserve list on request
Owners Crown Casino Pty Ltd & Guillaume Brahimi
Chefs Guillaume Brahimi & Graeme McLaughlin
Seats 75; outdoor seating; private room; bar
www.bistroguillaume.com.au

And ... Lunch deals are available Monday to Saturday.

Bistro Thierry

511 Malvern Road, Toorak **9824 0888**

FRENCH **14.5/20**

Maybe you're dreaming of a trip to Paris, anticipating a warm, wood-panelled brasserie with bentwood chairs and solicitous waiters in waistcoats, a menu crackling with golden frites and burnished duck skin, followed by chocolate souffle lovingly filled with unctuous hot sauce and rushed from the kitchen. In that case, make your first stopover Hawksburn Village. Bistro Thierry is like the best-of-French-brasserie experiences. Rich beef bourguignon under a shard of pastry, roast chicken with asparagus, steak frites, warm chevre salad, and even Moroccan tagine that every real Frenchie craves regularly are there to enjoy. But the kitchen also steps out confidently with delicate entrees like rare tuna with avocado mousse and horseradish foam, or the more adventurous blackboard specials. Crepes suzette, the lush souffle or caramelised tarte tatin feel obligatory - no passport required.

Open Daily noon-4pm, 6-10pm
Typical prices E $24 **M** $36.50 **D** $15
Cards AE MC V
Wine A well-tended and tempting list with a fabulous selection of French wines, from value to luxury, as well as some exciting smaller labels in the local selection; BYO Sun night (corkage $15 a bottle)
Owners Thierry Cornevin & Olivier Ferretjans
Chef Frederic Naud
Seats 65; outdoor seating
www.bistrothierry.com

And ... Sommelier Olivier Ferretjans, who hails from the UK's famous Waterside Inn, liked Bistro Thierry so much he bought in.

Bistro Vue

Normanby Chambers, 430 Little Collins Street, City **9691 3838**

FRENCH 15/20

Shannon Bennett's take on turn-of-the-century Paris ensures that Bistro Vue retains a flamboyant, romantic feel. It's got some growing room in its new space, thanks to the relocation of Bennett's flagship Vue de Monde, and at first it feels, well, big. But settle into a rich velvet banquette, and give over to the mood and exemplary service. Start with smoked trout on toasted brioche, enlivened by an artistic palette of capers, lime, shallots and onions. Or maybe classically prepared steak tartare, invigorated by truffle oil and cornichons. For mains, the plat du jour might be bouillabaisse; or David Blackmore's irresistible wagyu, accompanied by fat, golden Pont Neuf potatoes, watercress and an array of classic sauces. The highlight's dessert, especially the tarte tatin, its pan theatrically flipped at the table, exposing runny flavours of vanilla bean, cinnamon, creme anglaise and caramelised apple. Perfection. Like Paris itself, Bistro Vue has ups and downs, but the sum of the parts remains satisfying.

Open Mon–Sat 11am–late
Typical prices E $20 **M** $36 **D** $14
Cards DC AE MC V Eftpos
Wine A tight French-dominated list, with broad price depth ranging from $40 to $495
Owner Shannon Bennett
Chef Chris Bonello
Seats 150; private room; bar
www.vuedemonde.com.au

And … Feeling rich? Look out for truffle supplements for $60 a head.

Bistrot d'Orsay

184 Collins Street, City **9654 6498**

FRENCH/MEDITERRANEAN **13.5/20**

Whether you're supping on wine and charcuterie under the lights of the theatre next door, or settling in your bentwood chair for a lazy afternoon lunch, Bistrot d'Orsay feels like it belongs in a foreign holiday, but one you can happily enjoy any time. Banquettes, dark-wood panelling, vintage prints and subdued lighting are so textbook bistro they resemble set dressing rather than decor, but the atmosphere is warm and inviting. Pre-theatre peak times are handled with panache by a smart and savvy team, ensuring everyone feels like they have the best seat in the house. Classics such as delicate bouillabaisse partnered with a robust rouille show exemplary restraint, while mushroom gnocchi with chard, truffle and pecorino is unapologetically rich. Perfect, still-pink eye fillet calls for an extra jug of bordelaise sauce to dunk the crisp ends of thick-cut chips. A chilled sticky and French cheese – perhaps a creamy d'Affinois or savoury blue Saint Agur – may suffice for those with no room for encore.

Open Mon–Sat 9am–11pm
Typical prices E $21 **M** $34.50 **D** $18.50
Cards AE MC V Eftpos
Wine Thoughtfully annotated list covering European and local wines, many by the glass
Owners Kenneth Meere & John Tully
Chef Quinn Spencer
Seats 50; outdoor seating
www.bistrotdorsay.com.au

And … Build the timing of your visit (and use of shared bathrooms) around the schedule of the Athenaeum Theatre next door.

Blue Chillies

182 Brunswick Street, Fitzroy **9417 0071**

MALAYSIAN **13/20**

There's comfort to be found in the satisfying portions and real-deal spices of this Brunswick Street old hand. The charmingly worn interior is a relaxed mix of contemporary (dark wood, low lighting, slate-grey banquettes) and neat Asian grocery store style. Sharing is best, and entree specials such as fragrant pomelo and nashi salad with tangy belachan-lime dressing will ferry you straight to a sunny Langkawi beach bar. Others, like otak otak – aromatic banana leaf parcels filled with a moussey scallop and fish – may sing with spice, while the popular Nonya duck curry delivers deep, earthy flavours that cry out for a flaky roti mop. No lazy dessert shortcuts here – Asian-inspired coconut creme caramel with ginger icecream is a winner. Though service can dwindle when slow, it's obliging when prompted. Sure, there will always be more exciting, younger options along this strip, but this is a solid go-to spot that continues to age gracefully.

Open Daily noon–2.30pm; Mon–Thurs 6–10.30pm; Fri–Sat 6–11pm; Sun 6–10pm
Typical prices E $8 **M** $25 **D** $8
Cards AE MC V
Wine Brief, all-Australian and NZ list of well-known but quality producers
Owners Linh Cao & Ricky Ng
Chef Soo Lam Tan
Seats 90; outdoor seating; private room
www.bluechillies.com.au

And ... Weekdays, there's a two-course lunch special, including entree, main and glass of wine for $17.50.

Bluestone Restaurant

349 Flinders Lane, City **9620 4060**

CONTEMPORARY **14/20**

With its heritage-listed building and rough-hewn bluestone walls, this is one of Melbourne's enduring business eateries by day. The decor, with heavy gilt mirrors, has changed little in decades, but not so the menu. Chef Cody Cunningham has brought new geographies and vegetarian adventures to a menu that balances well-teamed contrasts. Alongside Hopkins River eye-fillet steak with goat's camembert butter you might find entrees like a sleek tuna tataki enlivened by wasabi emulsion and a gentle seaweed salad. You'll also find the signature dish of dill-and-parmesan-crusted baked Hervey Bay scallops; long-standing regulars demand they remain a menu fixture. Mains may be a sumac-dressed lamb rump uplifted by soft turmeric labna, or the ever-changing vegetarian tasting plate where you might find a vegan tagine, a pumpkin pastie or vegetable empanada. Dessert may be a rich, dense chocolate tart. And, in the bar downstairs there's more broad geography represented in tapas and pizza.

Open Mon–Fri noon–3pm; Mon–Sat 5.30–10pm
Typical prices E $22 **M** $38 **D** $14
Cards DC AE MC V Eftpos
Wine Wide range of reasonably priced Australian wine with some European offerings; 18 by the glass
Owners Valerie & Jason McLean
Chef Cody Cunningham
Seats 140; private room; bar
www.bluestonerestaurantbar.com.au

And ... Three specials make lunch here even more alluring, with a choice of deals: $35, $45 or $55 for one, two or three courses.

The Boathouse

7 The Boulevard, Moonee Ponds **9375 2456**

CONTEMPORARY **12/20**

The lovely riverside location is the main attraction of this accessible west-side outpost co-owned by *MasterChef*'s Gary Mehigan. The vast oblong dining room offers enough homely touches (cushioned sofas, plasma screen, dedicated kids' menu) to keep families happy, and the food focuses on simple, rustic mod-Med flavours. Picks from the mezze menu might include crisp school prawns with herbed aioli, grilled Hervey Bay scallops topped with smoky chorizo dice and chimichurri or a bubbling, golden wedge of grilled kefalograviera cheese. Solid mains like the succulent pork belly with salty crackling and creamed corn puree are a bona fide hit, while others, such as salmon fillet with green bean, orzo and grapefruit salad, may be blandly less so. Wood-fired pizzas are popular, and desserts a high point – think peanut-butter panna cotta with salted popcorn icecream. Slow and patchy service can be an issue, but is offset to an extent by the primo views and (in cooler months) roaring open fire.

Open Mon 9am–4pm; Tues–Fri 9am–late; Sat–Sun 8.30am–late
Typical prices E $14 **M** $28 **D** $15
Cards DC AE MC V Eftpos
Wine Brief, mostly Australian selection, almost all by the glass
Owners Gary Mehigan & Steve Bogdani
Chef Joshua Smallwood
Seats 300; outdoor seating; private room
www.theboat-house.com.au

And ... Take in the view from the Boathouse's spacious outdoor deck.

Bok Choy Brighton

300 New Street, Brighton **9592 0253**

CHINESE **12/20**

Bok Choy's epic-length menus twinkle with luxe ingredients like lobster, and vintage and reserve wines. The dining room's deep-plum walls, gilt-framed artworks and dramatic spotlighting lend a theatrical edge to the dimly lit interior. Food presentation occasionally shows a matching flourish (something occasionally lacking in the service) – 'Long Island' spring rolls are chopstick-length and presented upright in a parfait glass with orchids and herbs. The extensive Chinese menu is a real crowd-pleaser, swinging from live lobster to beer-snack prawn cutlets, butterflied and crumbed, although desserts can feel like an afterthought (banana fritters and icecream, bland choc mousse). Scallops, glossily tossed with sugar-snaps and baby corn, really zing with shards of fresh ginger, while spicy calamari is pillow-soft and delicately battered. A simple 100g fillet of wild barramundi in a sweet, dark sauce with coriander and bok choy makes a delightful light meal, while beancurd with mushrooms is total comfort food.

Open Daily 5.30pm–late; Tues–Sat noon–3pm; Sun 11.30am–3pm
Typical prices E $14 **M** $29.50 **D** $9
Cards DC AE MC V
Wine Includes a good array of reasonably priced Australian drops; BYO (corkage $8 a bottle)
Owner Multi Ling International
Chef Ken So Yee
Seats 80
www.bokchoychinesecuisine.com.au

And ... There's jolly trolley yum cha on Sundays.

Bokchoy Tang

Federation Square, City **9650 8666**

NORTHERN CHINESE **14/20**

The frenetic open kitchen here may be alive with wok tossing and noodle throwing, but the modern dining room is a spacious, civilised spot with views of the river and square. One of the founding restaurants of Federation Square, with a loyal following, it makes a feature of dishes from China's north and west. House-made noodles and breads are a highlight, whether crisp fried pancakes or pillowy steamed buns ideal for mopping up the numbing Sichuan pepper sauce accompanying a plate of crisp king prawns. Specialities include a la carte yum cha at lunch: dumplings tend to be fried, the pastry chewier, the spices more robust than the more familiar Cantonese. There are rich pickings for vegetarians, such as a dish of gently steamed white and black fungi, lotus seeds, enoki and shiitake mushrooms, bamboo shoots and tofu with a subtle, ginger-rich sauce. Tofu is a key ingredient in many dishes. Presentation can become rustic on occasion, but lack of refinement doesn't compromise flavour.

Open Daily 11am–3pm; Sun–Thurs 5–10pm; Fri–Sat 5–11pm
Typical prices E $14 **M** $28.50 **D** $9.50
Cards AE MC V Eftpos
Wine Reasonable selection of Australian and NZ wines with an emphasis on Victoria
Owner George Qing
Chefs Feng Liu & Neil Feng
Seats 150; outdoor seating; private room; bar
www.bokchoytang.com.au

And ... There are good express lunch deals with wine; and northern and western-style yum cha.

Bombay by Night

355 North Road, Caulfield South **9578 6150**

INDIAN **14.5/20**

Twenty-plus years in the business, a *Good Food Guide* stalwart and a *Cheap Eats* hall-of-famer. What else is there to say about Bombay by Night? Well, there's this: it's still damn good and arguably the best Indian food you'll find in Melbourne. It's a combination of the relaxed, Euro-inspired room with a low-key, jazz-inflected soundtrack, fabulously executed northern Indian classics – say, gobi pakoras (fried cauliflower in a lentil batter) or a coconut-based prawn curry with a lightness of touch seldom found elsewhere – with rotating specials that might include ultra-tender lamb cutlets marinated in hung yoghurt, served with a vindaloo-spiced mayonnaise. Mop it all up with the light and puffy naan bread and you'll be on the path to contentment – until you have the kulfi (mango or praline) for dessert, at which point you might think you've reached nirvana.

Open Tues–Sun 6–10pm
Typical prices E $8.50 **M** $18.50 **D** $8
Cards AE MC V Eftpos
Wine Plenty by the glass on a thoughtfully chosen list ranging from aromatic whites to big, bold reds; BYO (corkage $4.50 a head)
Owners Arvind & Jaspal Gandhi
Chef Ajay Pal
Seats 90; private room
www.bombaybynight.com

And ... Thanks to its location, parking is never a problem.

TOP 10 BUSINESS LUNCH

Becco
11-25 Crossley Street, City **9663 3000**
Super-stylish retro Italian looks, solid Italian comfort food and sharp service.

Bistro Vue
430 Little Collins Street, City **9691 3838**
France's greatest bistro hits given a modern twist against a subtly theatrical backdrop.

Caterina's Cucina e Bar
Basement, 221 Queen Street, City **9670 8488**
The legal set love the cellar location, classic Italian menu and great wine list.

Ezard
187 Flinders Lane, City **9639 6811**
Elegantly low-key, swish basement setting plus whizz-bang modern Asian flavours.

Flower Drum
17 Market Lane, City **9662 3655**
A deal-sealing reputation, top-flight Cantonese food and an unbeatable setting.

Grossi Florentino
80 Bourke Street, City **9662 1811**
Melbourne's grandest Italian dining room plus voluminous, luxurious food and wine lists.

Hanabishi
187 King Street, City **9670 1167**
Excellent quality raw fish plus an impressive big-name wine list attract a loyal business following.

P M 24
24 Russell Street, City **9207 7424**
Philippe Mouchel stands guard over some of Melbourne's best French bistro food.

The Press Club
72 Flinders Street, City **9677 9677**
A sophisticated, dark-hued room, modern Greek flavours and the sweet smell of success.

Rockpool Bar & Grill
Crown Complex, Southbank **8648 1900**
Brilliant steak menu, charming service and a knee-weakening wine list.

Bottega
74 Bourke Street, City **9654 2252**

MODERN ITALIAN **14.5/20**

Between Pellegrini's and Grossi Florentino at the top end of Bourke Street, Bottega might seem like the new kid on the block, but with a decade of service now under the belt, it too is entering the long-timer league. A well-oiled operation that always manages to keep things looking fresh, its dining room is smart and its staff professional. The nicely balanced modern Italian menu offers plenty of options. You might start with sweet scallops grilled with crisp pancetta and truffle vinaigrette, or head straight for great-sounding pastas (available in two sizes) – maybe hand-rolled strozzapreti with clams, mussels, prawns and calamari. Goat, roasted for 12 hours, arrives shredded and formed into a tile with burghul, mandarin, dates, almonds and a yoghurt dressing, while beef cheeks are braised in sangiovese and paired with creamy cauliflower puree. Chocolate desserts are always a standout, maybe a mousse with chocolate sponge, hazelnut praline and Amarena cherry.

Open Mon–Fri noon–3pm; Mon–Sat 5.30–11pm
Typical prices E $22 **M** $38 **D** $18
Cards DC AE MC V
Wine An impressive list of Italian and Australian wines to suit a range of budgets; 17 by the glass and a number of half bottles
Owner Denis Lucey
Chef Gabriele Olivieri
Seats 130; outdoor seating; private room
www.bottega.com.au

And ... Pre-theatre deals include a glass of wine and two courses for $40 or three for $50.

Bouzy Rouge

470 Bridge Road, Richmond **9429 4348**

EUROPEAN/PORTUGUESE **13.5/20**

Bouzy Rouge is kooky – in a good way – much like an endearingly eccentric aunt. A mismatch of mirrored bulls' heads, alligator-patterned banquettes and hanging brass water pots surrounds spacious, white-clothed tables. The long dining room feels like a hunting lodge (ornamental cattle heads, zebra prints) that's crashed into a fancy bistro – it's cosy and it's fun. That's echoed by genuinely enthusiastic and polished waiters who make navigating the weighty wine list and verbal specials easy breezy. Start with tapas: a burly Portuguese chorizo doused in grappa and brought flaming to the table. Whipped, velvety salt cod is king, best piled atop triangles of airy flatbread. A main course of squid-ink paella evokes a plunge in the ocean: plump seafood swimming in a sea of blackened rice. Barbecued quail, surrounded by an earthy artichoke and ancient grain salad, lacks the punch of the tapas. Finish by dunking churros in thick, molten chocolate.

Open Daily 11am–late
Typical prices E $17 **M** $33 **D** $16
Cards DC AE MC V Eftpos
Wine Long list of Europeans including Spanish and Portuguese wines, plus boutique locals; 32 by the glass
Owners Jose & Sandra De Oliveira
Chefs James Smythe & Jake Guthrie
Seats 70; outdoor seating; private room; bar
www.bouzyrouge.com.au

And ... Ask about the signature slow roasts designed for sharing.

The Brix

Rear, 412 Brunswick Street, Fitzroy **9417 6114**

CONTEMPORARY **14.5/20**

The Brix is a wildcard restaurant – a smart Fitzroy bistro that asks diners to commit to a five-course tasting menu without the conventional bells and whistles of 'fine dining'. It's a resolutely modern experience, from the designer fitout of macramé, wooden shingles and potted ferns to the food of Ashly Hicks, an enthusiastic exponent of the contemporary Spanish and Danish schools. The nightly set menu showcases his naturalistic cuisine, foraged ingredients, and clever plays on texture and temperature. There might be jerky-like strips of dried venison with beetroot, candied red chilli, crunchy pops of wild rice and a unifying base of goat's curd; a fat tranche of monkfish well matched to the dusky sweetness of onion, artichokes and celeriac; or sous-vide lamb loin and a confit tile of belly, with a beautifully balanced pale lamb jus, broccoli florets, raw leek, samphire and dehydrated black olive. A brief a la carte menu of French bistro classics runs alongside, but commit to the full journey for the best of the Brix.

Open Tues–Sat 6pm–late; Fri–Sat noon–3pm
Typical prices E $17 **M** $28 **D** $14; set menu $90 (5 courses)
Cards MC V Eftpos
Wine Short, sharp, interesting mix of Old and New World with a good selection by the glass
Owners Emma O'Mara, Keir Vaughan & Tom O'Mara
Chef Ashly Hicks
Seats 40; outdoor seating; private room; bar
www.thebrix.com.au

And ... The set menu is compulsory for bookings of five or more.

Builders Arms Hotel

211 Gertrude Street, Fitzroy **9417 7700**

CONTEMPORARY **14/20**

There might be steak, pie and a roast on the menu, but the hotel's part-owned by Andrew McConnell, so the dry-aged rib eye comes with killer house-made mustard or textbook tarragon-scented bearnaise, the fish pie's chunky with lightly smoked trout and prawns and topped with a golden pillow of pastry, and fork-tender shoulder of lamb is big enough to keep Fred Flintstone satisfied. With a clean, almost New England-like fitout of white wainscoted walls, charcoal banquettes and wooden floors, the Builders Arms looks like the tradies have just finished the job. Unfussy service gets the food out smartly while leaving you to pour your own wine. Look out for McConnell-style treats such as anchovy toast, ancient grain salad and crisp pig's ear crackling. With 2012 Young Chef of the Year Josh Murphy in the kitchen, this happily buzzy pub delivers downright good food, right through to a celestial dessert combining meringue, tangy curd sorbet, quince and candied herbs.

Open Daily noon–11pm; evening bookings for 8–12 only
Typical prices E $14 **M** $32 **D** $14
Cards AE MC V Eftpos
Wine Cocktails and beers on tap and in bottle keep company with a sophisticated list, all $40-plus
Owners Josh Murphy, Andrew McConnell & Anthony Hammond
Chefs Josh Murphy & Andrew McConnell
Seats 70; outdoor seating; private room; bar
www.buildersarmshotel.com.au

And ... There's a garden out back, with a rotisserie roasting meats.

Cafe Bedda

242 High Street, Northcote **9482 9420**

SICILIAN **14/20**

Bedda continues to fly the flag for the distinctive food of Sicily from atop fashionable Rucker's Hill. A gleaming electric pizza oven is the engine driving this soulful operation, turning out bubbling slabs of goodness – perhaps the 'Etna' flowing with mozzarella, hot salami, roasted peppers and olives, or the 'Cicoria': chicory, asiago, lemon and black pepper on a white base. But pizza, whether to eat in or take away, is only half the story. Hemmed in by walls of canned tomatoes, packets of pasta and bottles of Italian sparkling water, the kitchen pumps out Sicilian delights such as crisp saffron-tinted arancini stuffed with molten mozzarella, tomato and peas; almond-studded cous cous with a soupy seafood stew; or tubular schiaffoni pasta with an orange and cinnamon-inflected lamb ragu – a reminder of the Arabic influence on this island cuisine. Locals tend to express their pleasure volubly in the checkerboard-floored room, especially once desserts arrive: perhaps cannoli filled with sweetened, lemon-scented ricotta and licked with chocolate.

Open Tues–Sun 5.30–10pm
Typical prices E $8 **M** $27.90 **D** $11.50
Cards MC V Eftpos
Wine Wines from all over Italy dominate a concise list; 10 by the glass
Owners Patrick Ciccaldo & Hugo Diaz
Chefs Hugo Diaz & Daniele Carcangiu
Seats 58; outdoor seating
www.cafebedda.com

And ... Expect two sittings on busy Friday and Saturday nights.

Cafe Di Stasio

31 Fitzroy Street, St Kilda **9525 3999**

ITALIAN **16/20**

A meal here can feel like the start of something. For two decades, discussions have become deals, attractions bloomed into affairs and lunches stretched into dinners. There's an intensity and clubby intimacy about the tight L-shaped dining room with its dark carpet, slatted blinds to the street, and blotchy walls dotted with theatrical masks. Double-clothed tables are set with fine stemware and tea-lights glow from within paper-wrapped wine glasses. Sharp, formal waiters wear white jackets and deliver – along with the odd cheeky aside – simple, smartly executed Italian favourites. The carpaccio is a case in point – petals of raw beef with olive oil, shards of parmesan, leaves of rocket and a lemon wedge. Every ingredient is top-quality: simple and superb. Duck comes crisp-skinned with tiny shreds of spaetzle; suckling pig is variously moist, crunchy and chewy, accompanied by baked apple and a salty, anchovy-spiked pile of wilted chicory: seasonings may tend to err to the salty. Foamy zabaglione makes a warm, marsala-scented finish.

Open Daily noon–3pm, 6–11pm
Typical prices E $29 **M** $41 **D** $17
Cards DC AE MC V
Wine Long and Italian-accented; by-the-glass choices include owner's own label
Owner Rinaldo Di Stasio
Chef Steven Rofe
Seats 70; outdoor seating
www.distasio.com.au

citibank Privileges

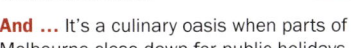

And … It's a culinary oasis when parts of Melbourne close down for public holidays.

Cafe Latte

521 Malvern Road, Toorak **9826 5846**

ITALIAN **14/20**

Cafe Latte's facelift means white walls, a new bar and a huge, beautiful suspended hoop light fitting designed by Marcos Davidson, decorated with birds and flowers. Loyal Latte regulars, some of whom have been coming since the early '90s, have been happy to reacquaint themselves with the menu's unpretentious, authentic, boldly flavoured dishes from the Puglia region, described by owner Luca Lorusso as the Japan of Italy. Thus, there's a focus on seafood, often served raw, as in tuna carpaccio with sweet-and-sour cauliflower. There's also crumbed, baked, smoked sardines sandwiched with caramelised onion, pinenuts and sultanas; fragrant seafood stew; or tender, white, paper-thin poached veal with anchovy aioli balanced by tart tomatoes, olives and capers. Gently rich veal ragu pennoni and soft, deep-flavoured ox cheek favour meat lovers, too. Traditional Italian desserts like tiramisu, panna cotta and zeppole never fail to please, especially the gooey cooked-to-order chocolate pudding that regulars happily wait to have delivered steaming fresh.

Open Mon–Sat 8am–10pm; Sun 8am–4pm
Typical prices E $19 **M** $36 **D** $16
Cards DC AE MC V
Wine Quality Italian and Australian list; 12-plus by the glass; BYO (corkage $20 a bottle)
Owner Luca Lorusso
Chefs Adriano Dimaso & Cataldo Rana
Seats 40; outdoor seating; private room; bar
www.cafelatte.com.au

And … Always open for coffee; you can even book for breakfast.

Cafeteria

36 Bluff Road, Black Rock **9589 2200**

EUROPEAN/MEDITERRANEAN **13/20**

Light, airy, buzzy, busy – that's Cafeteria in a nutshell. The week's sole dinner service, on Friday nights, offers Eugene Lavery's diverse, ever-changing menu that might include local yabbies with cauliflower skordalia and capocollo (cured pork), or perhaps 'traditional Irish stew, made by an Irishman'. But it's the daytime throng on which Cafeteria thrives. Seasonal, artfully plated antipasto might comprise asparagus with hollandaise, prawn and chorizo skewers, and cheese-filled, battered and fried zucchini flowers. Follow with the generously proportioned seafood risotto of mussels, clams and squid, with the earthy punch of saffron, or perhaps a roast beef and asparagus salad, a hulking lunch dish befitting big appetites. Desserts are mainly house-made, displayed behind glass, and might include macarons or dense, fudgy brownies. Breakfast runs until noon; if fried potato, black pudding, roast capsicum and poached egg isn't enough to encourage early(ish) rising, what is?

Open Sat–Thurs 7.30am–5pm; Fri 7.30am–10pm
Typical prices E $12.50 **M** $22.50 **D** $8.50
Cards AE MC V Eftpos
Wine Short list of predominantly NZ and Australian labels, with most by the glass
Owners Eugene Lavery & Eugen Ljutic
Chef Eugene Lavery
Seats 50; outdoor seating

And ... Six choices on the kids' menu shows they know it's not all about the grown-ups.

Carlisle Wine Bar

137 Carlisle Street, Balaclava **9531 3222**

ITALIAN **14.5/20**

There's vinyl on the turntable, and folks relaxing with a glass at outside tables; on appearances alone, this looks like a casual hangout. But, it's so much more. The wine list is expertly curated, the service is casual but attentive, and the kitchen excels at sending sharp, seasonal Italian dishes out into this slim, wood-warm restaurant. For a light bite, try an antipasto that might include char-grilled baby octopus, tangy slaw and a wedge of pumpkin-studded frittata, or perhaps a few tender twirls of pistachio-crumbed calamari. Mains feature a small array of quality meat dishes, including fish of the day, but it's the satin-smooth handmade pasta dishes that are the real showstoppers. Orecchiette with broccoli, peas and cherry tomato has a thrillingly fresh aroma, while spinach-and-ricotta gnocchi with gorgonzola cream is rich and heady, yet both are light enough to let you fit in a wicked Italian doughnut and a sip of sticky.

Open Mon–Fri 2–10pm; Fri–Sat noon–10pm
Typical prices E $18 **M** $29.50 **D** $13.50
Cards MC V Eftpos
Wine A tightly selected list by the sommelier owner, with a good span of varieties; 16 by the glass
Owner Steven Milic
Chef Jason Stilley
Seats 50; outdoor seating; bar
www.carlislewinebar.com.au

And ... The express lunch menu is brilliant value, including one course and a glass of wine for $18.

Carlton Wine Room

172–174 Faraday Street, Carlton **9347 2626**

EUROPEAN **14.5/20**

Lygon Street, Carlton, is one of Melbourne's best-known eat streets, but, paradoxically, most of the area's top restaurants are found in the surrounding streets. Take Carlton Wine Room, which opened in 2011 but already has an air of mature confidence. The deceptively large Victorian corner building sprawls over several levels, including an atmospheric bluestone cellar. The urbane Jay Bessell, one of three partners, guides diners through a wine list peppered with unusual varietals and idiosyncratic tasting notes and a clever, flexible menu that doesn't sacrifice flavour for technique. It kicks off with 'wine food' (antipasti) such as spicy cevapcici sausages, and tomato salad with crisp rice puffs and lush burrata (creamy mozzarella), then moves into dishes sized for pairing and sharing, among them satisfyingly earthy pork belly with white beans and baby turnips. The kitchen seems most at home with savoury dishes, but meringue with berries and a sweet-sharp balsamic syrup offers an excuse to read the wine list to the end.

Open Mon–Wed 5–10pm; Thurs noon–10pm; Fri–Sat noon–10.30pm
Typical prices E $17 **M** $35 **D** $15
Cards AE MC V
Wine Sterling list replete with half bottles, benchmark Australians and lesser known European wines
Owners Jay Bessell, Michael Tenace & Connie Cappello
Chef Matthew Silovic
Seats 130; private room
www.thecarltonwineroom.com.au

And ... Leave yourself in the chef's hands with the $56 three-course 'feed me' menu.

The Carringbush Hotel

228 Langridge Street, Abbotsford **9417 2918**

CONTEMPORARY **13/20**

Old-man pub or fine-diner? The Carringbush Hotel is both and that's part of the allure. In residential Abbotsford this grand old dame remains youthful despite its 142-year history. Squirreled at the rear, past the relaxed bar and memorabilia-heavy bistro, is a rustic exposed-brick dining room, bright with crisp linen and a courtyard view. The service echoes the hotel's sentiment: honest and professional. So too is the menu, with its pages of culinary definitions, a nod perhaps to chef Matt O'Meara's time at Bendigo fine-diner Whirrakee. A brittle zucchini flower comes swollen with salmon, bolstered by three fat scallops and a tri-colour of wasabi, squid ink and flying fish caviar. A tasting plate of duck liver pâté, chicken galantine and flawless scotch egg is impaired by a cloying dressing; better is wagyu scotch fillet, perfectly paired with dauphinoise and a lightly smoked pork belly salad. For dessert, poached plums are heightened by zesty lime yoghurt and macadamia shortbread.

Open Tues–Fri noon–3pm; Tues–Sat 6–9pm
Typical prices E $18 **M** $34 **D** $14
Cards DC AE MC V Eftpos
Wine Succinct, almost all-Australian wine list with agreeable pub pricing; 16 by the glass
Owners Mick Liszukiewicz & Greg Gross
Chef Matt O'Meara
Seats 45; outdoor seating; private room; bar
www.thecarringbush.com.au

And ... There's a neat bistro menu dished up seven days a week.

Casa Ciuccio

15 Gertrude Street, Fitzroy **8488 8150**

MEDITERRANEAN **14.5/20**

Effortlessly cool Casa Cuiccio, a skinny two-roomed space from the team who brought you Bar Lourinha, is confident, vibey and loads of fun. Gather around the beautiful timber bar in the atmospheric front room, have a chinwag with the chefs at the 'kitchen table', or chill in the quieter courtyard, festive with umbrellas and fairy lights. A compact ensemble of dishes for snacking and sharing might start with crunchy-soft chorizo and potato croquettes, or an anchovy 'montadito', a char-striped finger sandwich with a juicy white anchovy. Tender octopus tentacles come hot off the grill, but the big tickets here are the smoked coal-pit meats, slow-cooked for at least six hours. There might be suckling kid, or Black Angus rib, or a fantastic Boston pork butt rubbed simply with allspice, lemon thyme and garlic, plus a generous serve of small potatoes roasted whole in their jackets. Finish with a bowl of cool, caramel dulce de leche scattered with crunchy peanut praline. Service is whip-smart.

Open Tues–Thurs noon–11pm; Fri–Sat noon–1am
Typical prices E $10 **M** $32 **D** $12
Cards AE MC V Eftpos
Wine One of the city's best new lists: compact, competitive and snappy with locals and Europeans, plus a focus on independent, small producers
Owners Matt McConnell, Jo Gamvros & Simon Benjamin
Chef Matt McConnell
Seats 40; outdoor seating; private room; bar
www.casaciuccio.com.au

And ... Hang out upstairs at Bar Chooch.

Caterina's Cucina e Bar

Basement, 221 Queen Street, City **9670 8488**

ITALIAN **14/20**

This luncheon-only basement Italian restaurant is an institution in Melbourne for both its Italian fare and the hospitality of its namesake restaurateur. Regulars are greeted by name and stick to favourite orders despite a long list of daily specials. House-made pastas and risottos are authentic. Carpaccio of fillet of Angus beef comes with house-made mayonnaise, imported olive oil, shaves of grana padano and snapping fresh celery to add crunch. Slowly oven-braised meats change daily and may be goat, veal or lamb – all will leave you mopping up cooking juices and all come with not-to-be-missed semolina dumplings. Twice-cooked, on-the-bone duck leg is served with a boned duck leg. Lunch here can be short or spent lingering over great wines of the world from an excellent list of domestic and imported wine served by knowledgeable staff. Italian cheeses are well selected and treated seriously. Caterina Borsato flits from table to table adding her unique personal touch.

Open Mon–Fri noon–3.30pm
Typical prices E $22 **M** $35 **D** $16.50
Cards DC AE MC V
Wine Extensive, well-balanced and fairly priced list based on quality with Australia, France and Italy well represented; 16 by the glass
Owner Caterina Borsato
Chef Michele Usci
Seats 90; bar
www.caterinas.com.au

And ... Caterina is one of TV's longest-serving food presenters. Her *Regional Italian Cuisine* has been seen on Channel 31 for almost a decade.

Cecconi's Cantina

Basement, 61 Flinders Lane, City **8663 0500**

MODERN ITALIAN **15/20**

The luxe, dark and clubby basement space of Cecconi's boasts one of the more theatrical kitchens in Melbourne – wide-open and centre stage. Knowledgeable, professional staff and consistently well-executed food ensure that Cecconi's continues to hold a place among the ranks of our top Italian restaurants. The broad menu might see you kicking off with delicate kingfish carpaccio served with avocado puree, or perfectly executed seafood linguine – the freshest of seafood, and nicely dressed pasta with a touch of chilli heat. For main course, try perhaps poached John Dory with crab tortellini and clams or a simple veal cotoletta with a salad of savoy cabbage and apple. Artfully plated desserts might include deconstructed chilled apple crumble with walnut, apple puree and yoghurt sorbet, or citrus parfait with honey biscuit crumbs, passionfruit and a dusting of raspberry 'snow'.

Open Mon–Fri 8am–late; Sat 5.30pm–late
Typical prices E $27 **M** $44 **D** $18
Cards AE MC V Eftpos
Wine A smart, broad-ranging and hefty list; 24 by the glass
Owners Olimpia, Maria & Anna Bortolotto
Chefs Olimpia Bortolotto & Daniel Kranjcic
Seats 130; private room; bar
www.cecconis.com

And ... The more casual Cantina, to the left of the kitchen, is a great lower-price option for pre-theatre, lunch or light breakfast.

Centonove

109 Cotham Road, Kew **9817 6468**

ITALIAN **14.5/20**

The plate-sized flounder turns heads and is sold out by 8pm; the suckling pig has been a big hit too. But this handsome, long-time, well-loved local has plenty more to keep regulars returning. Menu mainstays might include steamed zucchini flower with crab, or lemon-crumbed veal. Pastas are house-made, with sauces that beg to be soaked up with crusty Baker D. Chirico bread. Service is informal but meticulous, glasses topped up, linen crisp. Much on the menu is excellent: a tasting plate includes vitello tonnato, carpaccio and figs with gorgonzola. Scallops are lifted by cauliflower puree and crisp pancetta. Lamb rack has lovely accompaniments, a palette of pea puree, burghul and goat's curd. But other dishes perhaps don't hit the same mark – fettuccine with porcini feels too lush with oil. Crisp-skinned barramundi atop fregola in a saffron, spanner crab and tomato broth seems shy with flavours. But desserts reward stayers: hazelnut ganache with chestnut millefoglie and honey icecream, or a classy little plate of petits fours.

Open Tues–Sat 11am–3pm, 6–10pm
Typical prices E $21 **M** $39 **D** $14.50
Cards DC AE MC V Eftpos
Wine A quality list that lingers in Italy; verticals and vintages, but with plenty of choice for all palates and budgets (including by the glass)
Owners Jesse & Kymberly Davidson
Chef Patrick Fletcher
Seats 80; private room
www.centonove.com.au

And ... Downstairs has buzz but upstairs is no poor relation, with big mirrors and chandeliers.

Charcoal Grill on the Hill

289 High Street, Kew **9853 7535**

STEAKHOUSE **13.5/20**

The Grill is so old-school it's cool. While Kew continues to sprout hip new places with exotic menus, this adorably formal veteran sticks with its red-painted walls and gilt-framed repro prints, and its relentless dedication to the equally red stuff that gladens a meat-lover's heart. What's not to like about a place that has a set formula and stubborn rules ('main course minimum $28') and some of the juiciest grain- and grass-fed fillet, rump and porterhouse steak in town? Devoted clients jabber loudly and happily until their meat arrives and then eat quietly, reverentially, before finishing with plump strawberry crepes. The long wine list is eccentrically tended like a garden – every wine affectionately described, meat-friendly wines highlighted and favourites celebrated. Service is excellent, with a real sense of a team determined to please – perhaps with a little complimentary 'palate cleanser' glass of wine, or with the proud, knowledgeable presentation of a groaning cheese tray, pulsing with sticky perfection.

Open Mon–Sat 6pm–midnight; Fri noon–4pm
Typical prices E $11 **M** $48 **D** $11
Cards DC AE MC V Eftpos
Wine Aged and rare wines plus some bargains; meat-friendly Europeans, and hard-to-find Australian shiraz and cab sav
Owners Peter & Dejan Derbogosian, Fabian Caminiti
Chef Fabian Caminiti
Seats 65; private room

And ... The cheeses come from celebrated French affineur Hervé Mons, and have been resting beneath the Rhone Alps.

Charcoal Lane

136 Gertrude Street, Fitzroy **9418 3400**

CONTEMPORARY **14/20**

Gleaming parquetry, fish-trap lightshades and splashes of abstract colour on the walls form a stylish setting for a laid-back clientele taking in Gertrude Street's passing parade through low Victorian windows. Slick staff deliver blushingly pink saltbush lamb loin with honey and mint 'vinaigrette', or perhaps a sticky wedge of glazed salmon, teamed with cured trout and tomato-cardamom sauce. Some dishes star distinctively Australian ingredients: you might find wallaby tartare with horseradish potato salad and Melba toast; a bowl of lemon-myrtle angel-hair pasta with West Australian marron, tomato and young basil; or paperbark-smoked barramundi fillet on parsnip cream. Vegetarians generally have an option in each course – perhaps an entree of fat, braised artichokes with a goat's cheese tart, a main of flowing polenta with wild mushrooms and coddled egg. Desserts – such as bittersweet 'frozen liquid chocolate' with cherry icecream – are as good as they sound.

Open Tues–Sat noon–3pm, 6–10pm
Typical prices E $18 **M** $34 **D** $15
Cards AE MC V Eftpos
Wine Australian, with a focus on boutique, cool-climate producers, plus a couple of Spanish sherries
Owner Mission Australia
Chef Andy Bedford
Seats 50; outdoor seating; private room
www.charcoallane.com.au

And ... The restaurant, which trains Aboriginal youth, takes its name from an old briquette factory at which local Aboriginal people used to meet.

Chez Bob

22 Beatty Avenue, Armadale **9824 8022**

FRENCH **13/20**

Here's a little touch of Paris: physically, gastronomically, linguistically, spiritually. The railway line slopes past a street with a hotchpotch of aged shops clinging to its east side. Among them is Chez Bob, with a bustling service bar, linen-clothed tables, bentwood chairs and French-speaking staff. The menu is Gallic and classic: oysters shucked to order, cured salmon, a terrine of the day. Seafood 'pie' is saucy, almost soupy, the dish crammed with scallops, mussels, prawns and white fish, then topped with puff pastry. Much of the cuisine looks to country France, with dishes such as braised rabbit or veal fillets Normande in a creamy sauce of mushrooms spiked with calvados. A hunk of eye fillet arrives as ordered, rare, pink and juicy, with perfect pommes frites alongside. Desserts are rich and profuse: creamy profiteroles, or there's classic creme brulee. Everything arrives with a flourish, a chat and a smile.

Open Tues–Fri noon–2.30pm; Tues–Sat 6–10.30pm
Typical prices E $19 **M** $35 **D** $14
Cards DC AE MC V
Wine Compact selection of French and Australian bottles, many by the glass; BYO Tues-Thurs (corkage $18 a bottle)
Owner Jean-Paul Tranquille
Chef Julien Perretto
Seats 55; outdoor seating; private room
www.chezbob.com.au

And ... Amp up the 'feels like France' factor with an aperitif of Kir Royale.

Chin Chin

125 Flinders Lane, City **8663 2000**

MODERN THAI **14/20**

'Boom!' go the flavours at Chin Chin – sour tamarind, tangy citrus – each dish bright and aromatic with authentic Thai tastes. They match the raucous vibe at this modern diner, a converted warehouse with exposed bricks and boards, a loud, mostly '80s, soundtrack, in-your-face service and usually a queue for tables packed tight. Benjamin Cooper's strong Thai cooking inspires the kitchen. From the barbecue might come magnificent salmon, lusciously soft and flavoursome with coconut red curry, lime and Thai basil in its banana-leaf jacket. Signature kingfish sashimi is juicy, fleshy and bright with lime, chilli, Asian basil and zigzags of coconut cream. You're warned about 'not-for-amateurs' jungle curry – it's hot but not outrageously so – a gingery, soupy brew with soft-cooked wild boar. Say 'feed me' and they'll dish up a customised spread for $66 a head. Sundae heaven is a tumbler of palm sugar icecream, crunchy salted honeycomb and lime syrup. First date, last date, city lunch – Chin Chin's bold, brash nature makes it an exciting place to dine.

Open Daily 11am–late; bookings for one table of 12 only
Typical prices E $15 **M** $28 **D** $13
Cards AE MC V Eftpos
Wine Fun, fresh list with well-matched whites, plus cocktails galore
Owner Chris Lucas
Chef Benjamin Cooper
Seats 100; bar
www.chinchinrestaurant.com.au

And ... Stuck in the queue? Wait downstairs at Chin Chin's basement Go Go Bar.

China Max

6 Keilor Road, Essendon North **9374 1988**

CHINESE **13/20**

Sometimes it's nice to get back to basics, and at China Max you can do just that. No jostling queues or touch-screens here. Instead, oriental timber carvings, red lanterns and the odd tinsel tassel identify this restaurant as old-school Chinese; and if the faded uniforms, well-worn menus and occasionally vague service underline its age, at least the quiet, unpretentious environment and classic Cantonese fare with flair conjure comfortable familiarity. To begin, a crisp iceberg lettuce cup filled with scallops and fluffy egg is an original take on sang choy bao, and a much nimbler option than the soft-shell crab, which may be a little oily for some tastes. For mains, a hotpot of pork ribs in a rich red sauce (made from red rice and spice) will have you effortlessly sucking meat off the bone, while a dish of Sichuan eggplant might be more sugar than spice. Desserts, such as lemon tart and custard buns, demonstrate ambitions stretching beyond the ubiquitous banana fritter.

Open Mon–Fri 11.30am–2.30pm; Sun 11am–3pm; Sun–Thurs 5–10.30pm; Fri–Sat 5–11pm
Typical prices E $8.50 **M** $22.50 **D** $8.50
Cards DC AE MC V
Wine A 300-plus list of European and Australian wines ranging from very affordable to special-occasion; six reds and whites by the glass; BYO (corkage $8 a bottle)
Owners William Lee & Paul Chan
Chef Paul Chan
Seats 80
www.chinamax.com.au

And ... There's a vegetarian banquet and menu.

Chocolate Buddha

Federation Square, City **9654 5688**

JAPANESE **12/20**

Low stools and communal tables replicate the traditional donburi dens of Japan, but the best seats in the house are at the outdoor tables overlooking Federation Square. The place is often thronged, with the kitchen pumping so fast that mains may beat starters to the table. Tempura pumpkin roll is a delightfully fresh take on vegetarian sushi, with shredded beetroot, avocado and lightly battered pumpkin. The soft-shell crab version is another inside-out winner, topped with capelin roe and served with herbed, house-made tartare. Elsewhere, the kitchen subtly tweaks more standard Japanese fare. A tasty, if pedestrian curry might come with arguably too-firm potatoes and slices of tender panko-crumbed pork loin. Silken tofu is just that, with Asian greens, beanshoots and mushrooms. Staggeringly, the bar might be out of both sake and plum wine on the same night, but such shortfalls are offset by the hard work of smiling, charming waitstaff.

Open Daily noon–11pm; bookings accepted on Fri and Sat nights only for groups of six or more
Typical prices E $13 **M** $20 **D** $12
Cards DC AE MC V Eftpos
Wine 21 wines available (20 by the glass), plus sake, shochu and plum wine, beers and cocktails
Owner Angela Mathioudakis
Chef Masayuki Yoshida
Seats 160; outdoor seating; bar
www.chocolatebuddha.com.au

And ... Former Taxi sushi chef Kin San has come on board as a consultant.

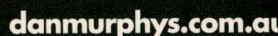

Choi's

186 Riversdale Road, Hawthorn **9818 2299**

CHINESE **13.5/20**

After more than 20 years here, Choi's still hums. It stays faithful to being a suburban Chinese, keeping BYO locals loyal with lemon chicken and baskets of dumplings, but, just as its decor is both elegantly oriental and boldly western, Choi's wears two faces. It's a special-occasion destination too, with a suit-clad sommelier, tablecloths and beautiful black and silver chopsticks with which to indulge in Choi's current enthusiasm for fusion cooking. One entree mixes prawns with blue cheese (crumbed and melting, it works!). Quail dumplings are a splendid diversion from mainstream Chinese entrees – big, deep-fried pastry pouches of meat, vegetables and spice. There's no messing with Peking duck though. It's as you want: large chunks of tender poultry with satisfyingly crunchy skin. Eye fillet has a gentle whisper of lemongrass. Tender scallops get a kick with garlic, chilli and ginger. Red beans and maple syrup: now there's a combo – a terrific one when brought together in the red-bean paste pancake for dessert.

Open Mon–Fri noon–3pm; Sun–Thurs 5–10pm; Fri–Sat 5–11pm
Typical prices E $11 **M** $26 **D** $10
Cards DC AE MC V Eftpos
Wine Long list, mostly Australian, Italian and French at reasonable mark-ups; BYO (corkage $4 a head)
Owner & chef David Yap
Seats 110
www.chois.com.au

And ... Check out the display cases of replicas of ancient Chinese artefacts.

Church St Enoteca

527 Church Street, Richmond **9428 7898**

ITALIAN **15/20**

A new chef had just stepped up here as the *Guide* went to press, and was making a solid start at this handsome, assuredly urbane spot. Pasta now plays a slightly more supporting role to meaty mains like bistecca fiorentina, slow cooked lamb and a chunky pink veal rib-eye dotted with perfect broad beans. Fish seems a reliable choice too, perhaps nettle-crusted blue cod sweetly paired with broccoli rabe and tender batons of cuttlefish. The Enoteca, with its timber floors, white-clothed tables, vintage prints and Art Deco details, has always been about style and well-founded confidence. Service is attentive and unobtrusive. The cooking represents modern and traditional Italian: try the carpaccio, a plateful of thin red circles of tenderloin beef topped with a tiny mixed salad that looks far too big a serving – until you eat it. Agnolotti filled with braised ox-cheek are sleek, round and packed with flavour. No room for dessert? Have a plate of pasticcini instead with excellent coffee.

Open Mon–Fri noon–3pm; Mon–Sat 6–10pm
Typical prices E $22 **M** $38 **D** $16
Cards DC AE MC V Eftpos
Wine Italian wines are the strength, from the length and breadth of the country, supported by Australian and some French
Owners Jim Ireland & Keith Snell
Chef Sebastian McQuarrie
Seats 80; private rooms; bar
www.churchstenoteca.com.au

And ... The private rooms are terrific. Pre-order a whole suckling pig and throw a party.

Ciao Cielo

171 Bay Street, Port Melbourne **9645 1568**

MODERN ITALIAN **14/20**

The arancini with slow-roasted duck take nine hours to make, according to the owners, but they'll barely last a minute when dished up. They're terrific, and alongside beetroot ravioli with bug tails, have become a menu fixture at this welcoming little main-street spot. The handsome Art Deco-style interior cleverly mixes old and new: leadlight windows and wood panelling with shiny black tables and a mirrored wall. Co-owner Kate Dickins is a warm host; maybe offering an extra splash of wine with an anecdote about her grandmother's cooking. There's plenty to excite on the small, modern menu. Pan-seared sardines on toasted ciabatta come with a smear of tangy house-made fennel and orange marmalade. Butterflied barbecued quail sit on a thick slice of smoky kaiserfleisch, with a crisp radish and radicchio salad. House-made cannelloni are filled with slow-braised lamb shoulder. Tiramisu is made with zabaglione folded through the mascarpone, and served the traditional way, from a bowl brought to the table. As Ciao Cielo's name translates, hello heaven.

Open Tues–Fri noon–3pm, 6–9pm; Sat 6–9.30pm; Sat–Sun 9am–2.30pm
Typical prices E $16 **M** $32 **D** $14
Cards AE MC V Eftpos
Wine Emphasis on Italian varietals, from Australian and Italian producers; well priced; 18 by the glass
Owners Kate Dickins & Bryan Nelson
Chef Bryan Nelson
Seats 35; outdoor seating
www.ciaocielo.com.au

And ... There are often by-the-glass specials.

Cicciolina

130 Acland Street, St Kilda **9525 3333**

CONTEMPORARY **14.5/20**

Loud, lively and full every night, this bistro is still sexy and familiar almost 20 years on, much like La Cicciolina – the minxish Italian porn-queen-turned-politician after whom it's named. Inside the dimly lit dining room, waitstaff greet the never-ending band of loyal locals by name and shoehorn them into swivel bucket chairs and banquettes around close-set timber tables. Virginia Redmond's French-inspired menu of fixtures has a rustic Italian accent, while blackboard specials add variety and seasonality. Signature soft, creamy lamb brains come bound in basil, eggplant and crisp prosciutto; blue swimmer crab-flecked souffle in rich champagne and chive velouté; and generous chunks of juicy crumbed veal on buttered chats. If something sweet beckons, creme brulee, sticky-date pudding and soft-centred chocolate fondant rank as favourites. Occasionally service is so-so, and not all dishes sparkle, but at Cicc' it's never just about food. There's a genuinely convivial, club-like, egalitarian feel about the place.

Open Mon–Sat noon–11pm; Sun noon–10pm; no bookings at dinner
Typical prices E $15.50 **M** $35.50 **D** $15
Cards AE MC V
Wine Long affordable list leaning to French and Italian varietals; 19 by the glass
Owners Virginia Redmond, Barbara Dight & Lisa Carrodus
Chefs Virginia Redmond & Michelle Elia
Seats 45; outdoor seating; bar
www.cicciolinastkilda.com.au

And ... Arrive by 6.30pm to avoid the wait-list.

Circa

2 Acland Street, St Kilda **9536 1122**

CONTEMPORARY 15/20

It's been reinvented more times than the little black dress, and Circa's current incarnation sees St Kilda's premier dining room at its most rollicking and fun. Service standards are undiminished but the sense of occasion has relaxed into a buzzy bonhomie. The broad, flexible menu is built around the capabilities of a wood grill: there's smoke but no mirrors. The ideas are an on-trend Pacific Rim grab-bag relying on punchy flavour combinations and multiple condiments. Execution is straightforward but flawless. A Korean/LA taco mash-up with spicy slaw and short rib is a culinary cacophany that works beautifully. Soba noodles are dressed with a powerful assembly of bottarga, caviar and sea urchin. Main plates relax into easy elegance: rice-crusted chicken and herbed white sausage both dressed with immaculate shiitake broth. Yakitori skewers (bacon-wrapped prawns with spicy pineapple) are such button-pushing delights that Circa starts to feel like a high-class snack stop as well as a fine-dining restaurant. Perhaps that's the whole idea.

Open Daily 7–11am, noon–4pm, 6–10pm
Typical prices E $18 **M** $40 **D** $15
Cards DC AE MC V Eftpos
Wine A formidable list topped with two pages of food-friendly wine in 100ml pours
Owners Tom Walker, Julian Gerner & Gerry Ryan
Chefs Paul Wilson & Jake Nicolson
Seats 90; outdoor seating; private room; bar
www.circa.com.au

And ... There's all-day grazing in the bar.

City Wine Shop

159 Spring Street, City **9654 6657**

EUROPEAN **13.5/20**

The wine wall is epic, exciting and ever-changing at City Wine Shop, catnip to thirsty punters who land at the long bar for a quick drink, but often finish up being fed at the communal table down the back, or at the cheek-by-jowl outside tables. It's a trip, all seamlessly facilitated by sharp, knowledgeable staff. Suave good looks with a warm, European edge extend to the menu. Marinated sardines come paired with vibrant salsa verde. Rustic smoked haddock croquettes and pillowy polenta chips (a menu stalwart) are perfect for sharing while sipping. Mains are more substantial. Thick chicken schnitzel comes with an Italian coleslaw freckled with parsley and radish, and finished with lemon. Orecchiette pasta is tossed through a robust ragu of slow-cooked beef with tomato and shaved parmigiano reggiano. To conclude, a zesty lemon tart served with clotted cream is simply wonderful. Alternatively, cheese, say 50g of stilton or Heidi raclette, seems a fitting finale. With a glass of sticky, of course.

Open Mon–Thurs 7am–10pm; Fri 7am–11pm; Sat 9am–11pm; Sun 9am–10pm; no bookings
Typical prices E $11 **M** $26 **D** $12.50
Cards DC AE MC V
Wine Cracking selection of 400 labels; corkage $20 a bottle for wines bought and consumed on the premises
Owners Con Christopoulos & Joshua Brisbane
Chef Ian Curley
Seats 54; outdoor seating; bar
www.citywineshop.net.au

And ... Check the website for wine events.

Coda

Basement, 141 Flinders Lane, City **9650 3155**

ASIAN **15/20**

Coda has great energy, something it has had from day one. Staff seem happy to be there, acting as casual-professional guides through a somewhat surprising menu that might put share-dishes like black pepper crab next to minute steak with lemon and capers. It's easy to stick with the Asian dishes – maybe spanner crab on a betel leaf with galangal, roasted chilli and lime – but then you'd miss out on a gorgeous salad of buffalo mozzarella, zucchini fritters, mint and peas. Roasted yellow duck curry is a huge flavour hit, with plenty of pepper to keep things interesting and floor staff busy topping up water glasses. Things can get loud by the evening's end. To conclude, beautifully presented dessert boards are every bit as good as they look and might include a frangipane and pear tart with drunken date icecream.

Open Daily noon–3pm, 6–10.30pm
Typical prices E $20 **M** $38 **D** $16
Cards AE MC V Eftpos
Wine 15-page list from around the world with knowledgeable staff to help navigate; 12-plus by the glass
Owners Adam D'Sylva, Mykal Bartholomew & Kate Calder
Chefs Adam D'Sylva, Julie Thai & Hendri Budiman
Seats 40; bar
www.codarestaurant.com.au

And ... Most folks plump for one of the three available set menus of between eight and 13 courses.

Collins Quarter

86a Collins Street, City **9650 8500**

EUROPEAN **13.5/20**

Behind an anonymous Collins Street doorway, it's party central for Melbourne office workers. Vernon Chalker, who applied his Midas touch to the city's bar scene (think Gin Palace, Bar Ampere, Madame Brussels), extends his realm to Collins Quarter, a combination of low-key bistro, courtyard bar and swanky champagne and cigar lounge. On a warm night, with the glass doors flung wide and crowd noise swelling in the courtyard beneath the magnolia tree, it's hard not to feel a smidgeon smug about having found the place. The menu, organised under headings Finger, Fork, Knife and Spoon, offers good-time food, no analysis required. You could order cocktails and snack happily on croquettes with gooey gruyere and jamon centres, or prawns in potato string vests with pungent anchovy mayo. Or settle into a booth and chow on steak with bearnaise sauce or chicken schnitzel lifted by rosemary and parmesan crumbs. Staff won't bat an eyelid if you adjourn upstairs to the decadent Ra Bar for faithful desserts like creme brulee and chocolate fondant.

Open Mon–Thurs 7.30am–11pm; Fri 7.30am–1am; Sat noon–1am
Typical prices E $12 **M** $25 **D** $10
Cards DC AE MC V Eftpos
Wine Pricey, fashion-forward list; about 15 by the glass
Owner Vernon Chalker
Chef Michael Nunn
Seats 70; outdoor seating; private room; bar
www.collinsquarter.com

And ... The Ra Bar has its own snack menu.

Comme

7 Alfred Place, City **9631 4000**

MODERN FRENCH **14.5/20**

The grand 1880s building, originally built as the German Club, has had more lives than a cat. In its present sleek incarnation, the restaurant is in a handsome large space dominated by a vast square bar. There are cosy quiet corners, but perhaps the best places are at the bare-topped tables, lingering over a meal and something from the considerable tome of a wine list. The mood is now French bistro, a single sheet menu listing dishes of various sizes and prices, including classics and clever updates. Mount Martha mussels are not marinière, but served with shreds of red capsicum and (less engagingly) charred sweetcorn. The old favourite of steak frites comes with a choice of cuts and size (onglet or sirloin); delicate Gippsland rabbit is dressed up with a crisp zucchini flower filled with pea and tarragon mousse, fresh peas and finely diced zucchini, and a wonderfully rich clear just-sticky jus. Desserts may include a rhubarb crumble souffle.

Open Mon–Fri noon–3pm; Mon–Sat 6–10.30pm
Typical prices E $18 **M** $32 **D** $17
Cards DC AE MC V Eftpos
Wine Extensive, divided between Australian and imported, with an emphasis on high-end French
Owners Frank & Sharon van Haandel
Chef Daniel Southern
Seats 60; private room; bar
www.comme.com.au

And ... Also open for coffee, continental breakfast and cake from 9am Monday to Friday.

The Commoner

122 Johnston Street, Fitzroy **9415 6876**

MODERN BRITISH **13/20**

It's been five years since the Commoner was born – a mere slip of a place in a narrow shopfront with polished boards and bentwood chairs – but the mission to share the vibrancy of modern British cuisine endures, along with a produce-driven menu that changes weekly, if not daily. Perhaps you'll find Scots-style black pudding, moist and spiced with cinnamon, nutmeg and clove, beside an egg yolk laid in a nest of creamy mash. Or fried zucchini flowers, stuffed with a sharp goat's cheese, over a tangle of blanched snow peas, cress, and for a touch of the Old Dart, julienned pickled onions. A lamb shoulder is boned, braised and rearranged into a fall-apart parcel with a block of chickpea puree and a radish salad. 'Pudding' might be a creme brulee given a floral burst of orange blossom, contrasting with sour rhubarb and light sumac shortbread on the side. And it may arrive with some antique serving spoons and cream in a gravy boat. These quirky but unselfconscious touches, along with attentive, smart service, make the Commoner a little gem.

Open Wed–Thurs 6–10.30pm; Fri–Sun noon–10.30pm
Typical prices E $14 **M** $32 **D** $13
Cards AE MC V Eftpos
Wine Broad list of good-value locals and imports, interesting cocktails and rotating craft beers
Owner Jo Corrigan
Chef Brook Petrie
Seats 50; outdoor seating; private room
www.thecommoner.com.au

And ... There are regular movie-themed soirees.

Cookie

Level 1, 252 Swanston Street, City **9663 7660**

MODERN THAI **13.5/20**

Hold on to your hard hats, diners – Cookie is one rowdy, flavour-fuelled and thoroughly fun ride. The lively pace of the adjoining bar area spills into the lofty Art Nouveau dining room, where dishes are drawn from a tome of a menu divided into bar food, small, medium and large dishes. Can't decide where to start? Ask one of the sprightly and well-versed waitstaff about the many modern Thai specialities from chef Karen Batson and, while they're at it, hints on the mammoth wine list. You might begin with spiced quail tempered by dazzling pickled watermelon husk and mint salad, or cracking tapioca dumplings sticky with chilli and plump with peanuts and pork mince. Medium dishes are generous – the jungle curry a mountain of moist duck, eggplant and bamboo shoots all tied together with the fire of chilli. If room allows, desserts traverse the globe from a richly rewarding tiramisu to banana fritters with invigorating coconut and honey icecream. Want to go again? Inhale, exhale, relax.

Open Daily noon–11pm
Typical prices E $13.50 **M** $28 **D** $13.50
Cards DC AE MC V Eftpos
Wine A hefty, eclectic and globetrotting list catalogued by country of origin; 60 by the glass
Owner Camillo Ippoliti
Chef Karen Batson
Seats 80; outdoor seating; bar
www.cookie.net.au

And ... Nab a seat on one of the Juliet balconies for a sparkling city vista.

Cornershop

11 Ballarat Street, Yarraville **9689 0052**

CONTEMPORARY **13.5/20**

After the invariably frenetic day trade, evenings at this popular cafe-restaurant are more sedate. With artsy lightshades throwing spectral shapes on the walls and attentive staff flitting among recycled wood tables, it's one of the west's most charming spots. David Danks' share-friendly dishes still mostly take their cues from the Levant, but there's a smattering of French and Asian flavours too. A terrine sporting hearty chunks of confit duck comes with crisp slivers of pide, while the sweetness of lightly charred Hervey Bay scallops is craftily offset by a splodge of salty taramasalata. Pan-fried sardines on a tumble of kipfler potato and spinach is a solid, if not mind-blowing, offering; better is roasted quail, dusted with polenta and served with a smear of zesty orange and peach chutney (you'll find it hiding with the hummus underneath the cress salad). A disc of black treacle cake, floating in vanilla-flecked custard with a side of clotted cream, makes a comforting finale.

Open Mon 8am–5pm; Tues–Sun 8am–10pm
Typical prices E $10.50 **M** $19 **D** $15
Cards AE MC V Eftpos
Wine Compact list of well-priced domestic and European wines; about 12 by the glass; plus a selection of craft beers
Owners Iain Munro, Alan & Jan Stephens, Simon Reed
Chef David Danks
Seats 60; outdoor seating

And ... Coffee and takeaways are available from the same team at the nearby Wee Jeanie.

The Courthouse

86–90 Errol Street (corner Queensberry Street), North Melbourne **9329 5394**

MODERN EUROPEAN **13/20**

The Courthouse menu has returned to its European bistro roots under new chef Zoe Birch, and the mid-sized dining room, with its Art Nouveau light fittings and woody wainscoting, makes a charming setting. An entree of crumb-topped mussels with a daub of rich romesco is a simple joy, and a single raviolo encasing a runny egg yolk and floating in a light bacon broth with scallop pieces impresses. And while a dish of plump gnocchi with wild mushrooms, a rich porcini cream, peas and shavings of truffled pecorino succeeds admirably, a roasted venison main might appear less inspiringly matched with a beet salad and a disc of baked ricotta, perhaps not the most perfect partner. Impressive desserts such as a dainty quince pie with smooth pomegranate parfait mount a credible defence, as does attentive but unobtrusive service. Little things like ageing tables that might be better hidden by linen mean the package may not have the finesse it once did. The verdict on this courthouse, though maybe not unanimous, is still positive.

Open Mon–Sat noon–3pm, 6–10pm
Typical prices E $17 **M** $27 **D** $15
Cards DC AE MC V Eftpos
Wine Eurocentric list with some heavy hitters
Owner Scott Thomas
Chef Zoe Birch
Seats 90; private room; bar
www.thecourthouse.net.au

And … The bar has 11 craft beers on tap, which change regularly.

The Crimean

351 Queensberry Street (corner Peel Street), North Melbourne **9329 3353**

EASTERN EUROPEAN **13.5/20**

You go behind the bar, rather than the Iron Curtain, to the lively restaurant here ... but once in the moody wood-panelled, communist-era-postered room, you'll feel like you've crossed borders. Steel mesh lightshades casting a mellow glow give it a seductive, brooding look – but when it's busy, noise-levels can feel more bawdy drinking-house than romantically retro. You might find yourself between a celebratory group and a babushka sipping vodka with her daughter. Hefty mains – say pink crisp-skinned duck breast atop creamy mamaliga (Romanian maize porridge), or melting lamb braised with orange and quince on buckwheat kasha – are assured, but it's the entrees that really warm the cockles. Sour cream and vibrant paprika butter complement crescent-shaped pork and beef pelmeni (dumplings). Dessert may include Crimean mess – chocolate icecream, meringue and sour cherries. Or finish by exploring the list of exotic vodkas and liqueurs on offer – affable staff are happy to help guide adventurers.

Open Tues–Sun 6–10pm; Sun noon–3.30pm
Typical prices E $12 **M** $30 **D** $13
Cards AE MC V Eftpos
Wine Features lesser-known varietals from Croatia, Slovenia and Hungary, plus some intriguing liqueurs
Owners Lazlo Evenhuis, Melissa Macfarlane & Frank Moylan
Chef Nathan Glover-Smith
Seats 70; bar
www.thecrimean.com

And … The front bar has a great snacky menu and some serious Eastern European liquor.

Cumulus Inc

45 Flinders Lane, City **9650 1445**

CONTEMPORARY 15/20

It's impossible to be all things to all people but Cumulus comes very close, adroitly straddling cafe and bar, bistro and fine-diner. No bookings means you'll need to wait (or lurk nearby), but once seated in the artfully raw, airy dining room or at the bar along the open kitchen, the charms of the menu emerge. It relies on unfussy flavour combinations, but with enough culinary pizazz to satisfy the sniffiest food snob. Typical is a beautifully bloody duck breast, perched on a mix of toasted barley, walnuts and pepitas, with lentils and dabs of turnip puree and plum. Sweet, crunchy, oily and earthy, it's a wonderful combination. Spiced cauliflower with goat's curd and pomegranate traverses similar territory, but you can go simpler still with a plate of superb cured meats or a bowl of Padron peppers, deep-fried and lushly salted. Given the quality of ingredients, Cumulus offers very good value, while cheery, helpful staff add to the unpretentious buzz.

Open Mon–Fri 7am–11pm; Sat–Sun 8am–11pm; no bookings, except for groups of seven to 14
Typical prices E $17 **M** $32 **D** $17
Cards AE MC V Eftpos
Wine Deep list especially strong on French and Italian labels
Owners Andrew McConnell, Pascale Gomes-McNabb & Jayden Ong
Chefs Andrew McConnell & Colin Wood
Seats 60; private room
www.cumulusinc.com.au

And ... Oyster fiends note: there are about six varieties available by the piece.

Cutler & Co

55–57 Gertrude Street, Fitzroy **9419 4888**

CONTEMPORARY 17/20

Great restaurant food needs to fulfill many obligations: it must be appropriate to the season, inventive, have wowee-yet-flawless technique, surprise the most cynical of diners, and above all be consistent from one sitting to the next. Add service that is systematic, reflects the character of a beautifully designed space, is subtle but always there, and you've got the formula for a constantly repeatable great occasion. Cutler & Co has all of this, which is high praise indeed. Head chef Andrew McConnell and co-chef Chris Watson work as one to drive and maintain such standards. An opener of scallops, chilled pea and sorrel soup is a masterpiece that surprises, illuminates and then challenges all parts of the palate. Mains such as slow-roasted chicken accompanied by an iron pot of gently cooked peas and lettuce, and beef strip-loin and braised short rib – each meat enhanced by the sous-vide cooking process – put on display technical skills that allow flavour, texture, imagination and generosity to combine to perfection.

Open Tues–Sun 6–11pm; Fri & Sun noon–2.30pm
Typical prices E $27 **M** $43 **D** $18
Cards AE MC V Eftpos
Wine Extensive list covering all vital regions; 16 by the glass
Owners Andrew McConnell, Pascale Gomes-McNabb & Frank van Haandel
Chefs Andrew McConnell & Chris Watson
Seats 100; outdoor seating; private room
www.cutlerandco.com.au

And ... The bar is a welcoming hotspot. Seats on the street add a nice touch.

Da Noi

95 Toorak Road, South Yarra **9866 5975**

SARDINIAN **14.5/20**

Da Noi's long-standing owner-chef Pietro Porcu is a man who has never lost faith in the pleasures of honest food cooked in traditional style. His Sardinian repertoire is a tonic for the modern soul. The degustation is the signature experience: decision-free and with the thrill of surprise. Black-clad waiters deliver a succession of marvellous dishes, traipsing up and down the precipitous stairs between the ground and first-floor dining rooms of this narrow terrace. First, a train of appetite-whetting morsels, which might include crumbed, roasted gummy shark marinated in a sweet, citrusy tomato vinaigrette, or punchy parmesan and zucchini fritters. Pasta follows, perhaps silken potato and pecorino-filled ravioli, topped with pungent slices of truffle. Mains may feature several meat dishes: delicate, rosy-centred lamb fillets, wrapped in prosciutto and stuffed with green olives, or fried and roasted quail served with figs, vincotto and blue-vein cheese. The dessert platter might include a swooningly tangy mint and apple sorbet and a velvety rich chocolate mousse cake.

Open Tues–Sat noon–4pm; Mon–Sat 6–11pm
Typical prices E $24 **M** $38 **D** $16; degustation $93
Cards DC AE MC V Eftpos
Wine A tantalising list of Italian regional wines; BYO lunch & Mon night (corkage $12 a bottle)
Owner Pietro Porcu
Chefs Pietro Porcu, Shoichi Ueda & Matthew Angelucci
Seats 55; outdoor seating; private room

And ... Menus change daily and dishes may use produce from Porcu's farm in Yarck.

Dalmatino

280 Bay Street, Port Melbourne **9645 6584**

CROATIAN/DALMATIAN **13.5/20**

The sights, smells and sounds of the Adriatic are dizzying once you're past Dalmatino's red-brick facade, the air heady with the scents of spices and grills. A pyramid of lemony octopus salad flecked with parsley and red onion might whiz past en route to a table of jocular diners enjoying the flavours of their homeland. Four cevapcici fingers arrive boosted by a subtly sweet eggplant and capsicum relish. It all comes together in a lofty space made snug by rich wooden furnishings, simple settings and dim lighting. Croatian wines feature, flanked by enough local and global heavyweights to satisfy most – informed staff are good guides. In the kitchen, it's not all tradition: a jade-green asparagus risotto is balanced with the bite of Maffra cheddar. Three veal eye fillets stand like soldiers on velvety lima bean and potato puree, heady with sticky rosemary jus. Occasional dishes may miss the mark, like a gluggy creme caramel. But for a Croatian sojourn on our shores, Dalmatino delivers.

Open Tues–Fri noon–3.30pm; Tues–Sun 6–11pm; Sat–Sun 8.30am–3.30pm
Typical prices E $17 **M** $29.90 **D** $14
Cards DC AE MC V Eftpos
Wine A well-priced Australian-leaning wine list with an inviting selection from Croatia
Owners Ino & Natko Kuvacic
Chef Ino Kuvacic
Seats 80; outdoor seating; bar
www.dalmatino.com.au

And ... Live music accompanies set-price, three-course Croatian dinners on Wednesdays.

Dandelion

133 Ormond Road, Elwood **9531 4900**

MODERN VIETNAMESE **15/20**

Just reading Dandelion's effervescent menu is enough to make your tongue tingle. Full of bright, fragrant herbs, top-notch produce and flavour-packed sauces (think red date and goji berry), Geoff Lindsay's modern Vietnamese offerings are broken down into 'nibbles', 'rolls', 'phos', 'curries' and 'grills'. Kick off with drunken chicken ribs in a crisp, spiced batter or perhaps the Buddha rolls, with chubby nubs of tofu and shiitake wrapped in rice paper. Wok-tossed king prawns are magnificently mammoth, doused in a tamarind caramel; the lauded barbecue pork spare ribs fall off the bone, justifiably popular for their messy succulence; and pho might feature mud crab, wagyu, or tofu with mushrooms and lily bud. The fitout is modern, with neutral tones and decorative greenery. Service can sometimes lack that assured quality, especially when pushing through two sittings, and some tables are more comfortable than others, but Dandelion is fresh, fun and an essential player in the neighbourhood. Bookings are essential.

Open Mon–Wed 5.30–10pm; Thurs–Sun noon–10pm
Typical prices E $18 **M** $35 **D** $16
Cards AE MC V Eftpos
Wine Crisp list of smart Australians and Europeans, categorised by body and sweetness; 15 by the glass
Owners Geoff & Jane Lindsay
Chef Geoff Lindsay
Seats 80
www.dandelion.ws

And ... With 48 hours' notice, book the 'family table' for crab or suckling pig.

The Deanery

13 Bligh Place, City **9629 5599**

CONTEMPORARY **13/20**

After a change of ownership in 2010, this large, longstanding laneway restaurant has become a cordial and hospitable venue for drinkers, diners and those having a bet each way. The same easygoing, well-priced menu runs in the ground-floor bar with its hideaway booths and in the mezzanine dining room, a comfortable, quiet zone flanked by wine cages. Lamb rolls work as drink nibble or entree: shoulder meat is curried, shredded and wrapped in brik pastry to create a bite both crisp and luscious. There's an emphasis on charcuterie and steak (the pork and chicken sausage is a juicy delight), but vegetarians are also showered with love in the form of a rich, intense mushroom souffle accompanied by a jug of gooey fondue cheese. Desserts are simple and fun: hazelnut and chocolate three-point sandwiches feature nutty meringue sheets layered with chocolate and cream. Unassuming but impeccable service underscores a solid city experience.

Open Mon–Fri noon–3pm; Mon–Sat 5–9.30pm
Typical prices E $13.50 **M** $29 **D** $12
Cards DC AE MC V Eftpos
Wine Well-organised and well-priced list offering accessibility and depth; good range by the glass
Owners Glenn Fletcher, Donelle Coates & Graham Sutherland
Chef Graham Sutherland
Seats 80; private room; bar
www.thedeanery.com.au

And ... Wine storage is available for those longing to collect but lacking a cellar.

The Deck

Upper level, Southgate, Southbank **9699 9544**

MODERN EUROPEAN **14/20**

This Southgate stalwart moved in 2011, and its new home is so Melbourne: small, narrow, in what almost looks like a leftover corner. Cosy and dark inside, outside there's the eponymous deck itself, which socks it to you with a spectacular city view that you never saw coming. The menu has French inspiration and meals are generous. Duck is a menu favourite – as parfait, it's silky and smooth with clarified butter. A fat duck sausage is beautifully seasoned. Duck breast main is lean, smartly accessorised with an onion tarte tatin, and a pan-fried, but slightly dry, puck of duck 'rillettes'. Moving away from duck, cauliflower soup with a sprinkling of Stilton is liquid velvet. Ocean trout maintains a deep pink, and, with tomatoes and brilliant green soybeans, fish never looked so pretty. You could quibble that a fondant, while delicious, lacks enough oozing chocolate. Creme brulee is perfect, though, and, endearingly, comes with bite-sized jam doughnuts.

Open Daily 5.30–10.30pm; Mon–Fri 8am–3pm; Sat–Sun noon–3pm
Typical prices E $17 **M** $34 **D** $14
Cards AE MC V Eftpos
Wine A solid selection to please a variety of palates, including several by 375ml carafe
Owners Robert Burgio & Giliberto family
Chef Chris Toogood
Seats 55; outdoor seating; bar
www.thedeckrestaurant.com.au

And ... There's a pre-theatre menu from 5.30pm to 7pm, and breakfast and great coffee weekday mornings (including takeaway).

Dino's

34 Chapel Street, Windsor **9521 3466**

MEDITERRANEAN/SPANISH **14/20**

If HG Wells' time machine had inspired a dining room for the Melburnians of downtown Windsor, Dino's would be it. The inviting apothecary-esque interior features vast cabinets and bottles, highly polished timbers and colourful stained glass; pockets of secluded tables create a mystical, covert magic. Taking its culinary cues from Spain, the tapas, raciones and salads are the most popular dishes, and the best. Spicy meatballs with pinenut crumble are more exciting than most. Calamari is crusted in polenta and fried; paired with a paprika aioli, it's unsurprising but good. Chewy haloumi finds welcome relief with piquant olives and parsley, while huge prawns are simply sauteed with fresh chilli and garlic. It's not boundary-pushing stuff, but it works. A quick deviation from Spain reveals a verdant risotto of lightly cooked asparagus and mint or a classic full-blood wagyu rump with green peas. Affable staff don't hurry for much but they're justly quick to advocate the luscious crema Catalana as a sweet ending.

Open Mon–Fri 7am–11pm; Sat–Sun 8am–11pm
Typical prices E $12 **M** $26 **D** $12
Cards DC AE MC V Eftpos
Wine An exciting European and Australian list rich in Spanish wines with about 15 by the glass; good value
Owner Francisco Valles
Chefs James Kenny & Fadel Fadlallah
Seats 60; outdoor seating; private room; bar
www.dinos.com.au

And ... Sundays from noon there's a Spanish barbecue and paella afternoon 'on the roof'.

DOC

295 Drummond Street, Carlton **9347 2998**

ITALIAN/PIZZERIA **12.5/20**

Some of Melbourne's best pizza can be found in this Victorian corner shopfront, so expect queues. It's nice to begin with DOC's other speciality – silken-centred buffalo mozzarella – maybe teamed with slivers of San Daniele prosciutto and a fistful of crostini. Then it's on to the main game – thin, perfectly chewy-crunchy pizzas, perhaps topped with truffle-oil-drizzled porcini, morel and field mushrooms and pecorino cheese; roasted peppers and hot salami; or heady gorgonzola with chicory leaves and lemon slices. Wash it down with an Italian micro-brewed beer. It must be said, this DOC felt a little ragged around the edges, the result, perhaps, of focus shifting to newer ventures nearby and on the Mornington Peninsula. On our visit the walls could have done with a coat of paint, the toilets needed a makeover, and the service faltered at times. Still, there are other rewards, including people-watching from outside tables. Say 'ciao' with desserts like Belgian white chocolate or strawberry pizza with icecream.

Open Mon–Thurs 5–11pm; Fri–Sun noon–11pm; no bookings, except for groups of seven or more
Typical prices E $17 **M** $21 **D** $10
Cards AE MC V Eftpos
Wine Local and imported Italian varietals, with more than 15 by the glass; BYO (corkage $8.50 a bottle)
Owners Tony Nicolini, Michael Costanzo & Robert De Santis
Chefs Michele Usci & Tony Nicolini
Seats 55; outdoor seating; private room
www.docgroup.net

And ... DOC denotes food and wine produced within certain regions of Italy.

Donovans

40 Jacka Boulevard, St Kilda **9534 8221**

CONTEMPORARY **15.5/20**

A restaurant that strives for consistency risks being underrated in a milieu that prizes novelty. But reliability is the key to a great restaurant and Donovans is as constant and steady as the wavelets tickling the beach it overlooks. For 15 years now, this dreamy beachy pile, with decor that's tweaked as the seasons roll, has been the place for luxurious but straightforward meals with Mediterranean flavours. Forest mushrooms are wood-roasted and their juices allowed to drizzle into tarragon-scented pecorino polenta. Subtle prawn and scallop ravioli are ramped up with a robust bisque. The barbecue dishes – steak, fish, chilli-flecked leader prawns – are persuasive arguments for simplicity as perfection, and the more complex plates (a lamb medley including juicy sausage and pull-apart shoulder; peppery and tender venison with buttery shortcrust pie) are elegant and thoughtful. The jitters that accompanied a changing of the kitchen guard have settled and Donovans is back to its easy, hospitable and generous best.

Open Daily noon–3.30pm, 6–10pm
Typical prices E $25 **M** $48 **D** $19.50
Cards DC AE MC V Eftpos
Wine Covers the great wine regions of the world accessibly, with by-the-glass and winery showcases
Owners Gail & Kevin Donovan, Richard Fisher & Jeannie Donovan-Fisher
Chefs Adam Draper & Emma D'Alessandro
Seats 132; private room; bar
www.donovanshouse.com.au

And ... The 'cubby house menu' is so delicious that parents often steal nibbles.

Easy Tiger

96 Smith Street, Collingwood **9417 2373**

MODERN THAI **15/20**

It might be small, but Easy Tiger packs kapow into everything it does, from its fabulously feisty food to the small, design-den digs where everything (from the backlit line of glasses along one wall to the mural of a deer riding a magic carpet) is deliberate, good-looking and smooth. It's something of a local hero, so expect two sittings (6pm and 8.30pm) to cope with demand. Communal dining (share-plates and tables) promotes a polite level of sociability. The real energy, though, is on your fork, or in your fingers, collecting one-bite starters like ma hor, a sticky palm-sugar-sweet mince patty on a pedestal of fresh watermelon. Among curries, there's radiant sour orange with smoked trout and roasted cherry tomatoes. Of the salads, five-spice duck and watermelon is a virtual confetti of betel, mint and coriander leaves – sweet, salty, spicy and sour with nam jim and spring onion. Coconut-cream pudding may leave you planning your next visit the minute you finish your last mouthful.

Open Tues–Sun 6–10pm
Typical prices E $12 **M** $28 **D** $14
Cards AE MC V Eftpos
Wine Short list of lighter-style, single-vineyard wines mostly from Victoria
Owners Jarrod Hudson, Suzanne Tyzack, Simon Hall & Brett McConnell
Chef Jarrod Hudson
Seats 34; outdoor seating
www.easytiger.co

And ... The banquets – nine courses for $65 (vegetarian, too) – are great value. Sunday nights are chef's banquet menu only.

Eau de Vie

Shop 1, 233 Chapel Street, Prahran **9510 0955**

MEDITERRANEAN **13/20**

This tiny bolt-hole with its front thrown open on to Chapel Street's midriff has the feel of a little neighbourhood bar – in Europe. Shoppers pop in for good coffee, a chat with the owner, and to share all-day dishes like hot, puffy pita, fried kefalograviera or discs of chorizo with poached pear. Tapas-style plates and a few mains to share are the evening fare, and make good drinking food whether you're at the small bar or the cafe-sized tables inside and out. Fine tiles of kingfish bathed in vibrant lime-leaf oil are a must, then maybe the wafer-thin beef carpaccio with sharp tartare condiments. A bronzed, crunchy croquette of finely chopped ham hock and minty pea puree is savoury, salty and even better with a chilled Peroni. More substantial is a comforting braise of tender rabbit, tomato, fennel and cheesy risoni. To follow, try a luxe chocolate and hazelnut terrine. The bunches-of-grapes light fitting channelling Beaujolais and vintage suitcases set the scene for savouring a little eau de vie.

Open Sun–Tues 8am–5pm; Wed–Thurs 8am–10pm; Fri–Sat 8am–11pm
Typical prices E $14 **M** $23 **D** $11
Cards AE MC V Eftpos
Wine Succinct list of popular locals and a few well-chosen internationals for interest; eight by the glass
Owner Dimitri Tsombanos
Chef Justin Beilin
Seats 35; outdoor seating; bar
www.eaudeviebar.com.au

And ... Morning after the night before? Try the breakfast of chorizo chipolatas, egg, pommes frites and coriander yoghurt.

Eighty One

81 High Street, Berwick **9768 9555**

CONTEMPORARY/TAPAS **14/20**

The first thing you notice about Eighty One is its magnificent vaulted wooden ceiling, enough to make interior designers buckle and swoon. This deceptively casual bar/restaurant pairs rustic with savvy in decor and food. The space is deftly segmented for cosy booth-like or fireside dining while still keeping a sense of air and expanse. The menu from chef Matt Major (ex-Donovan's and Hotel Lincoln) is bright and lively, with a handful of imaginative, wine-friendly snacks such as Middle Eastern prawn toast encrusted with zaatar, or smaller share-plates like squid stuffed with saffron quinoa. Mains are lusty and sumptuous: chestnut gnocchi comes with whole roasted mushrooms, broad beans and shards of parmesan wafer; the Otway pork belly accompanied by a whole baked apple. Desserts are desirable – a satin-smooth orange blossom bavarois gets a cheeky kick from a sprinkling of rose petals and pistachio candy. Servings are more than generous, as are the knowledgeable, conversational staff.

Open Tues–Fri noon–late; Tues–Sat 5pm–late; Sun 9am–late
Typical prices E $16 **M** $34 **D** $14
Cards DC AE MC V Eftpos
Wine Impressive, accessible list strong on Australians, plus NZ and French wines; 32 by the glass
Owner Catherine Charles
Chef Matt Major
Seats 100; outdoor seating; bar
www.eightyone.com.au

And ... High tea is held on Sundays from 2pm to 5pm.

Ellery & Co

46 Church Street, Hawthorn **9853 3533**

CONTEMPORARY **13/20**

This enveloping little restaurant makes a virtue of cosiness and a habit of comfort. By day Ellery does the eggs/pide/salad thing with verve, the coffee machine going full throttle. But at night the lights come down, the intimacy comes up, and you're face down in a plate of fritto misto with a lemony riesling in your hand before you know it. If you can't be bothered cooking after a hard day at the office – like many of the locals who wander in – you couldn't ask for more than a prawn cocktail: fat Crystal Bay babies reclining pinkly on crisp iceberg and house-made cocktail sauce. Friendly service is delivered casually, but no one seems to mind, and Black Angus eye fillet with green peppercorn sauce – yes, pepper steak – is style and comfort epitomised. Regulars won't let the crumbed veal or the seafood fettuccine leave the menu. Settling in? Stay for a bowl of lemon mousse, cream and fresh raspberries, or poached apricots with house-made vanilla icecream.

Open Mon–Fri 8am–3pm; Sat 8am–2pm; Sun 8.30am–2pm; Wed–Sat 5.30–9pm
Typical prices E $16 **M** $26 **D** $10
Cards MC V Eftpos
Wine About eight whites, seven reds, but each a cracker, and nearly all available by the glass
Owners Sharryn Knight & Talya Wright
Chef Siobhan Waters
Seats 36; outdoor seating; private room
www.elleryandco.com.au

And ... Elbow your way in during the day for steak and onion pide, or home-made jam on toast.

Embrasse

312 Drummond Street, Carlton **9347 3312**

MODERN FRENCH **15/20**

In a bijoux Carlton dining room of glossy black walls and statement silver lights, Nicolas Poelaert seduces diners with dishes that look as though they should be snapped, not scoffed. His time spent in the kitchen of Michel Bras has translated into a predilection for edible flowers, lush leaves and fresh-picked vegetables, enhanced by on-trend techniques such as sous-vide and smoking. The latter seems to be Poelaert's latest flourish, with wood smoke enhancing everything from the monogrammed bread rolls to a tile of ox cheek with raw, burnt and pureed onions, which arrives smoking under a glass cloche at the table. A main of maple roast pork is redolent with charry goodness, and a chunk of wagyu comes with a jet-black glaze of squid ink. Tender curls of carrot and a jumble of berries and elderflower are just some of the delicate accompaniments, demonstrating a light, respectful touch that's also at play in a dessert of lychee granita, white chocolate icecream and cheeky cherry jellies.

Open Wed–Sun 6.30–9.30pm; Fri–Sun noon–2.30pm
Typical prices E $21 **M** $40 **D** $19
Cards AE MC V Eftpos
Wine Cherry-picked choice of elegant Australian and European wines, priced at the upper end; 12 by the glass
Owners Nicolas & Tara Poelaert
Chef Nicolas Poelaert
Seats 50; private room
www.embrasserestaurant.com.au

And … Lash out on a degustation dinner, with five or more courses, from $95.

En Izakaya

277 Carlisle Street, Balaclava **9525 8886**

JAPANESE **13/20**

Endless plates of the signature seared tofu and eggplant landing on tables are proof of a loyal following – and new Tokyo-trained chef Makoto Motoyama ensures there are still plenty of fresh ideas at this neat little shopfront. The dynamism of his hometown reveals itself in a 'mispacho', a chilled creamy miso broth with raw salmon cubes and shreds of fried shallot that arrives in a martini glass. It's as delicious as it is pretty. So too is a crispy yam-skin-coated tuna roll, fried but still vibrant pink in the middle, while a generous pile of soft-shell crab is a textural treat. Heavier dishes such as sticky pork belly and blackened cod with a tangle of squid tempura come out when they're ready – not necessarily when you are – in the Japanese pub style. It's all part of the fun, and owner Andy Gray is never far away for advice on a sake or Alsatian riesling. In the true Japanese way, detail is everything.

Open Tues–Sat noon–2.30pm, 6–10pm
Typical prices E $10 **M** $17 **D** $8
Cards MC V Eftpos
Wine Playful list covering well-matched Spanish and French varietals, as well as izakaya classics shochu, sake and boutique beers
Owner Andy Gray
Chef Makoto Motoyama
Seats 40; outdoor seating; bar
www.enizakaya.com.au

And … Phone in an order for izakaya bites to eat at home.

Estelle Bar & Kitchen

243 High Street, Northcote **9489 4609**

CONTEMPORARY 15/20

With its pink, black and grey tiled walls, spindly legged furniture and tabletops made from a recycled bowling alley, the Estelle looks very much like the retro Northcote cafe it once was. There's still a laid-back, unpretentious feel to the place, but owner-chefs Scott Pickett (ex-The Point) and Ryan Flaherty (ex-Fat Duck, Arzak) deliver a tasting menu-only format (anything from three to nine courses) and a wine list enamoured of the Old World and sake. Pickett and Flaherty love a bit of molecular experimentation – sardine 'fossils', like misshapen, tastier prawn crackers, or compressed melon encased in a tube of clear potato starch – but never at the expense of flavour or substance. Think excellent cauliflower sausage teamed with curry-flavoured cauliflower cous cous, fat scallops served with salmon roe and black miso butter, venison with a bitter chocolate sauce or hugely addictive olive oil and vanilla sponge served with frozen sour cream. It's smart and interesting but best of all, a whole lot of fun.

Open Tues–Thurs 6–10pm; Fri–Sun noon–3pm, 6–11pm
Typical prices Tasting menus $70 (5 courses) to $110 (9 courses); lunch menu $50 (3 courses)
Cards AE MC V Eftpos
Wine A smart, flexible list with sake, beer and cider listed alongside a split of Old and New World labels
Owners Scott Pickett, Rebecca Harris & Ryan Flaherty
Chefs Scott Pickett & Ryan Flaherty
Seats 35; outdoor seating; private room; bar
www.estellebarkitchen.com.au

And … The chefs deliver some of the food themselves and don't mind staying for a chat.

Estivo

330 High Street, Kew **9853 1727**

CONTEMPORARY **14/20**

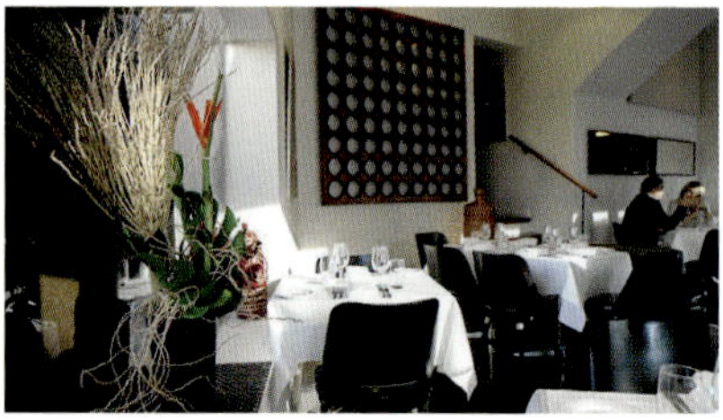

There was a time when really fabulous home cooks prepared classy, on-trend dinner parties for their friends. Now they probably go to Estivo for the same effect. This friendly local restaurant perfectly balances the 'let's get together!' vibe with a bit of funky creativity in the kitchen and obliging, efficient service. Despite a change in owner and chef in 2012, regulars expect to see something for everyone on the menu, and a bright canvas of colours on the plate. Sweetcorn soup with serrano ham croquette and piquillo peppers might get you started, or there are medium-sized dishes, maybe seared scallops served on a cloud of cauliflower foam with chorizo and almond brioche crumble. Mains span all tastes and may include veal with porcini and Puy lentils, baby snapper in harissa-infused broth or a hearty duck done two ways served with carrot puree. A honey panna cotta with strawberry soup is a suitably showy finish to Estivo's version of an elegant night in, with all of the chatter and none of the washing up.

Open Tues–Fri noon–3.30pm; Tues–Sat 6pm–late
Typical prices E $13 **M** $35 **D** $14
Cards DC AE MC V Eftpos
Wine A tempting mix, with some interesting regional Italian, French and Spanish wines
Owner Dana Hospitality Australia
Chef Kirti Amarendar
Seats 90; private rooms
www.estivo.com.au

And … Always the local, one of the popular uses for Estivo's two private rooms is christenings.

Eureka 89

Level 89, Eureka Tower, 7 Riverside Quay, Southbank
9693 8889

CONTEMPORARY **13.5/20**

There's a hint of celebrity dining here, with red-carpet entry and security guards to see you up to the 89th floor, where the black-and-red decor and low lighting ensure the focus is on the spectacular views of Melbourne. That lighting might make it difficult to read the wine list, but for an extra $55 or $80 per person, there will be selected wines with every course. The five- or seven-course menu changes seasonally and the cooking is in the modern style, with small dishes carefully crafted in their flavours and presentation. Ceviche of kingfish comes with precisely modulated tropical flavors, while boned quail rests on a smear of celeriac puree with a rectangle of potato gratin, a peeled grape and broad beans. There are some disappointments: a dessert of watermelon jelly and strawberry powder that's a little light on flavour, and a not quite melt-in-the-mouth chocolate casing for the raspberry bombe. Waiters may lack polish but are well meaning.

Open Wed–Sat 6pm–late
Typical prices Degustation $95 (5 courses), $130 (7 courses)
Cards AE MC V
Wine Predominantly Australian, with Victorian wines well represented, and not unreasonably priced; selected wines by the glass available to match food
Owner Paul O'Brien
Chef Michael Hartnell
Seats 50; private room; bar
www.eureka89.com.au

And ... A five-course menu is available midweek, seven courses are compulsory on Saturday, and payment is required on booking.

European

161 Spring Street, City **9654 0811**

EUROPEAN **15/20**

If the Windsor Hotel is Spring Street's grand dame, then the European is her dashing nephew, handsome with his dark-wood outfit and gilt-on-glass frontage, but chummy enough to keep tables close along the long, warmly lit room. Adroit, affable staff take care of dressed-up diners and post-show patrons, delivering artful continental starters: a sauteed calamari entree is in fact a mini paella, with the squid, smoky peppers and tomato-soaked rice sitting in a small cast-iron pan. Likewise prawns dressed in olive oil and herbs come 'potted' in a tin, accompanied by thin, crisp toast. Reinterpreted mains might include deconstructed coq au vin, the dish of lardons, parsley mash and poultry perhaps lacking the moisture of its stewy origins. Pasta dishes, whether linguine twirled through with crab and basil, or a rotolo of pumpkin and pinenut (as its own dish or the foundation for duck confit), sit perfectly between rural and refined. Regulars know desserts such as chocolate salty caramel are too rich to tackle alone.

Open Daily 7am–midnight
Typical prices E $21.50 **M** $35 **D** $16
Cards DC AE MC V
Wine A splendid Spanish, French and Italian collection, with forays north for riesling
Owners Con Christopoulos & Josh Brisbane
Chefs Ian Curley, Trent Kerr & Ben Keal
Seats 68; outdoor seating
www.theeuropean.com.au

And ... Leather couches and fortifieds await upstairs at the sibling Supper Club.

Ezard

187 Flinders Lane, City **9639 6811**

CONTEMPORARY **17/20**

Thirteen years on, this elegant basement restaurant still delivers arresting east-west dishes of alluring complexity. A consistent performer known for exemplary service, Ezard is top-class, high-end dining. The plush fitout and well-spaced tables allow for easy conversation, perfect for business, romance and celebration. As for the signature chilli caramel pork hock, resistance is futile. For an exhilarating adventure in colour, texture, flavour and harmony, take an eight-course tour stopping off in South-East Asia, moving through seafood to eight-score wagyu. Think swordfish shooter; citrus-cured salmon with sweet beet meringue and wasabi aioli; and a silky crab dumpling in luscious, aromatic tom kha. Next, coconut-grilled ocean trout on thick zingy gazpacho; sticky, slow cooked, five-spice Bangalow pork belly with apple pud and calvados jus; and Chinese-style roast duck with green chilli dressing on coconut rice. Finish with mango bavarois, slow-cooked peach and raspberry sorbet. Sublime.

Open Mon–Fri noon–2.30pm; Mon–Sat 6–10.30pm
Typical prices E $29 **M** $49 **D** $22
Cards DC AE MC V
Wine An impressive international list of established, iconic and emerging wines, and well-versed staff keen to advise
Owner Teage Ezard
Chefs Teage Ezard & Sharn Greiner
Seats 75; private room
www.ezard.com.au

citibank Privileges

And ... Try the express lunch and pre-theatre set menus, or the degustation for $150.

Fabulous Fine Food

161 McKinnon Road, McKinnon **9578 2238**

CONTEMPORARY **13/20**

Fabulous Fine Food is indeed fab, and owners Ross Parker and Anthony Green have created a welcoming, chic little space with a loyal local following. Fresh white walls offset dark bentwood chairs, and a square of carpet in the centre of the room works hard to soften the acoustics, especially at weekends when FFF is jumping. Service is warm and genuine, nailing the art of making customers feel looked-after but not smothered. Families comprise the early shift, when a nugget-free kids' menu is offered from 5.30pm to 6.45pm – things like grilled fish or house-made rissoles. Superb entrees may include steamed seafood gyoza in a soy broth, or crumbly spinach, cashew and goat's cheese 'cake' on a delicate saffron creme fraiche. Solid mains could be house-made potato gnocchi with a lamb ragu, or skinless salmon with a miso glaze on an Asian slaw with roasted peanuts. The hefty shortbread parfait sandwich deserves special mention, with manuka honey icecream and lavender sherbet – it's too good not to finish.

Open Tues–Sat noon–11pm
Typical prices E $19 **M** $38 **D** $16
Cards MC V Eftpos
Wine Compact list of 20-odd wines, most under $40; all by the glass; BYO Tues–Wed, except Dec (corkage $2.50 a head)
Owners Ross Parker & Anthony Green
Chef Anthony Green
Seats 42; bar
www.fabulousfinefood.com

And ... Try the lunch special from Tuesday to Saturday for $25.

Firechief

169 Camberwell Road, Hawthorn East **9831 1700**

ITALIAN/PIZZERIA **13/20**

The name might mistakenly suggest the soaring ceilings of this hip pizzeria were once part of a fire station. Rather, Firechief is a nod to the guys in charge of the burning ovens, ex-Ladro chefs Gabriel Espinoza and Daniel Barrese, who trained in Naples. This is no suburban takeout. It's serious pizza cooked three ways – wood-fired (to a strictly authentic recipe), on stone or in a modern conveyor oven. Purists can have their simply dressed, chewier margherita with a hint of char, while those who like it funkier can have braised saltbush Dorper lamb with goat's cheese, almonds and mint on a softer base, and kids a crisper modern creation, like Aussie with Otway bacon and free-range egg. There's a studied cafeteria feel – chequered lino floor, flitting young staff, a din – and a small list of other dishes that suits the cross-section of diners (young families, twentysomethings, older couples). Eclectic designer dabs include a 1930s Berlin brass chandelier. Sweet pizzas (maybe banana, caramel, chocolate and coffee cream) invite sharing.

Open Daily noon–3pm, 5–10.30pm
Typical prices E $13 **M** $22 **D** $12
Cards AE MC V Eftpos
Wine Compact list of Australian and Italian whites and reds; 12 by the glass
Owner Paul Mathis
Chefs Gabriel Espinoza & Daniel Barrese
Seats 100; private room
www.firechiefpizzeria.com.au

And ... Across the road from the Rivoli, it's perfect for pre-cinema dining.

The Firehouse

253-257 Maroondah Highway, Ringwood **9876 8100**

MEDITERRANEAN **13/20**

The firies and their trucks may have left the building, but there remains a burning passion within the quaint red-brick walls of this restaurant: to deliver food that is organic, sustainable, local and sensitive to allergies. You only have to look as far as the shared starter plates 'from the water', 'soil' and 'paddock'. Offerings can be mixed. Bruschetta of yabby and wonderfully sweet roast pumpkin, topped with a salty-nutty hit of almond romesco, bursts with flavour; Lebanese salad is less vividly flavoured despite seven main ingredients. More consistent are the heaped portions and rustic feel that carry through to the mains, which might include slow-cooked Red Angus oyster blade in a thickish Puerto Rican hot sauce with chunkily cut vegetables or moist, butter-roasted Balmain bugs on a panzanella salad with a hefty kick of dill. Desserts, like salted chocolate terrine, pack a mighty sweet punch. The floor runs with an efficiency that would make the former residents proud.

Open Wed–Sun 8am–11pm
Typical prices E $12 **M** $34 **D** $13
Cards AE MC V Eftpos
Wine Broad range of Australian and imported wines, many from standout smaller producers
Owners David & Scott Dungan
Chef Antony Henare
Seats 120; outdoor seating; private room; bar
www.thefirehouse.net.au

And ... More intimate and private spaces are available off the main dining hall.

Fitzrovia

155 Fitzroy Street, St Kilda **9537 0001**

CONTEMPORARY **13.5/20**

With its chic farmers' market styling and a chef who's worked at London's River Cafe, Fitzrovia was swiftly embraced by savvy St Kilda locals. Featuring pressed-metal ceilings, exposed brick walls and a large open kitchen with decoratively dangling pots, Fitzrovia is elegantly rustic – like its food. The grazing craze is avoided here – the emphasis, rather, is on comforting, fully fledged meals, using seasonal produce, with influences from the Mediterranean to the East. Breakfasts might include an indulgent creme brulee French toast, or simpler fresh figs and ricotta on grilled sourdough. For dinner, start perhaps with spicy Sichuan-style calamari. Less successful might be the too-chilly salmon rillettes with sourdough soldiers. Beef cheek braised overnight in Red Hill scotch ale is unforgettably tender. The fish might be an unusually hearty combination of roasted leatherjacket served with borlotti beans braised in Lardo di Colonnata (cured pork fat). Desserts such as a warm apple and cinnamon cake are delectably no-fuss.

Open Tues–Fri 7am–10pm; Sat–Sun 8am–10pm
Typical prices E $18 **M** $33 **D** $10.50
Cards AE MC V Eftpos
Wine An appealing list with user-friendly descriptions featuring reasonably priced boutique labels from Australia, NZ and Europe
Owners Paul Jewson & Marco Pugnaloni
Chef Paul Jewson
Seats 60; outdoor seating
www.fitzrovia.com.au

And … Breakfast is served until 3pm.

Flower Drum

17 Market Lane, City **9662 3655**

CANTONESE **17.5/20**

Rich, famous, infamous and ordinary, the 'Drum' has drawn them all with the city's finest Cantonese food for nearly four decades. Every night is a performance. Watching the procession of diners – dressed to impress or as casual as they come – is almost as engaging as the food itself. Expect great cooking in plush, plummy surrounds, and exemplary service, headed by Jason Lui, possibly the city's best maître d'. Chef Anthony Lui produces classic Cantonese dishes using the very best ingredients, from pearl meat to wagyu beef. Peking duck is a signature, the seafood often spectacular. You can spend a fortune, or dine without breaking the bank on dishes like delicate steamed dim sum, lightly battered and stuffed garfish served with shiitake sauce, stir-fried West Australian scallops or rice noodles stir-fried with Angus eye fillet. But specials are always worth exploring. As a finale, try the spun-sugar spectacle of Peking toffee apples teased out before your eyes.

Open Mon–Sat noon–3pm, 6–10.30pm; Sun 6–10pm
Typical prices E $18 **M** $30 **D** $16
Cards DC AE MC V Eftpos
Wine Top-class, top-end-heavy 24-page list; 14 by the glass
Owners Anthony Lui, Patricia Fung & William Shek
Chef Anthony Lui
Seats 120; private rooms
www.flower-drum.com

And … Feeling like a party? Book a table for eight to 10, pre-order the whole suckling pig for $500, and have it carved at table.

Fog

142 Greville Street, Prahran **9521 3155**

AMERICAN **14/20**

Fog is a scene – popular with a sleek set, who on busy weekends must pass burly security staff. Inside, a dramatic central staircase divides the stylish bar and smartly dressed tables. Floor staff do their best in the vast space but when noise levels reach a mojito-fuelled crescendo and the second sitting arrives, they can be stretched too far. It's fun, but the bar/restaurant balance can lean in the direction of the former. In the latter, the kitchen's heart lies in south-west America. A tart salsa of grilled pineapple is a clever foil for the briney freshness of rock oysters, and a salad of sweet prawns and mango is elevated with a hint of tequila and fiery chilli; the spiced rockling taco is a happy riot of flavour and texture; the popular grilled chicken pairs with feisty barbecue sauce and potato salad. Lavish peach, caramel and chocolate praline bar is worth extra time on the treadmill.

Open Tues–Wed 6–9.30pm; Thurs–Sat noon–midnight
Typical prices E $22 **M** $36 **D** $17
Cards DC AE MC V Eftpos
Wine Smart selection of higher-end local and European drops, 30 by the glass
Owner Sam Frantzeskos
Chefs Jeremy Sutphin & Cristopher Sutphin
Seats 140; outdoor seating; bar
www.fog.com.au

And ... The flashy cocktail lounge and courtyard make a sassy late-night rendezvous spot – just add bubbly and southern-fried chicken ribs.

France-Soir

11 Toorak Road, South Yarra **9866 8569**

FRENCH **14/20**

Settling in at this veteran bistro can feel like joining a lively party. A window-table blonde sips champagne, telling the gents on the next-door table about her trip to Paris. The gents greet a foursome coming through the brassy glass entrance. And isn't that so-and-so from the telly? But this long, mirror-lined room, busy as a train carriage at peak hour, is more than a neighbourhood hero with sharp service. For a quarter-century it has done a thriving trade in the classics: bubbling onion soup or juicy, charred steaks with a gravy boat of bearnaise. Goat's cheese on garlicky croutons with a tumble of frisee is another menu stalwart. Plump, pan-cooked scallops might come sans roe, with springy chunks of king brown mushroom. A tenderly cooked veal escalope is lapped by creamy mushroom sauce. Specials include fish and pork of the day and most mains come with textbook frites. Finish with île flottante, a single airy iceberg of soft meringue.

Open Daily noon–midnight
Typical prices E $19.50 **M** $35 **D** $13.50
Cards AE MC V Eftpos
Wine Encyclopedic list, plus BYO, except on Sat, holidays or for groups of six or more (corkage $14.50 a bottle; no corkage at lunchtime)
Owner Jean-Paul Prunetti
Chef Geraud Fabre
Seats 74; outdoor seating
www.france-soir.com.au

And ... Duck in for a fast pre-show dinner or drop by afterwards for supper.

Franco Choo's

179a High Street, Prahran **9529 7310**

ITALIAN **14/20**

Rustic, raucous and packed to the rafters most nights, this tiny trattoria is dishing up honest, home-style food, warm hospitality and well-paced service. It's snug but stylish informal dining. Good value, too. Mirrors add a spacious feel to rough-hewn timber tables, stools and bistro chairs. Chef Steven Choo's own striking wall-size photograph of a Piaggio three-wheeler laden with wooden cases at Sicily's Catania market inspired the recycled crate shelving lined with pedigree produce above the bar. Vibrant paintings by musician Kavisha Mazzella hang near the short blackboard menu. Two entrees, mains and desserts celebrate Calabria. Start with hearty char-grilled eggplant and pecorino involtini (rolls) doused in sweet, chunky sugo or juicy Berkshire pork subtly spiced with fennel seeds, tossed through fusilli and ricotta. Move on to slow-roasted Milawa free-range chicken and Dutch cream potatoes in marsala sauce or braised Gippsland lamb in robust borlotti bean ragu. To finish, fluffy zeppole (like doughnuts) on thick, eggy custard or green tomato jam tart. *Buonissimo.*

Open Tues–Sat 6–10pm
Typical prices E $14 **M** $25 **D** $12
Cards MC V Eftpos
Wine A judicious short list of Victorian Italian-style varietals; nine by the glass
Owner & chef Steven Choo
Seats 25; outdoor seating
www.francochoos.com.au

And ... Choo's does takeaway too.

The French Brasserie

2 Malthouse Lane (off Flinders Lane), City **9662 1632**

FRENCH **14.5/20**

Tall, dark and handsome, this striking laneway-dweller merges modern styling with a menu strong on French classics. Be seated at a dressed table against a backdrop of tall windows and Moroccan-inspired screens. There's a bar down the other side, and vintage French posters line the wall. Dense house-baked bread is offered with flavoured butter – perhaps anchovy and mustard. A glass of chablis sets the mood while you contemplate traditional starters such as garlic-butter snails, charcuterie, or beef tartare. Other dishes present broader flavours of the Med; maybe an entree of tender octopus on discs of potato and chorizo with pickled green chillies. Deeply flavoured bouillabaisse, heady with fennel, is packed with flathead, clams and prawns, while other mains span minute steak, filet de boeuf, duck a l'orange, and pork belly with apple puree. Staff are competent and maybe French-accented, too. Though it's hard to resist a French cheese finale, it's equally hard to say *non* to strawberry tart with creme patisserie.

Open Mon–Fri noon–3pm; Mon–Thurs 6–10pm; Fri–Sat 6–10.30pm
Typical prices E $18.50 **M** $37.50 **D** $16
Cards DC AE MC V Eftpos
Wine Mostly French labels, with some domestic and NZ wines; French and Australian drops by the glass
Owners Hadj Sadki & Claudio Perruzza
Chef Lionel Abello
Seats 110; outdoor seating; private room
www.thefrenchbrasserie.com.au

And ... The mezzanine's great for functions.

Gerald's Bar

386 Rathdowne Street, Carlton North **9349 4748**

EUROPEAN **14/20**

Behind lace curtains in Rathdowne Street's cutesy shopping village lies the ultimate clubby retreat, a narrow salon that appears to have evolved over decades but actually opened in 2007. Eccentric collectables (military field telephone, the grille from an old Wolseley car, a model ship) dot the walls, and bar staff alternatively spin vinyl and clamber up a ladder to fetch top-shelf digestives and spirits. Clipped to the ladder is a compact handwritten menu offering plates of cured meat sliced to order, cheeses or Sicilian white anchovies, starters such as a warm tumble of calamari, chorizo, rocket and toasted almonds or richly marbled beef carpaccio, and a few unpretentious but carefully prepared mains – three sweet pan-fried garfish under a scattering of capers and chopped parsley, perhaps, or twice-cooked pork belly with potato salad. Simple desserts might be refreshingly sharp lime sorbet or berries with house-made icecream. Come early for first dibs on the dishes and you may get to choose the evening's wines by the glass.

Open Mon–Sat 5–11pm; no bookings
Typical prices E $12 **M** $20 **D** $9
Cards MC V (minimum spend $200, otherwise, cash only)
Wine A wine buff's list offering interest at all price points; a small ever-changing array by the glass
Owners Gerald Diffey & Mario Di Ienno
Chef Peter Savage
Seats 50; outdoor seating; private room; bar

And ... In the rear parlour, Gerald's offers a $50-a-head shared degustation feast.

TOP 10 CHEAP THRILLS

Cafe Di Stasio
31 Fitzroy Street, St Kilda **9525 3999**
The $35 lunch special here remains one of Melbourne's true bargains.

Cafe Vue at Heide
7 Templestowe Road, Bulleen **9852 2346**
The Shannon Bennett experience without maxing out the card.

Florentino Cellar Bar
80 Bourke Street, City **9662 1811**
A gorgeous, atmospheric, timber-panelled piece of Melbourne restaurant history.

Hu Tong
14-16 Market Lane, City **9650 8128**
The third floor dining room adds fine dining style to the xiao long bao.

Kenzan @ GPO
350 Bourke Street, City **9663 7767**
The famed Japanese restaurant's canteen outpost keeps quality high and prices low.

Pei Modern Bar
Collins Place, 45 Collins Street, City **9654 8545**
Pei's bar plays it cool, simple and reasonable from breakfast to nightcap.

Rockpool Bar & Grill
Crown Complex, Southbank **8648 1900**
The bar, for times when the budget says wagyu burger rather than wagyu.

Royal Mail Hotel
Glenelg Highway (Parker Street), Dunkeld **5577 2241**
For those not in the mood (or money) for degustation, the bistro's an excellent alternative.

South of Johnson
48 Oxford Street, Collingwood **9417 2741**
The warehouse fitout looks a million dollars, the prices are pure cafe.

Yu-u
137 Flinders lane, City **9639 7073**
There's a reason the $18 lunchbox special books out every day.

Gigibaba

102 Smith Street, Collingwood **9486 0345**

TURKISH **14.5/20**

Tiny no-bookings Gigibaba is as buzzy as the Bosphorous on a summer's afternoon, so prepare to share. There are half a dozen tables, but backless stools at the white marble bar are a sweet spot, where casual yet cluey staff keep things ticking to a retro '60s-'70s-inspired soundtrack, despite rising noise levels and peak-hour queues. Around 20 neat dishes start small, perhaps with smoky flame-grilled eggplant swirled through tahini and yoghurt, bejewelled with pomegranate seeds. Golden grilled hellim cheese handmade locally is pillowy perfection. There are barbecue-kissed minced lamb kebabs, steamed eggplant-swaddled prawns, and nubs of lusciously salty roast goat on hummus. A *Guide* user-review rightfully noted of side dishes: 'if all vegetables tasted like this there'd be more vegetarians'. Exhibit A: tender broad beans tossed with white balsamic, olive oil, coriander and roast garlic – you'll mop the nana's china-style plate with bottomless Dench sourdough. Limited desserts might simply be almond baklava, best washed down with a fragrant brew of fresh mint tea.

Open Tues–Sat 6–10pm; bookings for 8–12 only
Typical prices E $10 **M** $22 **D** $11
Cards AE MC V Eftpos
Wine Dwells largely in Italy, Spain and France, available by 120ml, 300ml, 500ml and bottle; plus aniseedy raki and Turkey's beloved Efes beer
Owner & chef Ismail Tosun
Seats 42; outdoor seating; bar

And ... Want to guarantee a spot? Book the communal table for eight to 12.

Gills Diner

Rear, 360 Little Collins Street (enter from Gills Alley), City **9670 7214**

EUROPEAN **15/20**

The entrance to Gills Diner is up a 'where the heck are we going?' city laneway. Once a garage, formerly and still a bakery, it's a wonderfully atmospheric bolthole, with communal bare old timber tables, recycled schoolroom chairs, joint-jumping music on the turntable, and a blackboard menu. Professional, jeans-clad staff set you up from the stellar drinks list with French and Italian aperitifs, boutique beers, ciders and wines. In a group? Try the bargain antipasto trio (choose three from perhaps heirloom carrots, octopus and school prawns with salsa verde, quail with freekeh, chunky farmhouse terrine or plump zucchini flowers stuffed with quinoa, manchego cheese and tomato on romesco sauce). Full-flavoured pastas (perhaps mushroom pappardelle) are a menu mainstay but specials excel, like rich rabbit risotto or pan-fried and roasted poussin with harissa, confit fennel and potatoes, raisins, eggplant, and chorizo. To finish there's creamy goat's cheese from Gippsland, cow's milk cheese from Jura, Switzerland, or Gills' much-loved churros to plunge into chocolate sauce.

Open Mon–Fri 7am–late; Sat 8am–late
Typical prices E $19 **M** $34 **D** $12
Cards DC AE MC V
Wine Almost all-Victorian list, a model of clarity and selection; good choice of spirits, fortifieds, aperitifs, ciders and beers
Owners Con Christopoulos & Chris Kerr
Chefs Ian Alexander & Chris Kerr
Seats 55; bar

And ... Don't leave without a loaf of the bakery's crusty bread.

Gingerboy

27-29 Crossley Street, City **9662 4200**

MODERN SOUTH-EAST ASIAN **14.5/20**

Although it touts itself as a hawker-style Asian eatery, you're unlikely to find such chic surroundings in the alleyways of Bangkok, even if the pace can be as frenetic and the noise levels as high. The black bamboo-clad walls, efficient staff and funky soundtrack are the backdrop to chef Leigh Power's share-plates small and large, from the fragrant to the fiery – though some may find the latter too timid. Choose from such offerings as crisp prawns atop betel leaves with avocado and a tangy lime aioli, a feisty smashed green papaya salad or, on the larger side, perfectly roasted ocean trout with a smoked ginger and lemongrass dressing. An aromatic duck-leg red curry comes with a side of nuggety fried corn cakes to mop up the sauce. Desserts include tweaks on the traditional, such as banana fritters with cinnamon icecream, or the more adventurous coconut and chilli chocolate 'splice' with water chestnuts.

Open Mon–Fri noon–2.30pm; Mon–Sat 6–10.30pm
Typical prices E $15 **M** $36 **D** $16
Cards DC AE MC V Eftpos
Wine Globe-traversing list with lesser-known labels and decent by-the-glass options; quirky Asian-inspired cocktails
Owner Teage Ezard
Chef Leigh Power
Seats 66; private room; bar
www.gingerboy.com.au

And ... The swish bar upstairs has the same menu, and is where many hospitality folks land after they knock off.

Giuseppe Arnaldo & Sons

Riverside, Crown Complex, Southbank **9694 7400**

ITALIAN **14.5/20**

The Italians invented share-plates long before they became fashionable, and GAS works best if you have a crowd along to sample widely – the menu presented not in the usual entree-main convention but as a single sheet with 15 sections, the idea being you choose a little of what you like. Expect simple dishes done well: a basket of super-crisp school prawns; lovely tagliatelle with pancetta all'amatriciana; or a summery salad with witlof, anchovies and asiago cheese. Of the seven steaks, go for the magnificent bistecca fiorentina covered in salsa (to share) or the minute steak piled high with watercress. The walk-in crowd of casino-bound fun-seekers makes for a buzzy atmosphere despite the dark tiles and staff in lab coats, and while we get that it's a 'casual' affair (cutlery in holders at your table, menu placemats), service can have patchy moments. To keep the bill down, order cafefully – it's easy to get carried away.

Open Daily noon–4pm, 6–11pm; lunch bookings only
Typical prices E $18 **M** $30 **D** $16
Cards DC AE MC V Eftpos
Wine Midweight list with plenty of Italians and Italian varietals; house wines available by the glass (from $6) and carafe
Owners Robert Marchetti, Kimme Shaw & Tony Zaccagnini
Chefs Robert Marchetti, Hendri Salim & Jamie Hogg
Seats 140; outdoor seating; private room; bar
www.idrb.com

And ... Just enough room for a mouthful of dessert after all that? The cannoli three ways is perfect for sharing.

Golden Fields

Shop 2, 157 Fitzroy Street, St Kilda **9525 4488**

CONTEMPORARY 15/20

Last year's Best New Restaurant in the *Guide* is still a thrilling place to dine. A fresh, fun take on Asian cuisine combines with a deep understanding of restaurant theatrics: Golden Fields is noisy but poised, hip but striving to please. The food's mostly inspired by China. Poached chicken, glutinous rice noodles and cucumber ribbons are the cool, clean base for a dish that's mussed up with sesame paste and chilli oil. Shaved cuttlefish, earthy yam and chopped mussels combine in a gorgeously smoky, spicy starter. Grilled porterhouse is served rare with meaty mushrooms, a simple dish made outstanding with fabulous produce. Desserts are a highlight. Confit apple glistens alongside candied hazelnut and salted miso icecream. In all dishes, the control of flavour, texture and temperature is exemplary, ensuring each well-paced meal is something of a jazz masterwork, with all the building, bursting and restraint that such compositions entail. Every detail is considered, from the crockery to the kitsch lucky cat, creating an experience that excites and satisfies.

Open Daily noon–11pm
Typical prices E $14 **M** $32 **D** $12
Cards AE MC V Eftpos
Wine Adventurous list dotted with affordable, food-friendly European wines and a nice sideline in sake
Owner Andrew McConnell
Chefs Andrew McConnell & Todd Moses
Seats 80; outdoor seating; bar
www.goldenfields.com.au

And ... The famous (and fabulous) lobster rolls are available to take away.

The Graham

97 Graham Street (corner Esplanade West), Port Melbourne **9676 2566**

CONTEMPORARY **14.5/20**

There's a gentle calm to the Graham's dining room. Double-clothed tables, classic cutlery settings, subtle lighting and textured artwork set the scene for the charms of traditional entree-main-dessert. The sharp, experienced staff manage the floor deftly and chef Perry Schagen (ex-Taxi Dining Room) has created a contemporary, Asian-influenced menu. Maybe start with a truffled spanner crab salad with radish and nashi pear or freshly shucked oysters finished with yuzu-cured salmon and ponzu dressing. Mains may take a more conservative path with John Dory (perhaps pan-fried a touch too long), red pepper essence and artichokes or a textural dish of chicken, the sous-vide breast crumbed with brioche and garlic, the drumstick wrapped in filo pastry. For dessert, dark chocolate panna cotta is rich and playful, with peanut caramel and banana. The buzzy courtyard wine bar (heated and undercover) is a relaxed spot for pre-dinner drinks or a casual meal of shared dishes, such as potstickers, crab buns and Sichuan-spiced calamari.

Open Daily noon–3pm, 6–10pm
Typical prices E $20 **M** $38.50 **D** $16.50
Cards DC AE MC V Eftpos
Wine A lovely trek through Europe and Australia, taking in boutique wineries and interesting varietals; BYO Mon (corkage $10 a bottle)
Owners Tony, Amanda & Peter Giannakis
Chef Perry Schagen
Seats 60; outdoor seating; private room; bar
www.thegraham.com.au

And ... Express lunch (Monday to Friday $35) includes two courses and a glass of wine.

The Grand

333 Burnley Street, Richmond **9429 2530**

MODERN ITALIAN **15/20**

Ignore appearances. Within a shambles of mismatching pub architecture hides one of inner Melbourne's cosiest dining rooms, where you're welcomed warmly, like a friend to a party. Indeed, for your senses, it's quite the knees-up. Plump, fresh scallops pair harmoniously with their spinach and parmesan gratin. An entree of delicious prosciutto-wrapped rabbit loin remembers to bow to its companion, a spicy, caper-studded saute that drags frisée from wallflower to showgirl. Al dente tagliatelle might come with pork, fennel and sage ragu, and little lurking thrills of clove and cinnamon. Rib-eye steak is charry, black and pink in all the right places. The torn maltagliati pasta, flecked with breadcrumbs, comes with prawns, fennel and white wine – it's a deserving fixture on the menu. Finish by slurping brandy mascarpone with panettone bread-and-butter pudding, and reflect upon the virtues of simplicity. Here it's done admirably, in Grand style.

Open Daily noon–3pm, 6–9.30pm
Typical prices E $20 **M** $36 **D** $15
Cards DC AE MC V Eftpos
Wine Long international list with strong Italian bent, lots of choice sub-$70 plus some pricier 'occasion' wines; 25-plus by the glass
Owners David Yuncken, Ros Harvey, Barnie Bouchaud, Kevin Greenhatch & Valerio Nucci
Chef Jonathan Knight
Seats 55; outdoor seating; private room; bar
www.grandrichmond.com.au

And ... Wednesday night is $25 'duck and pinot' night in the pub lounge.

Grossi Florentino

80 Bourke Street, City **9662 1811**

ITALIAN **15.5/20**

Guy Grossi came to the Florentino in 1999, bringing with him proud family traditions of fine food and service. Now his personal brand – enhanced by his connection to an institution that's been part of Melbourne fine-dining since before the Depression – has spread to other restaurants, through books and television. Perhaps as a result, Florentino remains a benchmark of the ancient art of service, but is drifting as a benchmark of the total food experience. The extensive menu lists peerless ingredients, but the desire to mix timeless Italian classics with modern cooking flourishes – dusts, foams and such – does not always deliver the results expected with $39 entrees, and $56 mains. Tuna carpaccio with lemon snow and apple and fennel jelly is vivid and tart, while lobster tortellini may be more chewy than al dente. Fremantle octopus was too salty, while Glenloth pigeon came roasted perfectly, supported by ravioli filled with tender leg. The Mural room is as beautiful as ever – Melbourne will likely always have a soft spot for this cultured fine-diner.

Open Mon–Fri noon–2.30pm, 6–10pm; Mon–Sat 6–10.30pm
Typical prices E $39 **M** $56 **D** $26; degustation $140 (5 courses) to $195 (8 courses)
Cards DC AE MC V Eftpos
Wine Extensive and premium list covering the best of Australia and Europe; 22 by the glass
Owner Grossi family
Chefs Guy Grossi, Chris Rodriguez & Louis Naepels
Seats 100; private rooms
www.grossiflorentino.com

And ... Chocolate souffle is a signature.

Grossi Florentino Grill

80 Bourke Street, City **9662 1811**

ITALIAN **14.5/20**

Between the boisterous Cellar Bar and the grand Grossi Florentino, the Grill might seem in danger of suffering from middle-child syndrome. If you thought it wasn't swanky enough for the big night, or too pricey for pre-theatre pasta, you'd be wrong. Here's assured, eminently civilised, value dining - crowded with pollies, financiers, lawyers and Italian food lovers spending their own money. A tightly packed room with an open kitchen, simple white linen and assured service, the Grill has an extensive menu based around superb produce and technique. Select antipasti from a list of maybe sweet-and-sour eggplant, salt cod croquettes, salumi, and pressed mullet roe with lemon, parsley and chilli. The signature grill is fired up for dry-aged Angus steaks, Italian sausage or simple spatchcocked chicken with lemon and chilli. Favourites with the regulars are line-caught fish roasted in a bag, a 12-hour pork neck and the businessman's friend, the crumbed veal cutlet. Finish with traditional desserts, like gelato or tiramisu.

Open Mon–Sat noon–3pm, 5.30–11pm
Typical prices E $28 **M** $42 **D** $18
Cards DC AE MC V Eftpos
Wine Voluminous list, particularly strong on Italians, with excellent selections by the glass and half bottle
Owner Grossi family
Chef Matteo Tine
Seats 70
www.grossi.com.au

And ... Listen for the seasonal produce that makes its way into the specials (and for political and stockmarket tips from nearby tables).

Hako

310 Flinders Lane, City **9620 1881**

JAPANESE **14/20**

Hako has evolved with quiet distinction from a buzz-worthy laneway bolthole into a comfortably familiar piece of CBD furniture, perhaps no longer as hip but still happening. Its dark timber floor, whitewashed walls and rows of chunky ornamental sake bottles express a stripped-back sense of style that is ageing well, while waitstaff show cool composure but are never too cool. The menu is built around modern Japanese drinking food, but with a bow to culinary tradition. Novel izakaya-style morsels abound, perhaps crumbed pork fillet with sweet-sour tomato and fuji apple puree, or piquant chicken fingers filled with mentaiko roe and shiso leaf with dipping mayo. Slow-cooked beef ribs are as warming as thick socks, the fall-apart meat and soft carrot half-submerged in sticky sweet soy and peppercorn sauce. Bountiful moriawase is loaded with delectable sushi and velvety sashimi. Dessert choices are more minimal than the decor.

Open Mon–Fri noon–2.30pm; Mon–Wed 5.30–9.30pm; Thurs–Sat 5.30pm–late
Typical prices Small dishes $11, large dishes $25 **D** $7
Cards AE MC V Eftpos
Wine A good sake and shochu list, and serviceable mid-priced wine list favouring whites
Owners Masahiro & Ji-ah Horie
Chef Masahiro Horie
Seats 60
www.hako.com.au

And ... Killer bento boxes and lunch sets for hungry city workers.

Hanabishi

187 King Street, City **9670 1167**

JAPANESE **14.5/20**

Forget a fashionable address or slick designer interiors: the only flash you're likely to see here is in chef Akio Soga's knife skills with a piece of premium wagyu fillet or tuna belly. Hanabishi's focus is on authentic cooking, using the best seasonal produce – a path the restaurant has happily stuck to for more than 25 years, much to the pleasure of its suit-and-tie-skewed clientele. With a large menu on offer, a light, fresh starter may be in order: Soga-san's choice of sushi may include shimmering slices of snapper and kingfish; three kinds of Okinawa seaweed with rich sesame dressing; or razor-thin slices of raw wagyu beef. This should preserve the appetite for a basket of deep-fried soft-shell crab or crumbed loin of superbly tender kurobuta pork. Err on the healthy side with seafood, such as the popular Patagonian toothfish baked in cedar, and splurge on one of the worthwhile dessert tasting plates of six or nine treats.

Open Mon–Fri noon–2.30pm, 6–9.30pm
Typical prices E $20 **M** $38 **D** $14
Cards DC AE MC V Eftpos
Wine Exhaustive list that reads like a who's who of Australian labels, plus some French and NZ; choice of warm and cold sakes
Owners Akio & Eiko Soga
Chefs Akio Soga, Masahiko Iga & Shin Tsunazawa
Seats 70
www.hanabishi.com.au

And ... Collar the restaurant manager for chapter and verse on seasonal and special dishes or the sakes on offer.

Hare & Grace

525 Collins Street, City **9629 6755**

CONTEMPORARY **14.5/20**

Stepping into Hare & Grace is like entering a fairytale. Decked out by green-thumbed designer Joost Bakker, this dimly lit space features bunches of twigs hanging from the ceiling, avant-garde floral arrangements and plush, high-backed chairs fit for a king. Raymond Capaldi's adventure-filled menu delivers intriguing lists of ingredients that beg explanation. Enthusiastic staff are on hand to decipher dishes such as a light and pretty starter of plump yabby tails, green fruits and chenopodiums (vivid amaranth flowers), doused in a delicate jasmine tea poured at the table. Spruiked as the signature dish, an 'Eton mess' of oysters, cream, passionfruit and beetroot meringue strays into dessert territory. Comfort, rather than kitchen trickery, gets the meal back on track, with a main of pink lamb loin and fork-tender neck, enlivened with a carrot and orange gel. And, as in all good stories, there's a happy ending thanks to a standout dish of creamy lemon tart in a thin tahini shell.

Open Mon–Fri noon–3pm, 6–10pm
Typical prices E $20 **M** $40 **D** $18
Cards DC AE MC V Eftpos
Wine Succinct, largely Australian and NZ list, backed by creative cocktails and beers from the bar
Owners Raymond Capaldi, Jessica Stuart & Caitlin Ingram
Chefs Raymond Capaldi & Adam Liston
Seats 100; outdoor seating; private room; bar
www.hareandgrace.com

And ... For a speedy midweek lunch in the bar, pre-order your prawn sandwich or wagyu burger.

Hellenic Republic

434 Lygon Street, Brunswick East **9381 1222**

GREEK **14/20**

From the polished, well-drilled service to the glistening Greek grub, the Republic is slick. It takes a tight operation like this to turn out a couple of hundred well-fed and watered patrons a night. Hellenic Republic manages a casual control over its chatty, all-walks crowd who are slotted in close in the bright, white dining room. Most diners will have taken their waiter's lead and signed on as a table for the sharing menu. It's a Homeric spread that takes in around three-quarters of the menu. There's taramasalata and wedges of soft pita, the satisfying salty-sweet combo of saganaki topped with whole jammy figs, then seafood. Offerings might include crumbed, garlicky scallops in the shell or fillets of crisp-skinned, succulent salmon. But wait ... there's more. There's meat from the ironbark grill (or smoky calamari if you prefer), and your salad prayers may be answered with a spectacular mix of lentils, almonds and currants with cumin yoghurt – flown in from Greece. This is uncomplicated and undeniably fun dining.

Open Daily 5.30pm–late; Fri noon–4pm; Sat–Sun 11am–4pm;
Typical prices E $11 **M** $25 **D** $12.50
Cards DC AE MC V Eftpos
Wine Short list of almost all Greek wines, 12 by the glass, plus epic ouzo list
Owners Made Establishment & Travis McAuley
Chefs Travis McAuley & Johan Vanderwalle
Seats 120; outdoor seating
www.hellenicrepublic.com.au

And ... Check the website for regular events such as ouzo tastings.

Henry & the Fox

525 Little Collins Street, City **9614 3277**

CONTEMPORARY **13.5/20**

Like most good foxy lairs, this one's not easily stumbled upon. Camouflaged in a commercial sector, its verandah and woodsy Nordic-inspired dining room cater to business breakfasters, office lunchers and after-work diners. That's a charm and a challenge. Henry and the Fox, one of six restaurants opened in rapid succession by Paul Mathis, is fronted by the *Guide*'s 2011 Young Chef of the Year, Michael Fox. His mod-Euro lunch and dinner menu is designed to share, with no lines drawn between entrees and mains. You might start with sweet roasted bug tails and nubbly spiced cauliflower on smooth cauliflower puree, or terrific rustic rabbit terrine partnered with batons of rhubarb and toasted house-made brioche. Pork and lemony salsa verde can unexpectedly lack punch atop pizza, but slow-cooked lamb neck with earthy globe artichokes and pearl barley is appealing comfort food. It's cooking to catch this Fox's prey.

Open Mon–Fri 7.30am–late
Typical prices E $24 **M** $28 **D** $14
Cards AE MC V Eftpos
Wine A lively, globetrotting list; plenty to amuse after-work tipplers
Owner Paul Mathis
Chef Michael Fox
Seats 70; outdoor seating; bar
www.henryandthefox.com.au

And ... Barbecues on the deck, pizza and happy hours aim to lure the after-work crowd.

Hotel Lincoln

91 Cardigan Street, Carlton **9347 4666**

CONTEMPORARY **13.5/20**

Top food pubs tend to wax and wane in their ability to consistently nail the genre, but the Lincoln is 'in the zone'. Chef Ross Beeley's menu displays Moorish, Iberian and traditional French influences, which means you could start with an excellent iteration of duck rillettes with port-soused prunes or a dish of superb garlic-infused razor clams with chorizo, white wine and sherry. Like any good gastropub worth its salt there's a selection of quality steak options – here all Victorian and dry-aged in-house – and plenty of old shiraz to match. Generous mains might include a homely, golden-topped rabbit, bacon and prune pithiviers or the aromatic, slow-cooked goat tagine with green olives and preserved lemon. With its slate-grey paint job, lacquered white partitioning and understated stencil art, the stylish dining room attracts a relaxed, food-savvy crowd. Well-spaced tables, a thoughtful wine list and professional service elevate the experience well beyond pubby expectations.

Open Daily noon–3pm; Sun–Thurs 6–9pm; Fri–Sat 6–9.30pm
Typical prices E $17 **M** $35 **D** $12
Cards DC AE MC V Eftpos
Wine Excellent mid-sized list with an interesting smattering of European varietals; 10-plus draught beers including craft offerings.
Owners Antoinette & Jonathan Burfurd
Chef Ross Beeley
Seats 64; outdoor seating; private room; bar
www.hotellincoln.com.au

And ... The two-course weekend lunch is a great option for pre-footy or post-shopping dining.

Huxtable

131 Smith Street, Fitzroy **9419 5101**

CONTEMPORARY **14.5/20**

For pure exuberance it's hard to go past Huxtable. Two years in and the early dishes-to-die-for (molten jalapeno and cheddar croquettes, spicy ribs) are rusted-on classics. Chef Daniel Wilson keeps exploring, backed by a team that displays a judicious mix of Smith Street savvy and service smarts. The small pseudo-retro dining room has a buzzy hubbub and the share-friendly globetrotting menu plucks from hither and thither, redefining fine dining and fast food with equal vigour. Steamed cod with exotic mushroom and dashi braise is topped with a dazzling sesame and wakame crumb. Pork cheek is slow-cooked, smoked and served warm with a clever contrasting salad of Thai basil, finger lime and toasted coconut flakes. Underpinning the pop flavours and punchy combinations are careful cooking and a hospitable ethic that showers vegetarians and coeliacs with love. Dishes from the long 'land' section may include unmissable corn and black-bean stew with chipotle cream. Desserts (jam doughnuts, icecream and fudge sandwich) sweetly express the hip Huxtable spirit.

Open Tues–Sun noon–11pm
Typical prices E $5.50 **M** $23 **D** $15
Cards AE MC V
Wine Nimble list that's almost as peripatetic as the food
Owners Daniel Wilson, Dante Ruaine & Jeff Wong
Chef Daniel Wilson
Seats 40; outdoor seating; bar
www.huxtablerestaurant.com.au

And ... For quick bites and late nights, head across the road to Huxtaburger.

Ido Kitchen

166 Bridport Street, Albert Park **9699 8969**

VIETNAMESE **14/20**

Theo Do cooks the beef stock for his pho for up to 44 hours. That tells you a lot of what you need to know about his restaurant, which dishes up some of the city's brightest modern Vietnamese. A refugee's son, Do was working in the tax office in Canberra when the urge to cook struck. He learnt some of his cheffy moves from former business partner, iconic chef Greg Brown. Silk hanging lanterns, linen napkins, bentwoods and a banquette make a handsome setting for his food, vibrant with fresh herbs. Though upbeat, service can vary. Familiar favourites like sugarcane prawns and chicken salad crisp with cabbage and herbs are done well. But detours reward menu explorers with turmeric-marinated fish, slow-cooked pork with caramelised onion sauce, or soft chunks of beef braised with lemongrass and chilli. Stick around for elegant desserts – perhaps molten chocolate pudding, or a sphere of black-sesame icecream in coconut jelly, inspired by the street vendor's drinks of the chef's former homeland.

Open Tues–Sat 6–10pm; Fri–Sat noon–2.30pm
Typical prices E $14 **M** $28 **D** $12
Cards AE MC V
Wine Compact, well-priced list, around 12 by the glass; try Vietnam's Huda Beer
Owners Theo Do & An Nguyen
Chef Theo Do
Seats 42; outdoor seating; private room
www.idokitchen.com.au

And ... Want to try Do's pho? His Hanoi-style version is served at lunch only.

Il Bacaro

168–170 Little Collins Street, City **9654 6778**

ITALIAN **15/20**

From behind venetian blinds, Il Bacaro's golden glow beckons passersby. Step into the snug dining room and you'll be welcomed with a *ciao*. Modelled on a Venetian bacaro (wine bar), Il Bacaro has been the epitome of consistency since it opened in late 1995. Small tables draped with heavy linen squeeze around a horseshoe-shaped bar, a favourite haunt of solo diners. A hubbub of contentment and snippets of Italian provide the soundtrack. Chef David Dellai gently updates Italian classics, turning goat's cheese into foam and serving it alongside heirloom tomatoes or sending out sashimi-style kingfish and ocean trout with lightly pickled cucumber and black grapes, silver-served by polished staff. Duck, a signature, might be served with confit leg and pinkly roasted breast atop parsnip puree, and game makes a regular appearance in rustic dishes like prosciutto-swaddled rabbit or fall-apart braised goat. If it's on, don't miss Dellai's witty Violet Crumble homage, with agave nectar cheesecake, chocolate pop rocks and violet sorbet.

Open Mon–Sat noon–3pm; Mon–Thurs 6–10.30pm; Fri–Sat 6–11pm
Typical prices E $24 **M** $42 **D** $19
Cards DC AE MC V
Wine High-end Italians, Italian varietals and Australian benchmarks; satisfying options by the glass
Owners Graeme Ballentine & Joe Mammone
Chef David Dellai
Seats 45; bar
www.ilbacaro.com.au

And ... Don't skip dessert – the kitchen saves some of its best work until last.

Il Solito Posto

Basement, 113 Collins Street (enter from George Parade), City **9654 4466**

ITALIAN **14/20**

There's more than meets the eye to this top-end-of-town stayer. It presents a plain face to the street but turn the corner into a lane and you'll find a buzzing ground-level bar-bistro. Beyond the lunch crowd or evening theatre-goers propped at the bar are stairs down to the restaurant proper – a candlelit cave of timber tables, wine bottles lining the walls and woven wicker chairs. It's as charming as the waiters who weave around the room buttering up diners and delivering classically Italian dishes: perhaps salumi (cured meats); or insalata caprese using local buffalo mozzarella; or fried school prawns. House-made pasta is a speciality, from ravioli of braised quail, porcini and leek dotted with fresh grapes, to silky ribbons of pappardelle with spicy sausage and red peppers. Spatchcock may come wrapped in pancetta and sage; lamb is slow-cooked, with herbs and fresh peas. Sweets might include a lovely, fudgy chocolate pudding with dense salted-caramel sauce and strawberry icecream.

Open Mon–Thurs 7.30am–10.30pm; Fri 7.30am–11pm; Sat 9am–11pm
Typical prices E $17 **M** $37 **D** $16
Cards AE MC V Eftpos
Wine Quirky tasting notes accompany the list, 20-plus pages of mostly European and Australian wine
Owners Michael Tenace & Theo Poulakis
Chef Nathan Morfett
Seats 47; bar
www.ilsolitoposto.com.au

And ... The bistro offers breakfast daily, and there's a takeaway dining menu, too.

Ilona Staller

282 Carlisle Street, Balaclava **9534 0488**

CONTEMPORARY **14/20**

Saucy sister to St Kilda's Cicciolina, Ilona Staller (also named after the Italian-Hungarian porn star) has found a fitting home on Balaclava's lively, bohemian Carlisle Street. The Art Deco building, a former bank turned fast-food joint, has been gussied up with zebra-print bar stools and caged bird wall fixtures. Like the waiters, Staller is flamboyant and cheeky, serving bistro food with bite. Among classics, the 'bee sting' is a standout starter – a fried jalapeno chilli stuffed with feta, lime and pinenuts. It's delicate and delectable, as are entrees such as fatty, crisp pork belly, served with a zesty calvados jus. Lemon linguine, dotted with sauteed calamari, pinenuts, currants, tomato, spring onions and squid ink-infused panko crumbs, zings and sings, while less boisterous mains like kingfish fillet with prawn farce may not be quite as memorable. Desserts, including chocolate bombe – the meringue crust scalded with a blowtorch – offer sweet redemption.

Open Mon–Fri noon–11pm; Sat–Sun 9am–11pm
Typical prices E $17.50 **M** $34.50 **D** $15.50
Cards AE MC V Eftpos
Wine Very reasonable mark-ups on an exciting 10-page list, including 20-plus by the glass
Owners Virginia Redmond, Barbara Dight & Lisa Carrodus
Chefs Virginia Redmond & Jessica Van Nooten
Seats 100; outdoor seating; private room; bar
www.ilonastaller.com.au

And ... There are $10 kids' meals daily until 6.30pm; bookings for 6.30pm and 8.30pm dinner sittings.

Indian Palace

131 Church Street, Brighton **9593 1488**

INDIAN **12/20**

The Hindu god Ganesh serenely watches over diners at this casual spot. And save for the parade of stencilled elephants across a wall, interrupted only by a large flat-screen television with the volume turned to low, the sparse contemporary room is testament to the Palace's no-frills approach. This ethos also emanates from the kitchen, where a bevy of chefs turns out family-friendly Indian food from across the subcontinent: biryani, jalfrezi, korma and vindaloo dishes abound. However, it pays to delve into the menu's numerous pages to discover entrees like moist-centred navratan vegie pakoras, and subtly spiced fillets of fish marinated with green chutney and cooked in the tandoor. A stew-like bhuna features fall-apart chunks of beef in a ginger-laced gravy that's perfect for mopping up with flaky paratha, while a prawn patia comes with plump king prawns cooked in vinegar, brown sugar and spices such as ginger and cumin seeds. On warm nights friendly staff throw open the giant glass doors overlooking bustling Church Street.

Open Daily 5–10.30pm
Typical prices E $12.90 **M** $19.90 **D** $8
Cards DC AE MC V Eftpos
Wine Varied list of mostly Australian wines plus some from NZ; 12 by the glass; BYO (corkage $2.50 a head)
Owner Anuj Tyagi
Chefs Salik Ram Aryal, Rajan Pokhrel & Subash Khrel
Seats 50; outdoor seating; private room
www.indianpalace.net.au

And ... Nearly everything is takeaway too.

The Italian

101 Collins Street (enter from Flinders Lane), City
9654 9499

ITALIAN **15/20**

This clever suitor employs slow-burning charm. First impression: handsome, debonair, a prestigious address. Somewhere between red leather banquettes and the clink of corporate high-flyers' glasses, attraction begins. With house-cured ocean trout, or distinctive offal dishes, such as char-grilled veal tongue with white anchovies, you sense a solid style; no strutting its stuff with arty presentation but focusing on its core intent: to woo you with excellent food. The pursuit deepens with thick, char-grilled porterhouse, melted gorgonzola smeared on top and worked, with aioli, into rocket salad. Ligurian seafood stew excites with a sublime sauce containing saffron, chilli, olives and vermouth. Pastas include beef-cheek ravioli with a cavalier dollop of thick tomato sauce. You can almost feel the Latin lover finally allowing itself a roguish smirk of conquest with its devastatingly seductive tiramisu, and the panna cotta, smooth yet twinkling with mint. You're smitten.

Open Mon–Fri 7am–10.30pm; Sat 6–10.30pm
Typical prices E $25 **M** $38 **D** $16
Cards DC AE MC V
Wine A nine-page list of mainly Australian and Italian wines ranging in price from low to high; nine white and 11 reds available in half bottles – good for business lunches
Owner Roberto Scheriani
Chef Anthony Grafton
Seats 140; outdoor seating; private room; bar
www.theitalian.com.au

And ... At lunchtime, enter via the foyer of 101 Collins Street and enjoy the artwork.

Italy 1

823 Burke Road, Camberwell **9804 0944**

ITALIAN **13.5/20**

This sepia-toned, plump-cushioned restaurant has been given a fresh start with a view to pulling it back to its heyday. After a bumpy change of guard that shook a few loyal locals and temporarily closed its doors, chef and 10-year Italy 1 veteran Darren Venn has reopened his first love with a gentle polish of the dark timbers and a determination to return to the relaxed bistro concept that industry pioneers Geoff Slattery and Rick Davis created here more than 15 years ago. So the roast duck is a perfection of crisp skin and tender meat on radicchio, pear and walnuts; the calamari a soft golden tangle on a bed of rocket and aioli; and the tiramisu is more lushly alcoholic than ever. It's same-same but better under Venn's loving care, with sassy choices like pork belly or barramundi on the specials list. Glossy fior di burrata, oozing beside warm pear in crisp prosciutto, is Italy 1 on a plate.

Open Mon–Sat noon–10pm
Typical prices E $18 **M** $28 **D** $14
Cards DC AE MC V Eftpos
Wine Short, approachable, affordable list – mostly Australian with a few Italians for interest
Owners Darren Venn & Lichun Wu
Chef Darren Venn
Seats 60; outdoor seating
www.italy1.com.au

And ... Italy 1 stays open between lunch and dinner, with antipasti, arancini and more available for that pre-cinema nibble.

Izakaya Den

Basement, 114 Russell Street, City **9654 2977**

JAPANESE **14/20**

Factor in a mobile phone call if you're meeting first-timers at this hidden basement bunker. They'll almost certainly need help finding it, even if they decipher the word 'DEN' on the obscure sign outside. All is revealed 17 steps down, through the heavy glass door and black curtain to where the action is frenetic, the music up and the tall timber stools rarely empty for long. Head chef Yosuke Furukawa (the biggest man behind the bar) and his hyperactive team wear bandanas and beaming smiles and offer a menu of more than 30 sharing-style treats. Try the irresistible sweetcorn 'kaki-age' (steamed kernels served with green tea salt in a light tempura batter); or a bowl overflowing with crisp school prawns served with a light yuzu mayonnaise. Simple grills include barramundi with hajikami (pickled ginger shoot). Luscious house-made tofu may be lunchtime-only, but warm tofu cake with brown-sugar icecream, or the popular tower of dried apple wafers layered with icy apple sorbet are worthy consolation.

Open Mon–Fri noon–2.30pm; Mon–Sat 5.30pm–midnight; no dinner bookings except for five or more
Typical prices E $11 **M** $18 **D** $12
Cards AE MC V
Wine Enticing list of sake, umeshu and shochu by the glass, with origin, brewing method and flavour profile
Owners Simon Denton, Takashi Omi & Miyuki Nakahara
Chef Yosuke Furukawa
Seats 95
www.izakayaden.com.au

And ... The $18 lunch set menu is great value.

Jacques Reymond

78 Williams Road, Prahran **9525 2178**

CONTEMPORARY 18/20

It's easy to underestimate the pleasures of luxurious, old-school hospitality like that of Jacques Reymond. The welcome is warm, the room chic, the chairs comfy, the linen-dressed tables spaced for conversation, not eavesdropping. Every need is quietly anticipated. But traditional doesn't mean old-fashioned. Expect some of the city's very best service, but with wit and a wink. And Jacques Reymond's sophisticated food leaps confidently from European to Asian flavours in small, intricate dishes of many elements, dotted like jewellery on the plate. Scallop grilled with musky miso, rock lobster dumpling wrapped in bok choy, and caramelised sweetbreads are ensemble players in a single dish. Pigeon 'like a Peking duck' partners sweetly with silky purple garlic sauce; kingfish with ham and saffron foam. Four large menus (a la carte, degustation, lunch and vegetarian) rarely double up, proving the place's polish. The degustation remains a drawcard, as do gorgeous desserts, maybe a citrusy snow egg with creamy apricot bombe.

Open Tues–Sat 6.30–9pm; Thurs–Fri noon–1.30pm
Typical prices Degustation $135 (4 courses) to $190 (9 courses); lunch menu $55 (2 courses)
Cards DC AE MC V
Wine An appropriately significant list, with some lovely wines made specifically for the restaurant
Owners Jacques & Kathy Reymond
Chef Jacques Reymond
Seats 60; private room
www.jacquesreymond.com.au

And ... Spoil yourself with Dom Perignon champagne by the glass for $55.

Jorg

203 St Georges Road, Fitzroy North **9482 3002**

EUROPEAN **13.5/20**

Forget the frenetic buzz that often surrounds Fitzroy dining; Jorg is a cool, calm customer by comparison. The handsome once-a-warehouse space with soaring cathedral ceilings, designer light fittings and charcoal concrete floors, has typical industrial chic. But the feel is less fashion-forward, with low-key service, easy-listening music and an appealing, flexible menu, with 'small' and 'large' plates. All dishes have European heritage, such as asparagus spears with a rich coddled-egg mayo and crisp-crumbed but soft-hearted balls of goat's cheese, and a twice-baked nettle-flecked ricotta souffle. Four 'large' uncomplicated dishes (maybe roast pork loin, beef bavette, braised lamb and fish) are supplemented by a few specials, which could include whole flounder topped with salsa, fregola and frisee, and there's always a vegetarian option (and degustation), such as artichoke tortellini with sage butter. Desserts (maybe firm chocolate mousse with warm pistachio shortbreads) end the meal on a high note.

Open Tues–Fri 6–11pm; Sat–Sun 8am–late
Typical prices E $15 **M** $31 **D** $15
Cards AE MC V Eftpos
Wine Old World wines, including solid Australian labels; more than 12 by the glass
Owners Bryce Bernhardt, Michael Smith & David Cristiano
Chefs Bryce Bernhardt & Michael Smith
Seats 90; outdoor seating; private room
www.jorgrestaurant.com.au

And ... Weekend breakfasts include a few options for kids; Sunday is BYO (no corkage).

Journal Canteen

Mezzanine, 253 Flinders Lane, City **9650 4399**

SARDINIAN/SICILIAN **14/20**

The Canteen, not to be confused with street-side Journal Cafe, is the culinary haven up the stairs adjacent to the cafe. The rustic Italian menu is confident in its simplicity, the wine list is short and sweet, and the decor industrial chic: concrete floors, metal stools, bench by the window, communal tables with cutlery baskets. The obligatory antipasto might comprise a wedge of spongy pea frittata, plump olives, ribbons of zucchini, mushrooms and slow-roasted tomatoes. There's now a broader offering of house-made pastas, too. Consider a hearty bowl of capunti – canoe-shaped pasta with baked cauliflower and melting fontina. Or you might choose suckling pig lasagne, studded with fennel seeds and topped with basil pesto, or perfect pillows of ravioli filled with lemony-ricotta in a bright tomato sugo. There's always something meatier on offer, maybe a moist lamb shoulder and carrot puree, and in the evenings, perhaps porchetta. A joyous fig and ricotta tart with stove-top coffee make the perfect ending.

Open Mon–Wed 7am–4pm; Thurs–Fri 7am–10pm
Typical prices E $17 **M** $24 **D** $8
Cards None
Wine Short, one-page list of mostly Italian wine; about 10 by the glass
Owner John Vakalis
Chef Oscar Rigo
Seats 50

And ... Breakfast is available from 7am, and ask about good-value tasting menus at $38 for lunch, $45 for dinner.

The Kent Hotel

370 Rathdowne Street, Carlton North **9347 5672**

MEDITERRANEAN/ITALIAN **12.5/20**

What a pleasure it is to walk into an old local pub that has adapted to modern times. The Kent Hotel is a Carlton tradition and still has a local feel. But it has also been gracefully modernised with big, comfortable spaces, high ceilings, polished hardwood floors and solid furniture. The dining area more or less floats through the whole pub, with service provided by cheerful, efficient staff. There's a detailed blackboard as well as a full menu. Try the entree tasting platter for two, a generous dish crammed with a selection of tasters like five-spice duck shanks and beer-battered fish pieces. Quality seafood features in several dishes, notably the linguine tossed with Portarlington mussels and blue swimmer crab (plus fish, calamari and prawns). There's a selection of steak cuts, and pizzas and pastas – a forte, though not house-made. The noise level is lively, especially when the several large tables are full of happy diners. This is a warm, modern pub with top-notch food.

Open Mon–Sat noon–10pm; Sun noon–9pm
Typical prices E $12 **M** $27 **D** $14
Cards DC AE MC V Eftpos
Wine List of 200 Australian and international wines, often good value; 25 by the glass
Owners Tony Adamo, Lucy Adamo & Joe Setaro
Chef Nathan McKee
Seats 110; outdoor seating; private room; bar
www.kenthotel.com.au

And ... Craft beers (and a cider) on tap include Little Creatures, Mountain Goat and Brunswick Bitter.

Kenzan

Lower level, Collins Place, 45 Collins Street (enter from Flinders Lane), City **9654 8933**

JAPANESE **15/20**

Generations have enjoyed Kenzan, and, after more than 30 years, the so-called empress of Melbourne's Japanese restaurants maintains her reign. With a modernised look and expanded menu (reworked in 2011), Kenzan's tranquil dark-wood and lacquer finishes reflect the elegant finesse of its food. The menu still features favourites like tempura, tatsuta-age (fried, marinated chicken) and sukiyaki in refined fashion. And you'll always find more unusual fare on the daily specials, such as grilled, salted kingfish cheek (the simple cooking highlighting the particular tenderness and rich taste of this cut), or an exquisite spicy tuna and scallop salad. Eel is at its oily best in an entree of grilled eel and cucumber in sweet vinegar or the more familiar main dish with sweet soy sauce on rice. And Kenzan's always-popular sushi bar proves its mettle, with dedicated sushi chefs crafting exemplary sushi using high-quality seafood that's delicately arranged and subtly garnished.

Open Mon–Fri noon–2.15pm; Mon–Sat 6–10pm
Typical prices E $16 **M** $35 **D** $10
Cards DC AE MC V Eftpos
Wine Select list of mainly big-name Australians; 10 by the glass, plus a good range of sake, shochu and Japanese beer
Owners Kaz Murayama, Boeing Cho & Yuki Munehiro
Chefs Kaname Komatsu & Koichi Minamishima
Seats 100; private room; bar
www.kenzan.com.au

And ... The lunch menu includes wonderfully ornate two-tiered bento boxes ($35–$38).

Koko

Level 3, Crown Complex, Southbank **9292 6886**

JAPANESE **14.5/20**

There are few more spectacular dining rooms than Koko, with its serene central rock pool and view through Crown's dramatic giant flame jets to the city skyline. Prices, too, can be spectacular, such as $380 for the signature Mayura wagyu 300g striploin and mains hovering around $40. Koko's ambition, though, allows for dishes and produce rarely found outside Japan, such as the Mayura wagyu and the puffer fish, fugu, which is poisonous if not correctly prepared. Koko is a special-occasion kind of place, and a favourite for wedding proposals, but if romance is your intention, don't sit at the exciting teppanyaki where chefs sizzle top-notch seafood and meat. From the a la carte menu, you might try the simple stir-fried udon, lush with seafood, or miso-and-mustard dressed salad topped with crunchy fried salmon skin. Having strayed into more pan-Asian fare in recent years, Koko is back to being quintessentially Japanese and remains eminently striking.

Open Daily noon–3pm; Sun–Thurs 6–11pm; Fri–Sat 6pm–midnight
Typical prices E $25 **M** $45 **D** $15
Cards DC AE MC V Eftpos
Wine Diverse Japanese (and Australian) sakes; well-matched list of mainly Australian and NZ wines; around 24 by the glass
Owner Crown Casino Pty Ltd
Chef Norimasa Kosaka
Seats 150; private room; bar
www.kokoatcrown.com.au

And ... $88 three-course 'signature' menus offer entrees, sashimi and mains (including fugu).

Good food
should be enjoyed
free range.
LILYDALE
free range chicken.com.au

Komeyui Japanese Restaurant

396 Bay Street, Port Melbourne **9646 2296**

JAPANESE **14.5/20**

Sucking hot soybeans from their salted pod, a little wooden box of top-shelf sake at the ready – there's a lot to love about Komeyui. It's the vision of Hokkaido-born chef Motomu Kumano (ex-Kenzan) who designed the restaurant with harmony, health and tradition in mind. Aesthetics are considered, from the warmly lit, blond-timbered space and beautiful Japanese crockery to the stunning sashimi platter of kingfish, salmon, scallop and king dory with sheer daikon crisps and mini towers of wasabi. Rice is cooked in a hagama, a traditional cast-iron pot, and a shichirin (charcoal brazier) is used to grill luscious black cod, marinated for three days in miso, mirin or sake. Hokkaido specialities include a succulent foil-wrapped parcel of steamed salmon with white miso and beanshoots, and the soul-satisfying Berkshire pork curry hotpot, a miso-based brew, is kept warm at the table with a gas burner. Then, for dessert, there's silken sake brulee with a brittle top. Service is confident and friendly, just another solid aspect of this splendid spot.

Open Tues–Sat noon–3pm, 6–10pm
Typical prices E $15 **M** $25 **D** $15
Cards MC V
Wine High-end sakes, umeshus and shochus matched to the food; BYO Tues (corkage $10 a bottle)
Owners Motomu Kumano & Queenie
Chef Motomu Kumano
Seats 47
www.komeyui.com.au

And ... Call ahead to order the omakase (the chef's selection menu), and try Komeyui's primo lunch sets.

Koots Salle a Manger

479 Glenferrie Road, Kooyong **9822 3809**

MODERN FRENCH **15/20**

Owner-chef Patrice Repellin may have moved the family to the Mornington Peninsula, but the tree-change hasn't altered his cosy, elegant Gallic restaurant an iota. Expect the same salle a manger (dining room) with traditional touches – napery, upholstered chairs, and chandelier – as well as a warm greeting and attentive, knowledgeable service. Unchanged, too, is the first-class French food, at once classic and contemporary. An entree selection perfectly showcases Repellin's range – perhaps a shot of chilled gazpacho, goat's cheese foam quenelle on brioche, pork and prune terrine, and super-thin yellowfin tuna dressed with ginger, shallot and wasabi mayo. Mains, like roasted milk-fed lamb with stuffed zucchini flower fritters and eggplant relish, follow a more conservative course. A shared dessert platter returns to a joyful marriage of old and new: perhaps canelés bordelais (Bordeaux rum cake cooked for four hours), mango and hazelnut parfait layered with filo and jelly, or armagnac-soaked cherries on almond meringue crumble.

Open Tues–Fri noon–2.30pm; Tues–Sat 6–10pm
Typical prices E $19 **M** $38 **D** $18
Cards AE MC V
Wine First-class selection, mainly French and Australian; 12 by the glass; BYO Tues–Thurs one bottle a table (corkage $15 a table)
Owners Patrice & Catherine Repellin
Chef Patrice Repellin
Seats 45; outdoor seating; bar
www.koots.com.au

And ... A rear courtyard is casual but charming.

Kumo Izakaya

152 Lygon Street, Brunswick East **9388 1505**

JAPANESE **13/20**

At once beautiful and bubbling with energy, Kumo Izakaya is as coolly flamboyant as dining gets in Brunswick. The industrial-chic bar and diner with Art Deco flourishes is as big on seating options as it is on style, with booths, bar seating, a monster communal table and even a mezzanine on which to perch. It's as much a place to drink as eat, and the tipple that gets star treatment is sake. There's a dizzying selection, but savvy staff will steer you through it. Share-focused bar snacks are a mixed bag, from sumptuous slivers of wagyu beef tataki seasoned with ponzu to a humble jumble of whitebait tempura with spicy mayo to soak up the booze. A justifiable crowd fave is the fab pork-belly pie, rich braised pork chunks in mirin and soy encased in flaky pastry. A sake-infused sorbet flight will have dessert fans soaring.

Open Mon 5-10pm; Tues-Thurs & Sun 5-11pm; Fri-Sat 5-11.30pm; Sat-Sun noon-3pm
Typical prices E $10.80 **M** $16.80 **D** $14.80
Cards DC AE MC V Eftpos
Wine A highlight: a lavish list of more than 70 sakes, a short but varied wine list, plus Japanese micro-brewed beers
Owners Andre Bishop & Jo Fallshaw Bishop
Chefs Akimi Iguchi & Eriko Hamabe
Seats 126; outdoor seating; private room; bar
www.kumoizakaya.com.au

And ... Order omakase and let the house decide what you eat.

Kuni's

56 Little Bourke Street, City **9663 7243**

JAPANESE **13/20**

One of Melbourne's true stayers, Kuni's has maintained a steady traditional-Japanese course. For decades, it's been a reliably comfortable place to land, while all around it, the city is swept up in foodie trends: the Mexican food wave, dumpling obsession and artisan pizza. And while its plain, pine-furnished digs may not be the place for fad followers or event dining, it delivers decent Japanese standards with the occasional culinary curve ball (to reference Japan's favourite sport) in its own relaxed and understated style. Sushi and sashimi moriawase is fresh and varied. You might score snapper one day, dory the next. Kurumi tofu comes fried and covered in a slightly sweet walnut paste, while gyumaki (asparagus rolled in thin teriyaki beef slices) is given a moderate chilli kick. Almond jelly dessert may be cloyingly sweet; however, a nip of green tea will keep the meal on course.

Open Mon-Fri noon-2.30pm; Mon-Thurs 6-10pm; Fri-Sat 6-10.30pm
Typical prices E $10 **M** $28 **D** $10
Cards AE MC V Eftpos
Wine A shortish but still interesting list of mostly local, smaller label wines priced in the mid-range; BYO (corkage $10 a bottle)
Owner Jimmy Zheng
Chef Masa Kuriki
Seats 80
www.kunismelbourne.com

And ... The lunch sets have long pulled a crowd; a generation of city workers can't be wrong.

La Luna Bistro

320 Rathdowne Street, Carlton North **9349 4888**

MEDITERRANEAN **14.5/20**

Chef and hands-on meat man Adrian Richardson's easygoing ways and nose-to-tail food philosophy are always on show in his Victorian-era corner shopfront restaurant, where the butcher's block does heavy duty and house-made is the mantra. Illustrations of a pig and steer (each sliced into choice cuts, with tasting notes) feature on a blackboard wall in the lofty-ceilinged space with bentwood chairs, fence-wire chandeliers and much rawhide glam. Sausages are house-made, the charcuterie meats cured upstairs, and cubes of Atlantic salmon in a cucumber and apple salad are wondrously smoked on site. Dry-aged, on-the-bone rib-eye is a standout among well-rested, heavyweight steaks. Rolled pork loin is roasted and ringed in pleasure-giving crackling. But the finer points can delight too – piquant horseradish cream, hand-cut russet burbank fries, the outside herb garden – at this rustic-chic bistro, which charms with its big-hearted take on the food chain, right through to a tasting plate of desserts to share.

Open Tues–Sun noon–4pm, 6–10pm
Typical prices E $18.50 **M** $40 **D** $16.50
Cards DC AE MC V Eftpos
Wine A globetrotting list big on local and Italian reds, for a variety of budgets and tastes; 12 by the glass; tempting aperitifs; BYO (corkage $17.50 a bottle)
Owner Adrian Richardson
Chefs Adrian Richardson & Michael Slade
Seats 75; outdoor seating; private rooms
www.lalunabistro.com.au

And ... Look out for Richardson's pop-up smoking red gum Texan barbecue outside.

Ladro Gertrude

224 Gertrude Street, Fitzroy **9415 7575**

ITALIAN/PIZZERIA **13.5/20**

It's often tempting to say 'let's just get pizza', but Ladro's fine versions make those times an occasion. Their bottoms are thin (and gluten-free, if you like), and include toppings like mozzarella and 'carciuga' (anchovy and artichoke paste), and winning go-tos like puttanesca (anchovies, capers, chilli and olives). But the other half of Ladro's Italian menu is worth exploring, too. It includes impressive entrees like scorched white peach segments topped with gorgonzola, strewn with walnuts and drizzled with sweet balsamic. Simple, trattoria-style mains include a fish dish and a steak, plus risotto and house-made fresh pasta – maybe a delightful prawn-packed ravioli in a perky pea sauce set off with a smidgen of sweet mustard fruits. It's refined good-value grub in a noisy room with voices ricocheting around the sleek, hard-surfaced interior. Service may be a bit too casual (water glasses left empty, menu knowledge patchy), but expect sweet endings with desserts like vanilla-speckled panna cotta with salted caramel.

Open Mon–Thurs 6–11pm; Fri–Sun 5.30–11pm; Sun noon–3pm
Typical prices E $13 **M** $22 **D** $12.50
Cards DC AE MC V Eftpos
Wine An Italian-leaning list; BYO (corkage $15 a bottle)
Owners Sean Kierce, Ingrid Langtry, Frank van Haandel & Anthony Mussara
Chef Niko Pizzimenti
Seats 45; outdoor seating; bar
www.ladro.com.au

And ... Monday's $5 corkage goes to charity.

BYO RESTAURANT OF THE YEAR

Ladro Greville

162 Greville Street, Prahran **9510 2233**

ITALIAN/PIZZERIA **14/20**

The stark fitout of Ladro Greville bounces high-level hubbub around its whitewashed hard surfaces. Things get a shot of warmth via the casual yet professional service coupled with simple and expertly executed Italian food. Family groups are made especially welcome. There is no doubting that Ladro continues to serve some of this town's best pizza, but a menu detour en route is a must. Kick things off with a beautiful salad, maybe a vividly red, white and green caprese, or something a bit heartier, like creamy white polenta with asparagus, poached egg and pecorino. There's interest aplenty on the specials list: perhaps pizza of truffled salami with taleggio, anchovies and olives, or the roast of the day – perhaps amazingly tender spatchcock from the wood oven on saffron-and-pea risotto. It would be a pity not to order the bomboloni with their vanilla icecream and blood-orange syrup.

Open Mon–Thurs 6–11pm; Fri & Sun noon–11pm, Sat 5.30–11pm
Typical prices E $15 **M** $22 **D** $11
Cards DC AE MC V Eftpos
Wine A brief list of predominantly Italian varietals from Italy and Australia; BYO (corkage $15 a bottle)
Owners Sean Kierce, Ingrid Langtry, Frank van Haandel & Anthony Musarra
Chef Niko Pizzimenti
Seats 75; outdoor seating; private room; bar
www.ladro.com.au

And ... $5 BYO on Mondays with all corkage donated to Prahran Mission for their annual homeless Christmas lunch.

Lamaro's

273 Cecil Street, South Melbourne **9690 3737**

CONTEMPORARY **14/20**

Since its classy refurbishment in 2005, this historic pub in a leafy residential pocket has delighted locals with its clever mix of glamour and comfort. Despite a changing of the guard – the effervescent Pam Lamaro has retired and long-serving Shaun Sheridan now heads the kitchen – Lamaro's retains its urbane but relaxed vibe. The food, too, has kept the faith, and perhaps lifted a little. A lightly charred grain-fed eye fillet is moistly pink and served with a well-balanced bearnaise sauce. Several dishes show an Asian twist; perhaps three plump crescents of char siu pork gyoza enlivened with black vinegar dressing, or the ever-popular Sichuan duck, crisp-skinned and delicately spicy with a sweet pool of orange-blossom caramel. For dessert, perhaps a subtle espresso creme brulee with feathery almond foam. Servings are generous, waitstaff are friendly and knowledgeable, and the carpeted dining room – fully separated from the bustling bar – is a stylish sanctuary of warm autumnal tones, soft lighting and padded chairs.

Open Daily noon–late
Typical prices E $20 **M** $35 **D** $14
Cards AE MC V Eftpos
Wine Comprehensive list of predominantly Australian wines ranging from obscure to iconic, 30 by the glass
Owner Chris Morris
Chef Shaun Sheridan
Seats 120; outdoor seating; private room; bar
www.lamaros.com.au

And ... Check the website for regular events, from wine-led dinners to live music.

Lau's Family Kitchen

4 Acland Street, St Kilda **8598 9880**

CANTONESE **14.5/20**

This bustling bolthole is a generation away from the restaurant that made the Lau family name synonymous with fine dining in Melbourne. But brothers Jason and Michael Lau clearly learnt a thing or two about service from their father's Flower Drum. They have built a vibrant St Kilda canteen serving modern Cantonese food with calm yet bristling efficiency. The decor is simple timber and screens (which could do with a bit of sprucing up). In the evenings, the attentive service reflects a need to shift two sittings through the smallish dining room. The menu here is similarly compact, offering traditional Cantonese dishes plus some with flair or a new twist. The specials might include whitebait fritters served with salt-and-pepper chillies or chicken with asparagus and pinenuts. There are hints of the Laus' origins: delicate dim sum, garfish with mushrooms. Little wonder that many of the regulars here savour both the more relaxed atmosphere and the modest prices.

Open Daily 6–10pm; Mon–Fri noon–3pm; Sun 12.30–3pm
Typical prices E $12.50 **M** $26 **D** $10.50
Cards MC V Eftpos
Wine A modest list, mostly mid-range Australians; 14 by the glass
Owners Michael & Jason Lau
Chef James Lau
Seats 52; outdoor seating
www.lauskitchen.com.au

And ... For dessert, there's always banana fritter, though an extra entree might be a better investment.

Le Petit Bourgeois

330 Waverley Road, Malvern East **9571 0909**

FRENCH **13.5/20**

John Salisbury has manned the pans here for almost a quarter of a century. In that time, the children from the area's family homes have grown up and moved out, and the surrounding parks have weathered a few droughts, but little has changed here. John still dishes up traditional bistro-style French cuisine, while wife Wendy tends front-of-house. The enduring stripped-back decor, generously spaced tables and reliability in the kitchen are just as the locals like it. A popular kick-off to the meal is the plate of a dozen hors d'oeuvres, which may include Sichuan beans, blue goat's cheese tart, grilled quail or duck terrine. Mains may feature pink slices of rib-eye lamb fanned beside layered, creamy dauphinoise potato or a hearty portion of confit duck, paired with a salad of greens and orange slices. And a meal here wouldn't be complete without a souffle: choose one of three options – perhaps the Grand Marnier?

Open Tues–Sat 7–9pm
Typical prices E $19 **M** $33 **D** $15
Cards DC AE MC V Eftpos
Wine Small selection of wallet-friendly drops mainly from Australia, with a handful of French and NZ; BYO (corkage $4 a head)
Owners John & Wendy Salisbury
Chef John Salisbury
Seats 30
www.lepetitbourgeois.com.au

And ... Dust off that special bottle and take advantage of the very reasonable corkage here.

Lezzet

81 Brighton Road, Elwood **9531 7733**

TURKISH **13/20**

It can be as bustling as the Grand Bazaar at this ever-expanding Elwood eatery, which now straddles three shopfronts on busy Brighton Road. It gives culinary young Turk Kemal Barut more space to showcase his upmarket, modern twist on traditional Ottoman favourites. Start with a mezze platter that might include house-made dried beef bastourma, scallop and prawn mousse wrapped in crisp strands of kataifi pastry, and finger-licking good lamb ribs marinated in honey and sumac. It's hard to resist the super-tender, if subtly flavoured, Anatolian lamb cooked slowly for 18 hours, while Atlantic salmon wrapped in vine leaves, served with a pinot grigio reduction and splodges of date mousse (an example, perhaps, of too much action on one plate) is one of a plethora of seafood offerings. Service in the dusky ethnic-meets-decorator dining rooms is friendly if often flat-out. The kids are sure to like the selection of wood-fired Turkish pizzas – and you might have to fight them off when Barut's elegant take on baklava with mascarpone hits the table for dessert.

Open Tues–Sun 5.30–10pm; Sun noon–3pm
Typical prices E $15 **M** $28 **D** $14.50
Cards AE MC V Eftpos
Wine Mainly Australian and NZ wines divided into palate weight; plenty by the glass; BYO (corkage $8.50 a bottle)
Owner & chef Kemal Barut
Seats 115; outdoor seating; private room
www.lezzet.com.au

And ... Four- and five-course set menus encourage feasting.

Libertine

500 Victoria Street, North Melbourne **9329 5228**

FRENCH **14/20**

This compact, husband-and-wife-run bistro is modestly glam, not big-chequebook glam. Think close tables, gilt mirrors, chandeliers, candlelight, and a line-up of bottles above a velvet banquette. Service is cheerily down-to-earth and uncontrived. But Libertine's menu blows away expectations of the modest and down-to-earth with dishes that are beautifully designed, carefully executed and well proportioned. For a feather-light start, perhaps a tian of spanner crab alongside a big seared scallop and tangle of julienned, pickled kohlrabi. Or stay earthy with a chevre wedge and scattering of olive 'soil' lent sweetness with provençale-style vegetables. Mains tour seafood, beef, game, duck and maybe mushroom gougere. Though there's traditional heaviness – wagyu with sweetbreads or snapper fillet, herb gratin and richly sauced moules marinieres – there's lightness to some components to update classics. Seasonal fruits lift desserts above lovely: a rectangle of pink grapefruit jelly makes memorable a slice of lemon tart with yoghurt sorbet.

Open Fri–Sat noon–3pm; Tues–Sat 6–10pm
Typical prices E $19 **M** $36 **D** $15.50
Cards AE MC V
Wine Thoughtfully constructed list dominated by European labels with some excellent locals; BYO lunch & Thurs night (corkage $10 a bottle)
Owners Nicholas Creswick & Zoe Ladyman
Chef Nicholas Creswick
Seats 80; private room
www.libertinedining.com.au

And ... Outdoor dining and a bar are planned.

Little Thai Princess

285 Burke Road, Glen Iris **9885 4866**

MODERN THAI **12.5/20**

The setting is not exotic: there's a freeway, Glen Iris railway station, a few shops, and at the end, the Little Thai Princess. Thankfully you enter a quiet haven, classical piano music drifting, starched linen, and a charming welcome from elegant waitstaff. Over, perhaps, a glass of Alsace pinot blanc (it's a delightful wine list) you peruse a menu of tantalising possibilities. Try the platter-for-two entree for a browse: Thai fish cakes, vibrant prawns, quality curry puffs stuffed with minced chicken. Main courses include, of course, curries, ginger beef, whole barramundi and a lively pad Thai with tiger prawns, all anointed by those feisty, sparky Thai flavours that are so pleasing. Service might not be speedy on arrival but is well paced as a subdued and soothing evening unfolds. Visually, the food is a treat; gastronomically it is splendid. Desserts might include sticky black rice pudding, or mango or coconut icecream imported from Thailand. This is a little restaurant with big ambitions.

Open Tues–Sun 4–10pm
Typical prices E $9 **M** $22 **D** $7
Cards AE MC V Eftpos
Wine Concise list of Old and New World wines focuses on Thai-friendly aromatic varieties, reasonably priced; BYO (corkage $8 a bottle)
Owner Hye Young Lee
Chef Sung Min Lee
Seats 40; private room
www.littlethaiprincess.com

And ... Takeaway is justly popular with commuters on the way home.

Livingroom

12–18 Claremont Avenue, Malvern **9576 0356**

CONTEMPORARY **14.5/20**

Livingroom is perfectly named. Filled with friends and families, good wine, good food and good conversation, it sprawls cosily across three old shopfronts. It's comfy and convivial, and you could happily come every week, as some regulars seem to. Tables are undressed, but napkins are linen, and Darren Daley's cooking looks and tastes inviting. To start, pearly cured kingfish is sparked up with a little ginger and crab, while scallops partner silky dukkah-spiced pumpkin puree. Then hapuku is baked under a soft herb crust with sweet braised fennel quarters. A side salad of shredded cabbage, peas, mint and chilli is heavy with feta, but very moreish. Rabbit is a signature dish, and a showstopper, dramatically presented, perhaps wound with pancetta and filled with melting buffalo mozzarella. Chocolatey things seem popular to finish, or, in season, roasted fresh figs come with pecan icecream. Best of all, unlike your own living room, this one comes with a happy hour and personable service.

Open Tues–Fri 6–10pm; Wed–Fri noon–3pm; Sat 8am–10pm; Sun 8am–3pm
Typical prices E $20 **M** $38 **D** $16
Cards AE MC V Eftpos
Wine A good cellar selection, plus aged whiskies; BYO Tues–Thurs nights (corkage $12 a bottle)
Owners Alan Markham & Carolyn Liem
Chef Darren Daley
Seats 70; outdoor seating
www.lroom.com.au

And ... Share menus are top value. They do take-home meals, too.

Longrain

40-44 Little Bourke Street, City **9671 3151**

MODERN THAI **15/20**

Couples face a dilemma at Longrain. Sit side-by-side (like most), or opposite each other at the big communal tables? Perch, with cocktail, at the bar? Take a knee-high table for two near the entrance? Longrain can get loud, especially if you have a lively foursome up against you, and the music's keeping beat. But the food within this sassy converted warehouse is a conversation-stopper, bursting joyfully with chilli, coriander and kaffir lime. Hand-chopped beef tumbled with chilli and nutty roasted rice comes to pile on crackers or witlof leaves. Jungle curry creates converts, with tiny eggplants, soft chunks of barramundi, and perky holy basil. Egg-net blanketed pork, prawns and peanuts, and caramelised pork hock are delicious fixtures. Service is slick, though Longrain's bossy rulebook can frustrate - you won't get seated till your whole party has arrived. But it's the CBD's top Thai, and that's enough to make you forgive and forget, especially after a scoop of coconut sorbet.

Open Mon-Thurs 6-11pm; Fri-Sun 5.30-11pm; Fri noon-3pm; no bookings for groups less than six, except Fri lunch
Typical prices E $26 **M** $38.50 **D** $15
Cards DC AE MC V
Wine Compact but classy, matched to the cuisine
Owners Sam Christie, Martin Boetz, John van Haandel & John Sample
Chef Martin Boetz
Seats 100; bar
www.longrain.com.au

And ... Look out for a 'street food bar', scheduled to open upstairs in 2013.

Lord Cardigan

59 Cardigan Place, Albert Park **9645 5305**

CONTEMPORARY **14/20**

While the original Lord Cardigan was famed for his pompous style, this Lord Cardigan has more in common with the garment - warm, comfortable and year-round smart. Dominique Bolger works the floor with charm, chatting to diners and ferrying seasonal dishes cooked by husband John Singer from the kitchen. They make wonderful hosts. Once settled in the long, gold-toned dining room you might start with the signature rabbit pie, savoury bites of meat in perfect sour-cream pastry. Or perhaps your style is nori-wrapped house-picked crabmeat in a thin soda batter, paired with a zingy mango-papaya salad. King George whiting makes a heartier main when paired with sliced and fried potatoes, and a few greens may be needed for the roast lamb loin sliced over soft ratatouille flecked with basil oil - or perhaps some house sourdough to soak up the garlicky juices. Dessert doesn't disappoint; ricotta fritters with coconut sorbet is both rich and light. No unbuttoning required.

Open Tues-Sat 6-10pm; Thurs-Sun noon-2.30pm; Sat 8.30am-3pm; Sun 8.30am-2.30pm
Typical prices E $18 **M** $35 **D** $15
Cards AE MC V Eftpos
Wine Enjoyable list with great value; 14 by the glass; BYO Tues (corkage $10 a bottle)
Owners John Singer & Dominique Bolger
Chef John Singer
Seats 42; outdoor seating
www.lordcardigan.com.au

And ... At the weekend, lord it up with terrific breakfasts and the Sunday Roast.

Lupino

41 Little Collins Street, City **9639 0333**

ITALIAN **14.5/20**

Dancing with wolves is undoubtedly dangerous, yet little seems safer in Melbourne than booking this confident new Italian bistro. 'Lupino' is Italian for 'little wolf', which explains the neon wolf head above Lupino's wooden front door. The menu is classically familiar, the service is sure, the wines tick the regions, and yet the vibe and fitout is modern Melbourne in a reassuringly retro way. You might begin with baked polpetti drenched in sugo, or a generous serving of gnocchi swimming in rich gorgonzola cheese, or taglierini ribbons with prawns, mussels, tomato and torn basil. Sharing might prove difficult on small rectangular tables, but reach out nonetheless for liberal tagliata, chunks of porterhouse on a bed of drizzled rocket, or apply home-made chilli oil to fire up chewy pizza with Sicilian anchovies. Creamy tiramisu, or cassata with cherries will fortify you for roaming the Melbourne night. Lupino already feels as if it's been with us for years.

Open Wed–Sun 11.30am–10pm
Typical prices E $16.50 **M** $32 **D** $14
Cards DC AE MC V
Wine Decent wine list hits the right Italian and Australian regions; plus, of course, there's grappa
Owners Richard Lodge, Marco Lori & George Sykiotis
Chefs Marco Lori & Stephen Phillips
Seats 60; private room; bar
www.lupino.com.au

And ... If you're wondering about the big jars of Italian Nutella along the back wall, try the Italian doughnuts.

Magic City

871 Burke Road, Camberwell **9882 7788**

CONTEMPORARY **12.5/20**

This suburban pleasure parlour used to trade in pinball; now highballs are more its style. One of the first culinary-cool customers on the main drag of this leafy neighbourhood nearly a decade ago, today's Magic City delivers a menu of East and West food. That may mean starting with wok-tossed calamari with Thai basil, garlic shoots and peppercorns; or Spanish white anchovies and pecorino shavings on cos with a poached egg. But it can lead to confusion about what to expect – some dishes, like the pad Thai, lean towards more authentic flavours, while a beautifully roasted snapper with fish dumplings in a lightly flavoured lemongrass consomme has just a hint of Asian influence. Desserts follow a strictly Western route, like the surprisingly rich rubble of a partially deconstructed flourless chocolate cake with ganache, honeycomb debris and date-armagnac icecream. Service can go missing and sometimes lack a little charm, but there's plenty of the latter in the handsome, high-ceilinged room.

Open Daily 10am–late
Typical prices E $17 **M** $32 **D** $15
Cards AE MC V Eftpos
Wine Regularly updated list of popular locals supported by plenty of NZ and some European; BYO (corkage $10 a bottle)
Owner Clive Dornan
Chef Ben Corp
Seats 60; outdoor seating; bar
www.magiccity.com.au

And ... Pull in for a drink and bar snack after work, or breakfast at weekends.

Maha

21 Bond Street, City **9629 5900**

MIDDLE EASTERN **15.5/20**

You know you're in for a big occasion the moment you enter this sultry subterranean den. The long, inviting space is divided into several rooms: a moody bar, a richly coloured dining room with thick Persian carpet and a cushion-scattered banquette, and way down the back, hidden by an ornate laser-cut partition, a private room. Adroit staff take you through the food and wine options, which include an elaborate 'sultan's banquet', a more rustic soufra ('little eats') menu and a vegetarian feast, plus a wide-ranging wine list. Splurge on the six- or eight-course banquet and you'll discover how refined Middle Eastern food can be. Highly worked dishes might include tender scallops and juice-spurting 'pearls' of lime, bathed with cool coconut water at the table, and snapper with velvety corn custard and crab mousse rolled in sucuk sausage crumbs. Touches like sprinkling guests' hands with lemon-scented water and presenting an exit package of the fixings to recreate Maha's signature Turkish delight doughnuts are special indeed.

Open Sun–Fri noon–3pm; Sat–Thurs 6–10pm; Fri 6–11pm
Typical prices E $28 **M** $34 **D** $15
Cards DC AE MC V Eftpos
Wine Choice of arak, raki and the wines of Lebanon's Bekaa Valley
Owners Shane Delia & Made Establishment
Chefs Shane Delia & Nick Korceba
Seats 110; private room; bar
www.mahabg.com.au

And ... The Maha shop sells gift vouchers, ingredients and Shane Delia's cookbook.

Mahjong

165 Fitzroy Street, St Kilda **9534 8833**

CHINESE **13.5/20**

Aficionados of yum cha and Cantonese food may be used to dodging trolleys in dimly lit Chinatown enclaves, but this slick south-side restaurant, with its red lacquered chinoiserie, has all the creature comforts. Polished concrete floors, pavement tables, and calm, well-timed service create an urbane atmosphere for difficult menu decisions, and some diners may opt for mains in yum cha sizes to increase the options for sharing. Blue swimmer crab dumplings are delicate and fragrant, while biting through the petal-thin wonton of the ginger prawn dumplings results in a sweet, juicy explosion of flavour. Barbecued roast pork belly arrives cut sideways, revealing small circles of bone in some pieces, the surrounding flesh sweet and smoky. Chicken pie melds sweet puff pastry with a savoury leek and chicken filling to moreish effect. Desserts may change seasonally and might include a refreshing mango pudding or a coconut aloe vera version.

Open Sun–Thurs 11am–10.30pm; Fri–Sat 11am–11.30pm
Typical prices E $7.80 **M** $30 **D** $7
Cards DC AE MC V Eftpos
Wine Big-name producers as well as a diverse range of Old and New World varietals; about 12 by the glass
Owner Max Tsang
Chefs Wah Feng & Ying Lee
Seats 120; outdoor seating; private room
www.mahjongrestaurant.com.au

And ... Yum cha trolleys are only on Sundays; Mahjong Black (see next page) is a city sibling.

Mahjong Black

118 Little Collins Street, City **9650 8873**

CHINESE **13.5/20**

Say the word 'dumplings' and people perk up. Melburnians love them and Mahjong Black makes very fine versions. Add to this a sleek, dark fitout, stiff white tablecloths and chandeliers with long shimmering tentacles of light, and eating dumplings has never been so glam. The menu is mostly smaller dishes – waitstaff can advise on an appropriate number – so indulge your inner glutton and sample widely. Dumpling standouts include plump and juicy ginger prawn; slurpalicious 'juice pork' (xiao long bao); and the intricate steamed vegetable variation, each topped whimsically with diced carrot and mushroom, and pea and corn kernels. In the non-dumpling department, pre-folded Peking duck packages wrap succulent meat in fresh, supple pancakes, although a steamed eggplant dish might fall short in flavour. Desserts can be pedestrian (banana fritter, fried icecream), so consider another round of prawn dumplings – or unlock the mystery of the enigmatically named 'crab seafood fluffy', which turns out to be an eggwhite scramble.

Open Mon–Fri noon–3pm; Mon–Sat 6pm–late
Typical prices E $6 **M** $25 **D** $8
Cards DC AE MC V Eftpos
Wine Interesting, competitively priced list complements the cuisine, categorised by weight and character for easy navigation
Owner Max Tsang
Chef Huan Feng
Seats 80; bar
www.mahjongblack.com.au

And ... Try the 10-course degustation for $56.

Mama Baba

21 Daly Street, South Yarra **9207 7421**

ROMAN-GRECO **13.5/20**

Put a casual family pasta bar into a warehousey former nightclub and give the menu multiple cultural characteristics – maybe even a few highfalutin' gastro flourishes. That's Mama Baba. The family spin centres on co-owner-chef-mascot George Calombaris's folks, dividing the mainly house-made pasta menu into Greek (Mama) and Italian-Greek (Baba). It sets up an expectation for generous serves and honest flavours despite the contemporary-industrial interior. But the food is more conscious and contained: big tortellini (maybe a tad chewy in the folds) are plump with prawn mousse and meat with mild lobster-tomato oil and roast cherry tomatoes; soft mash-and-truffle pecorino ravioli sit in a light, white-wine duck-leg ragout with asparagus spears. Desserts cut loose: tiramisu comes as coffee icecream on a stick coated in chocolate and pressed with 'exploding' coffee pop-rock; from the trolley, cannoli is a biscuit wafer roll with caramel custard one end, vanilla custard the other. If that ain't lively enough for you, the giant bar with unobtrusive DJ ought to be.

Open Mon–Thurs & Sat 6pm–late; Fri & Sun noon–3pm, 5pm–late
Typical prices E $9.50 **M** $27 **D** $12.50
Cards DC AE MC V Eftpos
Wine Italian-leaning list; good range by the glass
Owner Made Establishment
Chefs Dominic Pipicelli & George Calombaris
Seats 130; bar
www.mamababa.com.au

And ... Those just starting solids are in good hands with Mama Baba's baby food.

Mama Ganoush

56 Chapel Street, Windsor **9521 4141**

MIDDLE EASTERN **13.5/20**

Expect a touch of the exotic at Mama Ganoush. The narrow dining room is emblazoned with elegant Arabic motifs, and the menu boldly swings across the Middle East and back again. There are Maloufs at the helm (Geoff works the floor while wife Amal takes charge in the kitchen) so expect confident, well-tuned flavours and humming service. You'll be encouraged to share dishes rich with Lebanese, Turkish and Syrian flavours, perhaps tender, cumin-dusted calamari with tahini mayonnaise or mammoth, yoghurt-smothered Turkish dumplings filled with spiced lamb. A fattoush comes with chunks of chevre offset by sweet baby beets and the welcome crunch of fried pita squares. There are two perfectly executed tagines to choose from (chicken or veg), and there's a crisp-skinned duck that's braised then fried and served with an almond rice alight with pomegranate jewels. The buttery baklava might be pure melt-in-the-mouth goodness but bolder dessert fanciers will be rewarded by choosing the chocolate and Turkish coffee icecream.

Open Tues–Sat 6–10pm
Typical prices E $15 **M** $30 **D** $14
Cards MC V Eftpos
Wine A short, reasonably priced, predominantly Australian list with the occasional European and Lebanese drop
Owners Geoff & Amal Malouf
Chef Amal Malouf
Seats 70; private room; outdoor seating
www.mamaganoush.com

And ... Eight-course banquets are $55.

Mamasita

Level 1, 11 Collins Street, City **9650 3821**

MEXICAN **14.5/20**

Yes, you may have to queue to snare a table, and it can get noisy. Now stop whining and pass the salsa because Mamasita is one of the most exuberant dining experiences you're likely to have. The owners have pinned the zeitgeist, yet Mamasita avoids taking itself too seriously, unless we're talking margaritas and tequila, which are taken very seriously indeed. The food is lip-smackingly fun, the char-grilled corn cobs, swathed in cheese, mayo, paprika and lime juice legendary. Tostaditas are morsels of pleasure, perhaps topped with avocado and crab. Invariably good are the tacos and quesadillas, with fillings that might include luscious huitlacoche (a corn fungus that is a Mexican delicacy), mushroom and zucchini or char-grilled chicken, coriander and cheese. More adventurous is the zesty ceviche of raw blue-eye, swimming in coconut milk, chilli and lime. For dessert, the sweetcorn icecream is on-theme, but better is the lemon chilli sorbet with mango. Kudos to staff who happily handle the crowds.

Open Mon–Wed noon–midnight; Thurs noon-12.30am; Fri–Sat noon–2am; no bookings, except groups of eight to 10 (groups offered a chef's selection banquet only)
Typical prices E $14 **M** $24 **D** $10
Cards AE MC V Eftpos
Wine The100-strong tequila menu is complemented by reasonably priced wines, mainly from Spain
Owners Matt Lane & Jason Jones
Chef Scott Eddington
Seats 96; bar
www.mamasita.com.au

And ... Arrive 5pm-ish to avoid queuing.

Maris

15 Glenferrie Road, Malvern **9500 0665**

CONTEMPORARY **13/20**

Locals often bring out a good bottle when heading to this smart-casual BYO-friendly husband-and-wife run bistro. The menu's undergone a change in the past year – now smaller, less Italian-inspired, more ambitious, and you may find suckling pig, wagyu beef and roast duck account for three of five mains. To whet your appetite, try chicken and foie gras parfait, with prune jelly and brioche. Too sweet? A busy tumble of calamari, chickpeas, chorizo, fennel, yoghurt and pomegranate satisfies more savoury cravings. Sher wagyu cheek is rich and tender, braised with red wine, star anise and coriander seeds. Using a variety of cuts from suckling pig can be hit-and-miss and picking for morsels of tasty meat may be fiddly; the dish comes with light pumpkin puree with a perky sprinkle of ground coffee. Desserts are good and simpler, a highlight being Valrhona chocolate crumble with house-made honeycomb icecream.

Open Tues–Fri noon–3pm; Tues–Sat 6–10pm
Typical prices E $18 **M** $38 **D** $16
Cards AE MC V Eftpos
Wine An easy-pleaser list strong on Australian and NZ wines, boosted by French bubbles, German whites and Spanish sherries; BYO (corkage $9 a bottle)
Owners Patrick & Gabby Craig
Chef Patrick Craig
Seats 40; private room
www.maris.com.au

And ... As well as making icecream in-house, Maris makes its own bread and butter.

Markov Place

350 Drummond Street, Carlton **9347 7113**

MODERN EUROPEAN **13.5/20**

Hidden behind a streetside bar, Markov Place has the feel of a private club, complete with leather-lined tables, Persian rugs, wine posters and modern grooves. A long central bar table blurs the distinction between bar and restaurant, and the menu, tweaked by new chef Trumble Dewé, has moved away from tapas to a choice of small and large plates of clever contemporary cooking, a relaxed way of eating that suits the young and stylish crowd. Plates are prettily presented – a wedge of cured ocean trout is matched with bright red baby beetroot and crisp potato, dabs of smooth goat's curd and a sprinkling of leek dust. And a side of sweet roast zucchini batons, crunchy almonds and mint is a refreshing match for a plate of crisp and salty Berkshire pork belly, spicy chorizo and golden potatoes. Noise may increase as the night progresses; well-groomed and efficient staff contribute to the buzzy atmosphere.

Open Tues–Sat 6–10.30pm
Typical prices E $14 **M** $26 **D** $14
Cards AE MC V Eftpos
Wine Broad list of mostly local and European wines; 15 or more options by the glass
Owner Guy David
Chef Trumble Dewé
Seats 60; outdoor seating; bar
www.markov.com.au

And ... A special fixed menu for two ($42 a head) includes seven shared plates from the a la carte menu.

Masani

313 Drummond Street, Carlton **9347 5610**

ITALIAN **13.5/20**

A block away from the commotion of Lygon Street, Masani's large, warm, comfortable dining room oozes family hospitality with dad in the kitchen and daughter out the front. It would be hard not to enjoy settling into the grand old dining room, with its high ceilings and chandeliers, for a big Italian feast. Pasta should definitely form part of a meal at Masani: maybe silky tortellini filled with shredded rabbit in a light sauce of peas and porcini, topped with yabbies; or large but surprisingly light spinach and ricotta-filled gnocchi with roast walnuts, nutmeg and an asiago sauce. From the oven, perhaps half a tender citrus-roasted Barossa Valley duck, with pears cooked in grappa, or a classic veal scaloppine with a knockout braise of sweetbreads and porcini. A grand finish of chocolate souffle is worth the wait. Sommelier Kara Maisano maintains an impressive wine list and delivers wine service with personality and charm.

Open Daily noon–3pm, 6–10.30pm
Typical prices E $22 **M** $35 **D** $16
Cards DC AE MC V Eftpos
Wine Long, spectacular list of mainly Italian and Australian wines at a range of price points; BYO (corkage $15.50 a bottle)
Owner & chef Richard Maisano
Seats 70; outdoor seating; private room; bar
www.masani.com.au

And ... The Artisan Express menu, Monday to Friday for lunch and dinner, offers great value.

Mask of China

115–117 Little Bourke Street, City **9662 2116**

CHINESE **12.5/20**

More than 25 years ago, Mask of China carved a niche serving Chiu Chow cuisine – a regional variation in the southern Chinese style that dominated the city's Chinese restaurants for decades. Chiu Chow is relatively light, with seafood as its speciality; expect abalone, crab and whole fish steamed or lightly sauteed. In comparison to the fiery Sichuan and rustic northern styles now more commonly found around town, Chiu Chow could seem almost bland. But it has a subtlety its northern counterparts lack, made possible at Mask of China by the use of fresh, high-quality ingredients, served with style and care. After a little cup of digestion-readying tea (a hallmark of Chiu Chow), you might start with a pomegranate dumpling – diced chicken in eggwhite pastry – named for its size and shape. Follow, perhaps, with spicy quail, deboned, pan-fried and tossed in five-spice. Apart from seafood, there's a smattering of meat dishes, including beef in peppery chinjew sauce. In season you may spot game, such as venison, wild boar and squab.

Open Daily 6–11pm; Sun–Fri noon–3pm
Typical prices E $13 **M** $35 **D** $12
Cards DC AE MC V Eftpos
Wine An extensive list covering high- and low-end, Old and New World; about 12 by the glass
Owners Yeung Pui Ming & Andy Tran
Chef Yeung Pui Ming
Seats 90; private room
www.maskofchina.com.au

And ... The set lunch menus (three courses for $35, five for $55) are available until 7pm.

Matteo's

533 Brunswick Street, Fitzroy North **9481 1177**

CONTEMPORARY 16/20

The sense of theatre that accompanies a meal at Matteo's begins the moment you pull aside the thick peacock-blue curtains and enter the dining room, an opulent space of textured wallpaper, plum velvet chairs and vivid paintings. Polished waitstaff draped in plum-coloured aprons stick to the silver-service script, delivering menus and pouring wine with aplomb. Brendan McQueen's modern cuisine leans towards the Orient, with dishes such as soy-glazed salmon tataki, smoky unagi (teriyaki eel), and fall-apart lamb shoulder with miso-glazed eggplant playing starring roles. Even the fresh-baked bread has an Eastern lilt, served with silken butter and a Japanese seasoning of seaweed, sesame and crustacean shells. More crowd-pleasing than cutting-edge, desserts might include vanilla bavarois with poached peaches, or a tasting plate of chocolate fondant, berry tart and nougat parfait. A stellar wine list plays a supporting role, loaded with Asian-food-friendly varieties (riesling and pinot noir), with a commendable spread of prices.

Open Sun–Thurs 6–9.30pm; Fri–Sat 6–10pm; Sun–Fri noon–2.30pm
Typical prices E $22 **M** $42 **D** $18
Cards DC AE MC V Eftpos
Wine Impressive list with local gems and heavy-hitting imports; BYO (corkage $20 a bottle)
Owners Matteo & Franca Pignatelli
Chefs Brendan McQueen & Samuel Forte
Seats 85; private room
www.matteos.com.au

And ... Menu options include a la carte, daily-changing degustations and Sunday lunch.

The Meeting Pool

7 Hillcrest Avenue, Eltham **9431 2681**

FRENCH 13/20

A visit to the Meeting Pool, in the magnificent grounds of the historic Montsalvat artists' colony, is more than just a meal. By day, artists, sculptors and jewellers can be seen working in their studios and, as evening descends, fat geese waddle in formation to their quarters while resident peacocks preen, just metres from the table. Like the restaurant, the carte is small with a short list of French provincial fare, such as cider-braised pork belly or a wild mushroom fricassee that combines perfectly with a soft, saffron-poached egg. Mains continue the theme, perhaps spatchcocked chicken with pancetta, baby onions and mushrooms, the juices best mopped up with freshly baked bread, or rabbit saddle stuffed with shallots and herbs and served on Puy lentils and a combination of cabbage and bacon. Dessert might be a 'salad' of candied fennel, strawberry and rhubarb with an orange tuile. On sunny weekends, the Meeting Pool's large courtyard is a lovely place to, er, meet.

Open Tues–Sun noon–3pm; Thurs–Sat 6.30–9pm; Sat–Sun 9–11am
Typical prices E $15 **M** $30 **D** $15
Cards DC AE MC V Eftpos
Wine A short, strong list of Australian and French wines; about 10 by the glass
Owner Montsalvat Utilities
Chef Paul Phelan
Seats 50; outdoor seating
www.montsalvat.com.au

And ... Take an art class or build your own guitar at one of Montsalvat's workshops.

Melbourne Wine Room

125 Fitzroy Street, St Kilda **9525 5599**

CONTEMPORARY **12/20**

Since the *Guide* last visited Melbourne Wine Room it has changed hands, with Karen Martini selling up after 15-odd years to chef Paul Raynor, of Middle Brighton Baths. Out went the old staff, and with them some of the buzz and confidence of the dining experience they had built. Another change is that all meals are now taken in the (often noisy) front bar. Regulars might also mourn the extinction of Martini's signature (vast) rib-eye; in its place there's a standard-sized fillet (200g) or a 400g T-bone and a number of other 'larger plates'. Expect competent but unsurprising offerings like Atlantic salmon with a watercress salad or an asparagus risotto. Entrees are a little more zingy: a crowd-pleasing serve of smoked salmon might come with a well-judged horseradish cream, there's a generous charcuterie plate for $20, and who doesn't love a big plate of carefully fried salt-and-pepper calamari?

Open Mon–Thurs 3pm–late; Fri–Sun noon–late
Typical prices E $16 **M** $28 **D** $12
Cards AE MC V Eftpos
Wine Still a strong list with many available by the glass
Owners & chefs Paul Raynor & Damian Snell
Seats 120; outdoor seating
www.melbournewineroom.com

And ... Melbourne Wine Room now has a cafe where the more formal restaurant used to be.

Mercer's

732 Main Road, Eltham **9431 1015**

CONTEMPORARY **15/20**

If you're not a local, it's worth travelling to this inviting cottage, with its comfortable dining room and white-clothed tables to enjoy Stephen Mercer's cooking, delivered with a fierce desire to delight and keep lifting standards. Some dishes remain at regulars' insistence, such as the Malaysian dancing prawns entree: five juicy offerings in a hot mayonnaise, with spicy eggplant crisps. Classic techniques are on show in main courses, typically meats done two ways. A crunchy, duck-and-mushroom cigar might accompany a slow-cooked breast with fig. Similarly, a rich chicken confit in duck fat complements a Milawa breast that's lifted by a crusty farce of mushrooms and truffles. The cooking is experienced and assured, flavours harmonising like a choir. No wonder, then, that desserts deliver: a large friand of berries might be accompanied by flavours of burnt butter, strawberries and pistachio. Ute Mercer leads friendly front-of-house service: this husband and wife are clearly still on-song.

Open Thurs–Fri & Sun noon–2pm; Wed–Sun 6.30–8.30pm
Typical prices Set menus $60, $75, $93
Cards AE MC V Eftpos
Wine Extensive list of quality offerings includes big-name Australian red wines of five to 10 years, keenly priced by restaurant standards
Owners Stephen & Ute Mercer
Chef Stephen Mercer
Seats 60; private room
www.mercersrestaurant.com.au

And ... Degustation menus offer a value-packed experience.

THE AGE
good food
Guide
Edited by Janne Apelgren
citibank
Samsung GALAXY SIII

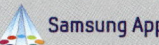

Heaven Gastro Lounge is located only five minutes from the Melbourne CBD, in the busy commercial hub of St Kilda Road. Featuring modern English Gastro Pub food with French, Italian & Asian influences. The style of the décor and ambience promotes "Heaven" as the perfect place for functions, private dining or after work drinks.

The restaurant is headed by Executive chef Sanjeev Johri who migrated to Australia in 2008. Sanjeev Johri has been a chef for more than twelve years and has worked in some of the finest kitchens in Melbourne including working for some celebrity chefs like Michael Lambie, Jacques Reymond and Tony Twitchett. Sanjeev has worked closely with his second chef Natalia Villalobos to modernise traditional gastro pub cuisine using various gastronomy techniques.

HEAVEN
GASTRO LOUNGE

add Heaven Gastro Lounge on facebook

Contact Us

580 Lower Ground Floor, St. Kilda Road,
Melbourne VIC 3004.

Landline: (03) 9041 2129,
Mobile: 0449 950 698
Email: info@heavengastrolounge.com.au
heavengastrolounge@gmail.com

Merchant Osteria Veneta

Rialto, 495 Collins Street, City **9614 7688**

NORTHERN ITALIAN **14/20**

Decent diners were long scant in the city's west end, but Guy Grossi's Merchant at the Rialto – a happy confluence of location, name and the Venetian menu – is perfectly pitched for this increasingly corporate zone. Open all day, it's a bustling place serving quality northern Italian fare, good coffee and aperitivi rich in Campari, prosecco and Aperol. With a carafe of soave, sweet-and-sour sardines, salumi, house-preserved artichokes, Venetian chopped salad, a steaming dish of tripe, polenta and, finally, a Campari semifreddo, you could easily be dining on a piazza in Verona. The casually styled place is designed for boisterous sharing, whether it's the dishes or Italian wines by the half-litre and litre. The menu spans 11 categories including rice, polenta and pasta. Try out-of-the-ordinary regional dishes such as the thick, round pasta bigoli (with a rich duck ragout) or an earthy braise of salt cod, artichokes and potato. Homely, lively and classy.

Open Mon–Fri 7–11am, noon–3.30pm, 4.30–10pm; Sat 5–10pm
Typical prices E $16 **M** $25 **D** $14.50
Cards DC AE MC V Eftpos
Wine All Italian with a focus on the Veneto region; strong range by the glass, half-litre and litre carafes
Owners Grossi & Grollo families
Chef Daniel Airo-Farulla
Seats 150; outdoor seating; private room; bar
www.merchantov.com

And ... It's good for breakfast, coffee or an after-work aperitivo.

Merricote

81 High Street, Northcote **9939 4762**

CONTEMPORARY **14.5/20**

In a skinny shop on a buzzy northside strip, chef Rob Kabboord and his sommelier wife, Bronwyn, have arrived at the formula for a model neighbourhood bistro, combining well-trodden Persian carpets, farm animal prints and a hefty gilt-framed mirror with good-humoured service, adroit cooking and a seductive drinks list. On the modern European menu, 'selection of snacks and charcuterie' might involve a timber board, rounds of fat-speckled salami and venison calabrese, pickled carrots and cornichons, and wondrously crisp triangles of lamb bisteeya. Among the modestly proportioned mains might be buttery blue cod fillet on mauve congo potato mash with crunchy-salty sea blight (a coastal semi-succulent) or a rosy piece of eye fillet with a mustard reduction. 'Dutch mess', a play on Eton mess, combines a nest of orange Persian floss with an orb of orange sorbet, orange goat's-milk icecream and segments. Like Merricote, it's the perfect combination of cleverness and charm.

Open Tues–Sat 5.30–10pm; Thurs–Sat noon–2pm
Typical prices E $18 **M** $29 **D** $14; degustation $75 (6 courses)
Cards AE MC V Eftpos
Wine A compact, fairly priced list that crackles with interest, including an unusually good range by the glass and carafe
Owners Rob & Bronwyn Kabboord
Chef Rob Kabboord
Seats 30; outdoor seating; private room
www.merricote.com.au

And ... Snacks and drinks are available in the courtyard, which is heated in cold weather.

The Metropolitan Hotel

36 Courtney Street, North Melbourne **9328 4222**

CONTEMPORARY **14/20**

It's comforting to know that there are still some lovely old pubs left, places that escaped having their character stripped out and gaming machines brought in. The Metropolitan Hotel's dining room feels as though nothing much has changed in its many years – and that's not a bad thing. It has a deservedly great reputation for its dry-aged steaks, but among all that is hearty on the menu, there is also finesse in the cooking – with the real surprise coming at dessert time. Perhaps start with a generous sharing board that might include house-cured charcuterie, smoked lamb ribs and scallop ceviche. Someone on the table must have steak for main; when you read that they're cooked in beef fat and come with burnt-onion puree, mushroom pâté and duck-fat potatoes, maybe everyone will. The aforementioned desserts arrive artfully presented on slate plates, and might include caramelised peach with prune and armagnac icecream, and brioche French toast.

Open Mon–Fri noon–3pm; Mon–Thurs 5–9pm; Fri–Sat 5–9.30pm
Typical prices E $16 **M** $35 **D** $16
Cards DC AE MC V Eftpos
Wine Meat-friendly, mostly Australian reds backed by a sound selection of whites, all with tasting notes
Owners Jeff & Suzanne Marshall
Chef Lachlan Cashman
Seats 80; outdoor seating; private room; bar
www.metrohotel.com.au

And ... The front bar is a great spot for a beer and a snack.

Mezzo

35 Little Bourke Street, City **9650 0988**

ITALIAN **13.5/20**

Some restaurants overpower the occasion, but Mezzo is a pleasant backdrop to your event. It's their food, your way. Want to mix up entrees into tasting plates? Pre-theatre dinner? Sure, no worries. In this big, airy, genial restaurant, good cooking fires up your party and is sometimes remarkable enough to interrupt conversation. Crumbed and fried fishcakes are nice, but won't change the subject. Fresh fig salad will, with gorgonzola, radish, lettuce and, best of all, candied walnuts. Smoked trout agnolotti, smothered with crayfish bisque foam, looks amusingly clumsy but is an excellent balance of flavours. Veal, stuffed with ricotta and caramelised shallots, harmonises with pickled pumpkin that's palate-tingling, sweet and tart, but the accompanying roasted cauliflower puree may miss the mark, leaning towards bitterness. Desserts may include sorbet made with imported blood peaches. Tiramisu – a fair rendition – adds a dollop of Kahlua jelly as a tasty touch.

Open Mon–Fri noon–2.30pm; Mon–Wed 5–9.30pm; Thurs–Sat 5–10pm
Typical prices E $18 **M** $37 **D** $18
Cards DC AE MC V Eftpos
Wine Focus on local wines and Italian varietals; nine white by the glass, six red; BYO (corkage $10 a bottle)
Owner Silvio Sgarioto
Chef Mirco Speri
Seats 80; bar
www.mezzobar.com.au

And ... It's half-price Oyster Hour, served at the bar, Monday to Saturday 5pm to 6pm.

The Middle Park Hotel

102 Canterbury Road, Middle Park **9690 1958**

BRITISH **13.5/20**

You'll first notice wood: the dark club-like panelling (from the MCG's former Long Room), the open kitchen's wood barbecue, or the chopping board brought to your table holding the day's top-grade steaks. Consulting chef Paul Wilson's menu is a meaty affair: terrines, scotch eggs, chops, sausages and a 1kg monster 'Black Angus club steak' to share. Maybe start with a flash-grilled tuna steak with savoy cabbage and ginger. Daily pot pie might be chicken and mushroom, thickly crusted, and with mash, or go for beef, expertly aged, char-grilled and rested. Stay on the steak-and-narrow – peri peri chicken (with stodgy corn cake) can be a dull affair. Good are the thrice-cooked chips and the 'world's best onion rings', thickly beer-battered and stacked like quoits. A quibble: service can feel more front bar than fine-diner if you're unlucky, with noisy table clearing and clunky drinks service. To finish, there's milky bread-and-butter pudding with jugs of Jamieson's whisky cream and hot apricot sauce. Wood, fire and comfort come together at MPH.

Open Daily 7am–1am
Typical prices E $18 **M** $34 **D** $15
Cards DC AE MC V Eftpos
Wine An admirable, Victorian-only list (except champagne); five of each colour by the glass
Owners Gerry Ryan, Tom Walker & Julian Gerner
Chef Nuno Gabriel
Seats 95; outdoor seating; private room; bar
www.middleparkhotel.com.au

And … There's a 'rare breeds' roast-a-thon at weekends, $55 a head, including dessert.

Mirka Continental Bistro

42 Fitzroy Street, St Kilda **9525 3088**

EUROPEAN **14/20**

On Fitzroy Street girls stagger in too-high heels and police lights flash. Viewed through Mirka's big picture window, the scene unfolds like a silent movie. Inside, it's a world away: waitresses swish about in slinky green frocks and artist Mirka Mora's frisky angels and serpents beam down from the walls. Five years after its relaunch under Guy Grossi, the ambience is warm and professional, as is service (although it can be distracted at times). Food may be 'continental', but it's more sophisticated than that. Light, fresh starters include creamy Russian salad of spanner crab, or flavoursome chicken and prosciutto pressed into a slice of terrine. For mains, perhaps sweet rock flathead fillet, with clams, piquillo peppers and borlotti beans. Tuscan kale's bitterness is set off by radish and salted ricotta in a revelatory salad. Tiramisu is lush and creamy but could do with a greater punch of liqueur and coffee. Its dramatic entrance is flawless, in a huge bowl from which a generous slice is scooped.

Open Daily 10am–10pm
Typical prices E $22 **M** $34 **D** $16
Cards DC AE MC V Eftpos
Wine Smart and snappy list of Old and New World labels; about 20 by the glass
Owner Grossi family
Chef Brad Bouhalis
Seats 70; outdoor seating; private room; bar
www.mirkatolarnohotel.com

And … Gluten-free bread is made in-house.

Mister Bianco

285 High Street, Kew **9853 6929**

ITALIAN **14/20**

Mister Bianco? An Italian laundry powder or a town in Sicily? A welcome addition to Kew dining? The answer's all three – and they're linked here in the spotless white tablecloths and the sparks of Sicilian flavour. Mister Bianco, sibling of the city's Mezzo, is a generous host, starting with stuzzichini – think meatballs, curls of semolina-dusted calamari, golden arancini. There's risotto and pasta (all house-made, like spinach and ricotta gnocchi with sage brown butter), and good char-grilled steaks. Mains show the excitement of the cooking, little twists of flavour turning the familiar into the enticing – a salted nut praline contrasting with the smoothness of rich red-wine-braised lamb neck, for example. A hearty veal cotoletta is dressed up with green peperonata and black garlic dressing, heirloom tomato salad enlivened by the addition of fennel, orange and radicchio. The mood is unpretentious, noise levels lively but manageable, the service friendly. And if tiramisu's on the menu, it's one of the city's best.

Open Mon–Sat 6–9.30pm; Wed–Fri noon–3pm (two sittings Fri & Sat)
Typical prices E $18 **M** $36 **D** $15
Cards DC AE MC V Eftpos
Wine Selection of Italian and Italian varietals, mainly from Victoria; wide spread of prices; 12 by the glass
Owner & chef Joseph Vargetto
Seats 70; outdoor seating; private room
www.misterbianco.com.au

And ... Shared-table menus are wonderful, and pastry chef Maria Lantelme does great special-occasion cakes.

Money Order Office

Basement, 5 Driver Lane, City **9639 3020**

CONTEMPORARY **14/20**

Deep below Little Bourke is a remnant of the days when Melbourne was 'Marvellous'. The former vault of the 1890s Money Order Office – which later became offices for prime ministers Menzies and Chifley – now houses chesterfield furnishings and racks of dusty wine bottles. Contemporary elements have been embraced here, too: Stevie Wonder turns up on the otherwise swingin' soundtrack, and modern decor touches give the place a natty feel. MOO's broadsheet menu is built to share, and works for both larger bar-focused groups and those wanting an intimate meal in a deep-set booth. A strength is Med-inspired fish dishes, such as marinated (not salty) anchovies blessed with a sweet hit of fennel jam, and ceviche with citrus-spritzed avocado. Quail on quinoa is barely livened by pomegranate molasses; not so slices of marvellous, red-centred roast lamb saddle, served with smoky eggplant and gleaming pepper, caper and tomato salad. Goat's curd mousse with spiced orange and figs keeps up the value of this vault's contents.

Open Tues–Fri noon–3pm; Tues–Sat 5pm–late
Typical prices E $12 **M** $22 **D** $9
Cards DC AE MC V Eftpos
Wine Small-scale wineries and comprehensive vertical selections are the stars on this list, with bottles secreted in all corners of the room
Owner Robert Baker
Chef Wayne Seberry
Seats 66; private room; bar
www.moneyorderoffice.com.au

And ... Duck down to MOO for happy hours, Tuesday to Saturday 5pm to 7pm.

The Montague

355 Park Street, South Melbourne **9690 9044**

CONTEMPORARY **13.5/20**

Most neighbourhoods beg for a local that works just as well for a casual meal with friends as it does for a proper sit-down dinner with all the trimmings. The Montague confidently manages to offer both with a relaxed front bar and a dining room with pretty Art Deco flourishes that's more cosy than formal. Former sous chef Brad Selkrig now handles the pans in the kitchen, but the menu with its various Asian excursions remains. Expect entrees like dainty char-grilled asparagus spears paired with cubes of crumbed goat's cheese, and delicate vegie-stuffed samosas with cumin-laced yoghurt. Asian flavours once again spar with more Western staples among the mains. There's the deservedly popular Montague burger, its wagyu beef patty teamed with beer-battered red onion rings, a daily pie (perhaps filled with chunks of snapper, scallops and salmon) and a tantalising barbecued young chicken dressed with wasabi leaf and sweet green papaya. If this is your local, consider yourself lucky.

Open Mon–Fri noon–3pm, 6–10pm; Sat–Sun noon–10pm
Typical prices E $15 **M** $27 **D** $15
Cards DC AE MC V Eftpos
Wine Extensive, user-friendly list of Old and New World with boutique Australians; BYO Mon (corkage $10 a bottle)
Owner Scott Thomas
Chef Brad Selkrig
Seats 35; outdoor seating; private room; bar
www.montaguehotel.com.au

And ... If you choose to sit in the front bar you can still order food from the main menu.

Moon Under Water

211 Gertrude Street, Fitzroy **9417 7700**

CONTEMPORARY **15/20**

This chic white dining salon behind the rollicking Builders Arms is named after a George Orwell essay on the qualities of a great pub. The room is pared back and elegant – close linen-dressed tables, black bentwoods – and so is the menu: only four set courses (plus cheese) are offered, leaving diners little decision-making. It's assured, and requires a level of trust. But patrons are in good hands: owner-chefs are Andrew McConnell, who's making Gertrude the city's top eat street, and Josh Murphy, the *Guide*'s 2012 Young Chef of the Year. Ultimately, the leap of faith is repaid: pearly raw scallops are paired with crisp blanched cabbage, dressed with buttermilk, mustard, apple and a hint of juniper; sublime beef short rib features a crisp crumb crust with a mustardy kick alongside sweetly piquant house-made relish. Poached meringue, with strawberry jelly, its sweetness tempered by rhubarb granita, sheep's milk yoghurt chantilly and fresh pomelo, is celestial. Orwell would have been well-pleased.

Open Wed–Sun 6–11pm; Sun noon–3pm
Typical prices Set menu $75 (4 courses)
Cards AE MC V Eftpos
Wine Leaning to small producers and natural wines; upmarket and Eurocentric. Wine matching (from $55)
Owners Andrew McConnell, Anthony Hammond & Josh Murphy
Chefs Josh Murphy & Andrew McConnell
Seats 60; private room
www.buildersarmshotel.com.au

And ... There's a vegetarian version of the set menu at this rising star.

The Moor's Head

Rear, 774 High Street, Thornbury **9484 0173**

MIDDLE EASTERN/PIZZERIA **13.5/20**

You needn't know your Middle Eastern ABC's (arak, bastourma, cumin) to order at this reinvented pizzeria. Sparky, knowledgeable staff happily talk you through the menu – or you can browse the glossary. Dishing up Middle Eastern toppings on chewy Italian-style bases – billed as 'inauthentic pizza' – the menu is split between manoushe, a Lebanese street snack, and boat-shaped Turkish pide. Simple starters kick things off, maybe mini capsicums stuffed with tangy feta, laced with honey and scattered with walnuts, or fresh radish sprinkled with salt and nigella seeds. Pizza names are inspired by famous actors and figures, such as the Omar Sharif, a three-cheese marvel with mint leaves and onions soaked in red wine vinegar, and the Fairuz, with tomato, haloumi, bastourma and parsley. Side salads add colour and crunch, such as chickpeas in tahini and yoghurt with parsley and almonds. And so does the tavern-style vibe, rowdy and fun, in a black-walled former radiator-repair shop. You'll likely hang around for halva, fairy floss or Turkish delight.

Open Wed–Sun 5.30–10pm
Typical prices E $7.50 **M** $18 **D** $8
Cards MC V Eftpos
Wine Compact drinks list (4 by the glass), plus locally brewed 3 Ravens beer and an 'arak of the day'
Owners Joseph Abboud & John Farha
Chef Joseph Abboud
Seats 40
www.themoorshead.com

And ... There's takeaway too.

MoVida

1 Hosier Lane, City **9663 3038**

MODERN SPANISH **16/20**

Ten years and countless imitators haven't quelled the crush Melburnians have on this Hosier Lane flagship; the original and most atmospheric of the MoVida stable. It's frenetic and fun: multiple sittings every day and months-long waiting lists for weekend nights. Savvy floor-staff steer diners through the options: tapas and raciones your way or the great-value tasting menu. Retro honey-blondwood features and sleek '70s accents paint a simple backdrop. It's with the tapas that the real magic begins – the spicy heat of the chicken escabeche, the crunch of salt-cod croquettes or a perfect romesco atop succulent prawn meat. A glistening tile of tender lamb breast is an unexpected gem and the anchovy and smoked-tomato sorbet combination continues to wow. A comforting braise of barramundi, white beans and clams might round out the savoury courses. Classic churros or a trifle of fresh orange jelly and caramel foam is the final choice – until next time anyway. You'll be back; it's irresistible.

Open Daily noon–late
Typical prices E $4.50 **M** $18 **D** $13
Cards AE MC V
Wine A fantastic Spanish range with some popular Australian labels; good selection by the glass
Owner MoVida Pty Ltd
Chefs Frank Camorra & David Roberts
Seats 42; bar
www.movida.com.au

And ... Seats can appear more often Next Door, which takes no bookings, has quick turnover and the same tapas magic (open Tuesday to Thursday from 5pm, Friday to Saturday from noon, and Sunday from 2pm).

MoVida Aqui

Rear, Level 1, 500 Bourke Street (access via Little Bourke Street), City **9663 3038**

SPANISH **15/20**

This MoVida sibling wears its awarded 'hat' at a jaunty angle. Whether at chunky wooden tables, propped on stools or around the buzzing bar, you experience masterstrokes of flavour, starring imported products such as Cantabrian anchovies, serrano and iberico jamon, Spanish cider, and lemony chillies called guindillas. The anchovies come with smoked tomato sorbet. What an idea ... smoky, icy, salty, tangy: sensational. In other dishes, ingredients, such as plump, Spanish, hand-filleted sardines, simply speak for themselves. Octopus is blanched and boiled, emerging silky soft, dressed with paprika. In traditional Spanish style, cider is added to a pot of prawns and garlic. *Olé* to that. Pork pepper sausage is joyfully fiery and adapted from a Catalan recipe. Then, tip your hat to a pot of golden churros and chocolate, or creme caramel and pestinos – the latter are deep-fried, cinnamon-dusted Spanish biscuits flavoured with fennel and clove, a recipe from chef Frank Camorra's mum.

Open Mon–Fri noon–3pm; Mon–Wed 5–10pm; Thurs–Fri 5–10.30pm; Sat 6–10.30pm
Typical prices E $4.50 **M** $22.50 **D** $16
Cards DC AE MC V Eftpos
Wine Strong focus on Spanish wines with a broad price range, plus the option of Spanish sherry tasting
Owner MoVida Pty Ltd
Chefs Frank Camorra & James Campbell
Seats 120; outdoor seating; private room; bar
www.movida.com.au

And ... On the same level is Paco's Tacos, MoVida's casual, all-weather taqueria.

Mr Hive Kitchen & Bar

Level 1, Crown Metropol, 8 Whiteman Street, Southbank **9292 8300**

CONTEMPORARY **14.5/20**

There's little trace of former occupant Mr Gordon Ramsay at Mr Hive, formerly Maze. Sleek, showy interiors have been replaced with warm hues, low lights and a rocking soundtrack. Service, too, seems more relaxed. While much looks different now, Brit chef John Lawson remains, producing dishes that are still finely tuned and high on technique, but with less trickery than the Maze days. There's a playfulness to the menu, too, in dishes such as 'black and blue tuna' (a top-notch starter of smoky, soy-glazed yellowfin) and 'crispy little pig', in which golden cubes of crumbed and fried pig's head are served with beetroot-stained watermelon and barbecue-style sauce. Generous mains include perfectly pink venison, red cabbage, and parsnip mash, and pan-fried snapper with samphire and smoked egg, the salty yolk sprinkled mimosa style over the dish. There's a decadent signature chocolate-bar dessert, with peanuts and caramel, or opt for the elegant praline souffle.

Open Daily 11am-11pm
Typical prices E $18 **M** $32 **D** $16
Cards DC AE MC V
Wine Interesting world-roaming assembly, with seasonal features of organic wines; 21 by the glass
Owner Crown Metropol Hotel
Chef John Lawson
Seats 115; private room; bar
www.crownmetropol.com.au/MrHiveKitchenandBar

And ... Need a sugary fix? Pastry chef Daniel Fletcher's sweet concoctions are the stars of a stand-alone dessert bar, open nightly.

Mr Wolf

9-15 Inkerman Street, St Kilda **9534 0255**

ITALIAN **14/20**

Its speciality is pizza and they're great, with unusual toppings and thin, crisp-edged crusts, but everything else exhilarates too. The atmosphere, amid mod, minimalist decor, is exuberant. Children through to seniors blend seamlessly, with waiters attuned to all needs. The most popular dish isn't pizza but delightful eggplant fritters – fleshy, deep-fried chunks, breadcrumb crunch, lemon-yoghurt mayo and roasted cumin. Karen Martini's sense of adventure is evident in the pizza combos. Broccolini and gorgonzola is wonderful, though the added pancetta may be fatty. One pizza features cauliflower, another has peas. It's about reclaiming the pizza for Italy, so no ham and pineapple, but enough mushroom, mozzarella and olive options for less experimental eaters. Other options include a lasagne, or maybe a casserole. Mousse is traditional and dense, made with good-quality dark chocolate, and 'dessert chocolate martini', made with chocolate sorbet, is so good you almost forget that gorgeous eggplant.

Open Tues–Fri & Sun noon–4pm; Tues–Thurs & Sun 5–10pm; Fri–Sat 5–11pm
Typical prices E $17 **M** $23 **D** $14
Cards AE MC V Eftpos
Wine Lots of Italian wines, plus a variety of Australian and French; BYO Tues night (corkage $7 a bottle)
Owners Karen Martini, Michael Sapountsis, Marcus Ellis, Emma & Damien King
Chefs Karen Martini & Ben Sisley
Seats 90; outdoor seating; private room; bar
www.mrwolf.com.au

And ... Have a drink at Mr Wolf bar next door.

Newmarket Hotel

34 Inkerman Street, St Kilda **9537 1777**

MODERN HISPANIC **14/20**

In the beginning, there were tile-walled pubs that did a basic counter meal. Then, there were gastropubs that brought fine food to the sociable pub experience. Then, there were Melbourne Pub Group pubs: a third generation of gastropub that services its hip 'hood with a thoroughly curated, themed food and booze-focused bar experience with a sometimes nightclub vibe. The Newmarket is California 'with a wink to the south'. Half the menu is drinks (a pitcher of Pimms, perhaps, or a boutique draught); the other half is dedicated to dishes with Latin attitude, redolent of lime, chilli and coriander. The menu's 11 sections let diners jump between little dishes like great roll-your-own soft tacos with soft-shell crab, lamb-filled roasted fig with goat's cheese, and quinoa and zucchini salad. Or go for meats cooked on the grill – there are seven steaks – or rotisserie, with things like lamb or pork. Concrete arches, like the ribcage of a whale, denote the dining area proper, but eating in the more casual inside-outside front section is also fun.

Open Daily noon–3pm, 6–11pm
Typical prices E $18 **M** $38 **D** $14
Cards DC AE MC V Eftpos
Wine Cocktail pitchers suit the vibe and there's a strong showing of Iberian, Spanish and Argentinean wines
Owner Melbourne Pub Group
Chef Andrew Logan
Seats 180; outdoor seating; bar
www.newmarketstkilda.com.au

And ... Got 16 mates? Book the Chef's Table for a spread at $75 a head.

Nihonbashi Zen

Basement, 87 Little Bourke Street, City **9639 7050**

JAPANESE **13.5/20**

This little bunker in Chinatown has long been the last word in Melbourne for kushiyaki: simple flame-grilled skewers that rise above average yakitori by virtue of quality ingredients. An entire king prawn is served in its shell with just a pinch of salt and a wedge of lemon, tender free-range chicken breast is laced with a sour-plum sauce and crisp shiso leaf. Complexity is not a feature of the rest of the menu, either, which favours big flavours. Aged Angus beef might be served in thin, rare slices, with minced daikon radish and a sharp ponzu, while a soft-shell crab with shiitake is liberally coated with spicy mayo. Despite austere appearances, Nihonbashi Zen is not so formal. There are white tablecloths, but also paper napkins and disposable chopsticks. And though prices can feel high for what is essentially a solid city diner, produce is top notch. Host Emmy Yano is warm, chatty and adept at guiding diners through the exclusive sake selection.

Open Tues–Sun 6–10pm
Typical prices E $18 **M** $41.50 **D** $9.50
Cards DC AE MC V Eftpos
Wine Mix of mainstream and boutique local wines, plus some fine high-end sakes
Owners Hiro & Emmy Yano
Chef Hiro Yano
Seats 28; private room
www.nihonbashizen.com.au

And ... There's a compact row of bar seating for solo diners, just like you'll find in countless restaurants in Japan.

No35

Sofitel Melbourne, 25 Collins Street, City **9653 7744**

CONTEMPORARY **14/20**

Enjoying the magnificent vistas that dining 35 floors up affords, you might not know the kitchen is working hard to simplify things. Chef Stuart McVeigh has traded 'formal upscale' for 'casual chic', offering less-fussy food than in years past, and in a more flexible format designed for sharing. Begin, perhaps, with excellent fresh oysters, served simply. Or there's kingfish ceviche, a visual splendour of avocado and lime greenery. For main course, a pan-seared fillet of blue-eye with dill and preserved lemon may come with a potted black cabbage, tomato, chilli and fennel side. Bourguignonne-inspired brisket is a melting texture of slow-cooked Blackmore wagyu with velvety carrot and potato purees in copper pots. Service can be slow, and the fitout remains formal, but gorgeous desserts set things right. Chocolate ganache with milk-chocolate mousse is so fluffy, bitter and indulgent, it may well distract you from those million-dollar views.

Open Daily 6.30–10.30am, 5.30–9.30pm; Wed–Fri & Sun noon–2.30pm
Typical prices E $19 **M** $38 **D** $17
Cards DC AE MC V Eftpos
Wine Big range of Old and New World wines, mid- to high-end; 20-plus by the glass
Owner Sofitel Hotel
Chef Stuart McVeigh
Seats 150; private room
www.no35.com.au

And ... Check the web for theatre dinner-and-show packages.

Nobu

Riverside, Crown Complex, Southbank **9292 7879**

JAPANESE **14/20**

If you like your sushi with a dash of theatre, Nobu is the ticket. The dark, clubby subterranean dining hall is a loud place to celebrate, and Nobu's global status lends a level of prestige and ambitiousness to the modern Japanese menu. Milky, translucent scallop sashimi comes dusted with dried red miso; sublimely plump and tender lamb cutlets are sauced with wasabi-tinged pepper gravy. Textural salads might be whole, fleshy shiitake mushrooms sprinkled with crunchy bonito flakes with a fruity, aromatic dressing or wood-oven baked squid with crisp-fried sweet pea tendrils and a basil dipping sauce. Desserts can feel too complex, such as the espresso cup of frothy Suntory whisky foam over layers of crushed coffee-bean crumble and icecream, although creamy house-made icecreams such as Earl Grey and azuki bean impress. Nobu's squad of waiters might not be altogether in sync, but they are enthusiastic and keep the dial firmly tuned to a setting that says 'fun'.

Open Mon–Thurs noon–2.30pm; Sun–Thurs 6–10.30pm; Fri–Sun noon–3pm; Fri–Sat 6–11pm
Typical prices E $22 **M** $42 **D** $18
Cards DC AE MC V
Wine Expansive list with strong international flavour; more than a dozen sakes including a tasting flight
Owners Nobu Matsuhisa, Robert De Niro, Meir Teper & James Packer
Chef Shane Chan
Seats 130; private room; bar
www.noburestaurants.com/melbourne

And ... A shortened 'tapas' menu is available upstairs daily from 3pm for walk-ins.

Noir

175 Swan Street, Richmond **9428 3585**

CONTEMPORARY **14/20**

Noir is dark, with fir-green walls and dimmed lighting, but not black as its name suggests, with a generous heart in the kitchen. The mood is easygoing, with bare tables and timber floors, but the linen napkins and good glassware are indications of a meal to be taken seriously. The large handwritten menu offers broad choice – more than you may expect from a small restaurant. Think traditional and add some smart touches: kingfish ceviche slices dusted with lemon and parsley resting on a rouille dressing, or roast duck breast and confit leg with just-soft-enough brussels sprouts, chestnuts and a celeriac puree. A roast rack of lamb comes with a pressed shoulder of lamb (which may be salty) and fondant potatoes. Finish with cheese, or a densely smooth orange creme caramel, lifted by poached rhubarb and basil shoots. Persuade the whole table to opt for the tasting menu ($80 a person). Waitstaff are well informed and attentive.

Open Daily 6–10pm; Fri–Sun noon–3pm
Typical prices E $18.50 **M** $38 **D** $15
Cards AE MC V Eftpos
Wine Handwritten, expansive view of Australia, NZ, France and the Iberian peninsula; 10 by the glass
Owners Peter Roddy & Ebony Vagg
Chef Peter Roddy
Seats 30
www.noirrestaurant.com.au

And ... There's a more limited choice at lunch: $24 for one course, $35 for two, glass of wine included.

Ocha

3 Church Street, Hawthorn **9853 6002**

JAPANESE **14.5/20**

The queue starts early outside Ocha and within minutes of the 6pm kick-off the place is humming. The interior is like a display apartment, the staff are friendly, if not all 'career waiters', and the devoted regulars barely glance at the menu. By 7.45pm there's a frantic rush to do it all again for the more relaxed second sitting. Why so popular? For a start, there's the Ocha go-to of prawn dumplings, crusted in rice flakes and served with green-tea salt. Then, the crunchy calamari legs with garlic and chilli and the popular beef with a wasabi mash gratin. The signature antipasto showcases the kitchen's most finessed work, maybe a wonderfully delicate poached quail egg, a perfectly assembled shiitake with prawn or a deeply subtle snapper consomme. Sashimi salad has a spicy chilli-miso dressing, a little bit Korean, and the tatsuta-age is perfectly fried. Some very un-Japanese and very engaging desserts might include doughnuts with green tea and white chocolate dipping sauce.

Open Tues–Fri noon–2.30pm; Tues–Sat 6–10.30pm
Typical prices E $15 **M** $33 **D** $16.50
Cards DC AE MC V
Wine Carefully selected list of Antipodeans and Europeans; interesting varieties and excellent range by the glass at good prices; BYO (corkage $7.50 a head)
Owners Yasu Yoshida & Michelle Rogerson
Chefs Yasu Yoshida & Paula Lawdorn
Seats 70; bar
www.ocha.com.au

citibank Privileges

And … Look out for monthly Monday degustations for $120 (10 courses).

O'Connell's Centenary Hotel

193 Montague Street, South Melbourne **9699 9600**

CONTEMPORARY **13/20**

Many gastropubs are so posh that to call them 'pubs' is a misnomer, but O'Connell's retains its heritage warmth and informality. Sure, the comfortable Art Deco dining room could use a freshen up, but the menu's solid, though chef Paul Cooper departed and was replaced by Daniel Cairns as we went to press. Expect well-executed 'favourites' (schnitzels, burgers and the like) as well as more complex dishes. Golden fishcakes might be made from salted cod poached in milk with a subtle touch of lemon myrtle. Or an assiette of baby goat, using nose-to-tail techniques; small discs of loin rolled in parsley and breadcrumbs, wood-grilled chunks of leg, rolled shoulder slow-cooked overnight, a croquette of miso-sweetened belly and a chermoula-spiced pithiviers made from the neck. Steak options may include a moistly tender wood-grilled Hopkins River scotch fillet, its flavour intensified by salt-brining. For dessert, perhaps a creamy log of subtly honey-flavoured iced nougat, given texture with crunchy caramel and crystallised pumpkin seeds.

Open Daily noon–3pm; Wed–Sat 6–9.30pm; Sun–Tues 6–9pm
Typical prices E $19 **M** $34 **D** $15
Cards DC AE MC V Eftpos
Wine Good range of price points, varieties and producers; 18 by the glass
Owner Centenary Co Pty Ltd
Chef Daniel Cairns
Seats 80; outdoor seating; private room; bar
www.oconnells.com.au

And … Tuesday is pie day, which might mean beef and Guinness pie and a drink for $20.

Okra

159 Camberwell Road, Hawthorn East **9813 1623**

ASIAN **12.5/20**

This polite and pleasing split-level eatery has been skilfully blending the spices of South-East Asia here in Hawthorn East for a decade. Not much has changed, and that's the way the locals like it. The formal, restrained decor, with thin linen tablecloths, timber floors and subtle lighting, makes an unobtrusive setting – perfect for the head-turning presentation of some dishes. The hor mok talay is a flaming tinfoil parcel of steamed seafood in a delicate red Thai curry mingling coconut milk with kaffir lime and lemongrass. Equally theatrical is a baked clay entree plate of oysters, also alight, each bathed in a sweet ginger broth. Despite the somewhat stiff setting, service is friendly and there's culinary finesse: iceberg lettuce cups of duck sang choy bao, Singapore chilli prawns on the end of a chopstick for dipping in creamy gravy, and grilled eye-fillet with caramelised tamarind sauce – a smoky profound pleasure. It's a happy collision of elements that ensures Okra's enduring popularity.

Open Daily 6–10.30pm; Tues–Fri & Sun noon–3pm
Typical prices E $13 **M** $20.90 **D** $14
Cards DC AE MC V Eftpos
Wine Sturdy list of dependable Oz and NZ drops; 22 by the glass; BYO (corkage $2.50 a head)
Owner Frederick Tseng
Chef Michael Tiu
Seats 80; outdoor seating; private room

And ... Slurp fish head soup, bowls of laksa, and seafood noodles from the special Sunday lunch street-food hawker menu.

Omni

349 Keilor Road, Essendon **9379 9497**

MEDITERRANEAN **12.5/20**

Modest Omni is the village trattoria, servicing an appreciative local clientele with generous flavours and homely service. A passion for great ingredients is evident in owner-chef Natalie Stivala's Spanish- and Italian-influenced menu, where you're likely to find some solid renditions of classic dishes such as patatas bravas and seafood paella alongside more creative numbers like excellent seared scallops with crisp capers, chilli and burnt butter. Approach the menu in the traditional entree-main way (with mains like spaghetti marinara and pumpkin risotto) or share and order as a series of smaller, tapas plates; chirpy young staff are happy to guide with recommendations. Desserts cover similar Mediterranean terrain; a terrific orange blossom-scented crema Catalana comes with a thoroughly smashable burnt toffee top. Latino spice and fire can be muted in some dishes, so if your preference is for autentico, tell the kitchen to cut loose.

Open Tues–Sat 6–10pm; Wed–Fri noon–2.30pm; Sat 9–11.30am; Sun 9am–3pm
Typical prices E $16 **M** $33 **D** $14
Cards AE MC V Eftpos
Wine Brief list, mostly well-known Australian and NZ labels, with a few Spanish and Italian numbers; 16 by the glass
Owner & chef Natalie Stivala
Seats 38; outdoor seating; private room
www.eatatomni.com.au

And ... Weekend breakfasts could include Spanish eggs poached in tomato salsa.

SANTA VITTORIA
PRODUCT OF ITALY
SANTA VITTORIA
ACQUA MINERALE

Os Kitchen & Wine Bar

531a Hampton Street, Hampton **9533 1922**

ITALIAN **14/20**

Simple is best? It's certainly the case at Os Kitchen, where cool tones, clean lines and straight plates add up to a boon for bayside diners. From chef Rachael Ginty's succinct menu, take, for example, the antipasto: a classic collection of frittata, grissini, little piles of marinated red capsicum, mushrooms and cauliflower, chorizo chunks and prosciutto fresh from meeting the gleaming meat slicer at the rear of the intimate dining room. Or perhaps a superbly crumbed Otway pork cutlet, served on a cabbage and lemon salad with an apple-cider jus. A crisp-skinned barramundi fillet is paired with a niçoise of potato, a soft-boiled egg half and the sharpness of baby capers. The informed, convivial service will steer you in the right direction if you want to take the sweet path – the tiramisu with a hefty espresso hit, or the trifle of peaches, raspberry sorbet and lemon verbena cream will leave you glad you did. Hampton has reason to be happy.

Open Tues–Sat 11.30am–3.30pm; Wed–Sat 5.30–9.30pm
Typical prices E $19 **M** $29 **D** $15
Cards AE MC V Eftpos
Wine Classy, interesting Old and New World list categorised by palate weight; 24 by the glass
Owners Alastair Dobbs & Marie Dobbs
Chef Rachael Ginty
Seats 35; outdoor seating; bar
www.oskitchenandwinebar.com.au

And ... Wine flights are on offer for the viti-curious.

Osteria La Passione

486 Bridge Road, Richmond **9428 2558**

ITALIAN **14/20**

Owner and chef Carmine Costantini really makes customers feel like guests. He glides between tables greeting diners at his humble osteria, which is homely yet handsome, with touches like white linen tablecloths and low lighting. But he's also working hard behind the scenes. Many of the ingredients for his good, simple food began life at his farm in Yea, from the olive oil to the salumi and even the house shiraz. There's no menu: just sit back and let capable staff deliver the day's set six courses. Dinner could start with crisp baccala fritters, followed by sweet-and-sour peperonata and house-made bread. A wintry zampone (sausage-stuffed pig's trotter) with lentils and a sweet drizzle of vincotto may follow. Next, pumpkin gnocchi with earthy pine mushrooms. The main may be meltingly tender roast pork neck with celeriac mash, while dessert is usually a classic, perhaps vanilla panna cotta with the perfect wobble. Here, tonight, you could believe you were in Emilia-Romagna.

Open Tues–Sat 6.30–9.30pm
Typical prices Set menu $75 (6 courses)
Cards MC V Eftpos
Wine Pithy list with a slant towards Victorian wines and Italian grapes; BYO Tues (corkage $25 a bottle)
Owner & chef Carmine Costantini
Seats 34

And ... Although there's no menu and dishes change daily, dietary requirements of all kinds are catered for – advise when booking.

TOP 10 LATE NIGHT

Bar Lourinha

37 Little Collins Street, City **9663 7890**
Dishes up the good Iberian stuff in style until 1am on weekends.

Carlisle Wine Bar

137 Carlisle Street, Balaclava **9531 3222**
The Carlisle and its rustic Italian food stay up late every night.

Choo Choo's @ The Toff in Town

Level 2, 252 Swanston Street, City **9639 8770**
Punchy Thai flavours available here until the wee small hours every night.

European

161 Spring Street, City **9654 0811**
Late every night, later at weekends, the Euro balances style and substance at any time.

France-Soir

11 Toorak Road, South Yarra **9866 8569**
This French institution stays open until midnight every night of the week.

Izakaya Den

Basement, 114 Russell Street, City **9654 2977**
The Den pumps out classic and modern izakaya food until midnight most nights.

Ling Nan

204 Little Bourke Street, City **9663 2347**
No frills, brilliant 'Hong Kong-ese' flavours, until 3am every morning.

Mamasita

Level 1, 11 Collins Street, City **9650 3821**
Keeps the tacos and tostaditas coming until 2am on weekends.

Sho Noodle Bar

Crown Complex, Southbank **9292 6885**
An island of late-night vibrant Cantonese flavour in a sea of pokies.

Supper Inn

15 Celestial Avenue, City **9663 4759**
This night-owl institution pumps out Cantonese flavours until 2am every night.

Otsumami

257 High Street, Northcote **9489 6132**

JAPANESE **12/20**

Take a laid-back inner-city cafe, turn it Japanese, and fill it with a young, boisterous crowd, and you have Otsumami. Large modern lanterns enliven an otherwise unremarkable shopfront with simple, undressed tables clustered either side of a small open kitchen. Otsumami takes Japanese staples (gyoza, sushi, tempura) and adds some inner-Melbourne twists. Fried squid is marinated in coriander, lemon and soy and tossed in mesclun leaves with grapefruit segments and a sesame dressing; siu mai dumplings are delicate, filled with tofu and shiitake; a sushi special of kingfish and salmon may come lightly torched and with a touch of wasabi mayonnaise. The best dishes are those furthest from old Japan, such as lemongrass yakitori-don, chicken cooked in sweet soy and lemongrass with spinach, or chicken gyoza with five-spice and coriander. While the service can sometimes be a little too laid-back, there's no questioning the quality of the produce. Say 'sayonara' with a char-grilled pancake with sweet azuki bean filling and green-tea icecream.

Open Tues–Sun 5.30–10pm
Typical prices E $11 **M** $18 **D** $8
Cards AE MC V Eftpos
Wine Small but carefully selected list of interesting Australian and NZ wines; small sake list
Owners Katrina Smith & Danielle Halligan
Chef Kohei Matsuzaki
Seats 50
www.otsumami.com.au

And ... Takeaway also available.

Paladarr

7 Rowe Street (corner Yarralea Street), Alphington
1300 725 232

THAI **15/20**

Paladarr is, in the best way, a traditional restaurant. Deliberate service delivers Chaloem Chaiseeha's polished northern Thai cuisine - some of the city's best - and the former State Bank premises have a certain prudential grandeur, even if the sweeping curtains and lush carpets are starting to look just a little tired. But that's a quibble, as the food is vivid, the menu urging diners not to pull back on the chilli in the house-made curry pastes. Prawns make an aromatic entree, seared and glossy with ginger, lemongrass and chilli making a tart, syrupy dressing. Wok-tossed, thin-sliced beef is tumbled with garlic and Thai basil. The daily fish might be gently steamed, herb-stuffed snapper drizzled with nam jim sauce feisty with fresh lime, while pieces of chewy-crunchy belly pork punctuate glossy Chinese broccoli, stir-fried with a hit of chilli. Desserts have a sophisticated touch, coconut rum cream and Ricketts Point ginger and lime icecream conjured into a parfait that tastes of the tropics.

Open Sun–Thurs 6–9pm; Fri–Sat 6–9.30pm; Sun noon–2pm
Typical prices E $14 **M** $29 **D** $14
Cards DC AE MC V Eftpos
Wine Globetrotting list with an emphasis on the aromatic; wine matching available with degustation
Owners Chaloem Chaiseeha & Bryan Derrick
Chef Chaloem Chaiseeha
Seats 80; outdoor seating; private room
www.paladarr.com.au

And ... Check Paladarr's lively website for gift certificates, birthday specials, cooking classes, events and the special Monday menu.

The Panama Dining Room

Level 3, 231 Smith Street, Fitzroy **9417 7663**

CONTEMPORARY **13/20**

It's almost de rigueur to have to climb two flights of dusty stairs to reach a hip bar in this town; but here, you get the darkly seductive bar as well as a retro-styled dining room. The restaurant's focus is on clever flavour pairing. A slow-poached egg teams perfectly with rich smoked trout and a fresh nasturtium and frisee salad, or opt for the Glenloth chicken sous-vide, grilled and served with sweetcorn puree, charry corn kernels and sweet baby leeks. Flavourful specials might include a mound of beautifully briny mussels and plump prawns with silverbeet and soft risoni in saffron broth. Desserts may not scale the same heights, but a dense banana loaf with choc-chip icecream and caramel popcorn will thrill a sweet tooth. Staff are efficient and knowledgeable if occasionally distracted, and patrons sensitive to noise should eat early as the happy buzz intensifies as the night wears on.

Open Daily 6–10pm
Typical prices E $14 **M** $26 **D** $14
Cards DC AE MC V Eftpos
Wine A considered list with a good choice of European labels; 17 by the glass
Owners James Langley & Laki Papadopoulos
Chef Dianne Kerry
Seats 75; bar
www.thepanama.com.au

And ... Every Wednesday night in the restaurant your second bottle of Italian wine is free.

The Pantry

1-5 Church Street, Brighton **9591 0393**

CONTEMPORARY **13.5/20**

It's buzzy, it's hip, and it's kid-friendly too. The Pantry is a daytime cafe-deli that transforms into a mid-range diner by night. It has a welcoming, casual vibe with a beachy feel of distressed leather banquettes, butcher's paper-covered table-tops and energetic waiters. With a menu that runs from tacos to fried chicken to pizzas (with more than a dozen varieties to choose from), you might not expect fireworks, but the calibre of some dishes is top-notch. Tacos are right on trend – soft shell filled with a smoky blend of chilli beans and barbecued corn; a cheffy riff on prawn cocktail (fried in kataifi) is just a mouthful or two but packed with flavour; and a main of pappardelle with lamb and chilli is a rich, balanced and satisfying meal-in-a-bowl. And while desserts may not be a strong point, such as a 'trifle' that's more akin to a chocolate pudding, the cocktail and craft beer list are bound to impress.

Open Mon–Wed 7.30am–5pm; Thurs–Fri 7.30am–10.30pm; Sat 8am–10.30pm; Sun 8.30am–5pm
Typical prices E $17 **M** $38 **D** $14
Cards AE MC V Eftpos
Wine Strong list with two dozen Victorian pinots; around 20 by the glass
Owners Daniel Vaughan, Dave Evans & Guy Mainwaring
Chefs Jeff Young, Paul Dodd & Matthew Head
Seats 80; outdoor seating
www.pantry.com.au

And … As the *Guide* went to press, renovations were afoot for a bar, private room and new-look deli.

Papa Goose

91-93 Flinders Lane, City **9663 2800**

MODERN BRITISH **14/20**

You'll never go hungry in this city strip, where Papa Goose rubs shoulders with buzzy big-namers (Coda, Cumulus, Chin Chin) and admirably holds its own. The space is instantly comfortable, with dark timbers, chocolate-coloured banquettes and statement lampshades that pour a moody silver light through the room. Well-crafted modern British fare is the go, served by waiters who whiz about the tables at a snappy pace. Starters might be rabbit croquettes to dunk in mustard-laced tartare sauce or prawn ceviche with dollops of sweet pea puree and wild rice crisps scattered on top, adding a lovely texture. There could be pork loin for main course, slow-cooked and served with scallop meat and compressed apple doused with rosewater. Desserts embrace the Old Blighty ethos – think banana toffee medley, which gives a nod to the classic banoffee pie and leaves you yearning a little for the mother country.

Open Mon–Sat 5.30–10pm; Tues–Fri & Sun noon–3pm
Typical prices E $19 **M** $39 **D** $17
Cards AE MC V Eftpos
Wine A smart selection of well-priced drops from Europe, Australia and NZ with a good range by the glass
Owners Neale White & John Adgemis
Chef Neale White
Seats 65; private room; bar
www.papagoose.com.au

And … To find the striking upstairs bar Loose Goose, head down the side laneway to the separate entrance.

Pei Modern

Collins Place, 45 Collins Street, City **9654 8545**

CONTEMPORARY **15.5/20**

Mark Best's Melbourne debut more than meets expectations, despite leaving the template for his gastro-temple Marque at home in Sydney. An accessible, all-day eatery, Pei Modern's impact belies its simple 'bistro' status, thanks to its crack service team and exciting, surprising food (executed by head chef Matt Germanchis). From luxe, rich and creamy almond gazpacho dotted with blue swimmer crab, red grapes and parsley, to steamed hapuku with corn kernels and sea urchin butter sauce, to the meaty grunt of grilled ox heart with bullhorn peppers and harissa, or the to-die-for comfort food of potato, bone marrow, coffee grounds and cured tuna, it's a convention-challenging experience, although more traditional pairings (from hanger steak with beetroot and Swiss chard to a spoon-licking dessert of crostoli with sauterne custard) are also to be found. Housed in the Sofitel forecourt with a cracking bar occupying one side of its cool Scandinavian fitout, Pei Modern is simply brilliant.

Open Daily 7.30am–11pm (closed Sun in winter)
Typical prices E $16 **M** $34 **D** $15
Cards AE MC V Eftpos
Wine Eclectic global list with particular affection for organic and biodynamic wines
Owners Mark Best, David Mackintosh & Peter Bartholomew
Chefs Mark Best & Matt Germanchis
Seats 55; outdoor seating; bar
www.peimodern.com.au

And ... It's named after globally renowned Chinese-American architect I.M. Pei, whose work includes Collins Place.

Pelican

16 Fitzroy Street, St Kilda **9525 5847**

CONTEMPORARY **13.5/20**

A lazy breakfast catching the sun through the porthole windows; an alfresco lunch of rosé and springy charred calamari; or a cosy seat indoors when the temperature calls for tempranillo and meatballs. One occasion can easily blend into another: you might intend no more than a drink, and then the waiter, invitingly, pops a menu on your table. Pelican set out 10 years ago to be one of those all-day, all-occasion places; any visit reveals they nailed it from the get-go. It retains its breezy beach-house deck and Euro wine-bar interior, and seasonally changing dishes jump effortlessly between Med, mid-East and Asia. You might start with freshly shucked oysters or a delicate scallop on carrot-and-ginger puree before moving on to heartier dishes such as juicy, shredded duck with pomegranate and walnut to wrap in warmed piadina, or deliciously layered pork-belly skewers. There are no mission statements or fads here, just well-executed dishes that feel right at any hour.

Open Daily 7.30am–11pm
Typical prices Shared plates $9.50–$19.50 **D** $6
Cards DC AE MC V
Wine Plenty of European and Australian drops to complement tapas-style dining; 21 by the glass, plus weekly specials
Owner Paul Olynyk
Chef Dai Duong
Seats 110; outdoor seating; bar
www.stkildapelican.com

And ... In keeping with the laid-back mood, dogs are welcome outside.

Persimmon

Ground level, NGV International, 180 St Kilda Road, City
8620 2434

CONTEMPORARY **14/20**

This coolly elegant, window-wrapped dining room takes a minimal approach to decor (low black ceiling, charcoal-grey banquettes) – all the better to take in the surrounding sculpture-garden views. The menu is a contemporary take on various cultural influences, explained effectively by friendly staff. A charcuterie plate of mushrooms, salami, prosciutto and grilled bread sets the scene for relaxed sharing alongside a kingfish sashimi with spring onions, pickled ginger and cashews. Penne pasta dressed in Persian feta, pinenuts and olives may be heavily salted and fail to ignite the same enthusiasm, although a main of smoked then braised lamb's neck is a revelation of sticky, dark, lacquered meat that falls apart in velvety shreds against a coleslaw of celeriac, cucumber and tarragon. Desserts keep up the modern edge and a creaming soda spider with vanilla and raspberry jelly is a playful and visually pleasing finale to an experience that satisfies all the senses.

Open Wed–Mon 11.30am–2.30pm
Typical prices E $22 **M** $30 **D** $16
Cards DC AE MC V Eftpos
Wine A short, sharp list that has a good selection of Australian and European wines; 15 by the glass
Owner Peter Rowland Catering, NGV
Chef Terry Clark
Seats 110
www.ngv.vic.gov.au/visit

And ... There's a succinct but appropriate kids' menu to refuel the little ones for more exploring after lunch.

Philhellene

551-553 Mount Alexander Road, Moonee Ponds
9370 3303

GREEK **14/20**

Philhellene oozes homely charm. Vintage maps and prints adorn red-brick walls and waiters dispense oodles of warmth alongside the provincial-style dishes that keep this spot one step ahead. If you're after the usual dip and pita fare, they're happy to oblige with perhaps a salty wedge of char-grilled kefalograviera cheese or rice-and-dill-stuffed dolmades. But even here the temptation to explore regional Greece and farther-flung outposts is too great. The pomegranate molasses and grilled red capsicum in the rodi dip render it a rich and heady mix. Many regional specials have Cypriot and Middle Eastern flourishes. You might find kalitsounia (it changes but might be spinach, feta and dill encased in a smooth deep-fried pastry shell) or a hearty fricassee with artichoke hearts and tender chunks of lamb bobbing in an egg-lemon broth speckled with beads of olive oil. Desserts are classic: loukoumades drenched in honey syrup or icecream with nuggets of chocolate and vanilla halva. Philhellene is as warm as a Greek mama's embrace.

Open Mon–Sat 5pm–late; Thurs–Fri noon–3pm; Sun noon–late
Typical prices E $13.50 **M** $26.50 **D** $10.50
Cards DC AE MC V Eftpos
Wine Greek wines, beers, spirits and liquors star
Owners John & Susie Rerakis, Manny & Alkistis Gerassimou
Chefs Toma Youkhana, Katina Rerakis & Helen Gerassimou
Seats 120; private room
www.philhellene.com.au

And ... There's live music on Sunday afternoons.

Pinotta

32 Best Street, Fitzroy North **9481 3393**

ITALIAN **14/20**

Just what the burghers of Fitzroy North needed: a local trattoria with plenty of class but no fuss. Andy Logue (ex-The Italian) has transplanted his simple, confident, rustic Italian cooking to a narrow, terrazzo-floored neighbourhood restaurant. A few linen-topped tables are squeezed into the front room, dominated by a long wooden bar. Out back, things are more spacious, with black banquette seating, a gas fireplace and fresh white walls hung with art. The handwritten seasonal menu may proffer carpaccio of thick velvety-soft beef with parmesan, capers and anchovies, topped with radicchio salad, or semolina-dusted and fried calamari. Mains could be a hunk of on-the-bone rib-eye with a veal jus, presented carved with a side of shoestring fries. Logue makes the pasta, such as pliant ricotta gnocchi in a lamb shoulder ragu or agnolotti stuffed with baby snapper. Desserts are equally classic, like the baked-to-order chocolate fondant: a firm crust and a dollop of vanilla icecream complementing a runny interior.

Open Wed–Fri noon–10pm; Sat–Sun 9.30am–10pm
Typical prices E $22 **M** $32 **D** $15
Cards MC V Eftpos
Wine About 60 Australian, French and Italian wines with plenty of pinot and nebbiolo
Owners Andy Logue & Heidi Modra
Chef Andy Logue
Seats 60; outdoor seating; bar
www.pinotta.com

And ... With a minimum spend you can book out the rear room for a private function.

Pireaus Blues

310 Brunswick Street, Fitzroy **9417 0222**

GREEK **13/20**

Piraeus Blues has been waving the flag for traditional Greek cooking for close to two decades and while the decor may be looking a little dated (family photos, traditional instruments), the Greek-style comfort food and warm service have lost none of their appeal. Dips and pita, calamari and pickled octopus kick off the conventional entrees list, but check the blackboard specials for Florinian saganaki, a dish of red peppers cooked in loads of olive oil until soft and sweet then flecked with salty feta. Lamb and seafood dominate the mains and a large slice of swordfish, perfectly char-grilled with sauteed spinach and creamy skordalia, is testament to the power of treating good produce simply. Lamb may come char-grilled or slow-cooked, the latter a bowl of tender lemon-infused flesh served with a crunchy bean, chickpea and capsicum salad. Serving sizes are bumper, a bonus when it comes to halva icecream, rich with chunky chewy sesame candy.

Open Mon–Thurs 5–10pm; Fri–Sat noon–11pm; Sun noon–10pm
Typical prices E $14 **M** $32 **D** $9.50
Cards DC AE MC V Eftpos
Wine A short list of mostly Australian and NZ wines with several under $35; BYO (corkage $8 a bottle)
Owners George & Flora Karanikos, Lazarus & Vicki Thomaidis
Chefs Flora Karanikos & Dipesh Thapa
Seats 200; outdoor seating; private room
www.piraeusblues.com.au

And ... Check out the banquets (including vegetarian) and the live music on Sunday afternoons.

Pizza e Birra

60a Fitzroy Street, St Kilda **9537 3465**

ITALIAN/PIZZERIA **13.5/20**

Pizza and beer: what's not to love? But there's more to this light-filled pizzeria than just dough and yeast. Antipasto of pickled anchovies with rocket, tomato, olives and shaved fennel, and mains of rib-eye with roast cauliflower, and spaghetti tossed with plump prawns and cherry tomatoes round out the menu. The main event, though, is what emerges from the wood-fired oven: charred and thin-crusted pizza, from lists divided into red (tomato base) and white (oil). The signature lasagne pizza comprises tomato, ham, basil, ricotta, mozzarella and parmesan, while for the white team, perhaps pieces of pork-and-fennel sausage on a garlicky, crushed green olive base. Tiramisu and panna cotta are classic, or try the special rustic ricotta and chocolate crostata (baked tart, fresh from the oven). Service could be more attentive and dishes can be slow to arrive, but the modern room is stylish with bentwood chairs, hanging globes and brown paper on tables. Got the kids? Head to the enclosed and heated deck.

Open Tues–Thurs 6–10pm; Fri–Sat 6–10.30pm; Sun noon–3pm, 5.30–10pm
Typical prices E $17.50 **M** $27.50 (pizza $19) **D** $13.50
Cards AE MC V Eftpos
Wine One page of Australian and Italian wines; more than 10 by the glass
Owners Silvana Iacobaccio & Mauro Marcucci
Chef Silvana Iacobaccio
Seats 50; outdoor seating
www.pizzaebirra.com.au

And … Ask about their BYO Wednesdays in winter.

P M 24

24 Russell Street, City **9207 7424**

FRENCH **15.5/20**

Philippe Mouchel's aim is to recreate the French bistro experience. He may have surpassed his goal. The kitchen punctuates the space created by towering ceilings and portions the restaurant into a more casual bar, kitchen-side eatery and an intimate space at the rear. Sit by the famous red rotisserie and watch the theatre of the kitchen as French technique meets modern creativity. No pretension here, just real flavours artfully combined. White anchovy and Meredith goat's curd transform humble roasted beetroot to a sweet and salty confection. The soft, deep flavour of spanner crab makes an unforgettable 'bolognese' sauce for capellini, while the rotisseried Milawa organic chicken with rosemary and preserved lemon is a menu hero that keeps regulars returning. Pommes frites are far from ordinaire, flavoured with garlic, parmesan and rosemary, and rich chocolate tart is enlivened by mango and passionfruit foam. Just when you think a perfect evening is over, giant snips of house-made strawberry marshmallow are a parting gift. The pride of staff is obvious and justified.

Open Daily 6–10.30pm; Sun–Fri noon–3pm
Typical prices E $23 **M** $37 **D** $16
Cards DC AE MC V Eftpos
Wine Sizeable list of quality French and Australian wines; 28 by the glass
Owner Made Establishment & Philippe Mouchel
Chef Philippe Mouchel
Seats 90; private room; bar
www.PM24.com.au

And … A bar menu runs weekdays (3–6pm); the rotisserie chicken is available as takeaway.

The Point Albert Park

Aquatic Drive, Albert Park **9682 5566**

CONTEMPORARY **15/20**

Beef is still king here. Dry-ageing cuts are displayed liked crown jewels in a glam glass refrigerator by the entrance, proving that steak remains a focus, despite a change of ownership. Front-of-house staff, led by Brian Lloyd (ex-Vue de Monde) and sommelier Jane Semple, run this lakeside restaurant with velvet smoothness. Lunching ladies and business suits by day and couples by night are seated at tables with ironed linen and sparkling glassware. Chef Justin Wise balances the beef-centric menu with modernist cuisine – slices of marron tail with an array of rabbit (including rack, loin, leg, kidney) and dehydrated cherries. Also consider succulent salt-crusted rock flathead with smooth-set lime milk custard, or a just-pink venison loin with celeriac and palm heart. The single hot slate tile of three different steaks – grain-fed, grass-fed and wagyu – is a beef buff's tasting plate, although the more finessed dishes tend to have the edge. Finish with a delicately sharp lime souffle with yoghurt sorbet.

Open Daily noon–3pm; Sun–Thurs 6–10.30pm; Fri–Sat 6–11pm
Typical prices E $26 **M** $48 **D** $18
Cards DC AE MC V Eftpos
Wine A beautifully curated list, broad with global choices and deep with past vintages
Owner Rabih Yanni
Chef Justin Wise
Seats 90; outdoor seating; private room
www.thepointalbertpark.com.au

And ... If meat's not your bag, a vegetarian degustation is available.

Post Office Hotel

231 Sydney Road, Coburg **9386 5300**

MIDDLE EASTERN **13/20**

As Melbourne's inner-city dining scene creeps steadily northwards, the Post Office is no longer on the fringe; its kitchen, however, continues to explore the frontiers of updated pan-Middle Eastern fare. Troy Payne, a protégé of Greg Malouf, has designed a menu to share, taking inspiration from the Levant, Caucasus and North Africa and giving it contemporary expression. The manti (pert little Turkish dumplings) might marry the mild marine flavour of scallops with the tartness of barberries; the juicy lamb racks, stuffed with sweetbreads and sucuk (Turkish sausage) then rolled and roasted, might come with a 'gazpacho' of pistachio and mint; or an earthy tagine of wild mushrooms and chickpeas, sweetened with dates, might be offset by creamy 'stinging nettle yoghurt whip' and crunchy kataifi pastry. The dining room, with artfully exposed brickwork, metallic orange wallpaper, and bright, enthusiastic staff, manages to keep the atmosphere of the surrounding pub appropriately distant.

Open Wed–Sat 6–10pm
Typical prices E $17 **M** $34 **D** $10
Cards MC V Eftpos
Wine Australian-dominated 13-page list plus wine, beer, spirits and cocktails from around the globe
Owners Danial Caneva, Shannon Vanderwert & Tex Perkins
Chef Troy Payne
Seats 60; private room; bar
www.thepostofficehotel.com.au

And ... Feel like kicking on? DJs and bands play regularly in the front bar.

Potsticker

58 Hawthorn Road, Caulfield North **9500 8819**

ASIAN **13.5/20**

Hong Kong natives Eric Wong (formerly of Armadale's Cina) and chef Paul Chan have opened a fine-dining restaurant in a building where past businesses have failed to stick – but the Potsticker looks destined to stay. The room is serious (white linen, plush carpet, fine wines) yet merry – in the centre of a 26-seat table is a majestic water feature, complete with pink-lit cherry blossom tree, goldfish and floating candles. Like the sparkly ties worn by black-clad waiters, it's a bit of fun. The menu, too, is playful – a contemporary combination of classic Cantonese, Malaysian, Nonya and Japanese cuisines. Handmade dumplings take many forms: juicy pork with laksa sauce, prawn with spinach-green skins, and fried seafood wontons on a Nonya-style orange, ginger, lemongrass and chilli sauce. Fleshy Peking duck is parcelled up with hoisin, spring onion and cucumber. Deep-fried king prawn is like a modern-day cutlet with a rich coconut 'sand' crumb. Better is the wild black flathead simply steamed with soy, ginger and shallots. Wong blends the imported teas, all part of the personal Potsticker touch.

Open Tues–Sun noon–3pm, 5.30–10.30pm
Typical prices E $9.80 **M** $25.80 **D** $10
Cards DC AE MC V Eftpos
Wine Familiar names from Australia, NZ and Europe on a well-priced list; BYO (corkage $8 a bottle)
Owners Eric Wong & Paul Chan
Chef Paul Chan
Seats 115
www.thepotsticker.com.au

And ... There's daily yum cha with more than 40 dishes.

Preserve Kitchen

32 High Street, Glen Iris **9885 4869**

CONTEMPORARY **13/20**

Unpretentious in every way, this light, white shopfront has wide windows and dark bare boards, its minimalist good looks and crisply dressed tables given warmth by a friendly atmosphere and service. Strong, clear flavours that linger are the key to every dish, including sumac-crusted, boned quail with shaved cucumber, pomegranate and flaked almond salad. Bruschetta toppings change each day – perhaps caramelised onions, truffle paste and just-cooked scallops. Earthy porcini and wild-mushroom risotto might be topped with wilted spinach and black truffle. Beetroot risotto and lemon yoghurt is so flavoursome it threatens to outshine its accompanying tender, pan-seared pink kangaroo loin. Traditional desserts each take a new flavour or two, like Attiki honey panna cotta with honeycomb crumbs and vincotto, or gooey chocolate fondant with muscatel icecream. So good. Preserve has acquired a liquor licence and a short, smart wine list but retained its generous approach to corkage, adding to the appeal of a neat neighbourhood package.

Open Tues–Fri & Sun 11.30am–3pm, 5.30–10pm; Sat 5.30–10.30pm
Typical prices E $17 **M** $30 **D** $16
Cards AE MC V Eftpos
Wine Short eclectic list from major Australian regions and a few internationals; BYO (corkage $5 a head)
Owner & chef Jason Aitken
Seats 65; outdoor seating; private room
www.preservekitchen.com.au

And ... Three set menus make big group bookings simple and economical.

The Press Club

72 Flinders Street, City **9677 9677**

MODERN GREEK 16.5/20

Tumble down the rabbit hole to an epicurean wonderland with a marvellously topsy-turvy approach to Greek cuisine. What's over the top to some will seem a celebration to others. Souvlaki might be rendered unrecognisable – pureed pita, yoghurt as jellied whey, cucumber-skin gel – but is delicious with its lamb cooked two ways and ouzo-soaked onions. Japanese-Greek fusion turns up when yellowfin tuna and daikon run into jellied watermelon and surprisingly alluring pickled watermelon rind. Chicken in lemon brine is cooked sous-vide, served with onion foam, lettuce puree and chicken-skin 'chips'. Salmon is a centrepiece of a seafood main featuring deep-fried calamari tentacles and smoky eel croquettes. Traditional galatoboureko is reinvented as a carnival of treats such as honey panna cotta, jellied mango-juice pearls and sprinkles of sugary filo. Both food and atmosphere preserve the energy that once pulsed through this iconic newspaper building. Polished waitstaff work the darkly glamorous room, helping the open kitchen break new stories about how we eat.

Open Daily noon–3pm, 6–10pm
Typical prices E $28.90 **M** $43.90 **D** $19.90
Cards DC AE MC V Eftpos
Wine Old and New World list runs to 30-plus pages; includes Greek wines poured with knowledge and flair
Owners George Calombaris, George Sykiotis, Tony Lachimea & Joe Calleja
Chefs George Calombaris & Joe Grbac
Seats 90; private room
www.thepressclub.com.au

And ... Get close to the action at the chef's table.

Punch Lane

43 Little Bourke Street, City **9639 4944**

CONTEMPORARY 14/20

As Punch Lane nears its 20th anniversary it's been reinvigorated by new appointments: chef Luke Croston (formerly at Reserve, and Restaurant Serge Vieira in France), and Simon Denman as sommelier. The room remains intimate and dim, with dark timber finishes, red leather chairs and plump cushions. Theatre-goers flock for fresh, modern flavours that can go the traditional entree-main route or present as share-plates. Snacks of prawn bonbons (rolled in brik pastry, then fried) with chilli and lime salt, and cheese fritters (like croquettes) make excellent drinking companions. Starters of pork rillettes and discs of coppa with bitter leaves and pistachios, and spanner crab with confit tomatoes and pickled yellow beetroot are as attractive on the plate as the palate. A dish of herb-crusted John Dory fillets on braised capsicum and chorizo balances delicate and bold flavours, as does tender sirloin and braised beef cheek with rainbow chard and blood plums. Playful desserts might include an airy chocolate mousse with tart poached rhubarb and lime curd.

Open Mon–Fri noon–3pm; Mon–Sat 5.30–10.30pm; Sun 5.30–9.30pm
Typical prices E $24 **M** $38 **D** $14
Cards DC AE MC V Eftpos
Wine Long pan-European list plus good Australian producers; about 20 by the glass
Owner Martin Pirc
Chef Luke Croston
Seats 65; outdoor seating; bar
www.punchlane.com.au

And ... The bar's good late night or pre-show.

Pure South

River level, 3 Southgate Avenue, Southbank **9699 4600**

CONTEMPORARY **14/20**

This riverside restaurant treats Tasmania as its larder and its inspiration, plucking the best of the island state's rich produce. There are plump Tasmanian Pacific oysters, Huon salmon and farmed venison. The sublime ingredients are treated well and the cooking is delicate, creative and meticulous. How about crackling-topped pork belly, from Winnaleah, with figs and walnut maple dressing; carpaccio of venison; char-grilled grass-fed Angus steaks; chicken ballotine; lamb double-rib cutlet? Desserts range from a simple but luscious apple tart to lemon myrtle creme brulee to coconut meringue, and there's a handsome selection of Tassie cheeses. King Island triple cream brie, Roaring Forties blue, Bruny Island cheese, sweet and hard are all served with pickled walnuts and spiced pear. Take an outside table (it's sheltered and heated), and you are right by the promenade and the coffee-coloured river. Service is warm and knowledgeable and the table linen is crisp as a Tassie morning.

Open Mon–Fri noon–2.30pm, 6–9.30pm; Sat 5.30pm–late; Sun noon–9.30pm
Typical prices E $20 **M** $38 **D** $16
Cards DC AE MC V Eftpos
Wine First-class list: Tasmanian particularly, Australian and European generally; plenty by the glass
Owners Philip Kennedy & Peter Leary
Chef Dwayne Bourke
Seats 100; outdoor seating; private room; bar
www.puresouth.com.au

And … At lunch on a weekday you can get two courses for $39, three courses for $49.

Quaff

436 Toorak Road, Toorak **9827 4484**

CONTEMPORARY **13/20**

Quaff is reliable and elegant, a place where Toorak locals dine habitually and where strolling shoppers land for a generous, well-mannered meal. Smart, straight-backed young waiters tend a comfortable room that's dressed with starched linen and panelled with dark wood. Added ambience comes courtesy of the great outdoors when Quaff throws open its folding front window. The menu hugs the conservative side of contemporary. Asian influences may be evident in starters like seared yellowfin tuna with a seaweed and carrot salad, or pork belly with glazed shallot and peanut brittle. For main, try roasted duck served with a generous amount of jus and two squirts of carrot and celeriac puree, or fish pie with a creamy white-wine and truffle sauce. Dessert could be a three-storey mango millefeuille, which may be a little clunky with mango-cream layered between thick pastry; the flavour, though, is spot-on. Street seating means you can stop for lunch, with a Number 8 tram on the side.

Open Daily noon–10pm
Typical prices E $19 **M** $34 **D** $18
Cards DC AE MC V Eftpos
Wine Excellent, broad-ranging list of Australian and French wines; 14 by the glass
Owners Bruce McConnell, John Psanis & James Klapanis
Chef John Psanis
Seats 60; outdoor seating; private rooms
www.quaff.net.au

And … Upstairs function rooms are popular for celebrations and 21st birthdays, with canapes or set menus.

Quanjude

299 Queen Street, City **9670 0091**

CHINESE **12.5/20**

The original Quanjude roast duck restaurant opened in Beijing in 1864. Its local namesake is an outpost of a franchise that sells more than two million ducks a year in China alone. Beijing's roast duck is a different bird to Melbourne's, where the signature dish is less fatty, hence it's a little dry and less flavoursome, albeit wrapped in excellent wafer-thin pancakes. It still comes carved at table with ceremony and skill, amid a lush fitout of vermillion and imperial gold, fine table linen and crockery, although service from uniformed waiters can be slow at times. While duck and its component parts - soup, tongues, webs and gizzards - form the centrepiece, other offerings range from the vinegary crunch of sour and spicy cucumber sticks, delicate and juicy soft-shell crab dusted with spicy salt, scallops braised in a surprisingly gentle Sichuan sauce to more prosaic dishes such as lemon chicken. Desserts include pineapple and banana fritters and out-of-house icecreams.

Open Daily 6–11pm; Sun–Fri noon–3pm
Typical prices E $9 **M** $35 **D** $8
Cards DC AE MC V Eftpos
Wine A strong list of local wines; several selections by the glass
Owner William Cheung
Chef Edward Xu
Seats 120; private room
www.quanjude.com.au

And ... History buffs should look for the photos of famous customers who have dined at the Beijing flagship.

Red Emperor

Shop M10, level 2, Southgate, Southbank **9699 4170**

CHINESE **14/20**

Red Emperor, a Southgate stalwart, has had a nip and tuck. It has moved to the floor below (but kept the river view), shrinking a little in size and donning a new crimson and cream colour scheme. Even the menu has had a little makeover, although tried-and-true favourites haven't gone anywhere, which is good news for lovers of this emperor's deft and vibrant Chinese cooking. While entrees and desserts tread familiar paths, the extensive menu sings with fragrant and heady provincial dishes like spicy ma po tofu, rice-wine chicken (served with the homely touch of folded-back foil, its accompanying bready 'silver thread' roll is perfect for soaking up the sauce) or bak kut the, a lush bowl of soft pork belly, meaty shiitakes and succulent beancurd in a herbal soup tingling with goji berries. Seafood is tank-fresh and vegetarians are refreshingly well catered for. Service is conversational and informative without dropping the ball.

Open Mon–Sat noon–3pm; Mon–Fri 6–10.30pm; Sat 6–11pm; Sun 11am–4pm, 6–10pm
Typical prices E $11 **M** $30 **D** $8.50
Cards AE MC V
Wine Broad-ranging list to suit all budgets, with a dizzying array by the glass
Owners Charles Ng, Raymond Cheung & Christine Yong
Chef Hon-Kau Hui
Seats 150; outdoor seating; private room
www.redemperor.com.au

And ... There's a range of excellent value banquets, including a couple for vegetarians.

Red Spice Road

27 McKillop Street, City **9603 1601**

MODERN ASIAN **12.5/20**

Dark timber floors, mood lighting, striking splashes of red, an enormous UFO-sized lantern – Red Spice Road is one sexy, stylish space. A largely thirtysomething crowd congregates on long communal tables to dissect the working week over big-flavoured dishes that favour South-East Asian cuisine's sweeter side. The pork belly is sublime with sticky pull-apart meat and crunchy crackling. Reverse the damage with the accompanying refreshing minty apple slaw. A Vietnamese-style shredded banana blossom salad is similarly light and zesty and comes with a sharp chilli bite, while glossy eggplant pieces are deep-fried and teamed with cashews 'kung po' style. Cracking through the passionfruit brulee with puffed wild rice (think sophisticated Rice Bubbles) is a delight, but the mint-and-chocolate parfait can be a touch stodgy. Service is friendly and efficient; slower pacing would enable diners to better relish the experience.

Open Daily noon–3pm; Mon–Fri 5–10pm; Sat–Sun 6–10pm
Typical prices E $16 **M** $34 **D** $14
Cards DC AE MC V Eftpos
Wine Asian-inspired cocktails, beers, Australian and NZ wines; many by the glass and carafe
Owner Apples & Pears Entertainment Group
Chef John McLeay
Seats 150; outdoor seating; private room; bar
www.redspiceroad.com

And ... Good-value 'early bird' weeknight dinners (between 5pm and 6pm, out by 7pm) offer three dishes for $25.

Richmond Hill Cafe & Larder

48-50 Bridge Road, Richmond **9421 2808**

CONTEMPORARY **14/20**

Elegant dishes, top produce, great wine and a captivating cheese room – it's little wonder this cafe-foodstore is still going strong after all these years. Its genteel, light-filled, wicker-furnished dining room complements dishes like a summery salad of prawns, prosciutto, watermelon, avocado and roasted white peaches with rye bread crisps. More hearty is roasted chicken with a Mediterranean vegetable stew, salsa verde, mixed beans and gremolata, while beautifully presented sage-stuffed pork belly with caramelised apples, smoked bacon, celeriac and mulled cider-soaked prunes reveals the kitchen's fine-dining flair. Add efficient service, and you have a delightful lunch-spot and place to enjoy a glass or two from the well-curated wine list. Perhaps linger over a cheese plate with fruit-and-nut loaf and signature-branded quince paste, or come for breakfast (available till 3pm). Then, load up with artisanal breads, olive oil, charcuterie, cheese and chocolates to take home.

Open Sun–Thurs 8.30am–5pm; Fri–Sat 8.30am–6pm (no weekend bookings, except for groups of eight or more)
Typical prices E $17.50 **M** $28 **D** $13
Cards DC AE MC V Eftpos
Wine Terrific list of Australian and European varietals; plenty by the glass, half bottle and carafe
Owner Louis Daoud
Chef Franco Caruso
Seats 70; outdoor seating
www.rhcl.com.au

And ... Check the website for details on cheese and wine matching workshops.

Richmond Seafood Tavern

5 Rae Street, Fitzroy North **9489 1974**

SEAFOOD **14/20**

Danny Cecchi began his seafood career managing Rubira's Seafood Restaurant before opening the Richmond Seafood Tavern nearly a decade ago. Now he has returned to the original Rubira's site but continues to call it the Richmond Seafood Tavern (in Fitzroy North). The decor has been lightened but the seafood remains fresh and carefully handled. Seafood chowder is thick and flavoursome and oysters are shucked on request. A half-and-half plate of chilli and garlic king prawns makes an excellent starter, but the best way to explore entrees is with a platter, which might feature natural, mornay and kilpatrick oysters, prawns, scallops, prawn rolls, salted snapper croquettes and some of the best calamari fritti in Melbourne. Fish can be ordered pan-fried, in a heavenly light beer batter, in breadcrumbs, or in Cajun spices or egg wash. A speciality is sweet-tasting garfish with balsamic-drizzled tomato and onion salad and super fat chips. Finish with pudding: perhaps self-saucing chocolate or sticky date.

Open Tues–Fri noon–4pm; Wed–Sat 6pm–late
Typical prices E $16 **M** $32 **D** $12.50
Cards AE MC V Eftpos
Wine Well-balanced, quality list of predominantly Australian and NZ wines with reasonable mark-ups and covering all price points; 12 by the glass
Owners Danny Cecchi, Simone Greaney & Jody Smith
Chef Abi Gatuteo
Seats 90; outdoor seating; private room
www.richseatav.com.au

And ... Platters can be tailored to suit tastes and budgets – ask your waiter.

River Kwai

Shop 3, 1310 Centre Road, Clayton **9545 5688**

THAI/BURMESE **12/20**

Rich red walls decorated with sweeping flashes of gold and carved wooden turtles warm this large but cosy dining room. The menu turns up the temperature, where Thai and Burmese dishes revel in more heat than sweet. Entrees are familiar Thai offerings, but a home-made spring roll with thin, hot, house-made sweet chilli is good, as is a tender, marinated prawn cloaked in a crisp pastry shell. Green pawpaw salad adorned with splayed, salted crab is an invigorating collision of warm, crisp crab and cold, zingy salad. Burmese flavours get a real run in the curry department (they favour a blend of onion, garlic and ginger, while Thai curries lean on coconut cream) – the chunky potato and prawn curry is a homely, fragrant, uncomplicated stew. A simple pad Thai lacks a little signature sweetness, but the light and moreish kaffir-lime panna cotta served with coconut icecream makes up for it.

Open Daily 5.30–10pm
Typical prices E $11.90 **M** $20.90 **D** $10.90
Cards MC V Eftpos
Wine Brief, almost exclusively Australian list of budget-friendly usual suspects; nine by the glass; BYO (corkage $7 a bottle)
Owner Julia Phahonvanich
Chef Pratana Phahonvanich
Seats 70
www.riverkwai.com.au

And ... For full immersion, try the seven-course set menus available in full Thai or Burmese options.

Rockpool Bar & Grill

Crown Complex, Southbank **8648 1900**

CONTEMPORARY **16.5/20**

Squint and you can almost make out *Mad Men*'s Don Draper in the corner cradling a whisky, because Rockpool has Manhattan-like qualities, with double-height ceilings and claret-coloured banquettes. Equally impressive and seductive, it's apt for business lunches or romantic dinners. Though dry-aged, wood-fire grilled meat is the restaurant's stock in trade, the broad menu offers a wealth of options, from confit duck to crisp-fried flathead, shucked-to-order oysters and an elegant starter of raw tuna, ocean trout and kingfish with fresh wasabi and finger lime. Though a generous, juicy rotisserie chicken may tempt you to stray away from the paddock, it's the beef – world-class wagyu, grass- or grain-fed, from minute-steak to rib-eye – that lures most. Sides are terrific, perhaps wagyu-fat garlic and rosemary potatoes, bitey Warragul greens or cheesy macaroni. A huge service team means the odd hitch occurs: sticky wine perhaps arriving with the last bite of a luscious fig tart. Otherwise, like Don, Rockpool is a smooth operator.

Open Daily 6–11pm; Sun–Fri noon–3pm
Typical prices E $30 **M** $49 **D** $21
Cards DC AE MC V Eftpos
Wine A serious 50-plus-page list, including museum vintages and little-known boutique labels; handled and aged with care
Owners Neil Perry, Trish Richards & David Doyle
Chefs Neil Perry & Will Cowan-Lunn
Seats 200; private rooms; bar
www.rockpool.com/melbourne

And ... The petits fours are luscious, like passionfruit marshmallow and chocolate bark.

Rose Bar & Diner

309 Bay Street, Port Melbourne **9681 8550**

CONTEMPORARY **13.5/20**

Rose Diner is a smart, modern dining room in a revamped pub, but its food is nostalgia-inspired. The owners – with gastropubs Royal Saxon and Little Creatures on their CVs – have kept the building's bones, exposing bare brick, and adding black bentwood chairs, olive greens, and well-spaced Tasmanian oak tables. The menu reboots some classics, with an English skew. Think vol au vents, perhaps filled with snapper and dill. Steak diane uses Gippsland Black Angus porterhouse, sauced with cream, brandy and dijon. There's usually a pie, perhaps a pithiviers filled with quail, wood-smoked pork belly and mushrooms, a deep purple knob of apple jelly on the side. Welsh rarebit croquettes are crisp and crumbed, and Hervey Bay scallops – plump, pan-roasted and tender – are luscious in their simplicity. You'll need sides, and the hand-cut chips are brilliant. For afters, there's 'Mum's English trifle', with groggy sponge, custard, cream, berries and banana. Service is young and upbeat.

Open Mon–Thurs noon–late; Fri–Sat noon–1am; Sun noon–11pm
Typical prices E $10 **M** $27 **D** $14
Cards AE MC V Eftpos
Wine A sparky, well-priced list of Australians with a good range of European offerings from Austria, Spain and Italy, plus beers and cider on tap
Owners Ash Cranston, Steed Sherriff & Blake Oakley
Chef Stephen Drake
Seats 60; outdoor seating; private room; bar
www.rosediner.com.au

And ... There's also upstairs bar Cherry Rose and Little Rose cafe out back.

Royal Saxon

545 Church Street, Richmond **9429 5277**

ITALIAN/PUB DINING **13.5/20**

When the Royal Saxon opened to much Facebook-generated fanfare in 2009, it was a minor victory just getting past the queues of Nudie- and Scanlan-clad bodies. These days, while the Saxon may no longer be Richmond's zeitgeist bar, the atmosphere remains keen, as do the culinary standards. Saxon by name but Italian in nature, the menu – printed on paper placemats – runs from excellent thin-based pizzas (topped, say, with pork belly, stretched-curd caciocavallo cheese, garlic, rosemary and fennel) to more cheffy items. A Sicilian-style salad of octopus and celery hearts, cut mandoline-thin and layered with chilli and lemon, is delightfully zesty, while heartier appetites will be sated by a roasted Berkshire pork shoulder wrapped in salty prosciutto and served with cannellini beans and wilted spinach. There are iconic dishes, too: penne carbonara, tiramisu. The Saxon's sassy fitout – fig-tree-dominated courtyard and deliberately raw 'urban ruin' design – creates various nooks and spaces for drinkers and diners. 'Like' this pub.

Open Mon–Sat noon–11pm; Sun noon–10pm; no bookings
Typical prices E $16 **M** $32 **D** $13
Cards AE MC V Eftpos
Wine No mere 'pub list', and deep (100-odd), adventuring from Spanish cavas to French gamays, and the expected Italian and Italianate varietals
Owners Paul Olynyk & Julian Gerner
Chef Glenn Laurie
Seats 65; outdoor seating; bar
www.royalsaxon.com.au

And ... City views from the upstairs balcony.

Rumi

116 Lygon Street, Brunswick East **9388 8255**

MIDDLE EASTERN **13.5/20**

Rowdy, buzzy and unfussy, Rumi is the perfect neighbourhood restaurant, a modern Middle Eastern stronghold. Service is straightforward and friendly, the decor casual (compressed concrete tables, wooden school chairs), and the authentic, rustic share-plates arrive with pace. Order up a spread and start on crisp pastry cigars filled with a salty mix of haloumi, feta and kasseri (a signature dish) and charry quail kebabs with shallots and garlic sauce. Move on to freekeh salad with toasted slivered almonds and tart pomegranate dressing; Persian lamb meatballs cooked in a sweet tomato and saffron sauce; a side of green beans sprinkled with crumbly sheep's milk cheese; or fall-apart lamb shoulder slow-roasted on the bone, served with a little jug of sweet mint sauce. And for dessert? Maybe date pastries and mint tea or Lebanese coffee. Rumi isn't the place where they'll take your coat or top up your wine, but it is the place for a relaxed group catch-up, a casual date or an early-bird family dinner. It's fun, upbeat and authentically Levantine.

Open Daily 6–10pm
Typical prices E $12.50 **M** $21 **D** $7.50
Cards MC V Eftpos
Wine Short list featuring half a dozen Lebanese wines; excellent range of anise-scented arak
Owners Joseph & Natalie Abboud
Chef Joseph Abboud
Seats 100
www.rumirestaurant.com.au

And ... Rumi's banquets are top value and a great way to sample the signature dishes.

Sails on the Bay

15 Elwood Foreshore, Elwood **9525 6933**

CONTEMPORARY **12.5/20**

'On the bay' can describe anything within a sniff of a salty breeze; here, the description is literal. Sails' huge windows are one metre from the sand, giving unimpeded views of beach-walkers, swimmers and scavenging seagulls. The nautical theme continues inside with 'sails' strung up in the style of a grand marquee. Linen tablecloths and padded chairs deliver a dressed-up look that makes this a popular place for weddings and functions. The food has formality too, at times magnified by fussy touches. A sardine entree presents two whole fish atop a smear of basil puree, their heads resting on cherry tomatoes, with a dob of tomato sorbet and two piles of almond and garlic crumble. For mains, ocean trout cooked sous-vide might lack the strength of flavour of its accompanying braised fennel risotto. A dessert of apple compote is more successful, lifted with a silky vanilla panna cotta. Service is friendly but can lack polish given the prices. Oh, but the view ...

Open Daily noon–3pm, 6–9.30pm
Typical prices E $22 **M** $42 **D** $15.50
Cards AE MC V Eftpos
Wine All Australian regions and varieties well represented; 17 by the glass; BYO Mon–Thurs Jan–Nov (corkage $10 a bottle)
Owners Derek & Monica Fuller
Chef Kelvin Shaw
Seats 120; private room
www.sailsonthebay.com

And ... Two-course lunch plus a glass of wine and coffee is $40, Monday to Saturday.

Saint Peter's

6 Melbourne Place, City **9663 9882**

ITALIAN **13.5/20**

No longer a seafood-focused fine-diner, Saint Peter's is now a jaunty Italian trattoria. This new, casual persona suits the laneway locale and split-level room with classic wood-and-white finish. The short menu is a kind of homecoming for chef Maurice Esposito, who is cooking the regional Italian dishes he was raised on, using Victorian produce. You'll still find a smattering of seafood, such as an intricate entree of calamari hood filled with a whole prawn and seasoned with rosemary salt. More home-style mains might include sweet Dory fillets on a relatively heavy kidney-bean bed, or a saffron-stained spaghetti special tossed with prawns. All pastas and risottos, perhaps wagyu lasagne and portobello mushroom risotto, come in two sizes – good for the lunch crowd. Italian desserts might include Sicilian almond and orange cake. Everything on the one-page wine list is available by the glass, but only three whites and three reds are opened at any time – first in have first choice. It's a fun, social set-up that sees the Saint loosening its halo a little.

Open Mon–Fri noon–3pm; Mon–Sat 6–11.30pm
Typical prices E $16 **M** $29 **D** $15
Cards DC AE MC V Eftpos
Wine A brief list of mostly Italian DOC-certified wines; BYO (corkage $15 a bottle)
Owner & chef Maurice Esposito
Seats 70; outdoor seating; private room; bar
www.stpetersrestaurantandbar.com

And ... Finish with affogato and flavour it with the liqueur of your choice.

San Telmo

14 Meyers Place, City **9650 5525**

ARGENTINIAN **14.5/20**

Argentinian tucker is not too familiar in Victoria, but San Telmo could change all that. Few expenses were spared in making this wood-and-leather shrine to charcoal-seared beef as authentic as can be: the parrilla or grill, crafted there and assembled here, is magnificent. Breakfast aside, a meal here revolves around flame-grilled beef, ideally secondary cuts such as flank or hanger steaks, meaty ribs and delicate, fire-kissed sweetbreads – all cooked over Mallee root coals, all offered with lashings of house-made mild chimichurri sauce or perky salsa. Supporting acts are hardly second fiddles: deep-fried pastry empanadas, especially the cheesy ones, are superb, as are addictive corn and polenta chips with chipotle chilli mayo. Flame-roasted vegies and lively salads (think palm heart, pear, jamon and mozzarella) complete the picture. There's pudding, of course: seductive dulce de leche flan should be compulsory; the alfajor cookies are nearly as good.

Open Mon–Wed 8am–11pm; Thurs–Fri 8am–midnight; Sat 9am–midnight; Sun 9am–11pm
Typical prices E $14 **M** $35 **D** $14
Cards DC AE MC V Eftpos
Wine All-Argentinian list of whites and reds from the modest to the opulent; good selection at both levels by the glass, but don't miss the malbec
Owners Dave Parker, Micky Parker, Jason & Renee McConnell
Chefs Mike Patrick & Chris Moran
Seats 75; outdoor seating; private room; bar
www.santelmo.com.au

And ... Breakfasts run from empanadas to hazelnut bread with caramel, labna and apple.

Sapore

3-5 Fitzroy Street, St Kilda **9534 9666**

MODERN EUROPEAN **14.5/20**

When the name of your restaurant means 'flavour' in Italian, expectations are immediately high. Thankfully, this St Kilda stalwart hits the nail on the head, delivering mod-Mediterranean fare with flavour aplenty. The tightly packed dining room (mind the glassware as you squeeze between tables) packs a punch, too, with curvaceous rust- and mustard-coloured walls, an infectious buzz, and friendly, if sometimes distracted, service. A shared starter (perhaps salumi with pickled carrots, arancini on a smear of creamy goat's cheese, and beef carpaccio strewn with a zingy mix of capers, cornichons and micro cress) shows a generosity of spirit: lashings of food; lashings of taste. Main courses are similarly bold, such as wonderfully rich ossobuco served with parsley-flecked risotto, golden nubs of confit garlic, and a heady saffron broth poured at the table. The kitchen doesn't hold back in the dessert department, either, with intensely sweet banana bomboloni served with a slick of salted caramel.

Open Daily noon–3pm, 6–10pm
Typical prices E $19 **M** $38 **D** $14
Cards DC AE MC V
Wine Extensive wine list with astute local options and standout Italians, with 18 available by the glass or carafe; BYO Sun night (corkage $10 a bottle)
Owners Luisa Lucchesi & Simon Moss
Chefs Simon Moss & Chris Lillico
Seats 120; outdoor seating; private room
www.sapore.com.au

citibank Privileges

And ... Finish the meal in proper Italian fashion with grappa and an espresso.

Sarti

6 Russell Place, City **9639 7822**

ITALIAN **15/20**

Wild boar. Suckling pig. Chestnuts. Pig's ear. It may sound like the menu of an Italian hunting lodge, but two wallaby dishes are a giveaway you're actually in the back of Bourke (Street); in fact, Russell Place, and the surroundings are far less rustic. The floors are freshly glossy, there's a long bar, tweed and leather banquettes, and jaunty red details such as a beautiful bunch of glass chillies. Appealing little starters or stuzzichini are charmers meant to share. Some are a bite, like silverbeet rolled around kingfish with a hit of sour, citrusy yuzu; some are several bites, think delicate wallaby carpaccio with a crunch of native pepper and malt, or prawn carpaccio with aromatic mandarin oil. Duck-egg pappardelle tangles with wild boar ragu, nuggets of veal stew come with artichoke and crisp, doughy cauliflower 'cous cous'. Service is polished but unstuffy. Pistachio panna cotta with a ball of caramelised popcorn to pull apart, or sugary, warm, puffy doughnuts will catch any prey.

Open Mon–Fri noon–3pm; Mon–Sat 6–11pm
Typical prices E $18 **M** $39 **D** $15
Cards DC AE MC V
Wine Take yourself to Tuscany for lunch with a long list of Italians, plus plenty of locals, with side trips to France and Spain
Owners Joe Mammone, Riccardo Momesso & Michael Badr
Chef Riccardo Momesso
Seats 80; outdoor seating; private room; bar
www.sartirestaurant.com.au

And ... There's a $100 tasting menu; explore Riccardo Momesso's book *Antonio & Lucia*, too.

Scopri

191 Nicholson Street, Carlton **9347 8252**

ITALIAN **14.5/20**

Pride in the food of Italy's various regions shines forth at this little gem, discreetly set on a stretch of Nicholson Street that doesn't see a lot of foot traffic. There's a happily subdued atmosphere in the pleasant dining room with its whitewashed walls, stiff napery, dark wood and framed Barbaresco posters. Dinner might begin with well-rested quail, pancetta-wrapped, grilled and licked with sticky vincotto, then proceed through delicate John Dory-stuffed squid-ink ravioli in crayfish bisque (seafood is a feature in the primi piatti) or a gelatinous wet roast of kid in white wine with aromatic vegetables. Risotto, offered in two sizes, comes with proudly house-made tomato passata and smoked ricotta. Perhaps conclude with a cannolo, a thin pastry cylinder filled with coffee gelato, sweetened ricotta and hazelnut zabaglione. The wine-matching expertise and unforced hospitality of co-owner Anthony Scutella should ensure you step back out to the street with a sense of genuine warmth.

Open Tues–Fri noon–3pm; Tues–Sat 6–10pm
Typical prices E $20 **M** $34 **D** $14.50
Cards DC AE MC V Eftpos
Wine This non-partisan list is as likely to showcase pinot grigio from the Yarra Valley as from Alto Adige; BYO (corkage $10 a bottle)
Owners Anthony Scutella & Alison Foley
Chef Salvatore Caccioppoli
Seats 50; private room
www.scopri.com.au

And ... Watch the website for special-menu one-off events.

Gary Mehigan, Celebrity Chef

Scusami

Mid-level, Southgate, Southbank **9699 4111**

ITALIAN **13/20**

Above the river, spot-lit Melbourne before you, baby grand behind, it's clear why Scusami remains a special-occasion favourite. But in a city of hip, bare-tabled stars it's equally clear Scusami is old guard. Linen is starched; so are the usually attentive staff, and the chef is in the kitchen rather than on TV. The food is elegant and flavoursome, without breaking new ground. Start with warm olives and rosemary, or parmesan with house-made grissini, crostini and reduced balsamic, or soft, paper-thin DOC prosciutto interspersed with rockmelon slivers on a vincotto-dotted plate. Hefty mains include beautifully seasoned, sliced veal pan-fried with seasonal vegetables (maybe globe artichokes and asparagus). Or seafood panzanella: crouton salad with mussels and king prawns, zinging with basil and tomato-balsamic dressing. There's tiramisu, or try the rich pyramid of chocolate mousse with a raspberry hit. The tab can be up in expense-account territory, but Scusami is also a place to splurge. After all, the view's priceless.

Open Sun–Fri noon–3pm, 5.30–10pm; Sat 5.30–10.30pm
Typical prices E $25 **M** $45 **D** $18
Cards DC AE MC V Eftpos
Wine A long, mostly Australian and NZ list with some Italians; 12 by the glass; BYO (corkage $40 a bottle)
Owners Jonathon Alston, Emily Spinks & Fiona Spinks
Chefs Jonathon Alston & Joey Tababa
Seats 100; outdoor seating; private room; bar
www.scusami.com.au

And ... Adjoining L'Osteria is perfect for a pre-theatre quick bite or if Scusami is full.

Seamstress

113 Lonsdale Street, City **9663 6363**

MODERN ASIAN **14/20**

In this city's great culinary tradition, Seamstress takes 'tucked away' to a whole new level. Three levels, in fact: even once you've found the former garment factory, there's a staircase threading you to two bars or the dining room, playfully fitted out with fabrics, coathangers, suspended bouquets and locker boxes. Compartmentalisation continues with a menu split into 'S', 'M' and 'L'. But instead of doing the math, let perky staff determine portions and pacing, leaving you to settle in with snake-bean and sweet-potato wonton softened by pea foam, or twice-cooked five-spice quail sharpened by cucumber and pickled ginger. The weaving of flavours never creates confusion, and flexible dish sizes mean both 'S' and 'L' groups can enjoy hands-on, tempura-like soft-shell crab freshened by sugar snaps and chilli sauce. But you might decide some dishes, such as pork neck with glass noodles, bitter melon and soy-imbued mushrooms, or spiced chocolate pudding with whiskey sabayon, are too good to share.

Open Mon–Fri noon–2.30pm; Mon–Sat 6–11pm
Typical prices E $19 **M** $38 **D** $15
Cards AE MC V Eftpos
Wine A local range well suited to the food; ask the staff for guidance
Owner Tally Konstas
Chef Chris Terlikar
Seats 50; bar
www.seamstress.com.au

And ... The good service and tailored look continues upstairs at the Seamstress cocktail bar.

Senoritas

16 Meyers Place, City **9639 7437**

MEXICAN **13/20**

Day of the Dead celebrations collide with a macabre pop-culture aesthetic at Senoritas, a laneway bar-eatery where a cadaverous statue greets diners and flickering votive candles set the mood. One of the most recent additions to the city's thriving Mexican food scene boasts of its authenticity via the citizenship of the head chef. Soft corn tortillas are steamed over cooking meats before being filled, perhaps with shredded pork, pickled onion and house-made habanero salsa, or fried trevally with a salsa made with beer. They're sized (and priced) as bar snacks, which makes sense when tackling the list of real-deal margaritas and Mexican beers and tequilas. Ceviche – perhaps prawn with mango, or kingfish and scallop – might be a little underpowered in the acid department, unlike a flavour-packed pozoles – shredded pork in a hearty broth with hominy (corn kernels) and salad greens, or a classic chicken mole with chocolate-spiked pounded sauce. Finish on a sweet note with sugar-drenched baguette pudding topped with queso fresco.

Open Mon–Fri noon–3pm; Mon–Sat 6pm–late
Typical prices E $9 **M** $32 **D** $7
Cards AE MC V Eftpos
Wine Short and global, augmented by Mexican beers and tequila
Owners Linda Temani, Tom Gunson, Matteo Bruno, Matt Gillman & Zaac Woodhead
Chef Hugo Reyes
Seats 65; bar
www.senoritas.com.au

And ... It's claimed entrees were favourites of Mexican artists Frida Kahlo and Diego Rivera.

Sette Bello

540 Springvale Road, Glen Waverley **9574 8000**

ITALIAN **14/20**

Sometimes, from the moment you walk through the door, you know it's going to be good. With its modern design, polished wooden floors, high ceilings and generous windows, Sette Bello has an aura of graceful energy and spacious comfort from breakfast time until after dark. Welcoming, efficient, knowledgeable staff serve classic and modern Italian food. Try beef carpaccio, dressed with olive oil, capers, parmesan and Corella pear, or seared slices of tuna with mango salsa; other entree choices might include salt-and-pepper calamari on a salad of radicchio and rocket. For mains, fish of the day may be a hunk of roasted snapper fillet, juicy and succulent, simply served with lemon; an equally good half-duck could come double-roasted with orange glaze and sweet-potato puree. You might prefer rabbit braised in the Sicilian style with almonds and raisins, or one of several pasta offerings. Desserts include tiramisu laced with Strega liqueur, or you might choose a platter of three cheeses.

Open Mon–Fri 7am–10pm; Sat–Sun noon–10pm
Typical prices E $18 **M** $35 **D** $15
Cards AE MC V Eftpos
Wine More than 20 pages of Australian, Italian and French wines; museum releases from selected producers; 18 by the glass
Owners Frank Ciorciani, Peter & Elvis Chiaravalle, Joe DiCintio
Chef Joe DiCintio
Seats 85; outdoor seating
www.settebello.com.au

And ... On warm nights you can have a table on the roomy outside terrace.

The Sharing House

35 Dukes Walk, South Wharf, Docklands **9245 9800**

CONTEMPORARY **14/20**

The Sharing House is exactly what the name says: a place where the lengthy menu is tailored for sharing and a chilled-out vibe introduced by the Lego-covered bar and astroturf wall is brought home by young and enthusiastic staff members. Chef Mark Briggs plays down his past as a chef at Vue de Monde with dishes such as the Lancashire hotpot and a super-fun rabbit and cauliflower 'popcorn' with Marie Rose sauce, but occasionally he lets his fine-dining flag fly. Ocean trout gravlax with jellied, freeze-dried and compressed apple is pretty as well as tasty; ditto the gnocchi with crisp sweetbreads, spanner crab and a brown-butter sauce. But mostly you'll find retro classics with oodles of modern style: ossobuco spaghetti bolognaise, duck a l'orange and deconstructed treacle tart for dessert. Owner and serial restaurateur Paul Mathis has a love of the conceptual, and this one – a pioneer of the new South Wharf precinct – captures the zeitgeist.

Open Daily noon–4pm, 6pm–late
Typical prices E $12 **M** $24 **D** $12
Cards AE MC V Eftpos
Wine A good global selection across a wide price spectrum
Owner Paul Mathis
Chef Mark Briggs
Seats 85; outdoor seating; bar
www.thesharinghouse.com.au

And ... The Sharing House is a decent bar as well; there's a great global wine list.

Shira Nui

247 Springvale Road, Glen Waverley **9886 7755**

JAPANESE **14.5/20**

It says much about owner-chef Hiro Nishikura's food that after 10 years his small, inconspicuous restaurant in Glen Waverley remains one of Melbourne's must-try places for Japanese. Dine contentedly from the a la carte menu at a table, or opt for the chef's rightfully praised sushi selection (omakase). If the latter, you'll prop at the counter and leave the largely seafood procession entirely in the nimble hands of Nishikura and his animated crew. Typically, the degustation-style menu runs to nine courses – two pieces per round – with theatrics (think flashing blades and blowtorch) and helpful direction, such as when not to add soy. Included might be glistening slices of wonderfully fresh cod with flying-fish roe and a hit of wasabi, melt-away sirloin strip or daikon-swaddled mackerel marinated in sweet vinegar – all over sticky sushi rice. For larger appetites and deeper pockets – the omakase option isn't cheap – there's no need to stop. Sixteen stands as the house record.

Open Tues–Sat noon–2pm, 6–10pm
Typical prices E $17 **M** $25 **D** $13
Cards DC AE MC V Eftpos
Wine Small, affordable list of 10 wines (five each of white and red) and four by the glass; also sake and Japanese beer
Owner Hiro Nishikura
Chefs Hiro Nishikura, Eiki Ando & Yung-Ju Lee
Seats 25

And ... Be sure to book as the limited seating means the restaurant is often full.

Shoya

25 Market Lane, City **9650 0848**

JAPANESE **15.5/20**

Imagine six levels devoted to Japanese fine-dining. Shigeo Nonaka did, and he has created a stunning experience from the ground up: each level variously dedicated to relaxed yakiniku barbecue, to modern Japanese dining, right up to the karaoke bar. Three giant calligraphy works (representing 'imagine', 'observe' and 'experience') hang in the lowlit middle floors, which are split into table or traditional low-table seating, patrolled by watchful staff. It's here that Nonaka, at the sushi counter, oversees his nouvelle Japanese degustation menus (a la carte also available). Every dish is beautifully balanced and enriched by soft, delicate flavours and contrasting textures, such as diced pan-fried abalone with a smooth monkfish liver pâté and home-made cream cheese; slow-braised, fall-apart ox tongue; sashimi in a frosted glass bowl; or the signature deep-fried quail egg wrapped in a scallop mash. 'Imagine, observe and experience': Shoya shows imagination, is a sight to behold and is a singular experience to savour.

Open Daily noon–2.30pm; Sun–Thurs 6–10.30pm; Fri–Sat 6–11pm
Typical prices E $15.50 **M** $28 **D** $12; degustation $100–$180
Cards DC AE MC V Eftpos
Wine Almost 250 wines; plus sakes and shochus
Owners Ron Lim & Shigeo Nonaka
Chef Shigeo Nonaka
Seats 120; private room; bar
www.shoya.com.au

And ... There are three omakase degustation menus, ranging from 12 to 14 courses.

Siam 1

65 Koornang Road, Carnegie **9571 7334**

THAI **14/20**

At its best Thai cuisine is at once aromatic, spicy and spellbinding. It's also relatively hard to find in Melbourne. Hallelujah, then, that wine bar-restaurant Siam 1 is rectifying matters with its elegant take on traditional fare in a classy (if a little cramped) setting. Chef and co-owner Wichit Jimmy Maneeboon has a deft hand with the spicing, and can ramp up the heat without allowing it to dominate. Cases in point are the som tum (shredded green papaya with snake beans, tomato, garlic and roasted crushed peanuts) and the 'crying tiger' beef salad, its hot-sweet-salty-sour flavours getting along famously. Sharing is the way to go here, and while there's plenty of seafood on offer, you'd be more than satisfied by the refined, fragrant roasted red duck curry with pea eggplant and chunks of fresh pineapple, or the crisp chunks of pork belly with a zesty sauce of tamarind, fried shallots, red onion and mint. Add informed and unobtrusive service, and you have quite a find.

Open Mon–Thurs 5.30–10.30pm; Fri–Sat 5.30–11.30pm; Sun 5.30–10pm; Thurs–Fri noon–3pm
Typical prices E $14 **M** $27 **D** $12
Cards AE MC V Eftpos
Wine Thoughtful list of Old and New World offerings; 14 by the glass; BYO (corkage $10 a bottle)
Owners Wichit Jimmy Maneeboon & Chris Barnett
Chef Wichit Jimmy Maneeboon
Seats 42; bar
www.siam1.com.au

And ... BYO on Monday night and pay no corkage.

Silks

Level 1, Crown Complex, Southbank **9292 6888**

CHINESE **14.5/20**

A major makeover of the menu and a new chef have injected fresh life into this most opulent of Chinese restaurants. The elegant dining room is still dominated by a silk Mongolian tent, which gives way to a fine view over the Yarra, but the focus is firmly back on the plate. A fresh approach points to the full compass of Chinese cuisine. From the north comes the crunch of jellyfish or garlic cucumber, followed by tangy, thinly sliced pork and beancurd in chilli oil. Sichuan's fiery hot-and-numbing food is represented by versions of ma po beancurd and diced chicken in dried chilli. Simple stewed barramundi with black fungus reflects the more refined cuisine of Shanghai, while the vibrant flavours of Cantonese cuisine remain evident. With main courses hovering around the $55 mark and ranging into triple figures, this is not a budget option. But amid tough competition, and despite sometimes mechanical service, Silks looks on track to regain its former lustre.

Open Daily noon–3pm; Sun–Thurs 6–11.30pm; Fri–Sat 6pm–midnight
Typical prices E $18.50 **M** $55 **D** $13.50
Cards DC AE MC V
Wine Extensive, expensive list of local and international wines; 30-plus by the glass
Owner Crown Casino Pty Ltd
Chefs Peter Chan & JinHua Jiang
Seats 120; private room
www.silksatcrown.com.au

And … Dawdle at the entry and check out the display of porcelain and other antiquities.

The Smith

213 High Street, Prahran **9514 2444**

CONTEMPORARY **14/20**

Take every dining trend of the past 12 months and roll them into one frenetic package. The result is the Smith, a gastropub that shamelessly cherry-picks from the global food zeitgeist. After his lengthy tenure at Taxi, chef and co-owner Michael Lambie is having irreverent fun with his Thai-Jap-Viet-Cal-Mex-French-influenced menu at this reborn corner pub just off Chapel Street, where the line of demarcation between drinkers and diners isn't always clear. Whether it's tempura-battered soft-shell crab or foie gras parfait, robust flavours are the order of the day. Lambie's career-defining way with Asian flavours provides the best compass point. Thai pawpaw salad heavy on the dried shrimp, or master stock-poached baby chicken with son-in-law egg and feisty nam jim are standouts. But then, so are the fajitas, which might come with braised wagyu beef, avocado and spicy corn, and the retro English sundae, knickerbocker glory. Thinking global and acting local, the Smith takes crowd-pleasing to a whole new level.

Open Daily noon–late
Typical prices E $18 **M** $36 **D** $16
Cards AE MC V Eftpos
Wine A broad international collection at some big mark-ups; 22 by the glass
Owners Michael Lambie, Scott Borg & George Sykiotis
Chefs Michael Lambie, Brad Simpson & Zach Cribbes
Seats 140; outdoor seating; private room; bar
www.thesmithprahran.com.au

And … A reliable place for celebrity-spotting.

Society

23–29 Bourke Street, City **9639 2544**

ITALIAN **13/20**

There's an egalitarian feel to the three levels of food and drink at top-of-the-town Society, although affable staff can make you feel as though you're part of a club. The street-level dining room, with a mural of the regions of Italy wrapping the room, has an air of Art Deco with cream-and-black colourings, and tealights dappling the linen tablecloths. Settle into a booth and let the waiters recommend a wine to accompany an Italian menu that takes in the classics. To share, you may find arancini with mozzarella and peas or an entree of creamy burrata cheese, well-balanced with blistered cherry tomatoes and dried olives. Pasta is a highlight – handmade pappardelle with ox-cheek ragu is just al dente, giving enough structure to the intense braised meat, and the huge dessert platter takes in mango semifreddo, raspberry sorbet and chocolate fudge – and saves the decision-making for choosing a digestive in the multi-roomed bar upstairs.

Open Mon–Fri 8am–11pm; Sat 11am–11pm
Typical prices E $19 **M** $38 **D** $18
Cards DC AE MC V Eftpos
Wine An approachable list with big-name labels from Australia and Italy
Owners Paul DiMattina & Giuseppe Uva
Chefs Giuseppe Uva, Matthew Toal & Cary Thomson
Seats 80; outdoor seating; private room; bar
www.societyrestaurant.com

And ... A great spot for a pre-theatre dinner, with two courses for $35.

Sosta Cucina

12 Errol Street, North Melbourne **9329 2882**

ITALIAN **14.5/20**

Sosta Cucina is the Italian stallion of Errol Street. Smooth good looks, sharp service, crisp linen and candlelight are backed by dishes that exude straightforward and seasonal Italian tradition with flair. It's a handsome package. A modern take on vitello tonnato is sensational, a leaning row of poached veal and just-seared tuna discs sit happily in a mayonnaise thick with capers and lemon. Or try heart-warming pappardelle ribbons that tangle with melting lamb ragu rich with wine and pecorino shavings. There's the assaggi section too, buoyant with a selection including fresh oysters, delicate prosciutto with buffalo mozzarella, and wonderfully oily Sicilian anchovies. Mains may break from tradition, like barramundi fillet on a lick of pureed beetroot, bright alongside earthy golden beets, sea asparagus and mandarin. Desserts are a must, in particular hot doughnuts filled with pastry cream, rolled in cinnamon sugar and served with a puddle of melting milk chocolate for dipping. Sweet.

Open Tues–Sun noon–3pm, 6–10pm
Typical prices E $18 **M** $34 **D** $14
Cards DC AE MC V Eftpos
Wine A smart, sharp list of mainly Australian and Italian mid-priced varietals; BYO Tues–Thurs & Sun (corkage $15 a bottle)
Owner Maurice Santucci
Chef Paolo Masciopinto
Seats 60; outdoor seating; private room; bar
www.sosta.com.au

And ... Appealing 'early bird' and lunch meal deals offer two courses for $28.

Spice Temple

Riverside, Crown Complex, Southbank **8679 1888**

MODERN CHINESE **15.5/20**

A darkly handsome space of low-slung lanterns, sleek black furniture and portraits by local photographer Earl Carter, Neil Perry's dining room seduces the moment you walk through the door. Sassy staff glide through the Sino-chic space, delivering cocktails inspired by the Chinese zodiac (the Rabbit of gin, jasmine tea and salted cucumber is a standout), along with helpful advice – yes, you can order a small serve of that knockout 'numbing pork' with Sichuan pepper. Perhaps the best advice that can be shared, however, is to pre-order the tea-smoked duck. Given 24 hours' notice, the kitchen team can conjure up a platter of plump, smoky duck breast and thigh, lacquered with soy and served with Peking pancakes. Heat fiends should seek out the dishes marked in red, including prawn dumplings with black vinegar, and a jumble of egg noodles with bacon and chilli. For more delicate tastes, opt for the asparagus with salted duck egg. Put out any lingering fires with a watermelon granita, or the soothing milk cake scattered with nubs of pomegranate.

Open Daily noon–3pm, 6–11pm
Typical prices E $20 **M** $35 **D** $15
Cards DC AE MC V Eftpos
Wine Perfectly pitched list with light, aromatic whites from near and far, plus reds that are up to the chilli challenge
Owners Neil Perry, Trish Richards & David Doyle
Chefs Neil Perry & Ben Pollard
Seats 150; private rooms; bar
www.spicetemplemelbourne.com

And ... Yum cha is served daily, noon to 3pm.

Spoonful

543 High Street, Prahran **9521 5212**

CONTEMPORARY **12.5/20**

Dozens of cookbooks crowd shelves by the open kitchen at the rear of this terraced Victorian shopfront. Some are glossy, others thoroughly thumbed, evidence of owner Melly Beilby's years of experience and eye for the new. Seasonal flowers, wicker chairs and Chinese lanterns have a lived-in feel as backdrop for two communal tables and several smaller ones buzzing with lunching friends, all welcomed by friendly if not always watchful staff. Sauteed chicken liver salad spiked with vincotto is a well-loved perennial on the constantly changing menu. You might also find smoked trout salad, a generous pile with shaved fennel, beetroot and pea shoots. Indian-spiced lamb burger may be a little lean, needing its accompanying kasoundi and raita for moisture. Light and lovely spinach and ricotta gnocchi might come studded with cherry tomatoes and a sprinkle of lemon zest. Seasonal desserts from the cabinet, such as a fig and frangipane tart, show a light hand with pastry.

Open Mon–Sat 7.30am–4pm; Sun 8am–4pm
Typical prices E $14.50 **M** $22 **D** $8.50
Cards MC V Eftpos
Wine Brief list, Australian, NZ and French; a handful of lunch-friendly choices by the glass
Owner Melly Beilby
Chef Dan Bryan
Seats 30
www.spoonful.net.au

And ... Luscious breakfasts are served daily until noon, and private dinners are offered by arrangement.

TOP 10 PIZZA

Cafe Bedda
242 High Street, Northcote **9482 9420**
Plenty of southern Italian temptation here but thin-crust pizzas are hard to pass up.

DOC
295 Drummond Street, Carlton **9347 2998**
Charred edges, imported ingredients, simple combinations and a boisterous crowd.

Firechief
169 Camberwell Road, Hawthorn East **9831 1700**
Paul Mathis's colourful pizza barn boasts three different pizza ovens and lots of charm.

400 Gradi
99 Lygon Street, Brunswick East **9380 2320**
Authentic Neopolitan pizza here attracts swarms of Melbourne's Italian chefs.

Ladro
224 Gertrude Street, Fitzroy **9415 7575**
& 162 Greville Street, Prahran **9510 2233**
Northside or southside, Ladro's hand-shaped wood-fired pizzas always impress.

The Moor's Head
Rear, 774 High Street, Thornbury **9484 0173**
Joe Abboud's 'inauthentic' pizzas use beautiful Lebanese ingredients to great effect.

Mr Wolf
9-15 Inkerman Street, St Kilda **9534 0255**
Karen Martini's pizzas are a lesson in keeping it simple with quality ingredients.

Pizza Verde
62 Piper Street, Kyneton **5422 7400**
Great attitude, crust and toppings make this a must-do pitstop.

Scoozi
136 Union Road, Ascot Vale **9370 0100**
This Sicilian gem loves a wood-fired crust and an authentic ingredient of the San Marzano tomato kind.

Supermaxi
305 St Georges Road, Fitzroy North **9482 2828**
Rita Macali works wonders with beautiful ingredients and a finely tuned electric oven.

St Katherine's
26 Cotham Road, Kew **9207 7477**

MEDITERRANEAN **14.5/20**

St Katherine is a patron saint of lawyers and librarians, young women and students. All of them, plus partners and kids, crowd mosaiced communal tables and individual blondwood ones in this ample whitewashed restaurant, one of six in the family of George Calombaris and associates. Energetic young staff deftly handle greeting and seating, fetching platters and jugs of sangria. Geared towards family-style sharing, Shane Delia's menu is a rollicking mix of dude food (snacky burgers, sticky ribs, fried chicken in stripy buckets) and dishes from around the Mediterranean (Lebanese lamb sausage, canoe-shaped Turkish pide). Best to opt for a shared menu. The generous $39.50-a-head Quick Kat's menu is a tonne of garlicky fun: mezze like warmed olives, gorgeous creamy tarama, crunchy eat-all prawns, pide filled with spicy minced lamb, then hunks of roasted chicken and lamb and more. They'll tweak it to accommodate dislikes and allergies. There's sweet nostalgia to finish, including soft-serve icecream with sticky toppings, and doughnuts oozing hot cherry jam.

Open Mon–Fri noon–4pm, 5.30–11pm; Sat–Sun 11.30am–11pm
Typical prices E $15 **M** $25 **D** $15
Cards DC AE MC V Eftpos
Wine Compact, pricey, mostly Australian list; decent range of beers, ouzo and raki
Owners Shane Delia & Made Establishment
Chefs Shane Delia & Lucas Sansome
Seats 180; private rooms; bar
www.stkatherines.com.au

And … There's a huge function space upstairs.

The Station Hotel

59 Napier Street, Footscray **9687 2913**

CONTEMPORARY **14/20**

The Station announces its raison d'être before you actually arrive with a tantalising waft of charcoal grill that leaks out on to the street. Steak is the focus at this modern pub with pared-back decor. The crowd is a mix of local families, couples and groups; and 'crowd' they do – bookings for the smart (but loud) dining room are essential. Start, perhaps, with a rich, earthy chicken-liver parfait or octopus carpaccio crowned with a deep-fried Moreton Bay bug-tail. Then, that much-vaunted steak; perhaps a 500g Gippsland rib-eye, expertly charred and rested, with salad and seriously good, twice-cooked chips. The ample skill of the kitchen shows up in a pig's trotter braised into gelatinous glory, boned and wrapped around a mousse of chicken, morels and veal sweetbreads and finished with a wild mushroom sauce. Old-school desserts, like a velvety creme caramel with soused strawberries, are flawlessly executed, like the service from warm, well-drilled staff.

Open Daily noon–2.30pm, 5.30–9.30pm
Typical prices E $15 **M** $32 **D** $14
Cards AE MC V Eftpos
Wine Solid list of mostly mid-level locals and imports; 20 by the glass
Owners Sean Donovan & Greg Fee
Chef Sean Donovan
Seats 70; outdoor seating; bar
www.thestationhotel.com.au

And ... Love oysters? Look out for half-price Tasmanian and South Australian oysters from 3.30pm to 5.30pm.

Steer Bar & Grill

Olsen Hotel, 637–641 Chapel Street, South Yarra
9040 1188

STEAKHOUSE **15/20**

The massive wooden sculpture of a fit young bull greets you at the front door. The waiter holds a large heavy wooden platter loaded with a dozen different cuts of steak. This is what Steer is about – great steak, great wine, great service. The room itself is a mix of natural wooden floors, concrete columns, modern art and black and red furniture on the ground floor of the Olsen Hotel. Take a seat at the communal table by the kitchen or a more secluded spot on the red banquette and admire the polished marrow bone cutlery holders. Start, perhaps, with a matzo ball soup – a hand-formed morsel of cracker and schmaltz (chicken fat) in a delicate chicken consomme, or a sweet, rich croquette of pickled lamb's tongue and sweetbreads. The steaks are among the best in town, kissed with the fiery grill, perfectly rested and served with a top range of house-made condiments. Dessert could be a great slice of New York-style baked cheesecake or pieces of some of America's finest artisan cheese.

Open Daily 6–10pm; Fri noon–3pm
Typical prices E $12 **M** $45 **D** $14
Cards AE MC V Eftpos
Wine A wine list of admirable proportions that lends itself towards fine dining; BYO Mon night (corkage $13.50 a bottle)
Owners Alex Moulieris & Robert Webber
Chef Shaun Nielsen
Seats 120; outdoor seating; private room; bar
www.steerbarandgrill.com.au

And ... Look out for New York deli classics like chopped liver and the Reuben sandwich.

Stokehouse

Level 1, 30 Jacka Boulevard, St Kilda **9525 5555**

MODERN MEDITERRANEAN **16/20**

Ask us to recommend a restaurant for a very special occasion and Stokehouse would always be up there. Why? The feel-good factor – it manages to feel both fancy (as it should at these prices) yet relaxed, with an airy room that enhances that knockout bay view, and staff who affect a breezy attitude without missing a beat. The menu, too, aims for accessibility, even offering fish and chips (whiting fillets) as a main, presumably for risk-averse maiden aunts. Elsewhere, the chef isn't afraid to experiment: think pasta with braised rabbit and corn in a super-rich jus, a tumble of barely seared tuna with yoghurt and cherry tomatoes, or a clever take on kingfish ceviche, with salted grapes and sunflower seeds. Some don't quite wow, like a high-effort quail saltimbocca that's a bit fiddly, but generally expect bold flavours and beautiful presentation. Dessert? Go for a slice of the classic bombe, meringue and white-chocolate parfait encasing strawberry sorbet – stunning.

Open Daily noon–2.30pm, 6–10pm
Typical prices E $27 **M** $45 **D** $18.50
Cards DC AE MC V
Wine Long, curated list with strong international selections
Owners Frank & Sharon van Haandel
Chef Oliver Gould
Seats 135; outdoor seating; private room; bar
www.stokehouse.com.au

And ... Get there slightly early and take your aperitif on the balcony – very romantic.

Sud

219 King Street, City **9670 8451**

ITALIAN **13/20**

There's nothing pretentious in this intimate 40-seater. Dipping bread in sugo is encouraged, and friendly staff like to chat. Themes are constant despite a daily-changing menu. Begin in Puglia with orecchiette pasta and calamari tubes swimming in brothy, sweet sugo: business types need not fear being overwhelmed by garlic. Or evoke Sardinia with large herbed and fried sardines, freshened with dill, fennel and radicchio. Chef Mark Taylor's generous signature main is duck, maybe steamed and roasted, with sweet-potato mash and apple-balsamic segments to mop up jus. For mains there might be scotch fillet with witlof, or sometimes prawn risotto or pork with cotechino. Honesty remains through desserts, perhaps simple home-made nougat and pistachio semifreddo, two finger biscuits fallen across a creamy block like ancient pillar ruins. In a city precinct that's somewhat bland by day (think office blocks, law fims) yet salacious by night (think lights, clubs), Sud doesn't shoot for the stars but cheerily strikes a reliable balance of southern Italian comfort.

Open Mon–Fri noon–3pm, 6–9pm
Typical prices E $19 **M** $35 **D** $13
Cards DC AE MC V
Wine An extensive list covers the Italian regions; some sumptuous half bottles of Australian wines
Owner Vincenzo Tomaino
Chef Mark Taylor
Seats 40
www.sud.com.au

And ... You can book the whole restaurant for a private or business function.

Left to right: • Pablo Tordesillas - *Ortiga, Brisbane* • Darren Robertson - *Three Blue Ducks, Sydney* • Jake Nicolson - *Circa, The Prince, Melbourne* • Dan Hong - *Ms G's + El Loco, Sydney* • Brent Savage - *Bentley Restaurant & Bar, Sydney* • Peter Manifis - *Incontro + Beluga Claremont, Perth* • Shaun Presland - *Saké Restaurant & Bar, Sydney*

FAMOUS PORKSTARS

When it comes to PorkStars, this magnificent seven and their masterful command with pork, it is no wonder gluttony is one of the seven deadly sins. This sinful seven's diverse gastronomic and cultural backgrounds are the envy of others in creating lustful pork dishes that are the first word in imagination and temptation. Be a PorkStar and get some pork on your menu.

www.porkstar.com.au

PORKSTAR™

AUSTRALIAN Pork™

Supermaxi

305 St Georges Road, Fitzroy North **9482 2828**

ITALIAN/PIZZERIA **14.5/20**

From its cool black and white decor – a terrific terrazzo floor, moody pendant lights and central bar – to service that sparkles with brio, Supermaxi is loud with stylish machismo. It's a perfect fit for Rita Macali's food – classy, robust, modern Italian fare without a whiff of preciousness. Justifiably renowned thin, cut-your-own pizza comes crisp-yet-chewy and topped with, say, tomato sugo and fior di latte kicking with olives, anchovies, capers and chilli. It's not all about the pizza, though. A handsome plate of thinly sliced wagyu bresaola (salt-cured, air-dried beef) topped with rocket, capers and shaved parmesan or a classic combination of juicy crumbed veal cutlet with tangy coleslaw are spot-on. So are desserts such as the signature golden slab of deep-fried custard sweetened with honey and vanilla icecream. Service may fray a bit when the place is pumping, but the hospitable buzz and staff's easy banter make it hard not to feel part of la dolce vita.

Open Tues–Sun 5.30–10.30pm
Typical prices E $15 **M** $33 **D** $13
Cards AE MC V Eftpos
Wine Neat, short list features drops from throughout Italy; about a dozen by the glass; BYO (corkage $20 a bottle)
Owners Rita Macali & Giovanni Patane
Chef Rita Macali
Seats 80; bar
www.supermaxi.com.au

And ... When booking, feel free to specify whether you'd like to sit at a table or up at the bar.

Sushi Bar Aka Tombo

205 Greville Street, Prahran **9510 0577**

JAPANESE **14/20**

If this hushed little sushi bar was any more low-key it would sing bass at the opera. Pale green walls, plinky muzak, a pair of tables for two and a row of white chairs along the bar form a perfectly plain palette for chef Akira Kageyama to display his artistry. There is theatre in the sight of him turning a whole daikon radish into a metre-long parchment before shredding it, then dissecting fresh fish into immaculately sculpted sushi and sashimi to be presented moments later on a gorgeous ceramic plate. Japanese standards are given enough flair to put them several cuts above most similar restaurants, such as beautifully smoky eggplant, deep fried and marinated in soy, in umami dashi broth, or a delicate wakame salad with seaweed, crisp green beans and wafers of fiery red radish doused in a light vinegar and topped with sesame seeds. The specials list contains highlights, too, perhaps a richly flavoured grilled teriyaki kingfish steak.

Open Tues–Sat noon–2.30pm; Tues–Sun 6–9.30pm
Typical prices E $8 **M** $22 **D** $9
Cards DC AE MC V Eftpos
Wine Good sake list and Sapporo draught on tap, plus a modest list of local and overseas wines
Owners Akira & Keiko Kageyama
Chef Akira Kageyama
Seats 16; private room

And ... Great dessert options include slippery creme caramel and brown-sugar icecream.

Syracuse

23 Bank Place, City **9670 1777**

MODERN MEDITERRANEAN **13.5/20**

There's been a changing of the guard at this long-time elegant CBD stalwart, but there's still a lot to love in Syracuse's soaring dining room, the opulent excess of plush curtains, pillars and chandeliers balanced by bentwood chairs and bare tables. It's something of a temple to wine, with bottles lining the walls and a well-curated list that nudges 30 pages. That's not to say the food's an afterthought, though it's perhaps less ambitious than previously, with tried-and-true Mediterranean flavours the top picks. Share-plates run from scallops and morcilla (the Spanish version of blood sausage) to bresaola (cured, air-dried beef) with a punchy, rough paste of olives and anchovies. You could happily make a meal out of these small tastes (throw in some terrine, plump lamb cutlets or a beetroot salad with lentils and goat's cheese), or treat them as entrees before moving on to, say, whole rainbow trout or a big, bold plate of duck confit or suckling pig (for two). Wrap things up with a light dessert of violet icecream, honeycomb and berries, or a trio of cheeses and another glass of wine.

Open Mon–Fri 7am–11pm; Sat 5–11pm
Typical prices E $22 **M** $40 **D** $15
Cards DC AE MC V Eftpos
Wine Serious assembly of local and global gems, with a killer cognac and eau de vie selection
Owner RNRB Group Pty Ltd
Chef Hugh Sanderson
Seats 75; outdoor seating
www.syracuserestaurant.com.au

And ... Breakfast and lunch are also on offer at this Bank Place all-rounder.

Takumi

32 Bourke Street, City **9650 7020**

JAPANESE **13/20**

You might walk in feeling romantic, seduced by the low light; by night's end you have sauce all down your shirt, a full belly, and the kind of childlike smile that comes with a cheerful sense of achievement. Sumibi yakiniku (Japanese charcoal grill) can have this effect. Takumi specialises in cook-it-yourself meals and in wagyu beef: the premium plate comes with slices of rib-eye, porterhouse and tongue so thin that two quick sizzles is enough. Start by using a block of beef fat to coat the cooking surface and meat: it adds immense flavour. There's seafood to cook too, from squid to abalone, plus vegetables to soak up any juices. Lively young waiters emphasise sake; the house variety is terrific value. Sake snacks dot the meal, mostly exotic, such as anglerfish liver pâté. End with a Japanese sweet plate with a themed trio of icecream, parfait and pastry.

Open Daily 6–10pm; Mon–Fri noon–2pm
Typical prices E $15 **M** $35 **D** $6
Cards DC AE MC V Eftpos
Wine Short, mostly Australian list plus a handful of big, red vintages; sake list includes tasting notes
Owner Nao Uchiyama
Chef Taka Arai
Seats 50; bar
www.takumi.com.au

citibank Privileges

And ... Three barbecue set menus at varying price points take the guesswork out of ordering.

Taxi Dining Room

Level 1, Transport Hotel, Federation Square, City
9654 8808

CONTEMPORARY **14.5/20**

Taxi is no shrinking violet. Perched above Fed Square, the lofty dining room mixes jaw-plummeting vistas with look-at-me furnishings, including orb-like chandeliers, industrial mesh panels and daring disco lights. Tony Twitchett's menu cherry-picks flavours and techniques from Japan, China, Thailand and beyond to create bold, cutting-edge food. Chopsticks replace cutlery for starters of sake-cured tuna in punchy yuzu dressing, and tempura-prawn sushi wrapped in yuba (soy-milk skin) and served with dabs of miso mayo. Crisp-skinned barramundi partners tempura soft-shell crab, sparked up with a punchy little salad, and mayo spiked with sriracha chilli sauce; but a fragrant coconut curry might be marred by too-tough duck. Dreamy desserts, perhaps caramelised pear with delicate pear sorbet and a drizzle of Pedro Ximenez, show a return to form. Service, too, is tight and highly tuned – time is given to linger over aperitifs and wines between courses, making for a well-paced dinner even when there's a full house.

Open Daily noon–3pm, 6–11pm
Typical prices E $27 **M** $46 **D** $20
Cards DC AE MC V Eftpos
Wine A heavy-hitting encyclopedic list, loaded with stellar drops from around the world; hefty selection of dessert wines, digestifs and sakes
Owner Transit Pty Ltd
Chef Tony Twitchett
Seats 115; outdoor seating; private room; bar
www.taxidiningroom.com.au

And … Get a taste of Taxi with a lunchtime bento menu; four courses for $45.

Tea House on Burke

911-913 Burke Road, Camberwell **9882 9088**

CHINESE **13/20**

It's easy to see why Tea House on Burke is such a comforting cocoon: a spacious dining room, peaceful ambience and unfailingly polite, smooth service make for a highly enjoyable experience. Over a decade since opening, the (mostly) Cantonese menu is bedded down and confidently executed. An entree of fried garfish stuffed with diced carrot and celery is crisp and light; equally pleasing is the slinky rice noodle roll, filled with sliced celery and doused in a sweet soy sauce; and a main of battered prawns in a creamy wasabi sauce – curiously accompanied by sweet chilli sauce and fresh mango – is a guaranteed crowd-pleaser. Less thrilling may be a tender, soy-simmered duck that can lack the promised five-spice aromatics. Desserts generally tread the well-worn fritter path so, for something more, try the pan-fried red bean pancake that's boosted by fresh banana.

Open Sun–Fri noon–3pm; Sun–Thurs 6–10.30pm; Fri–Sat 6–11pm
Typical prices E $8 **M** $23 **D** $7
Cards DC AE MC V
Wine Fairly priced, mostly local list with a premium selection for diners with deep pockets; BYO (corkage $9.50 a bottle)
Owners Sum Cheung, Ruji & Kam Chen, Shannon Chan
Chefs Sum Cheung & Kam Chen
Seats 100; private room

And … There's a separate menu for vegetarians.

Tempura Hajime
60 Park Street, South Melbourne **9696 0051**

JAPANESE 15/20

One of the most refined dining experiences in Melbourne is built around deep-frying. There are 12 seats, three choices, and the owner-chef is just a metre away all night. Osaka-born Shigeo Yoshihara has a 20-year dedication to tempura. Those who enter this nondescript shopfront are here for Japanese culinary art, the freshest seasonal produce battered, deep-fried and precisely arranged on a plain bench. A wedge of sweetcorn is elevated to the sublime. Hot oil and batter accentuate perfectly the subcutaneous fat of freshwater eel. The night begins with sashimi and a delicate amuse-bouche of poached chicken with ground sesame. And then tempura. Yoshihara-san's performance is as exquisite as a top-end sushi chef (skills he also displays with delicately draped sushi post-tempura). The tempura progresses through more elaborate items like scallop sandwiching a layer of sea urchin, and white mushroom with a prawn mince. A refreshing shot glass of plum wine comes halfway through a night of exquisite simplicity.

Open Tues–Fri noon–2pm; Tues–Sat 6–10pm
Typical prices Lunches $24–$36; dinner set menus $75 (tempura), $85 or $92 (7 or 10 pieces tempura and sushi)
Cards AE MC V
Wine Short list of well-known Australians, complemented by good range of sake and shochu
Owner & chef Shigeo Yoshihara
Seats 12; bar
www.tempurahajime.com

And ... Exquisite lunch bentos move beyond the tempura purity of the evening.

Tender Trap
Shop 2, 266 Blackburn Road, Doncaster East
9842 3466

CONTEMPORARY 13/20

Perhaps one of Doncaster's most ambitious restaurants, Tender Trap is a sleek, grey-rendered, sometimes noisy space serving elegant, generously proportioned food. In terms of price and fine-dining smarts, it pits itself against top places closer to town. Service is professional, though not necessarily smiley, and while the dishes look beautiful, some can lack depth of flavour, as in a risotto of heirloom carrots and globe artichokes with a race-worthy fascinator of fine-sliced radish and carrot and charred spring onions. Expertly cooked grass-fed Angus rib-eye is treated reverentially, centre stage on a massive white platter with a knob of butter – whipped with fermented black garlic and parsley – and a minimalist steel cup of fat chips beside. Complex, multi-faceted desserts are bold, such as thin rectangles of brownie-like cake interspersed with golden shards of honeycomb and pistachio-green blobs of anglaise. Looks too good to eat, tastes too good not to.

Open Mon–Fri noon–3pm; Mon–Sat 6–10pm
Typical prices E $19 **M** $34 **D** $14.90
Cards DC AE MC V
Wine Mid-sized, approachable list of mostly Australian wines; about 20 by the glass; BYO Mon–Thurs (corkage $10 a bottle)
Owners Chris Moraitis & Nick Fragoulis
Chef David Stewart
Seats 75
www.tendertrap.com.au

And ... Three-course set menus are on offer for tables of 10 or more for $66 and $76.

The Terminus Hotel

492 Queens Parade, Fitzroy North **9481 3182**

PUB DINING **13/20**

There's been a shift in the kitchen of this handsomely furnished hotel; chef Michael Tillotson is now at the helm and his modern, unpretentious pub menu gets the thumbs-up. There's a healthy dose of Hispanic and Med influence (think chipotle, romesco, ceviche), but you're just as likely to find flavours from Japan or Korea – as with specials like the smoky, tender Korean barbecue beef skewers with kimchi puree. Quality steaks are a feature (and excellent) and the slow-cooked pork belly, maybe partnered with a tangy apple-fennel slaw, is done to luscious, salty perfection, its plus-sized portion a joy for big eaters. Desserts – such as pretty berry-strewn white chocolate icecream with raspberry sorbet and meringue – are a delight, exhibiting flavour balance and visual flair. Service, while welcoming, can be a little sketchy, but when it comes to the food, wine and atmosphere trifecta, the Terminus confidently delivers.

Open Mon–Thurs 6–9.30pm; Fri–Sun noon–2pm, 6–10pm
Typical prices E $13.90 **M** $35.90 **D** $11.90
Cards AE MC V Eftpos
Wine Brief but quality list of mostly boutique producers with an impressive selection of well-priced local and European wines by the glass
Owners Russell, Stephen, Alison & Paul Griggs
Chef Michael Tillotson
Seats 80; outdoor seating; private room; bar
www.terminus.com.au

And ... Pre-dinner, settle into the cosy front bar with a pint of craft beer from the rotating roster of local brews.

Town Hall Hotel

166 Johnston Street, Fitzroy **9416 5055**

ITALIAN **15/20**

With its austere Victorian exterior and dark-wood bistro interior, there's nothing flashy about the Town Hall Hotel. But that just allows the food to do the talking. Veteran chef Harry Lilai brings an infectious enthusiasm to his cooking: good, unpretentious mostly Italian dishes prepared with care. A menu of small, medium and large plates allows for easy, casual eating. 'Small' could be egg-dipped prawns wrapped in zucchini and prosciutto, while 'medium' might offer comforting soft polenta with chunks of baccala in a creamy sauce, or fried quail with the sweet and spicy combination of red grapes and chorizo. True to its pub heritage, there's a range of steaks, including grass-fed Angus sirloin with all the trimmings, and carafes of decent wines. Keep an eye on the mirror for seasonal specials such as silky ravioli with pine mushroom, toasted pinenuts and currants in brown butter. Classic desserts such as self-saucing chocolate pudding and tiramisu are superior examples of the species.

Open Tues–Sat noon–11pm; Sun 11.30am–4pm
Typical prices E $17 **M** $30 **D** $15
Cards AE MC V Eftpos
Wine A balanced wine list to suit all wallets and palates, including wine by the carafe
Owners Harry & Michelle Lilai, Stuart Neil
Chef Harry Lilai
Seats 65; private room; bar
www.townhallhotel.net.au

And ... The cellar (pictured above) offers private dining.

The Treasure Restaurant

482 Springvale Road, Forest Hill **9803 2388**

CHINESE **13/20**

The Treasure Restaurant is proof that excellent food can be served alongside pink paper napkins and faded wall murals. Not much is new in this big, long-serving food hall, and when it comes to the recipes, that's a good thing. The 13-page menu is mostly authentic Cantonese, for instance, aromatic shredded-duck soup as entree, thickened with just the right balance of cornflour and stock. Beyond starters think in communal terms. Roasted pigeon with peppered salt is presented as in the homeland – plated head and all, skin crisp, flesh moist. Try fresh seafood from the tank, such as spring onion and ginger crab served on a bed of short egg noodles. There are steamed oysters in black-bean sauce, too. Otherwise, pan-Asian faves include Thai green curry, teriyaki, laksa and char kway teow. Service is friendly, if occasionally naive on wine choices. And you could come over all nostalgic at dessert with offerings like banana fritters and toffee apples.

Open Mon–Fri noon–3pm; Sat–Sun 11am–3pm; Sat 5.30–11pm; Sun–Fri 5.30–10pm
Typical prices E $8 **M** $25 **D** $7
Cards AE MC V Eftpos
Wine Half-page inexpensive all-Australian list, with two red and five white by the glass; BYO (corkage $2 a bottle)
Owner The Treasure Fortune Pty Ltd
Chef Victor Li
Seats 140

And … The Treasure serves yum cha every day, with two sittings at weekends: 11am to 1pm and 1pm to 3pm.

Triple King

540 Whitehorse Road, Surrey Hills **9830 2111**

CHINESE **13/20**

Triple King is a symbol of the suburban revolution against mediocre Chinese restaurants; its sophisticated and immensely enjoyable Cantonese cuisine saves you a trip to Chinatown. Try a selection of dumplings, bursting with flavour; juicy Peking duck; or cooked oysters smothered in tasty sauces, such as simple lemon or chilli-balsamic. Chef's specials include pork spareribs in a punchy orange sauce, shredded beef in mandarin sauce, and king prawns in champagne sauce. Oxtail is stewed slow and long with red wine in a claypot, simple but succulent and a definite fingers job. Service is efficient and gentle, linen tablecloths and space between tables add to the general atmosphere of luxury and pleasure, and noise levels are acceptable. One slight drawback is a rather thin wine list, although there's a good choice of wine by the glass and it's also BYO. Triple King is a suburban gem – comfortable, professional, and you'll be pleasantly surprised by the modest bill.

Open Tues–Fri & Sun noon–3pm; Tues–Sun 5–10.30pm
Typical prices E $8 **M** $25 **D** $8
Cards DC AE MC V
Wine A modest selection, few by the glass; BYO (corkage $3 a head)
Owners John Lee & Martin Wong
Chef Martin Wong
Seats 80; private room

And … The bottle shop directly opposite has a huge range of wine and beer.

True South

298 Beach Road, Black Rock **1300 878 360**

ARGENTINIAN **13.5/20**

South American food and Black Rock brews are a happy marriage in this large, modern beer hall. Chef Mauro Callegari draws on a culinary background that includes Italian rustic, Argentinian barbecue and contemporary fine dining to create a pleasing array of snacks and feasts. Two types of house-made chorizo star on the menu: a version with smoked ham hock is stuffed in cornbread and smothered with garlic aioli to create the street snack 'choripan'. The other sausage, a fragrant, garlicky blend of pork and beef, is served with a balanced, fresh chimichurri sauce. Meat features – the locro stew of white corn and pumpkin served with pressed, fried pork belly is a sticky, succulent triumph – but it would be easy to make a meal of vegetable dishes here. Roasted carrots dressed with coriander, peanuts, honey and chilli are typically thoughtful and unfussy. Desserts include an excellent version of 2012's favourite tooth-rotter, dulce de leche. Service is keen and friendly, neatly wrapping a tasty bayside package.

Open Tues–Thurs & Sun noon–9pm; Fri–Sat noon–10pm
Typical prices E $12 **M** $36 **D** $13
Cards AE MC V Eftpos
Wine Beer is a major focus but the easygoing wine list includes some Argentinian wines by bottle and glass
Owners Grant & Suzanne Dow
Chef Mauro Callegari
Seats 140; outdoor seating; private room; bar
www.truesouth.com.au

And ... There are brewery tours every Saturday.

Tutto Bene

Mid-level, Southgate, Southbank **9696 3334**

ITALIAN **13/20**

It's all about the risotto – and the view – at Tutto Bene. Inside, dark-wood furnishings and close-set tables create a homely, Italian feel, but the best seats are on the deck – a stunning vantage point looking across the Yarra River to Flinders Street Station. There are up to 11 risottos on offer, from a straightforward blend of mushrooms and herbs to a brilliantly orange butternut pumpkin variation, to the more creative wagyu rump and tomato sugo or gorgonzola, pear and chestnut honey, all presented elegantly in a purpose-built risotto plate. Entrees do double duty as drinks snacks and risotto torch-bearers – quenelle-shaped tubes of calamari come stuffed with the stuff, and impressively crunchy ricotta-filled zucchini flowers feature scattered crumbs of crisped rice for textural balance. Pastas and main courses are traditionally simple – slow-cooked lamb with chickpeas is just that, in a copper pan. Desserts are resolutely Italian – panna cotta, tiramisu and award-winning gelati.

Open Daily noon–3pm, 6–11pm
Typical prices E $16.50 **M** $36.50 (risottos $27) **D** $14
Cards DC AE MC V Eftpos
Wine Comprehensive list with focus on organics
Owners Tamara Volkoff & Louis Pampliega
Chef Leandro Panza
Seats 85; outdoor seating; bar
www.tuttobene.com.au

And ... Good bread comes with house-label olive oil, which you can buy by the 500ml bottle ($24).

Union Dining

270 Swan Street, Richmond **9428 2988**

EUROPEAN **14.5/20**

There's joy at the heart of Union Dining. The dining room is good looking and comfortable, the waiters bubble with enthusiasm, and the food ethic is generous, seasonal and careful. A slow, wet lamb stew is emblematic of Nicky Riemer's cooking. Premium meat is the bedrock of a simple braise that's lovingly, expertly layered with oregano, green chilli and pecorino, all of which act as nuanced applause for the hero meat on the bone. Some dishes add refined technique to their list of accomplishments: there's always a terrine as rich and flavourful as it is pretty (combinations include veal, duck liver and pickled cherries), and there are dishes that balance sweet and savoury, raw and cooked, as with a lively sardine escabeche and a deluxe just-cured ocean trout with crisp shallots. Salads are meals in themselves, tossed with plenty of herbs, protein and grains, and always judiciously dressed. Desserts – a crowd-pleasing chocolate tart, say – are yet another encouragement to simply enjoy.

Open Tues–Thurs 6–10pm; Fri–Sat noon–10pm; Sun noon–9pm
Typical prices E $18 **M** $34 **D** $16
Cards AE MC V Eftpos
Wine A list that's as enamoured of the highways and byways of Europe as the food menu, plus plenty of mid-priced local wines
Owners Adam Cash & Nicky Riemer
Chef Nicky Riemer
Seats 80; outdoor seating; private room; bar
www.uniondining.com.au

And ... Skewers and spritzers are served on the rooftop terrace.

Va Tutto

226 Upper Heidelberg Road, Ivanhoe **9499 7769**

ITALIAN **13/20**

Still looking like a crisp, chic retro '60s film set near the top of the Ivanhoe strip, Va Tutto has accumulated regulars since opening in 2005. Menu choices abound. In the mood for classic Italian? The warmth of (long, thin) chitarra pasta nestled in sweet sugo sauce with herbed meatballs awaits. Ravenous? There are massive steaks, maybe tender scotch fillet in a striking copper serving dish with roasted whole potatoes. Asian flavours? They abound, including slightly crisp vegetarian dumplings with beancurd, bok choy and Asian mushrooms. Simply the usual? That would be the four-way duck, including a steamed bun with soy and a crisp leg on sweet roasted pear. Dessert also offers global choices, but going Australian wins out with pavlova presented like a sticky, sweet snowman topped with fruity flavours of berries and passionfruit. Va Tutto began assuredly as an outpost of what was happening in the city; the emphasis now feels comfortably more familiar than edgy.

Open Tues–Fri & Sun noon–2.30pm; Tues–Sun 6–10.30pm
Typical prices E $22 **M** $35 **D** $17
Cards AE MC V Eftpos
Wine Good selection of affordable, predominantly Australian and NZ wines, with a few Italian options
Owners Paul & Myrto Recinella
Chef Paul Recinella
Seats 140; private room
www.vatutto.com.au

And ... An expansive daily specials list might even include a Sri Lankan goat curry.

Vasko

111 Upper Heidelberg Road, Ivanhoe **9499 8111**

MEDITERRANEAN **13/20**

Vasko Dzanovski didn't just have a family, he staffed a restaurant. There are Dzanovskis everywhere – in the kitchen, waiting tables and smiling out from artfully reproduced family photos. It's a customer-service plus. If one wine is unavailable, for instance, anyone has authority to offer better for the price. Your meal could read like a Dzanovski recipe album, with 'Vasko bruschetta' (tomato, basil, red onion, pesto, olive tapenade) to start. Proceed to 'the Balkan' (a family version of a pork, veal and onion burger) as a main, then to sticky loukoumades – cinnamon doughnuts with honey, chopped walnuts and vanilla icecream. Savoury dishes have a complexity of flavour from recipes perfected over generations: feather-light ricotta gnocchi is coated in subtle pesto, resting on rich napoli. Dishes are simply, elegantly plated to match the interior. Clever architecture achieves an intimate local feel with banquettes and small tables, but easily morphs into a big, glam function space.

Open Mon–Fri 11am–3pm; Mon–Thurs 6–10pm; Fri–Sat 6–11pm
Typical prices E $15 **M** $30 **D** $14
Cards AE MC V
Wine Short, well-chosen list of mostly Australian and New Zealand wines under $50; 15 by the glass
Owner Dzanovski family
Chefs Daniel & Vasko Dzanovski, Manny Capones
Seats 140; outdoor seating; private room; bar
www.vasko.net.au

And ... The $19.90 lunch deal includes one course and a glass of house wine, or tea or coffee.

VicAsia

95 Victoria Avenue, Albert Park **9690 2390**

CHINESE **14/20**

VicAsia is as far removed from your local cheap-and-cheerful Chinese restaurant as pure wool is from polyester. Amid a sea of elegant chinoiserie calm (and music that's even more easy-listening than Kenny G, if that's possible), black-aproned, well-informed waiters glide between tables dispensing advice on the fabulous wine list and the lengthy, Cantonese-heavy menu that spreads its wings from Japan to Malaysia. Start, perhaps, with flash-fried calamari or light-as-air eggwhite stir-fried with West Australian crabmeat before delving into the easily shareable larger dishes. These may include well-cooked slices of crisp-skinned duck with a spicy mandarin sauce (hoisin sauce and chilli), and lightly battered, five-spiced pieces of King George whiting that can be a little overwhelmed by the chopped spring onion, capsicum, shallots and red chilli under which they sit. Desserts don't tend to defy stereotypes here, but the Chinese sweet pumpkin pancake with icecream or the orange and honey creme brulee are worthy finales.

Open Tues–Sun noon–2.45pm; Sun–Thurs 6–10.30pm; Fri–Sat 6–11pm
Typical prices E $10 **M** $28 **D** $12
Cards DC AE MC V Eftpos
Wine Outstanding 43-page list, with friendly mark-ups; a dozen by the glass; BYO (corkage $15 a bottle)
Owner Colonial Leisure Group
Chefs John Lei, Chuen Lo & Tsu Yin Kuang
Seats 40; outdoor seating; private room
www.vicasia.com.au

And ... Upmarket it may be, but it's still popular with the takeaway crowd.

Vivace

317 Bay Street, Brighton **9596 9511**

ITALIAN/CONTEMPORARY **14/20**

There's a lovely spirit to Vivace – it's a slick, sleek dining room with handsome windows to the street, but there are wild, expressive paintings on the walls and service is warm and friendly while never missing a beat. Start with warm house-made bread, maybe flecked with olive, while you peruse a menu of handmade pastas and excellent seasonal produce. There's a spotlight on quality meat, with a supporting cast of flavours curated with great flair. Start with oysters under a snowfall of melon and vodka granita, or a couple of large, succulent prawns with haricot beans, mint and grapefruit. An entree of terrine might be made with duck, pork and prunes, while a main of perfectly pink Gippsland lamb rump might come with a spicy house-made sausage. Pastas are silken and inspired: herbed gnocchi often comes with slow-cooked meat: perhaps pork, pear cider and broccolini. Mains are generous but you won't regret finishing with petits fours – light, sticky nougat, mini-eclairs and float-away cocoa-rolled truffles.

Open Mon–Thurs 5.30–9pm; Wed–Fri noon–3pm; Sat 5.30–9.30pm
Typical prices E $20 **M** $38 **D** $16
Cards AE MC V Eftpos
Wine A broad list with an emphasis on Italian reds; 20 by the glass; BYO Mon (no corkage)
Owner Chris Favaloro
Chef Daniel Redhead
Seats 100; outdoor seating; private room; bar
www.vivace.com.au

And ... Lunch specials (including a glass of wine) are available Wednesday to Friday.

Vlado's

61 Bridge Road, Richmond **9428 5833**

STEAKHOUSE **12/20**

This place is beyond fashion. It operates in a parallel universe in which restaurants do one thing, but superbly. At Vlado's, that thing is steak. Nothing else matters, nothing else is especially good. But the steak – a dense, thick fillet, a slab of grass-fed rump, a doorstop of marbled porterhouse – is meat of exemplary quality cooked to perfection. The redoubtable Ivan Glavas has long been the late Vlado's grill-double, and the restaurant remains on the same track after the baron of beef's passing in May 2012. There is no real choice, apart from the cut, size and degree of doneness of the steak, which, though vast, is clearly not meat enough as each meal begins with a lively sausage and a jumble of seared meat shrapnel – slices of calves' liver, slivers of pork neck and more. Then steak – cooked with neither lubricant nor seasoning, served with house mustard or fiery horseradish. A salad of slaw, tomatoes and lettuce accompanies, and strawberry crepes finish. Strange, austere, quietly wonderful.

Open Mon–Fri noon–3pm; Mon–Sat 6–11pm
Typical prices Set menu $88
Cards DC AE MC V
Wine One-page list with realistic prices, a few blockbusters and two admirable house wines by the glass
Owners Nina & Michael Gregurek
Chefs Ivan Glavas & Elliot Valkivic
Seats 90; private room
www.vlados.com.au

And ... Observe as steaks are hammered into submission by white-gloved hands.

Vue de Monde

Level 55, Rialto, 525 Collins Street, City **9691 3888**

CONTEMPORARY 🍽🍽🍽 **18/20**

Like Grand Final seats or tickets to a megaband arena spectacular, dining here does not come cheap. Take a deep breath and spend up to experience something special – the theatre and luxury of this restaurant 55 floors above the city. Vue reflects global trends, but with a Melbourne edge. It's fun, too, as chefs present dishes filled with boomer nostalgia, like Cona-brewed pumpkin 'cuppa soup', or musk stick and lamington petits fours. At its best, Vue's food can be sublime, witty, theatrical, decadent and utterly delicious, as in buttery marron tail, or 'eggs on toast' (duck yolk, celeriac puree, gorgeous onion and thyme sauce, truffles), and ethereal tonka bean souffle. Attention to detail is phenomenal, from 100-year-old Grange vines as rests for the Christofle cutlery to bespoke cheese trolleys, kangaroo-hide tables and rare teas. Some bookings are set-length, and best avoided for the full experience, while lack of a printed menu can make tracking costs tricky, but these are quibbles. For a big night out, there's nothing like it.

Open Mon–Sat 6–9.30pm; Tues–Fri & Sun noon–2pm
Typical prices Four-course menu $150; degustation (about 10 courses) $250
Cards DC AE MC V
Wine Walk through the cellar as you arrive; one of the city's most impressive lists, now more affordable too
Owner Shannon Bennett
Chefs Shannon Bennett & Cory Campbell
Seats 72; private room; bar
www.vuedemonde.com.au

And ... The adjacent Lui Bar stays open until 3am on Friday and Saturday nights.

Walter's Wine Bar

Upper level, Southgate, Southbank **9690 9211**

CONTEMPORARY **13.5/20**

When Walter's opened 20 years ago in the then-new Southgate complex, a wine bar was a relative novelty. Walter's has become a fixture on the Melbourne dining scene, and the wine list continues to hold its own, though the feel these days might be more restaurant than bar. Views of the Yarra and across to Melbourne's city centre remain a key attraction, with tourists and locals alike vying for balcony seats. Some dishes – such as fish and chips – have stayed on the menu since day one. They are supported by entrees such as roasted Hervey Bay scallops with prosciutto and a touch of chilli and garlic, or duck-and-mushroom risotto with white truffle oil. Mains may include battered baby barramundi and home-made tartare sauce, or puff-pastry mushroom pie containing shiitake, field and button mushrooms and Meredith goat's cheese. Service can be variable, but a signature souffle – perhaps accompanied by a splash of something sticky or fortified – should bring the meal to a sweet end.

Open Mon–Fri noon–late; Sat–Sun 9am–late
Typical prices E $26 **M** $40 **D** $19
Cards DC AE MC V Eftpos
Wine Excellent list from Australia, NZ, Italy and France; outstanding fortifieds; innovative, good-value wine flights
Owners Maria Bourke, Philippa Shaw & Dane Shaw
Chef Dane Shaw
Seats 100; outdoor seating; private room
www.walterswinebar.com.au

And ... It's a handy, comfortable retreat for post-theatre supper and drinks.

Wayside Inn

446 City Road, South Melbourne **9682 9119**

CONTEMPORARY **14/20**

The owners of Footscray's Station Hotel have tweaked a winning formula to bring accessible pub-style dining to the south. The Wayside offers a pleasing experience at fair prices; the setting is a 1915 hotel that's been brightened and shined but not at the expense of its corner-pub soul. Hard surfaces cause clatter but tables are well spaced and there's a semi-secluded mezzanine. A good-value 'fruits de mer' list and a handsome red rotisserie in the open kitchen point to the edible highlights. The skewered, slowly roasted meats are succulent and intensely flavoured, whether it's beef rib and bearnaise for two, or other meats (venison, organic lamb, Boer goat, suckling pig, Aylesbury duck, Glenloth chicken) that appear according to a daily roster. There's a fine selection of grass- and grain-fed steak and pride taken in consummate chips. Chef Donovan has his classical techniques down pat so look out for such dishes as pork terrine, chicken liver parfait and chocolate marquise, all of which have their wits about them.

Open Tues–Sun noon–3pm; Tues–Sat 6–9.30pm
Typical prices E $15 **M** $36 **D** $12
Cards AE MC V Eftpos
Wine A list as accessible as the food, with 15 wines by glass and carafe, and a decent range under $50
Owners Sean Donovan & Greg Fee
Chefs Sean Donovan & Josh Rudd
Seats 80; outdoor seating; private room; bar
www.waysideinn.com.au

And ... The front bar is the spot for classy fish, chips and cheeseburgers.

Wildflower

1 Theatre Place, Canterbury **9888 6662**

CONTEMPORARY **14.5/20**

As the name suggests, Wildflower is an unruly bloom at odds with its environment, delivering a modern dining experience amid the period charms and village air of Maling Road. In the kitchen, there's fresh creative force and technique courtesy of South African-born, UK-trained Graham Jefferies (ex-Pettavel). Complex, balanced constructions with multiple components and wide-ranging ingredients mark seasonally changing dishes. You might start with zingy grapefruit-cured kingfish with Japanese influences (red shiso leaves, the citrus fruit yuzu, and a powdery dashi 'snow'); or pink duck breast in white eggplant puree, with turrets of kohlrabi capped with nori powder, samphire (seaweed salad) and crunchy squid-ink crumble. Desserts keep up the pace: perhaps a wonderfully smooth chocolate cream with passionfruit gel and hazelnut crepe crumb, or deconstructed tropical cheesecake with cashew, coriander and lemongrass syrup.

Open Tues–Sat noon–2.30pm, 6pm–late; Sun noon–3pm
Typical prices E $19 **M** $39 **D** $16
Cards DC AE MC V Eftpos
Wine Small, quality list of predominantly Australian labels; 11 by the glass; BYO Tues–Thurs (corkage $7.50 a head)
Owner Tony Weis
Chef Graham Jefferies
Seats 65; outdoor seating; private room
www.wildflowerrestaurant.com.au

And ... Lunch specials are also available: two courses for $35, three for $45.

Yak Bar Pasta Artigianale

150 Flinders Lane, City **9654 6699**

ITALIAN **14.5/20**

Yak's room is bright and colourful, with splashes of green and purple paint and panels of floral fabrics above the banquettes that line the walls, giving it a youthful, modern feel. And there's no mistaking Yak's passion for pasta – you can see it drying though the kitchen window – from light pillows of lemony agnolotti filled with pureed potato that comes in a buttery sage sauce, to a heart-warming, rustic tagliolini with braised rabbit falling off the bone and black olives. The signature dish is vincisgrassi (lasagne of rump, sweetbreads and lamb's brain), which takes two days to make. Elsewhere, starters evoke the Med, such as shaved white zucchini with char-grilled calamari, or house-made Calabrian sausage and smoked scamorza cheese. Specials might include meaty mains such as roast, crisp-skinned half-duck with semolina gnocchi, or braised lamb shanks with lentils. The tiramisu is a worthy rendition; otherwise, complete the carb-fest with doughnuts stuffed with pistachio icecream.

Open Tues–Fri noon–3pm; Tues–Sat 5.30–10pm
Typical prices E $15.50 **M** $33 **D** $12.50
Cards DC AE MC V Eftpos
Wine Compact list of Australian, NZ and Italian labels; 30-plus by the glass
Owners Leo Gelsomino, Chris McIntyre & Linda Durnan
Chefs Leo Gelsomino & Dario Di Clerico
Seats 80; outdoor seating; bar
www.yakbarfood.com.au

And ... From 7am Monday to Friday pop in for a breakfast of coffee, toast, bagels and croissants.

Yu-u

137 Flinders Lane, City **9639 7073**

JAPANESE **15/20**

Yu-u's disdain for publicity, deliberately obscured entrance and beautifully designed basement fitout convey an impression of exclusivity, when in fact the experience of dining here is about as relaxed and earthy as a visit to your local Japanese, only way more awesome. A smoky yakitori grill forms the beautiful room's centrepiece, delivering delectable chicken morsels such as breast with pickled plum sauce and thigh with charred spring onion, the perfect match for draught beer or chilled sake. Elsewhere, it's simply excellent izakaya-style morsels, such as slaveringly fatty wagyu beef rolls wrapped round spring onion in a rich teriyaki, or thinly sliced scotch fillet with slippery capsicum and enoki mushrooms in a sticky barbecue sauce. All are presented promptly and with little fuss by the unflustered staff. Dessert, such as a house-made creme caramel, is good but not a highlight. Lunch is strictly a bento-box affair.

Open Mon–Fri noon–2pm; Mon–Thurs 6–9.30pm; Fri 6–10pm
Typical prices E $9 **M** $19 **D** $8
Cards AE MC V
Wine Excellent and nicely priced sake list; a short and equally affordable wine list
Owners Yoshiki Tano & Miho Nakao
Chef Yoshiki Tano
Seats 28; private rooms

And ... It's shoes off and half a world away from the city bustle in one of the private rooms.

GOURMET CAFES

Crafternoon

By Dani Valent

Batch Espresso

Shop 1, 320 Carlisle Street, Balaclava **9530 3550**

Still trucking and still awesome, this Balaclava old-timer's food and coffee are always on song. Standards are given clever twists, as with the cumin and lemon fried eggs.

The Boatbuilders Yard

23 South Wharf Promenade, South Wharf, Docklands **9686 5088**
theboatbuildersyard.com

The indoor-outdoor riverside shed is a fine spot on a still day. Eat eggs early, then prawns, pasta or pork chop, and loiter by the barbecue for fancy snags.

Chez Dre

Rear, 285–287 Coventry Street, South Melbourne **9690 2688**
chezdre.com.au

The menu here has a French accent, thanks to pastry chef Andrea Reiss, and runs from croque monsieur to brioche French toast and macarons, to be enjoyed inside or in the courtyard under the peppercorn tree.

Coffeehead

8 Railway Parade, Camberwell **9831 1400**
coffeehead.com.au

A variety of local roasters are showcased here, and there's a chirpy, well-priced food menu to boot. Larger groups should beeline for the lovely round marble table near the enormous kitchen and roasting room.

Common Galaxia

130–136 Victoria Street, Seddon **9689 0769**
commongalaxia.com.au

Named after a plucky local fish, the second cafe from the Dead Man Espresso team runs along similar lines: a classy space for food that's simple and elegant plus coffee crafted with rigour and passion.

Cooper & Milla's

1094 High Street, Armadale **9500 8127**

The salads and baked goods here are balanced, inspired, seasonal and sparklingly fresh. That's why it's possible to forgive the cramped tables and the premium prices.

Crafternoon

531 Nicholson Street, Carlton North **9077 6998**

At this sweet concept cafe, the food menu is flanked by a list of craft activities: your smaller companions can collage while you caffe latte. The food is fresh, cheap and delectably kid-friendly too.

Dr Jekyll

107 Grey Street, St Kilda **9525 5999**

drjekyll.com.au

Bright and spacious with a great rear deck floating in the greenery, this doctor delivers fine tunes, good vibes and scrambled eggs with just the right amount of jiggle.

Fifteen Pounds

21-23 Railway Place, Fairfield **9482 4481**

Fairfield often feels like the country, never more so than under the lemon tree in the rear garden here. Consider the 'pound dog' with chorizo and the rustic jam tarts.

Hobba

428 Malvern Road, Prahran **9510 8336**

hobba.com.au

An old garage is now a funky cafe with plywood booths and smashing food. Slow-poached eggs come with guaranteed ooze, and lunches are proper alluring meals like braised lamb with smoked almond dukkah.

Kitschen Pantry

128 Mansfield Street, Thornbury **9484 0503**

Produce grown in the owner's garden, just up the road, stars in many dishes at this cute retro cafe with a tiny kitchen, a big heart and ace icecream spiders.

Little Byrd

160 Union Road, Ascot Vale **(no phone)**

Homespun and handcrafted, this bird is a beauty – from the fabulous spinach pie to the saucepan lid mural. It's not big but seating on the wide pavement eases the crush.

Luxbite

38 Toorak Road, South Yarra **9867 5888**

luxbite.com.au

Lots of folk hit and run for the perfect macarons, but it's also nice to sit in the sleek cafe where the mix-and-match savoury and sweet menu makes it easy to build a feast from elements such as cinnamon waffle, pork belly and brie.

Manchester Press

8 Rankins Lane, City **9600 4054**

8oz.com.au

A laneway, a warehouse, a simple menu, a queue. Does it get any more Melbourne than that? But this place is worth the (short) wait for its large and lively setting, classic bagels (smoked salmon, pastrami) and low-fi salads.

Marmalade & Soul

162 Queens Parade, Fitzroy North **9486 2740**

marmaladeandsoul.com

A restaurant approach at cafe prices means this stripped-back old pub is a big win for diners. Raymond Capaldi's food is creative: think five-rice curry porridge for a sustaining brunch.

Martha Ray's

85 Brunswick Street, Fitzroy **(no phone)**

A turntable spins cool tunes in a calm, minimalist space, while the open kitchen pumps out fragrant and interesting food at keen prices. Breakfast might mean corn chowder; lunch could be eggplant and smoky tomato baguette.

Middle Fish

122 Berkeley Street, Carlton **9348 1704**

Fun and original, this big, buzzing Thai cafe serves brown rice soup and crunchy mussel omelette for breakfast; curries and spicy salads for lunch. The coffee with condensed milk is sweet and strong, and the red booths are prime position.

Miss Marie

45 Beetham Parade, Rosanna **(no phone)**

missmariecafe.com.au

A heaping pile of baked beans is emblematic of Miss Marie: generous, full-flavoured and fuss free. The home-made biscuits and cakes need special mention, especially the moist, spiced carrot cake.

My Sister Says

118 Bridge Street, Port Melbourne **9646 1117**

A dainty cake display is a constant lure at this cutie-pie cafe. Many of the excellent savoury and sweet bakes come from sister cafe Servery and Spoon in Malvern; the friendly welcome is all their own work.

Oasis Bakery

Shop 9, 993 North Road, Murrumbeena **9570 1122**
oasisbakery.com.au

The Middle Eastern pizzas and wraps are good, but consider the well-priced braises, soups and seafood dishes at this busy canteen. Be warned: a quick browse in the Middle Eastern grocery often results in a full trolley.

Oli & Levi

Shop 2, 20 Coromandel Place, City **9650 0501**

The welcome is dazzling at this alley cafe with one long communal table and a food cabinet full of baguettes and pastries. The egg tarts are perfect for a morning smash and grab.

Olie & Ari

133–135 Were Street, Brighton **9592 2929**

At this corner cafe, there's plenty of pram room, loads of natural light and Armenian accents on the menu. The coffee is excellent and the almond croissants are wicked.

Ora

156 Pakington Street, Kew **9855 2002**

Friendly is good but when it's combined with efficiency it's even better. Excellent food, coffee and a stellar service ethic make this small cafe a hot option.

The Pour Kids

1e Winter Street, Malvern **9077 3847**
thepourkids.com.au

The modern retro fitout says 'Come in, enjoy', and the menu backs up the promise with terrific offerings that show technique and care, like fresh sardines on toast with spiced bean paste and shaved fennel.

Pure Italian

249b Belmore Road, Balwyn North **9857 3961**

There's an art to making something new feel rusted on and cosy and this endlessly appealing hangout knows all about it. Order classic pasta and polenta from the paper wall scroll or browse the antipasto fridge for treasures.

Roller Door Cafe

13 Stawell Street, West Melbourne **0449 208 681**
rollerdoor-cafe.com.au

Personal and charming from the rugged frontage to the higgledy-piggledy courtyard, Roller Door also wins for its simple menu of eggs and ciabattas (with, say, house-glazed ham).

The Scented Garden Cafe

2a McAdam Square, Croydon North **9725 2299**
thescentedgardencafe.com.au

Everything's organic at this peaceful cafe where the courtyard is shaded by a lemon-scented gum tree. The food is simple but thoughtful, with soups, focaccia and home-made cakes starring.

Spout

48 Glen Eira Road, Ripponlea **9523 8155**

If ever a shopping strip was crying out for a cafe, it was this one. Locals leapt instantly and keep coming back for dishes like pan-fried challah (braided egg bread) with vanilla mascarpone, and Moroccan schnitzel sandwich.

Threefold

381 Flinders Lane, City **9614 8194**
three-fold.com.au

Wholefood salads, braises and pies are deliciously arranged on a marble countertop; on-the-money sandwiches (sausage and sauerkraut – yes, please) are assembled behind the scenes at this petite, civilised weekday dining room.

Wallis & Ed

1 Bourke Street, City **9633 6265**
wallisanded.com

Part of the Windsor Hotel, there's all-day dining and drinking in this smart, elevated dining room with classy and creative breakfast dishes like chestnut and barley porridge.

The Age Good Cafe Guide is available through goodguides.com.au

BEST BARS

The Everleigh

By Michael Harden

The Aylesbury Rooftop

Level 5, 103 Lonsdale Street, City **9077 0451** theaylesbury.com.au

This pint-sized eyrie with fab cityscape views and a great line in cocktails and craft beer also boasts its own little kitchen, the source of great Spanish-leaning snacks ranging from quality jamon to classic churros.

Bar Americano

20 Presgrave Place, City **(no phone)** baramericano.com

Channelling Italian espresso bars right down to its compact dimensions and mostly standing policy, Bar Americano focuses on doing a small number of things brilliantly, be they classic cocktails, Italian wine, good coffee or punchy bar snacks.

Bar Ampere

16 Russell Place, City **9663 7557** barampere.com

Vernon Chalker's latest drinking establishment has a hidden back bar, a secret entrance to next-door Gin Palace, a futurist theme, an absinthe fountain, snacks that include a smoking eel cigar, an all-French wine list and an all-Spanish sherry one.

Bishop of Ostia

77–79 Nicholson Street, Brunswick East **9388 8858** bishopofostia.com.au

Ostia's pig's ear sandwich teamed with something from the cute selection of all-Victorian beer makes for one of those ain't-life-grand moments. A finely crafted cocktail in the decked courtyard area makes you hold that thought.

Black Pearl

304 Brunswick Street, Fitzroy **9417 0455**

Boasting some of the city's finest bartenders and best booze, Black Pearl and its upstairs table-service counterpart, the Attic, offer a cocktail lover's paradise. Best of all, it's friendly, unpretentious and a whole lot of fun.

Boire

92 Smith Street, Collingwood **(no phone)** boire.com.au

Catherine Chauchat's sharply focused wine bar has a pared back elegance that perfectly matches the rustic French food (everything from roasted buttered chestnuts to duck) and a wine list of mostly small French producers.

EDV Melbourne

1 Malthouse Lane, City **0412 825 441**
eaudevie.com.au/Melbourne

An offshoot of Sydney's Eau de Vie, this sophisticate offers an excellent, humorously annotated cocktail list, low-lit upholstered comfort and a degustation menu with matching cocktails.

The Everleigh

Level 1, 150–156 Gertrude Street, Fitzroy **9416 2229**
theeverleigh.com

There are platters of meats and cheeses to be had at this glamorous, speakeasy-inspired candlelit bar, but the main focus is the cocktails – meticulous classic things of beauty served in antique glassware.

Gertrude Street Enoteca

229 Gertrude Street, Fitzroy **9415 8262**
gertrudestreetenoteca.com

There's a beautiful simplicity at work here, both in Brigitte Hafner's compact menu of finely crafted bar food (her terrines are legendary) and in the room itself, reassuringly lined with excellent wine to drink in or take with you.

Hell of the North

135 Greeves Street, Fitzroy **9417 6660**
hellofthenorth.com.au

Behind a bright yellow door lies this serene, smoothly decorated bar that's anything but hellish with its sharp cocktail list, craft beer, geographically diverse wines and French bistro-leaning food.

The Junction Beer Hall & Wine Room

15 Hall Street, Newport **9391 8188**
junctionnewport.com.au

A smart makeover, which includes a mural ode to John Brack's *The Bar*, has seen the Junction morph into two venues, one upholstered and loungey, the other vibrant and noisy. Both offer well-cooked pub faves.

The Kodiak Club

272 Brunswick Street, Fitzroy **0431 947 910**
kodiakclub.com.au

Fans of American whiskey and American bar snacks of the buffalo wings/pork slider/onion rings kind will find plenty to love at this saloon with its 100-plus collection of rare and aged bourbon and rye.

The Lui Bar

Level 55, Rialto, 525 Collins Street, City **9691 3888**
vuedemonde.com.au/the-lui-bar

There's plenty at Vue de Monde's bar to keep you happy beyond the pretty lights and drop-dead views – a whisky trolley, a cocktail made in honour of Lola Montez, a staggering wine list and Shannon Bennett's clever bar food.

Siglo

Level 2, 161 Spring Street, City **9654 6631**

One of the original and arguably best rooftop bars in town, Siglo mixes parliament and cathedral views with an Old World-favouring wine list, whisky, cocktails, cigars and hit-the-spot snacks.

The Toff in Town

Level 2, Curtin House, 252 Swanston Street, City
9639 8770 thetoffintown.com

This wonderfully louche den of imbibing has lengthy lists of quality beer (mostly imported), wine and cocktails. It also serves excellent Thai comfort food until the wee hours.

Umami Sake Bar

7 Victoria Avenue, Albert Park **9699 9022**

An excellent list of sake, chilled staff who are happy to help the uninitiated, a serene, lantern-strewn room and Japanese snacks of the gyoza and yakitori ilk make Umami one of the city's more peaceful and relaxed watering holes.

The Waiting Room

Crown Complex, Southbank **8679 1800** twrbar.com

With owner Neil Perry lurking about, you know the food here (a mix of Mexican and American classics) is going to be spot-on, but the drinks, especially the finely crafted cocktails that deliver some inspiring food/drink matches, keep that standard consistent.

The Woods of Windsor

108 Chapel Street, Windsor **9521 1900**
thewoodsofwindsor.com

A flexible beast with a penchant for moody Americana (taxidermy, antiques, beards), the Woods keeps the quality high with both food (grab a crab sandwich) and booze – a list full of whiskey, Euro wine and old-school cocktails.

The Age Good Bar Guide is available through goodguides.com.au

HILLS & YARRA VALLEY

TarraWarra Estate

Bella Vedere

874 Maroondah Highway, Coldstream **5962 6161**

REGIONAL 15.5/20

When the Apocalypse arrives, it would seem anyone stranded at Bella Vedere will be set for survival. Its woven-vine bordered garden bursts with produce, the spoils of which are displayed inside on a wide wooden table – a pile of red tomatoes, a splay of artichoke flowers. The aroma of baking hits as soon as you enter the olive-hued abode, and beyond a corridor of comestibles and freshly baked cakes is a fish-bowl 'country house' kitchen. It's busy with cooks clanging copper pots, keeping up with the plates of goat braised with tomatoes, cinnamon and white wine; paccheri (pasta tubes) filled with sardines, olives and capers; pork loin spiedino (skewers) with pinenut, garlic and currant soffrito, which are whisked to lunchtime crowds by waistcoated staff. Dinner on Saturday night remains the famed domain of chef Gary Cooper, who creates a set menu based on what he can get his gardening gloves on.

Open Wed–Sun 8.30am–5pm; Fri 6–10pm; Sat 7.30–11pm
Typical prices E $18 **M** $38 **D** $16; Sat dinner menu $105
Cards AE MC V Eftpos
Wine A superb selection divided into two parts: winemakers of the Yarra Valley; and winemakers beyond (Europe)
Owners Gary Cooper & Tim Sawyer
Chef Gary Cooper
Seats 80; outdoor seating; private room
www.bellavedere.com.au

And ... Garden produce like tomatoes and mushrooms appears in breakfasts, too.

Eleonore's

Chateau Yering, 42 Melba Highway, Yering **9237 3333**

CONTEMPORARY 15.5/20

Chateau Yering's vast gardens and impeccable 1854 chateau set high expectations for a meal at Eleonore's. The opulent setting invites big-night dining (a proposal, or significant anniversary), but as the string quartet plays on CD and candles brighten, any evening becomes a special occasion. Entrees might include pea tortellini paired with yabbies and saddle of rabbit, or veal loin accompanied by deliciously salty tastes of jamon and tuna croquettes. You may find mains of venison, two generous maroon rectangles, with horseradish dashes, beetroot, and chocolate jus. Or dense truffled polenta, with light pea mousse and rich slow-cooked egg. And, while a seared John Dory fillet with confit red capsicum may be cooked a touch too long, dessert returns to form. A banana parfait resplendent with mango sorbet, passionfruit, coconut and sago displays truly fresh tastes. Dainty trolleys, for cheese and petits four, are wheeled by bright, smiling young staff.

Open Daily 6.30–10pm
Typical prices Set menus $85 (2 courses), $98 (3 courses)
Cards DC AE MC V Eftpos
Wine A broad list showcasing Yarra Valley wines and well-known internationals, particularly from NZ and France
Owners Len & Elly Milner
Chef Mathew Macartney
Seats 120; private room
www.chateauyering.com.au

And ... No denim, and collared shirts for gents please. Try for Table 1, the best window view.

Healesville Hotel

256 Maroondah Highway, Healesville **5962 4002**

MODERN REGIONAL **14/20**

Seasonality is key in the kitchen at this timeless Edwardian beauty in the heart of town. Produce grown in the kitchen garden is picked and plucked daily and might end up as a delicate tomato consomme, bright with celery and elegant tomato-jelly cubes. Or jamon ribbons may be intricately entwined in a vibrant herb and apple salad, finished with crisp pork-belly slivers and an artistic smear of tomato. Service can become a little lax; pass the time studying the sturdy wine list or soaking up the hotel's considerable charms. The stunning old-world surrounds are resplendent with wicker chairs, graciously set tables, and huge flower arrangements – fitting of a special-occasion restaurant such as this. A fat snapper fillet complements the grand sense of occasion, flattered by a zucchini puree freckled with fregola and mint. Pavlova with candied rose petals bodes well for a tokay. Chink-chink to the grand old dame.

Open Wed–Sun noon–3pm, 6–9pm (daily during summer)
Typical prices E $16 **M** $36 **D** $16.50
Cards MC V Eftpos
Wine A 29-page tome celebrating Yarra Valley and Eurocentric wines
Owners Michael Kennedy & Kylie Balharrie
Chef Ben Arnold
Seats 70; outdoor seating; private room; bar
www.yarravalleyharvest.com.au

And ... There's a hearty bistro menu served daily from noon to 9pm.

Innocent Bystander

336 Maroondah Highway, Healesville **5962 6111**

CONTEMPORARY/PIZZERIA **14/20**

Innocent Bystander has one speed – full throttle. Inside this contemporary timber, glass and steel shed, it's a choose-your-own-adventure. There's the cellar door, the cheese room and a wood-fired bakery – all in bright and comfortable surrounds. Families and day-trippers file into spacious booths for tapas, pizza and large rustic offerings. Molten mozzarella balls ooze beneath olive and sourdough crumbs; house-cured ocean trout is vibrant with horseradish cream and chubby grapes. Pizzas' pillowy organic-sourdough crusts aren't overloaded with flavours; tomato, chilli and mozzarella, enlivened with spiced pork sausage, for example. Bigger meals, like duck and mushroom pie, are more imaginative, parked on a carrot puree lively with coriander. Sweet endings may come as a decadent wedge of flourless chocolate cake. Staff are welcoming, mischievous and seriously cluey, ensuring this multi-faceted and sometimes boisterous business idles smoothly.

Open Mon–Fri 10am–10pm; Sat–Sun 8am–10pm
Typical prices E $13 **M** $24 **D** $10
Cards DC AE MC V Eftpos
Wine Aside from the house varieties there's a weighty list that champions boutique wines and some heavy hitters
Owner Phil Sexton
Chef Trevor Schneider
Seats 100; outdoor seating
www.innocentbystander.com.au

And ... Separate gluten-free and kids' menus.

Locale

De Bortoli Winery, 58 Pinnacle Lane, Dixons Creek **5965 2271**

ITALIAN **14.5/20**

Short of taking a trip to Tuscany, you would be pressed to find a vinous version of Italy that beats Locale. Being surrounded by rolling hills of grapes is a good start, and there are one or two Roman columns. It's a stylish whitewashed setting with cushioned chairs and historical photos of the estate. But it's the menu that proudly waves the tricolore. Spoils of a kitchen garden abound, from the rosemary flecked on complimentary bread to deliciously al dente baby zucchini and peas beneath a generously seasoned pan-roasted lamb saddle. The kitchen's skills shine in classic Italian dishes: risotto (a wonderfully wet dish with wild rabbit, estate chardonnay and thyme) and gnocchi (solid, not stodgy, made with potato and parmesan, sprinkled with pinenuts and red capsicum strips). If you can't decide between finishing with dessert, coffee or a fortified, try all three: Italian doughnuts to dip in a DIY affogato (coffee-redolent Black Noble wine added, at table, to vanilla icecream).

Open Thurs–Mon noon–3pm; Sat 6.30–10pm
Typical prices E $17 **M** $35 **D** $16
Cards DC AE MC V Eftpos
Wine A showcase of De Bortoli's range, past and present, plus a peppering of the winemaker's favourites
Owner De Bortoli family
Chef Heath Dumesny
Seats 120; outdoor seating; private room
www.debortoliyarra.com.au

And ... Locale offers whole-table set menus: four courses $58 (accompanying wines $26); six courses $75 (accompanying wines $40).

Mandala Wines

1568 Melba Highway, Dixons Creek **5965 2016**

CONTEMPORARY **14/20**

Bring your camera: the glass box of a dining room sporting 180-degree vineyard views is gorgeous. Tables smartly dressed with crisp linen and fine glassware epitomise understated elegance. Infuse that with knowledgeable, warm service and an easily navigable wine list championing mainly Mandala wines: bliss. The short seasonal menu may include delicate scallop carpaccio lifted by a lively combo of ginger, lime and coriander. A beetroot salad is a kaleidoscope of colour, balanced by creamy goat's cheese blobs and radiant cabernet dressing. Slow-cooked beef short-ribs may have you sucking the bones to extract every skerrick of flavour, their richness tempered by a tart lemon puree. At dessert, a pistachio cake may be slightly parched but is boosted by fat strawberries poached in sparkling wine and a golf ball of sensational yoghurt sorbet. Perhaps pick up a souvenir from Mandala's cellar door, and you have here one great little vineyard escape.

Open Fri–Sun noon–3pm; Sat 6–9pm
Typical prices E $17 **M** $35 **D** $15
Cards AE MC V Eftpos
Wine A one-pager of predominantly Mandala wines; plenty by the glass
Owner Smedley family
Chef Neil Cunningham
Seats 70; outdoor seating; bar
www.mandalawines.com.au

And ... There's a tasty bar menu available in the comfortable lounge area.

Oakridge

864 Maroondah Highway, Coldstream **9738 9900**

CONTEMPORARY **14/20**

A crunchy gravel drive leads to immaculate vines and a bird-filled lake – no wonder stylish Oakridge is so popular. (So popular that the dining room was set to double in size as we went to print.) Expect panoramic views, a bright setting, fresh-faced staff, local produce and Yarra Valley wines. Chef Ritchie Boucher does good things with prime local produce, presented with understated flair. Entrees may include plump sauteed duck livers on mushrooms, toasted brioche and semi-soft Yarra Valley gemello cheese; or seared salmon on a nashi, radish and sorrel salad with a mild horseradish creme fraiche. Mains could be house-made gnocchi with local figs, baby spinach, caramelised onion and taleggio cheese; fall-off-the-bone cassoulet-style duck leg; or oh-so tender Gippsland lamb with tomato jam glaze, cous cous, mint salsa verde, local feta and an intriguing savoury olive 'cigar'. Before you turn back down that driveway, give serious consideration to icecream flecked with vanilla bean atop a warm calvados-caramelised apple tart.

Open Daily 11am–5pm
Typical prices E $16 **M** $33 **D** $12
Cards AE MC V Eftpos
Wine A short list composed exclusively of Oakridge Yarra Valley wines; many available by the glass
Owners D'Aloisio & Atlas families
Chef Ritchie Boucher
Seats 120; outdoor seating
www.oakridgewines.com.au

And ... There's a good value set menu at weekends, plus wine and food events.

TarraWarra Estate Restaurant

311 Healesville-Yarra Glen Road, Yarra Glen **5962 3311**

CONTEMPORARY **14/20**

The setting is splendid – a striking contemporary art museum, expansively grassed grounds, an award-winning winery. The restaurant is just as smart, but also casual, indoors or on the terrace. Friendly staff suggest wine-food combinations. Chardonnay lovers might start with house-cured salmon, twisted generously across avocado with sweet paprika. A vegetarian main triumphs in flavours (if not looks): two crunchy eggplant strips in chickpea-and-coriander batter, atop almond skordalia, quinoa salad and honey-cardamom syrup. Alternatively, paella-style chicken baked with bomba rice in a terracotta pot is cosy, yet may be a tad dry. Pinot noir enthusiasts might start with charcuterie – rich chicken-liver parfait, mustard fruits and air-cured local beef. Naturally, duck must follow, perfectly seared then moistened by lentil stew with apple. Desserts might include firm lemon polenta cake or even TarraWarra wine sorbets. Like the modern art next door, there's a commanding array and setting, and much to admire.

Open Tues–Sun noon–3pm
Typical prices E $18 **M** $35 **D** $15
Cards DC AE MC V Eftpos
Wine Focus on TarraWarra's wine stable (no beer or champagne)
Owner Besen family
Chef Robin Sutcliffe
Seats 40; outdoor seating; private room
www.tarrawarra.com.au

And ... The first Sunday of every month is Burgundy Sunday; BYO French burgundy at $10 a bottle corkage

Yering Station Wine Bar

38 Melba Highway, Yarra Glen **9730 0100**

CONTEMPORARY **14.5/20**

Though established way back in 1859, this old vineyard isn't showing her age, with modern lofty glass walls, sculptural water features and padded black seating spaced to hold groups of all sizes. She's had a lot of work done, and the decorative turns feature on dishes, too, especially entrees like wagyu beef tataki with its parmesan tuile, and the dessert assiette, with ribbons of chocolate twisting above treats like green-tea and lychee dacquoise. For mains, however, the kitchen has toned down the ornamentation, leaving diners with wonderfully uncluttered flavours, such as rich red tuna with perfectly seared edges, comfortably sharing the wide plate with a line of smoked eel nori rolls. Japanese influence is well utilised here, especially in summer, but tender eye fillet with a molasses-like jus and horseradish remoulade proves Yering Station cuts it in any season. Although welcoming, service can have lapses, but what's the hurry when views are this good?

Open Mon–Fri noon–3pm; Sat–Sun noon–4pm
Typical prices E $23 **M** $38 **D** $16
Cards DC AE MC V Eftpos
Wine Showcasing this premier Yarra Valley winery, with plenty of options by the glass
Owner Rathbone family
Chef Laura Webb-James
Seats 100; outdoor seating; private room; bar
www.yering.com

And ... The pick for an all-family affair, with playground and special menu for kids, a stately view, and fortifieds for grandfolks.

Essenza Yarra Valley

new

191b Maroondah Highway, Healesville **5962 4613**

CAFE

Two Sydney lads have refurbished a Healesville alley to fit half-a-dozen tables, one pew and a team turning out locally sourced, Italian-inflected fare. Their terracotta pot-baked muffins (zucchini and dill) and brilliant breadboard platters (roasted pistachios, goat's cheese, fresh ricotta, prosciutto ...) encapsulate the Yarra Valley. There's also locally roasted coffee and sweets such as orange poppyseed cake with mascarpone icing.

Open Daily 7.30am–5.30pm **Typical prices E** $15 **M** $20 **D** $7 **Unlicensed** essenzayarravalley.com.au

Hargreaves Hill Brewing Co

25 Bell Street, Yarra Glen **9730 1905**

CONTEMPORARY

Within the handsome bones of an old bank, this brewery is as much a gastronomic destination as a must-visit for beer buffs. The tasting paddle calls for crunchy hot chips with aioli from the bar menu, while long lunchers are lured with herb-crusted rare venison, pan-fried kipfler potatoes and goat's cheese; mash-topped fish pot-pie; and a wicked deconstructed cheesecake.

Open Mon–Sat 11.30am–late; Sun 8.30am–4pm; **Typical prices E** $16 **M** $35 **D** $13 **Licensed** hargreaveshill.com.au

Immerse Restaurant

1548 Melba Highway, Dixons Creek **5965 2300**

CONTEMPORARY

This vineyard spot is popular for weddings, but isn't just about the 'I dos' – seasonal food is done well here too. The menu includes dishes like pan-fried gnocchi with shredded roast duck and hazelnuts or meltingly tender Otway free-range pork belly with pumpkin puree and mustard fruits. The airy dining room has a stone fireplace and there are brekkie and kids' menus too.

Open Fri–Sat 6–9pm; Sat–Sun 9–10.30am, noon–2pm **Typical prices E** $17.90 **M** $33 **D** $15 **Licensed** immerse.com.au

Mt Rael Restaurant

Mt Rael, 140 Healesville-Yarra Glen Road, Healesville **5962 1977**

CONTEMPORARY

The menu changes with the seasons at Mt Rael and so does the 180-degree view. The constant is excellent local produce crafted with technique and creativity. Buxton creamy smoked trout pithiviers matches a crisp celeriac salad, and six-hour braised goat is as tender as you'd expect. Local Kennedy & Wilson chocolate comes in a fondant or try house-made ginger glace icecream.

Open Wed–Sun noon–3pm; Fri–Sat 6pm–9pm; Sat–Sun 9–11.30am **Typical prices E** $17 **M** $29 **D** $16 **Licensed** mtrael.com.au

Rae's Restaurant

Balgownie Estate Vineyard, 1309 Melba Highway, Yarra Glen **9730 0700**

CONTEMPORARY

Rae's is looking sharp these days, with chef Mathew Hart now in the kitchen and a fresh leadership team. By day, it's a family-friendly spot; by night, candles flicker in the dining room, back-lit by a spectacularly illuminated eucalypt. Snappy entrees include baby calamari with a chilli-scotch-caramel syrup. Mains could be honey mustard pork belly with caramelised apricots or a seriously good top-grade steak.

Open Daily 7–10.30am, noon–3pm, 6–10pm **Typical prices** Set menus $60 (2 courses), $70 (3 courses) **Licensed** balgownieestate.com.au

Ripe

376–378 Mount Dandenong Tourist Road, Sassafras **9755 2100**

CONTEMPORARY

Ripe is a lovely excuse for a daytrip, and if you're local, there's no excuse needed to stop by for delicious stuffed baguettes (perhaps chicken, brie and chilli cranberry relish), risotto, porterhouse or penne pasta. House-made cakes are impressive – there are more than 10 – from rocky-road cheesecake to carrot cake; just right to pair with a dark Lindt hot chocolate.

Open Daily 8am–6pm **Typical prices E** $9 **M** $19 **D** $5.50 **Licensed**

Sweetwater Cafe

Chateau Yering, 42 Melba Highway, Yering **9237 3333**

CONTEMPORARY

Chateau Yering's light-filled conservatory cafe, overlooking the gardens, might dish up tomatoes and basil, picked on the property, with burrata, followed by slow-cooked pork with trimmings, then gateau. Monday to Saturday offer good value with a fixed-price lunch including a glass of local wine. Unsurprisingly, Sundays are more crowded, both for lunch and a delicious high tea (2.30 to 4.30pm).

Open Daily 7.30am–4.30pm **Typical prices E** $18 **M** $35 **D** $18 **Licensed** chateauyering.com.au

Woods Sherbrooke

21 Sherbrooke Road, Sherbrooke **9755 2131**

CONTEMPORARY/ASIAN

Wind your way up the mountain through the tall forest and fern glades to this quaint restaurant, with its two glorious curved windows. Asian flavours inspire the menu: perhaps creamy Sri Lankan curry of tender beef, or a shiny crisp-skin duck leg atop sticky purple cabbage. Homely desserts, such as hot crumble, its chunky apple stained purple with blueberries, don't disappoint.

Open Fri 11am–11pm; Sat 9am–11pm; Sun 9am–5pm **Typical prices E** $17 **M** $34 **D** $15 **Licensed** woodssherbrooke.com.au

Zonzo

Train Trak Winery, 957 Healesville-Yarra Glen Road, Yarra Glen **9730 2500**

ITALIAN/PIZZERIA

If the vineyard, rolling landscape or distant dark swell of the Yarra Ranges aren't enough to seduce you, the smell of wood-fired pizza, which dominates a menu big on Italian favourites, might just do it. Perhaps a traditional margherita or more adventurous pork-and-fennel sausage with taleggio. With seating on the outdoor terrace and inside by the fire, Zonzo is deservedly popular.

Open Wed–Sun noon–4pm; Fri–Sun 5–10pm **Typical prices E** $15 **M** $22 **D** $14 **Licensed** zonzo.com.au

MORNINGTON PENINSULA

Fork to Fork at Heronswood

Bistro Maison

45 Mount Eliza Way, Mount Eliza **9787 6111**

FRENCH **14/20**

This suave and intimate upstairs/downstairs bistro is a romantic Gallic affair with bay and city glimpses. Chef Bernard McCarthy is best-known as owner of Salix at Willow Creek, and the wine list here features some canny local and French picks – part of why Bistro Maison has such a loyal following. Those sharing petite and popular tables for two might tete-a-tete over garlic snails, beautifully plump and creamy seared scallops or a classic, comforting gruyere and goat's cheese souffle. Meaty offerings may include a wonderfully tender slow-roasted lamb shank or a char-grilled eye fillet that comes perfectly rare and rested. The rustic theme continues with the plat du jour and classic offerings such as saucisson provençale or a full-flavoured boeuf bourguignon. There's the odd faux pas, a bouillabaisse may be disappointingly low tide, but otherwise this youthful 'maison' has become a chic home. And for sweets? But of course, there's creme brulee.

Open Mon–Sat 6–9.30pm
Typical prices E $16 **M** $32 **D** $14
Cards AE MC V Eftpos
Wine A proudly peninsular selection with selected French wines too; 15 by the glass; BYO Mon–Tues (corkage $5 a bottle)
Owners Bernard & Rachael McCarthy
Chef Bernard McCarthy
Seats 60
www.bistromaison.com.au

And ... Ask about the midweek La Belle Table, a themed shared long-table regional feast for $75 a head.

DOC Mornington

22 Main Street, Mornington **5977 0988**

PIZZERIA **14/20**

'Conceived in Italy, born in Carlton, now living happily in Mornington': the blackboard motto sums up this (relative) newcomer to the DOC family nicely. This peninsula outpost of the burgeoning pizza and pasta empire appeals immensely for its no-nonsense cooking of top-notch imported produce and a frenetic atmosphere oiled by the brusque charm of the small army of Italian waiters. Pizza is the main boasting point of the paper placemat menus plonked on the communal tables: crisp yet pliable bases needing only the simplest of toppings, like tiger prawns, endive and fresh chilli with a touch of mozzarella and sugo. Wooden paddles come bearing the softest cured meats from the hanging room – San Daniele prosciutto with a globe of Italian buffalo mozzarella, white anchovies and shaved fennel is a meal unto itself. Pasta such as a meaty lasagne mightn't hit the heights of the Lygon Street DOP pasta sibling, but finish on a flourish with warmed panettone drizzled with chocolate balsamic.

Open Daily 9.30am–10pm; no bookings, except for groups of seven or more
Typical prices E $16 **M** $21 **D** $11
Cards AE MC V Eftpos
Wine A well-priced selection of Italian beers and a tight list of Australian and Italian wines
Owners Tony Nicolini, Robert Di Santis & Michael Costanzo
Chef Tony Nicolini
Seats 80; outdoor seating; private room
www.docgroup.net

And ... Stock up on produce from the adjoining store – plus local fruit and veg.

La Petanque

1208 Mornington-Flinders Road, Main Ridge
5931 0155

FRENCH 15/20

Going up the garden path is rarely so rewarding: it leads to a restaurant whose inviting barn-like rooms look on to old cypress pines and across the slopes of the Main Ridge valley. Owner Philippe Marquet is the friendly, informative host. The menu moves comfortably between France and the Mornington Peninsula – local olive oil and vegetables share the table with French salt and French cheeses. A meal here is a leisurely and serious experience, with white cloths, fine glassware, and imaginative cooking. A prune-studded slice of rabbit terrine served with rabbit rillettes is balanced by sharp cornichons and crisp toast; a salad of winter vegetables, bright with all colours of beetroot, carrots and herbs, looks as fresh as a summer's morning. Crisp-skinned snapper, just cooked, comes with Mount Martha mussels, and fennel mousseline. Desserts are deliciously clever, maybe crepes filled with spiced Red Hill apples, paired with green apple sorbet and squares of apple balsamic jelly.

Open Daily noon–3pm; Fri–Sat 6.30pm–late (closed Wed–Thurs noon–3pm in winter)
Typical prices E $25 **M** $42 **D** $18
Cards AE MC V Eftpos
Wine Hefty list, focusing on Mornington Peninsula and French wines, with suggested food matches.
Owners Philippe & Judy Marquet
Chef Stuart Deller
Seats 60; outdoor seating; private room
www.lapetanque.com.au

And ... The fixed-price weekday lunch choices are excellent value.

The Long Table

Red Hill Village, 159 Shoreham Road, Red Hill South
5989 2326

CONTEMPORARY 15/20

Overlooking cherry orchards, the Long Table's split-level dining room is modern, casual and cosy. Its mismatched bare wooden tables and eclectic collectibles don't foreshadow the explosion of flavour from owner-chef Andrew Doughton's constantly evolving menu, a list of playful, flavoursome and iconoclastic dishes. The meal might start with a sharing plate of school prawns with smoky paprika, pork crackling and miso-flavoured mayo, or an entree of crabmeat roll with crisped chicken skin and sweetcorn mayo. Snapper may be salt-baked whole, served on a bed of seaweed with local shoreline leaves. Dessert could be a plate of different textures of chocolate – from smooth delice to bubbly chocolate bar – that has the cocoa-bean quota turned to 11. This young chef knows how the palate works and how to make food both flavourful and fun. Relax, ignore any gaps in the service, and enjoy one of Mornington Peninsula's most exciting restaurants.

Open Wed–Sun 6–9.30pm; Sat–Sun noon–3pm
Typical prices Fixed-price menus $45 (2 courses), $58 (3 courses), $70 (4 courses)
Cards MC V Eftpos
Wine Concise peninsula-biased list with an eye to Europe, with pleasingly moderate mark-ups; BYO Sun night (no corkage)
Owners Andrew Doughton & Samantha Fitzgerald
Chefs Andrew Doughton & Simon Hanmer
Seats 90; outdoor seating; private room; bar
www.thelongtable.com.au

And ... A great tapas menu runs all day at weekends and from 4pm weekdays.

Max's at Red Hill Estate

53 Shoreham Road, Red Hill South **5931 0177**

CONTEMPORARY **14/20**

From this unfussy, many-windowed dining room set high on the ridge of Red Hill, the views are outstanding, in fact, some of the peninsula's best. Diners in groups and pairs form a content crowd, happily ordering the succulent honey-and-thyme roasted quail with baked fig and buttery local blue cheese, and matching it with a crisp estate chardonnay. The robust flavours continue with a terrifically crisp-skinned duck breast, or a pink-centred lamb fillet crusted in dukkah and plated with rustic pea mash. A citrus-curd dessert may look spectacular, with its garland of meringues, but it may fail to work on the palate – tipping to too-sweet. Zabaglione made with the estate's sparkling is better. Young service can sometimes be unsophisticated, but that view across netting-trussed vines to Western Port and the knobby end of Phillip Island more than compensates.

Open Daily noon–5pm; Fri–Sat 6.30–11pm
Typical prices E $20 **M** $38 **D** $17
Cards DC AE MC V Eftpos
Wine Short, sharp list that spruiks Red Hill Estate's wines, plus a handful of local beers and cider; 12 by the glass
Owner & chef Max Paganoni
Seats 100; outdoor seating
www.maxsrestaurant.com.au

And ... During summer and in fine weather, grab a beanbag, one of Max's 'platters on the paddock' antipasto plates and a bottle of plonk, and plonk down to take in the vistas.

Montalto

33 Shoreham Road, Red Hill South **5989 8412**

CONTEMPORARY **15.5/20**

There's beauty everywhere you look. It's in the vines and orchards, the abundant vegetable gardens and, of course, the modern sculpture exhibition that grows every year as the annual acquisitive prize adds to the collection. And then there are the families who wander the gardens, take in the art and eat at the casual piazza. The restaurant, though, is all fine food and silver service. Each plate offers an artistic blend of flavour and technique such as scallop boudin graced by a gentle bacon and shiitake foam, or rich-flavoured rabbit terrine seasoned by pistachio butter and served with moreish house-made walnut bread. Velvety verjuice beurre blanc coats satiny confit salmon and accompanies potatoes too humbly described as crushed. Desserts make full use of the orchards, and a chocolate marquise with honeycomb and coffee icecream will make you swoon. And you can enjoy strolling it off on the estate's 'wetlands walk'.

Open Daily noon–3pm; Fri–Sat 6.30–11pm (extended hours in summer)
Typical prices E $21 **M** $39 **D** $19
Cards DC AE MC V Eftpos
Wine Smart 10-pager with wines from near (estate and Australia) and far (France and Italy); 16 by the glass
Owners John & Wendy Mitchell
Chef Barry Davis
Seats 100; outdoor seating; private room
www.montalto.com.au

And ... See the sculpture entries as well as the permanent exhibition from February to April, and have a pizza in the piazza at weekends.

Paringa Estate

44 Paringa Road, Red Hill South **5931 0136**

CONTEMPORARY **14/20**

Chef Julian Hills (ex-Courthouse Hotel, North Melbourne) has lifted Paringa several notches. The food is ambitious, without being overworked, with a lightness of touch and refined technique. Dunk warm house-baked rolls (sourdough, olive, a malty dark roll made with Red Hill beer) into local olive oil or smear with white anchovy butter. Adventurous touches – perhaps yellowfin tuna paired with translucent calamari (confited sous vide, and shaved) or local berries with a light, crumbly sheet of dehydrated choc mousse – add interest. Quail breast might come boned, rolled and cooked to a deep pink, then cut into three fat little coins, and served with a 'brulee' of foie gras and morello cherries. For mains, duck may be a twice-cooked breast and a braised leg. For dessert, sticky lemon cake and wild blackberry sorbet may feature. The dated, low-key dining room with terracotta tiled floor and cellar door sales at the rear lacks the wow factor of other winery restaurants and was being tweaked at press time. But the outlook compensates, with vines and a flock of waddling geese.

Open Wed–Sun noon–3pm; Fri–Sat 6–9pm
Typical prices E $19 **M** $38 **D** $14
Cards MC V Eftpos
Wine Short list of Europeans, plus the multi award-winning estate wines
Owner Lindsay McCall
Chef Julian Hills
Seats 65; outdoor seating
www.paringaestate.com.au

And ... You can buy *Lindsay's Reserve*, a DVD chronicling four seasons at Paringa.

Port Phillip Estate

263 Red Hill Road, Red Hill South **5989 4444**

CONTEMPORARY **14/20**

The entrance is a great sweeping curve of rammed concrete that rises from this rural Red Hill ridge. The drama of the architectural exterior is surpassed by the natural beauty of the forested valley below, sweeping down to Western Port Bay, the sky often home to a pair of wedge-tailed eagles. Inside, tables are set with white linen and service is relaxed, sometimes too low-key. A wine list that reads like a love letter to Europe can threaten to outshine the food at times, a standard grilled steak maybe shown up by a superlative red. Start with stunning Tassie oysters with rice-wine dressing, or a plate of wood-smoked ocean trout enriched with a little crabmeat and avocado. A meaty morsel of roasted grouper pairs with saffron-infused white beans and mussels. Finish with velvety, smooth chocolate pudding and drunken cherries. The striking design and aesthetics can sometimes be let down by detail (flowers could be fresher, windows could be cleaner) and more attention would move the dial here from good to great.

Open Wed–Sun noon–3pm; Fri–Sat 6.30–9pm
Typical prices E $21 **M** $38 **D** $17
Cards AE MC V Eftpos
Wine Their own, other fine Australians, plus extensive range of Old World wines; burgundy a speciality
Owner Gjergja family
Chef Simon West
Seats 85; outdoor seating; private room
www.portphillipestate.com.au

And ... At weekends, lunches and dinners are set price: $78 or $85 (two or three courses).

The Rocks

Mornington Yacht Club, 1 Schnapper Point Drive, Mornington **5973 5599**

SEAFOOD **14/20**

Celebrating 10 years in business with a makeover and a fresh pitch, the Rocks is now a better proposition than ever. With unimpeachable views of the marina, the seafood restaurant embraces the location with whimsical ocean-detritus chandeliers and a now-open kitchen through which diners can spy tanks of live sea creatures that make up a good portion of the menu. The occasional fuss (a mayo-dominated spanner crab cannoli) is balanced by some pleasingly big flavours with a multi-textured grilled octopus salad on a mild chilli sauce base. When it comes to the flappingly fresh mains, most of which come off the grill, the kitchen favours simplicity: check out the locally caught yellow-eye mullet with a smoky paprika sauce for a lesson in produce-driven excellence. Carnivores have a couple of options such as steak or braised lamb shoulder, and desserts may include chocolate and peanut parfait with salted caramel. Staff are some of the best on the peninsula.

Open Daily 8am–9.30pm (closed Sun nights June–Aug)
Typical prices E $22 **M** $31 **D** $14
Cards AE MC V Eftpos
Wine A broad church, including local heroes, with a good selection by the glass
Owners Robert & Lisa De Santis
Chefs Xavier Nalty & Shane Smith
Seats 80; outdoor seating; private room
www.therocksmornington.com.au

And ... Paper menus double as colouring-in material for the little ones – just ask for crayons.

Salix at Willow Creek

166 Balnarring Road, Merricks North **5989 7640**

CONTEMPORARY **14.5/20**

From the elevated, carpeted dining space to the linen tablecloths and upholstered chairs, Salix exudes calm and sophistication. 'House-made' peppers the short French-leaning menu, as in bread, charcuterie and icecream, along with produce from top-notch local suppliers (such as Main Ridge Dairy), all lifted with thoughtful and inventive touches. Boned quail, for example, is wrapped in jamon then pan-roasted, and served with cavolo nero (black kale) made crisp in a dehydrator, and a piquant cherry and pear salad. Pan-roasted pork fillet and a wedge of slow-cooked pork belly sit atop layers of thinly sliced buttery potato and a smear of fennel puree, and a moist mound of shredded duck-leg confit is paired with rich lamb-shoulder rillettes, a bacony duck-liver parfait and a ragout of delicate flageolet beans. Feeling decadent? Share the dessert assiette, a wooden board laden with assorted sweets such as honey bavarois, Belgian chocolate tart and peach tarte tatin.

Open Daily noon–3pm; Fri–Sat 6–10pm
Typical prices E $22 **M** $38 **D** $15
Cards DC AE MC V Eftpos
Wine Estate labels are supplemented with 10 whites and four reds from other Australian, NZ and European producers; 10 by the glass
Owners Bernard & Rachael McCarthy
Chef David Walford
Seats 70; outdoor seating
www.willow-creek.com.au

And ... The adjoining bistro and deck are casual and family friendly.

Stillwater at Crittenden

25 Harrisons Road, Dromana **5981 9555**

CONTEMPORARY **14.5/20**

Stillwater's dining room – with its panoramic windows capturing shimmering lakes, roaming ducks and lazily swaying willows – validates the restaurant's name. Simple white linens and hanging bundles of golden lightbulbs keep the interior simple, and the service is similarly relaxing, with warmed rolls and dukkah arriving to accompany your first glass. Using seasonal produce from the kitchen garden and local organic suppliers, the contemporary menu is masterful in its ability to orchestrate flavours without diluting their essence. A small chunk of pork belly is crisply bookended, and topped with tingling romesco. A caesar salad is deconstructed, with a pancetta crisp, draped Spanish anchovy and a slow-cooked egg the texture of custard. The baked rotolo filled with spiced pumpkin tastes like autumn with its stained-glass crumble of mustard fruits on top, while the Angus eye fillet is presented simply on a board, crowned with a coin of herb butter and accompanied by a salad with candied shallots.

Open Sun–Wed 9am–5pm; Thurs 9am–10pm; Fri–Sat 9am–11pm (Thurs 9am–5pm in winter)
Typical prices E $22 **M** $36 **D** $15
Cards AE MC V Eftpos
Wine A lively wine list with many estate-grown and local heroes, plus interesting European options
Owners Zac & Jacqui Poulier
Chefs Zac Poulier, Kat Shine & Rodney Graham
Seats 100; outdoor seating; private room
www.stillwateratcrittenden.com.au

And ... There are midweek lunch specials and value weekend fixed-price menus.

BEST REGIONAL WINE LIST

Ten Minutes by Tractor

1333 Mornington-Flinders Road, Main Ridge **5989 6080**

CONTEMPORARY **16/20**

A tractor is this winery's mascot, but rural rusticity is left at the door. The bar, with an open fire in winter, beckons. Then a dining area, immaculate as a designer penthouse, but relaxed, with its varnished timber, big windows and rolling vineyard view. Chef Stuart Bell's seasonal menus draw on a kitchen garden and organic local growers for dishes like a brilliant vegetarian entree – roasted corn, silken tofu, witlof and rosemary oil with satiny sweetcorn velouté poured at table. Cape Grim eye fillet accompanies slow-braised beef cheek, with parsnip and horseradish, and onion with red wine jus. Hapuku arrives parmesan-crusted on cauliflower puree with baby leeks, enoki mushrooms and chive-and-chardonnay sauce. Main Ridge pears come several ways in one dessert – caramelised, folded through pear mousse, as pear cannoli – with ginger and champagne jelly and popcorn icecream. Like many dishes, it's a visual and culinary composition. This modernistic temple to wine and food is well worth a pilgrimage.

Open Wed–Sun noon–3pm; Thurs–Sat 6.30–9pm
Typical prices Fixed-price menus $68 (2 courses), $88 (3 courses), degustation $120 (6 courses)
Cards AE MC V Eftpos
Wine Recommended wines from all over in an annotated leather tome, not just local or estate; fine chardonnay, pinot noir and burgundies star
Owner Martin Spedding
Chef Stuart Bell
Seats 50; outdoor seating; bar
www.tenminutesbytractor.com.au

And ... Try the special six-course degustation.

Terminus at Flinders Hotel

Corner Cook & Wood streets, Flinders **5989 0201**

NORTH AFRICAN/FRENCH **15/20**

The Flinders Pub has served cockies, surfies, yuppies and townies and now the newish owners are targeting foodies. The old band room has been gentrified with cool grey and earth tones, stone fireplaces and garden courtyard dining areas with large rooms opened up to feed the summer crowds but also creating intimate spaces. Algerian-born French chef Pierre Khodja is at the pans cooking food made with French technique and subtle use of North African ingredients. You might start with green and white asparagus with onion marmalade and shanklish (Lebanese soft cheese). Main course could be crisp-skinned snapper fillet with pearl cous cous and saffron-infused sauce, or a pan-seared beef fillet with a little beef borek with rich shallot puree and red-wine jus. Finish with a hot souffle with Turkish delight flavours matched with silky halva icecream – stunning. Terminus is emerging as a hot new destination for peninsula dining.

Open Wed–Sat 6–9pm; Sat–Sun noon–3pm (closed Wed–Thurs in winter)
Typical prices E $26 **M** $39 **D** $17
Cards DC AE MC V Eftpos
Wine A smart and compact collection of Mornington Peninsula greats, Victorian classics, Aussie icons and European favourites; 15 by the glass
Owner Zig Inge family
Chef Pierre Khodja
Seats 40; outdoor seating; private room; bar
www.flindershotel.com.au

And … Stay overnight at the new onsite boutique accommodation.

Acquolina

26 Ocean Beach Road, Sorrento **5984 0811**

ITALIAN

In summer this seaside eatery overflows with happy holidaymakers. House-made pasta is king, like glossy parcels of beef casoncelli with porcini cream sauce, enjoyed indoors among the Tuscan colours and butcher's paper, or in the low-lit back courtyard. Italian-accented staff may recommend specials, like sumptuous roasted spatchcock. Try the tiramisu; it's as good as everyone says.

Open Thurs–Mon 6–10pm (daily in summer) **Typical prices E** $17 **M** $33 **D** $15 **Licensed**

Brass Razu Wine Bar

13 Main Street, Mornington **5975 0108**

BAR DINING

Luxurious, labyrinthine Brass Razu is a wine bar for all moods (astroturfed alfresco, peacock-hued fireside salon, gilt-framed dining room) with a menu of mainly locally produced light bites to match. Red wines pair jubilantly with 'a little nibbly Spanish plate' of empanadas and olives, beer sits well with a chorizo-topped pizza, or indulge with champagne and French blue.

Open Mon 4–11pm; Tues–Wed & Sun noon–11pm; Thurs–Sat noon–midnight **Typical prices E** $13.50 **M** $20 **D** $7.50 **Licensed**

Ciao Bella

new

2998 Frankston–Flinders Road, Balnarring **5931 3098**

PIZZERIA

At this bustling family-friendly pizza shack you'll find daily-changing blackboard specials that might include simple crumbed and fried sardines or linguine with lemon-cured salmon and Flinders tomatoes. But it's mainly about the thin-crust pizzas – like 'Bob's' (named after a local) with Shaw River buffalo mozzarella, baby spinach, parmesan and tomato, or another starring mushroom, taleggio and truffle oil.

Open Wed–Sat noon–3pm; Tues–Sat 5–9.30pm; Sun 11.30am–4pm (daily in summer) **Typical prices E** $18 **M** $24 **D** $12 **Licensed** ciaobellapizza.com.au

Counting House

new

787 Esplanade, Mornington **5975 2055**

CONTEMPORARY

A warm greeting sets the tone at this renovated cottage-turned-restaurant. A table on the open deck is perfect for oysters, champagne and sea views, while the cosy yet minimal dining rooms suit the compact, uncomplicated menu that features deft renditions of a herb-crusted lamb rack, roasted corn-fed chicken with macaroni cheese, and a rich side of potato dauphinoise.

Open Tues–Sun noon–3pm, 6–11pm **Typical prices E** $18 **M** $32 **D** $12 **Licensed** countinghouse.com.au

Dee's Kitchen

new

19 Pier Street, Dromana **5981 4666**

MIDDLE EASTERN/MEDITERRANEAN

Off the main drag, with a low-key fitout (concrete floor, bare wood tables and naked light bulbs), this cafe/provedore lets the food say it all. Perhaps spicy shakshuka eggs (until 3pm), or tender lamb shoulder roasted for 16 hours. Choose a bottle from the wine wall and share a platter of salumi or house-made dips, or pop in for take-home lasagne.

Open Daily 8am–3pm; Thurs–Sat 6–9.30pm **Typical prices E** $16 **M** $28 **D** $5 **Licensed** deeskitchen.com.au

Fed-Up Fish Cafe

1571 Point Nepean Road, Rosebud West **5986 4716**

SEAFOOD

There's no shortage of fish shacks along this beachside highway but, despite its '*Happy Days* goes to the seaside' decor, this family-run place is the one to stop at. Whitebait fritters are webs of tasty little fish, while prawn and trevally spring rolls are fragrant with herbs. There's chowder, whole grilled flounder, a chunky crayfish and mango cocktail, and a joyous array of house-baked desserts.

Open Wed–Sun 5.30–9.30pm; Fri–Sun noon–2pm **Typical prices E** $15.90 **M** $31.90 **D** $10.50 **Licensed**

Fork to Fork at Heronswood

105 La Trobe Parade, Dromana **5984 7318**

MODERN REGIONAL

Simon Buckley (ex-La Petanque) now mans the pans at this thatched-roof cottage with its renowned kitchen garden. House platters highlight the day's (and season's) finest; smaller dishes may include heirloom beets with walnut and horseradish, snapper with silverbeet and Tuscan kale, or sugar-cured ocean trout with fennel and coriander emulsion. Delicate chocolate pudding, its centre oozing like lava, is a lush finish.

Open Daily 10am–4pm **Typical prices E** $16 **M** $28 **D** $13 **Licensed** diggers.com.au

Foxeys Hangout

795 White Hill Road, Red Hill **5989 2022**

SHARE-PLATES

Floor-to-ceiling windows make the most of the vineyard panorama at this small, bustling cellar door. Inside or on the deck winemaker-chef Tony Lee's rustic share-plates complement attractive stripped-back, blondwood aesthetics. Amiable staff deliver smoky roast capsicum with white anchovies, rich duck rillettes, plump Flinders tomatoes strewn with feta and mint or barbecued quail.

Open Sat–Sun 11am–5pm (and public hols); no bookings **Typical prices** Share-plates $11 **Licensed** foxeys-hangout.com.au

La Baracca Trattoria

T'Gallant Winemakers, 1385 Mornington-Flinders Road, Main Ridge **5931 1300**

ITALIAN

In summer it's open windows, in winter expect open fires. Either way, the converted barn invites you to relax, crack open a bottle, and graze. Robust flavours abound in the modern Italian food, with dishes such as confit duck tart with lardons and sticky currant relish, or glazed roasted chicken with romesco sauce and charred zucchini. There's a casual pizzeria (Spuntino Bar) onsite, too.

Open Mon–Fri noon–3pm; Sat–Sun noon–4pm **Typical prices E** $16 **M** $32 **D** $15 **Licensed** tgallant.com.au

La Campagna

176 Rogers Road, Cape Schanck **5988 5350**

ITALIAN

New owners at this modest dining room in grand natural surrounds let the seasons dictate what's on the home-style menu. Tasting plates might feature house olive products or mushrooms steeped in 30-year-old balsamic. Try tender meatballs smothered in caramelised red onion or succulent eggplant layered with potato. Then, dense choc-macadamia torte before you hit the road.

Open Fri–Sun noon–2.30pm **Typical prices E** $24 **M** $28 **D** $12.50 **Licensed**

Loquat

3183 Point Nepean Road, Sorrento **5984 4444**

CONTEMPORARY

When fish and chips just won't do, the weekender crowd descends on this charming converted cottage like a flock of noisy (bejewelled and coiffed) seagulls. The food is reliably good: an entree of char-grilled quail is first brined with brown sugar for extra colour and sweetness; an ocean-trout main cooked sous vide is suitably tender; a Callebaut chocolate fondant provides a sweet, oozy finish.

Open Thurs–Sun 6–9pm (extended hours in Jan; closed Aug) **Typical prices E** $17 **M** $34 **D** $15 **Licensed** loquat.com.au

Merricks General Wine Store

3460 Frankston-Flinders Road, Merricks **5989 8088**

CONTEMPORARY

Hearty breakfasts, house-made cakes, wine tasting from three local vineyards or perhaps a lingering lunch? Merricks sets a high benchmark for 'country pitstop'. Perhaps try smoked trout kedgeree or a pork pie in the bustling cellar door bistro, or head to the farmhouse-style dining room for twice-cooked confit duck or freekeh pilaf with shredded lamb shank. At both, expect generous, wine-friendly serves and top-notch local produce.

Open Daily 9–11.30am, noon–3.30pm **Typical prices E** $19 **M** $36 **D** $14 **Licensed** mgwinestore. com.au

Morning Star Estate

1 Sunnyside Road, Mount Eliza **9787 7760**

CONTEMPORARY

Dining on the enclosed verandah of this century-old mansion surrounded by rose gardens, manicured lawns and grapevines feels like a special occasion. Inside, too, it's fine dining on freshly shucked oysters or plump mussels in tomato sauce. Crisp-skinned young chicken is juicy and served with luxuriously buttery mash; a Cointreau panna cotta is a splendid finish.

Open Wed & Fri–Sun noon–3pm; Fri–Sat 6–8.30pm (extended hours in summer) **Typical prices E** $19 **M** $36 **D** $18 **Licensed** morningstarestate.com.au

Morning Sun Vineyard

337 Main Creek Road, Main Ridge **5989 6571**

ITALIAN

The vine-covered courtyard surrounding this small restaurant and cellar door provides delightful views. Estate wines accompany a tight menu, designed to share. The platters (bruschetta and antipasto) and wood-fired pizzas are as authentic as they come, or there might be flavoursome lamb meatballs in rich napoli with oregano and sour cream. Nonna Claudia's polenta fries deserve their high acclaim.

Open Fri–Mon 9.30am–5pm (daily in summer) **Typical prices** Share-plates $18, pizzas $23 **D** $12 **Licensed** morningsunvineyard.com.au

Red Barn at Box Stallion

64 Tubbarubba Road, Merricks North **5989 7444**

CONTEMPORARY

This unique restaurant is set in converted horse stalls, so you could say it literally shares a stable with the tasting room. Start with hearty soup, maybe tomato and basil. Open pork pie may be served on red cabbage, or prawns on a saffron risotto and topped with lemon, garlic and parsley. All are matched with value estate wines.

Open Daily noon–3pm **Typical prices E** $18 **M** $28 **D** $11 **Licensed** boxstallion.com.au

The Sisters

151 Ocean Beach Road, Sorrento **5984 4646**

CAFE

Kitchen-garden plots overflowing with produce are a sign of the goodness to come at this strip of gastronomy. Sit beneath market umbrellas in the inviting courtyard and order from the day's cook-up. Perhaps a hearty eggplant parmigiana, cheesy veg frittata or a chickpea salad with Persian feta, bacon and just-picked spinach. Flavours are robust and the made-here sweet things, such as frangipane tart, are wonderful.

Open Mon–Tues, Thurs–Fri 8am–4pm; Sat–Sun 8am–5pm (reduced hours Easter–Nov) **Typical prices M** $16 **D** $12 **Licensed**

Smokehouse Sorrento

182 Ocean Beach Road, Sorrento **5984 1246**

ITALIAN/PIZZERIA

Buzzy Smokehouse packs in all-comers with its swift, amiable service, easy menu, and family vibe (textas and colouring-in provided). Simple seafood dishes, from crisp-skinned roast trout on beetroot salad to golden fish and chips, threaten to upstage the thin-crust pizzas (maybe with lamb and rocket) from the wood-fired oven. Gelati with Mars Bar sauce helps keep kids (and adults) happy.

Open Wed–Sun 6–9.30pm (extended hours in summer) **Typical prices E** $15.50 **M** $26.50 (pizzas $18.50) **D** $12.50 **Licensed**

Spoon

Shop 1, 84 Mount Eliza Way, Mount Eliza **9787 7710**

EUROPEAN

This smart dining room serves up classy bistro fare to appreciative local families and date-night couples. After zucchini flowers stuffed with lemony ricotta perhaps opt for house-made gnocchi with braised oxtail, heirloom carrots and gremolata, or the simplicity of pan-fried snapper. Service could be more attentive, but desserts, which tread the pudding and panna cotta path, do so in fine style.

Open Tues–Sat 5.30–10pm; Wed–Fri noon–3pm **Typical prices E** $15 **M** $29 **D** $12 **Licensed & BYO** spoonatmteliza.com.au

Steam

Shop 4, 2257 Point Nepean Road, Rye **5985 7700**

MODERN ASIAN

At night, terrific Asian share-plates are the way to go at this stylish, funky, low-lit bunker. Enjoy oysters plucked from tanks by the bar, sesame-crusted tuna sashimi or spiced pork belly with apple and daikon salad. Service can misfire, with cutlery and drinks going missing one one visit, but desserts with oomph (maybe banana and white chocolate parfait) bring things back on course.

Open Mon–Fri 6–10pm; Sat–Sun noon–late **Typical prices E** $12 **M** $22 **D** $12 **Licensed** steamrestaurant.com.au

Tulsi

74 Station Street, Somerville **5977 6733**

INDIAN

Warm, earthy colours, attentive staff and a proudly local wine list are the backdrop for dishes with a pleasing hit of spice. Try golden samosas with a chunky blend of potato and pea, dory fillets with tamarind zing in a Kerala curry, or a chicken vindaloo that has a fiery kick. Team them with excellent stuffed breads and finish with sweet pistachio kulfi.

Open Wed–Mon 5.30–10.30pm **Typical prices E** $13 **M** $18 **D** $7.50 **Licensed & BYO** tulsi.com.au

Vines of Red Hill

150 Red Hill Road, Red Hill **5989 2977**

MODERN REGIONAL

Vines? You bet there are. Undulating vineyards are visible through the big windows of this airy dining room. A tasting plate, including pillowy eggplant beignets, is the perfect introduction. Octopus niçoise is prettily deconstructed and mushroom tortellini is featherlight, while mains feature sturdier options such as corn-fed chicken with polenta.

Open Tues–Sat noon–3pm; Sun 10.30am–3pm; Fri–Sat 6.30–11pm **Typical prices E** $15 **M** $35 **D** $15 **Licensed** vinesofredhill.com.au

GEELONG & BELLARINE PENINSULA

The Ol' Duke

Kelp Cafe

67 Lonsdale Street, Point Lonsdale **5258 4797**

CONTEMPORARY **14.5/20**

Stylish Kelp, with its minimalist beige-grey interior and city-slick vibe, is patrolled by a chic young staff, ferrying good coffee, French toast and seafood linguine by day, and more serious food by night. Dinner might begin with duck (in the forms of a meaty ras el hanout-scented terrine and a buttery parfait, the richness of each cut by pickled radish); proceed to a cheese souffle (with mushrooms, truffled polenta, shallot cream and caramelised carrot puree) or spatchcocked chicken rubbed with the chilli spice mix berbere, pan-baked and served with artichokes, smoked oyster mushrooms, leeks and house-cured bacon; then conclude with such suitably elaborate riches as the Banoffee pie (fresh banana with cinnamon toffee, macadamia biscuit and real vanilla icecream). The chef's Caribbean roots are subtly visible in his inclination towards warm spicing and the use of house-smoked ingredients.

Open Daily 8am–late (reduced hours in winter)
Typical prices E $17 **M** $38 **D** $16
Cards DC MC V Eftpos
Wine A worldly list is augmented by special bottles from the owner's cellar; BYO (corkage $20 a bottle)
Owners David & Lee Osborne
Chef Kasin Francis
Seats 54; outdoor seating

And ... Much of the art on the walls is for sale.

Loam

650 Andersons Road, Drysdale **5251 1101**

CONTEMPORARY **16.5/20**

Whether the rolling olive groves you see from Loam are lit by the moon, lashed by the rain or sparkling in summer, it's a sunny place to be, warmed by the easy country hospitality of an on-song service team and Aaron Turner's inspired cooking. The room's a simple box on a farm on an unmade road. Tables are bare and a produce-laden bench is the centrepiece, but it's beguiling. Submit to innovative set menus of four to nine courses. Whatever you've singled out from a card listing the day's ingredients, alluring dishes will follow. Spanner crab with sweetcorn custard and beach plants. Sweet bay bug with curls of pigs' ear crackling, tapioca and lush broth. The tenderest Angus short rib with a ribbon of beetroot, apple vinegar and sprigs of yarrow. Smoked, house-churned butter, for potato sourdough. The surprising conclusion is one of the year's most brilliant desserts, onion icecream with honeycomb – stunningly sublime.

Open Thurs & Sun noon–4pm; Fri–Sat noon–5pm, 6.30–11.30pm (Wed noon–4pm Dec–Feb)
Typical prices Set menus $60 (4 courses), $100 (7 courses), $125 (9 courses)
Cards AE MC V Eftpos
Wine Terrific wine matches; up to 22 by the glass, with a lively list favouring locals, and, increasingly, natural wines
Owners Aaron & Astrid Turner
Chef Aaron Turner
Seats 40; outdoor seating
www.loam.com.au

And ... They'll recommend local accommodation, and book taxis.

Napona

24 Hodgson Street, Ocean Grove **5256 3153**

CONTEMPORARY **14/20**

The owners say 'napona' means 'his wave' in the language of the Charomu people of the Marianas Islands, which tells you absolutely nothing about this exciting restaurant with its broad alfresco timber deck, and exhilarating menu of breezy, modern Asian and Mediterranean dishes. Young chef Will Swinton worked with Andrew McConnell at Cumulus, and it shows in the serious charcuterie platter loaded with warm, lush pork-cheek terrine, chorizo, serrano ham and cornichons; the crunchy, golden deep-fried school prawns with basil and aioli; and the house-made fettuccine tossed with fresh local fish and shellfish. It's sometimes hard to tell if what you order will be delicate, such as sashimi kingfish served with a slash of pea and wasabi puree, or full-bore satisfying, such as pink lamb rump paired with chickpea salad, goat's curd and dukkah. A fruity trifle of mango, ginger and orange sweetly layered in a glass tumbler is anything but a mere trifle. Eating in the Grove is definitely looking up.

Open Sun–Mon 8am–4pm; Tues–Sat 8am–late
Typical prices E $14 **M** $33 **D** $13
Cards MC V Eftpos
Wine Good, concise, Victorian-led list; BYO (corkage $15 a bottle)
Owner & chef Will Swinton
Seats 40; outdoor seating
www.napona.com.au

And ... Drop in for coffee and Istra ham-and-egg brekkies.

Oakdene

255 Grubb Road, Wallington **5255 1255**

CONTEMPORARY **14/20**

'Country eclectic' might best describe the setting in which you'll dine at Oakdene, but don't let the charismatic mash-up of regional art gallery and log cabin distract from the serious ambition in the kitchen. There's an endearing eccentricity to the objects peering out from every ochre nook of this boldly coloured and hospitable dining room, but genuine purpose in the menu, which might list sweet curls of local crayfish, keeping enoki and pumpkin 'tofu' company in a pure ham broth; wagyu carpaccio in a harmonious crowd of truffled pecorino, potato galette, soft egg gribiche, watercress and pungent horseradish 'snow'. Mains might feature local seafood (Queenscliff kingfish and Portarlington mussels) with native finger lime; slow-cooked kurobuta pork belly with white sausage, lentils, witlof and shiitakes; wagyu steak from the grill; or a salad of raw and cooked beetroot in buttermilk with candied walnuts. Desserts, such as a banana toffee cream pie with salted caramel icecream, round things off perfectly.

Open Wed–Sun noon–2.30pm; Wed–Sat 6.30–10pm
Typical prices Set menus $58 (2 courses), $69 (3 courses)
Cards AE MC V Eftpos
Wine Apart from the odd guest from the Coonawarra, Margaret River or France, most wines are from Victoria, especially Oakdene itself
Owners Bernard & Elizabeth Hooley
Chef Marty Chichester
Seats 80; outdoor seating; private room
www.oakdene.com.au

And ... There are classes for aspiring cooks.

The Ol' Duke

40 Newcombe Street, Portarlington **5259 1250**

CONTEMPORARY **14/20**

The Ol' Duke has stood sentinel overlooking the Bay since the 1850s. Broad decking and a whitewashed block-fronted facade invite patrons to beguile sunny days, while inside, a buzzing, eagerly staffed dining area encourages lingering over lunch or dinner. Kick off with cumin-tinged, flash-fried calamari, bulked up with nutty chickpeas and lightened by celery heart and lemon, or the obligatory Portarlington mussels, perhaps served one of four ways (with parsley and white wine, laksa lemak and noodles, a 'Chinese' broth with ginger and coriander or tomato and chorizo). The locavore commitment extends to flathead, simply beer-battered and served with aioli, and excellent eye fillet from Ballarat, char-grilled and accompanied by a golden mat of roesti, peppercorn jus and a salad of tomato, parsley and leek. Finish with blood plums, coconut icecream and strawberry sauce - pretty good. Here's a toast to this cracking little seaside inn's future as well as its past.

Open Thurs–Fri & Mon 9am–9pm; Sat–Sun 8am–9pm
Typical prices E $19 **M** $35 **D** $15
Cards AE MC V Eftpos
Wine The Bellarine gets a significant boost, with a smattering of good choices from Australia's great wine regions and abroad
Owners Adam & Jody Paine
Chef Tristan Bibby
Seats 95; outdoor seating; private room; bar
www.theolduke.com.au

And ... At the heart of the beautiful old hotel is a ballroom, which can hold 80 for functions.

Scorched

17 The Esplanade, Torquay **5261 6142**

MIDDLE EASTERN **15/20**

Middle Eastern flavours work spiffingly at this sweet little shopfront facing Zeally Bay, so much so that James White and Vanessa Joachim often run two sittings at weekends to cope with the crowds. This won't surprise anyone who's had White's crisp fried school prawns buzzed up with chilli salt, or his moreish little duck pies (miniature bisteeya pastries laced with sweet cinnamon). Everything comes tapas-style to share, from delectably crisp salt cod fritters with aioli, and plump, seared scallops in potato skordalia to long-flavoured, slow-cooked ox cheek with roasted shallots. It's smooth sailing all the way from the Zeally Bay sourdough bread sticks, ready to dip into dukkah spice and olive oil to the smooth peanut parfait with whipped chocolate and salted caramel, a chic way to finish. Relaxing by day, buzzy by night, it's the ideal place to dine after a day on the sand.

Open Wed–Thurs 3–9pm; Fri–Sat 11.30am–9pm; Sun 11.30am–3pm
Typical prices Share-plates $4–$34 **D** $12
Cards AE MC V Eftpos
Wine A fairly priced, three-page list with a smattering of local wines and plenty of global offerings including German rieslings, Iberian whites, NZ pinots and Spanish riojas; BYO (corkage $25 a bottle)
Owners James White & Vanessa Joachim
Chef James White
Seats 55; outdoor seating
www.scorched.com.au

And ... When the sun is shining, snaffle a table outside.

2 Faces

8 Malop Street, Geelong **5229 4546**

CONTEMPORARY **14/20**

The faces in question belong to Simon Yarham and Timothy Mitchell, partners, co-owners, and chef and floor manager respectively, who have been at the helm here since opening in 1999. The dining room dates back to 1857, and is a glorious fusion of kitsch and opulence, its purple walls lined with photos of the pair's family and friends. There's kitsch on the cocktail list too, which employs liqueurs such as Midori and Malibu, but when it comes to the food, it's fresh, inventive and delicious. Starters like tempura soft-shell crab on a piquant Thai-style pomelo salad set the bar high, but mains uphold the standard. Chickpea-battered vegetables with plump chestnut ravioli swim in sweet soy butter, while slow-cooked lamb is complemented with merguez sausage, currants and rich almond cream. Dessert, like chocolate souffle with a gooey truffle centre, is a sin worth indulging in, and the effervescent Mitchell, who works the floor most nights, feels like a friend by the meal's end.

Open Tues–Sat 6–11pm
Typical prices E $23 **M** $36 **D** $15
Cards DC AE MC V Eftpos
Wine Around 50 well-priced mostly Australian wines (11 by the glass), with a focus on local and regional producers
Owners Simon Yarham & Timothy Mitchell
Chef Simon Yarham
Seats 50
www.2faces.com.au

And ... The house chilli jelly and pistachio dukkah are available to take home.

Vue Grand

46 Hesse Street, Queenscliff **5258 1544**

CONTEMPORARY **14.5/20**

Don't be fooled by the high, sky-blue ceilings, statuary lamps, leadlighting and other signs of antique grandeur: here you'll find some of the finer contemporary food on the Bellarine. A respectful, technically accomplished approach recognises ingredients' merits and combines them brilliantly. An amuse-bouche might be poached quail egg in pure, sweet ham broth, sympathetically teamed with micro-diced shiitake and baby herbs. Then, rabbit loin (sourced up the road at Lara) with a vibrant mint pea puree topped with buckwheat, blood sausage, cuttlefish and confit rabbit leg; or maybe a hapuku fillet, the flakes of fish mingling with the juices from chorizo, wild mushrooms and clams. Desserts, perhaps seasonal berries with yoghurt pearls and vivid berry consomme, possibly raise the bar even higher at Vue Grand, as does professional, cheerful service and an upbeat atmosphere.

Open Wed–Sat 6–11pm; Sun noon–4pm
Typical prices E $18 **M** $38 **D** $18
Cards DC AE MC V Eftpos
Wine A balanced, cosmopolitan and modestly priced list (many around $60) with plenty of local offerings, including regional beers and separate sections for 'Geelong pinot noir' and 'Geelong shiraz'
Owners Anthony & Ross Closter
Chef Lyndon Betts
Seats 80; private room; bar
www.vuegrand.com.au

And ... The already-extravagant dining room is only a portion of the old Victorian ballroom.

Athelstane House

4 Hobson Street, Queenscliff **5258 1024**

CONTEMPORARY

This guesthouse-restaurant was established in the 1860s. The menu's simple but appealing: Coffin Bay oysters, duck and plum dumplings, local flathead lightly beer-battered, and a hefty wagyu beef burger. Local produce, like Portarlington mussels and Point Lonsdale tomatoes, features. There's friendly service, and a relaxed seaside mood in the good-looking dining room or at outdoor tables.

Open Daily 8.30–11am; Wed–Sat 6–8.30pm; Sat–Sun noon–3pm **Typical prices E** $12 **M** $23 **D** $10 **Licensed** athelstane.com.au

Barwon Edge Boathouse

40 Windsor Road, Newtown **5221 2200**

CONTEMPORARY

On the banks of the Barwon, this bright, open diner is a relaxed refuge. Below it, walkers and rowers pass, and kids run on the lawns (watch out for snakes), while grown-up diners share silky pâté, brioche and cornichons, try fragrant chermoula-spiced braised lamb, or dig into choc-cherry trifle. Staff do a great job, and there are wood-fired pizzas on Sunday afternoons.

Open Mon–Wed 9am–5pm; Thurs–Sun 9am–9pm **Typical prices E** $16 **M** $28 **D** $12 **Licensed & BYO** barwonedge.com.au

Baveras Brasserie

Cunningham Pier, 10 Western Beach Foreshore Road, Geelong **5222 6377**

CONTEMPORARY

The view from this brasserie at the end of Cunningham Pier is peerless, an unfettered expanse taking in Corio Bay, the yacht club and Geelong's foreshores and skyline. You might begin with a lasagne of blue swimmer crab encircled by delicate crab bisque, followed by eye fillet on a bed of baby root vegetables and caramelised shallots, then maybe hot chocolate souffle cake to further sweeten the outlook.

Open Mon–Sat 6–9pm; Mon–Thurs 9–11.30am, noon–3pm; Fri–Sun 8am–3pm **Typical prices E** $17 **M** $34 **D** $15 **Licensed** baveras.com.au

The Beach House

Eastern Beach Reserve, Geelong **5221 8322**

CONTEMPORARY

Enjoy knockout bay views of Eastern Beach's iconic pool from this historic gable-roofed one-time kiosk where professional, attentive service and linen-dressed tables set the mood. Rockling fillets may be a little overcooked, but risotto-stuffed calamari accompanying them is tender and lovely. Char-grilled lamb loin may come with pea- and pinenut-studded cous cous. End with a postprandial stroll on the promenade.

Open Fri–Sun noon–3pm; Wed–Sat 6–9pm **Typical prices E** $17.90 **M** $37.90 **D** $14.50 **Licensed** easternbeachhouse.com.au

Bellbrae Harvest

45 Portreath Road, Bellbrae **5266 2100**

CONTEMPORARY

A mudbrick farmlet cottage with waterlily-filled dam and meandering geese is the last place you'd expect to find molecular gastronomy. Yet chef David Veal's ambitious menu includes house-cured ocean trout with liquid pea spheres, gnocchi with olive dust and frozen parmesan, and a deconstructed beef wellington – pastry crust presented as a pile of crumbs. Local produce and wines feature.

Open Fri–Sun 11.30am–3.30pm; Fri–Sat 6–10pm **Typical prices E** $16.90 **M** $36 **D** $15 **Licensed** bellbraeharvestrestaurant.com.au

Bistro @ 310

310 Moorabool Street, Geelong **5221 0000**

GREEK

This historic bluestone building turns taverna with polished floors, Greek-inspired artwork and, in the background, traditional music. If you opt for the banquet, obliging professional staff will deliver dips, good house-made bread and spanakopita, followed by smoky grilled seafood, chicken, fall-apart slow-cooked lamb and salad, finishing with Hellenic-style pastries and fresh fruit.

Open Tues–Sun noon–2.30pm, 6–10pm **Typical prices E** $8 **M** $28 **D** $3.50 **Licensed** bistro310.com.au

Black Bull Tapas Bar & Restaurant

48 Moorabool Street, Geelong **5229 6100**

SPANISH

Whether throwing back a Moritz and a few tasty tapas or settling in for a full meal, you could almost believe you're on the Costa del Sol here. There's a holiday-like buzz, attractive bare brick walls, and prompt friendly service. Try tapas like Portarlington mussels with white wine, cream and parsley, entrees like lamb skewers, and, perhaps, traditional paella for main.

Open Mon–Fri noon–2pm; Mon–Thurs 5.30–9pm; Fri–Sat 5.30–late **Typical prices E** $9 **M** $30 **D** $18 **Licensed** blackbulltapas.com.au

Couta Boat Cafe

59 Hesse Street, Queenscliff **5258 4600**

CONTEMPORARY

History is tangible at this 1902 Edwardian guesthouse. It's in the iron lacework above the patio seating and in the ceiling rose of the cosy dining room with attentive service. Prime the palate with a tasting plate (mussels, spicy chorizo, scallops); move on to hearty lamb shank or seafood stew. Finish with refreshing lemon-meringue tartlet with aromatic basil icecream.

Open Daily noon–3pm, 6–9pm **Typical prices E** $16.90 **M** $26.90 **D** $10.90 **Licensed** queenscliffinn.com.au

Customs House

new

Basement, 57-59 Brougham Street (facing waterfront), Geelong **5246 6500**

CONTEMPORARY

This historic 1856 waterfront bluestone has classic charm. Original arched interconnecting rooms boast polished floors, tan leather banquettes and rich burgundy drapes, while the bar's homely club chairs, books and open fireplace add to the appeal. Try seared hapuku with zingy orange fennel salad, or grilled wagyu rump, but for a wow finish it's the chocolate fondant with peanut praline.

Open Mon–Fri 9am–11.30pm; Sat–Sun 8am–11.30pm **Typical prices E** $18 **M** $36 **D** $18 **Licensed** customshouse.biz

Fishermen's Pier

Yarra Street (Corio Bay end), Geelong **5222 4100**

SEAFOOD/CONTEMPORARY

Every seat's a winner here – all tables provide a Corio Bay view and a superlative seafood banquet. Moreton Bay bugs anointed with vanilla, saffron, kaffir lime and shallot are a treat; so too top-quality hapuku and barramundi fillets, simply grilled. The service is excellent. Adequate desserts (maybe hummingbird cake), a good wine selection, starched linen tablecloths, and a graceful atmosphere complete the package.

Open Daily noon–2.30pm, 6–9pm **Typical prices E** $20 **M** $40 **D** $15 **Licensed** fishermenspier.com.au

Jack & Jill Restaurant

247 Moorabool Street, Geelong **5229 9935**

CONTEMPORARY

Here's a novel approach: you design your meal from a list of mini-meals. Choose three or four small dishes, and they'll all arrive on the one plate. It's like tapas but you don't have to share. And you may not want to share braised rabbit ravioli in orange butter, asparagus spears wrapped in parmesan omelette, or local mussels in tomato broth.

Open Wed–Fri & Sun 10am–9pm; Mon–Tues 5–9pm; Sat 4pm–late **Typical prices** three-dish plate $30.50 (lunch $25.50), four-dish plate $35.50 (lunch $31.50) **Licensed** jackandjillrestaurant.com.au

Jack Rabbit Vineyard

85 McAdams Lane, Bellarine **5251 2223**

CONTEMPORARY

Spectacular Corio Bay views are the most obvious drawcard here. There are fans in summer, a fire in winter, and the decor's whimsical. Youthful staff ferry crab and prawn dumplings in cucumber 'gazpacho'; sweet-potato gnocchi, lime-blackened snapper (local, like much else on the menu) on a white bean salad. Dessert – perhaps pears poached in Jack Rabbit rosé with a limoncello parfait – is reason to linger on the deck.

Open Daily noon–2.30pm; Fri–Sat 6–9pm **Typical prices E** $17 **M** $35 **D** $15 **Licensed** jackrabbitvineyard.com.au

Joseph's

Mansion Hotel & Spa, Werribee Park, K Road, Werribee **9731 4130**

CONTEMPORARY

In an old seminary, Joseph's offers stunning views of the estate's manicured gardens. Service is professional, and formal. A modern European menu changes seasonally and might include a trendy 'superfood' salad (sesame seeds, avocado and broccoli), a grass-fed Black Angus sirloin with bitey horseradish slaw, and a decadent peanut butter parfait and chocolate sandwich.

Open Mon–Fri noon–2pm, 6–8.30pm; Sat–Sun noon–2.30pm, 6–9.30pm **Typical prices E** $20 **M** $42 **D** $16 **Licensed & BYO** lancemore.com.au/mansion/restaurant

Man Bo

361-363 Moorabool Street, Geelong **5221 7888**

CANTONESE

With its opulent oriental decor and ornate ceiling there's lots that's large about this spot – including the menu and wine list. If decision-making creates angst, opt for a trusty banquet to sample flavoursome quail sang choy bao, zingy ginger prawns, Peking duck and beef stir-fry. Desserts include banana fritters and fried icecream – predictable but fun.

Open Tues–Sun 11.30am–3pm, 5–10pm **Typical prices E** $10.50 **M** $24 **D** $8.50 **Licensed** manbo.com.au

Mr Hyde

11 Malop Street, Geelong **5223 1228**

CONTEMPORARY

The old bank that is now home to Mr Hyde cuts a striking figure, with six metre-high ceilings and a dimly lit dining room furnished with fat chesterfields. Amiable, earnest staff serve seasonal, regional specialities (grilled Drysdale haloumi with tapenade and citrus segments) and ever-popular Turkish-style pizzas (lamb and feta) from the well-priced tapas-style menu. There's a fab bar room too, serving excellent cocktails.

Open Mon–Fri 10am–3pm; Wed–Sun 6–9pm; Sat–Sun 9am–3pm **Typical prices E** $12 **M** $24 **D** $12.50 **Licensed** mrhyde.com.au

Riviera on Yarra

73 Yarra Street, Geelong **5223 2808**

CONTEMPORARY/TEPPANYAKI

It's teppanyaki up top under new owners here. Added is a smart new upstairs bar featuring set menus for the teppan. Elegant contemporary downstairs dining remains, with well-spaced linen-dressed tables and stylish appointments. Begin with a tasting platter combining sesame-crusted scallops and watermelon wakame salad, yakiniku pork belly and other morsels, and, to follow, soft-cooked beef cheek with pillows of potato gnocchi and gremolata.

Open Tues–Sat noon–3pm, 6–9.30pm **Typical prices E** $12 **M** $26 **D** $13 **Licensed** rivieraonyarra.com.au

Telegraph Hotel

2 Pakington Street, Geelong West **5222 2471**

CONTEMPORARY

This 19th century pub, furnished with dark-wood tables and spotless carpets, delivers top-notch, well-executed pub grub. Dig into generous, good-value dishes like juicy wagyu burger with beetroot slaw and fries, or a delicious lemon-and-parsley crumbed pork schnitzel with tangy jus. Service can be patchy, but desserts like a lime coconut icecream sandwich sweeten the deal.

Open Daily noon–2.30pm, 6–9pm **Typical prices E** $15.50 **M** $25.50 **D** $11.50 **Licensed** thetelegraphhotel.com.au

360Q

2 Wharf Street, Queenscliff **5257 4200**

CONTEMPORARY

Right on the water, 360Q is modern, spacious and seafood-inclined. There may be a tasting plate of tempura whiting, marinated octopus, char-grilled Moreton Bay bugs, cucumber-wrapped oyster and Canadian scallop. Pan-fried snapper may be enhanced by artichokes, asparagus and chilli-coriander sauce. Add gracious service, gentle sound levels, and a good wine selection – and you have a feel-good experience.

Open Thurs–Mon noon–3pm; Fri–Sat 6–9pm (reduced hours in winter) **Typical prices E** $18 **M** $34 **D** $13 **Licensed** 360Q.com.au

WESTERN VICTORIA

Gladioli

A la Grecque

60 Great Ocean Road, Aireys Inlet **5289 6922**

GREEK **15/20**

Kosta Talimanidis stands on the verandah loudly welcoming guests as if they were members of his own family. But then, after 35 years on the Great Ocean Road, including 27 at the legendary Kosta's in Lorne, the Talimanidis clan has accumulated a vast, extended family. While Kosta is busy kissing babies on the outdoor deck or inside the split-level colour-splashed dining room, his wife Pam is in the kitchen turning out beach-house, surfside-friendly food bearing varying degrees of Greekness. The best idea is to just cover the table with everything from a shimmering salmon gravlax with silky mayonnaise and kid-friendly fried Queenscliff calamari with oregano and lemon to rustically Greek baked beans topped with hearty loukaniko sausages and chunks of feta. Service can get stretched, but this is holiday food - great holiday food - so relax. Simple grilled local fish is a no-brainer, as is the pear and custard teacake - or a little baklava.

Open Daily 9-11.30am, 12.30-2.30pm, 6-10pm (closed May, June, July)
Typical prices E $18 **M** $32 **D** $14
Cards DC AE MC V Eftpos
Wine A seriously good list of quality labels with house wines by Nick Farr of Bannockburn
Owners Pam, Kosta & Alex Talimanidis
Chefs Pam & Alex Talimanidis
Seats 80; outdoor seating
www.alagrecque.com.au

And ... Drop in for coffee - it's some of the coast's best.

Chris's Restaurant

280 Skenes Creek Road, Apollo Bay **5237 6411**

EUROPEAN **15/20**

You'd have to be hang-gliding to find more jaw-dropping views than those from this dramatic fine-diner high above Bass Strait. It's burnt down in a bushfire, survived tourism downturns and held fast to owner Chris Talihmanidis's vision since 1979, despite being in a spot where staff can be hard to come by and the road is cliff-hugging and serpentine. The dining room is an airy space of light timber and white linen, and service is well intentioned, though sometimes lacking polish or knowledge. Still, this is one of Victoria's great dining destinations, its mod-Med menu studded with stayers like feta and spinach-stuffed calamari tubes, and rabbit, rolled with prunes and pistachio then wrapped in vine leaves. Rare ocean trout comes with a pistachio crust and swipe of satiny tahini-tinged aioli. For dessert, house-made icecreams are lush with Greek flavours like honey and lavender, mastic and pistachio praline. It's no surprise this romantic eyrie is a favourite for proposals and weddings.

Open Daily 8.30-10am, 6-8.30pm; Sat-Sun noon-2pm (extended hours in summer)
Typical prices E $22 **M** $40 **D** $16
Cards AE MC V Eftpos
Wine A list strong on local wines, plus some Greeks; about a dozen by the glass
Owner & chef Chris Talihmanidis
Seats 90; bar
www.chriss.com.au

And ... Stay the night. There's onsite accommodation, and more within walking distance at another small resort.

BEST NEW REGIONAL RESTAURANT

Gladioli

14 High Street, Inverleigh **5265 1111**

CONTEMPORARY 15/20

A tiny hamlet 20 minutes' drive from Geelong yields this regional treasure: a forward-thinking restaurant showcasing the refined food of local hero Matt Dempsey (ex-Pettavel and Baveras). The spruced-up Victorian weatherboard provides a neutral slate for Dempsey's elegant presentation as he mixes classic European flavours with contemporary kitchen tricks. Pink-centred medallions of duck with perfectly seasoned cooking juices, cherry puree, baby leek and tiny pickled turnips give a modern twist to a classic combination; pan-fried trumpeter with linguine-soft ribbons of translucent calamari, baby onions, mussels and seaside succulents on caramelised onion puree is a precise juggling of multiple elements. The rare over-stretch – maybe gummy sheets of tapioca that don't flatter their prawn and mayo-bound picked crab fillings – is lessened when followed by satisfyingly conventional desserts. Finish with strawberries and thickly textured balsamic foam on white chocolate panna cotta. With personable waiters and a casual charm, Gladioli is worth the journey.

Open Thurs–Sun noon–3pm; Wed–Sat 6pm–late
Typical prices E $23 **M** $41 **D** $16
Cards AE MC V Eftpos
Wine Compact selection focused on locals; 10 by the glass
Owners Matt & Kate Dempsey
Chef Matt Dempsey
Seats 55; outdoor seating
www.gladiolirestaurant.com.au

And ... There are good-value set menus of five courses ($75) or eight courses ($100).

La Bimba

125 Great Ocean Road, Apollo Bay **5237 7411**

REGIONAL 14/20

This airy, boisterous upstairs room overlooking Apollo Bay, with its faintly Arabic decor, is one of the Great Ocean Road's best spots to sample local produce – much of it from the owners' Otway farm and truffiere. You might kick off with a salad of seasonal greens, pickled baby beets, green beans, walnuts, local blue cheese and truffle honey dressing. Follow with home-grown lamb slow-roasted with figs, onion, confit garlic and cinnamon – deliciously unctuous. A local fisherman stocks the daily specials board, say silver dory or trumpeter baked with chermoula on fragrant cous cous, or spicy school prawns sizzling in sherry. The signature paella is another seafood bounty – for two. Finish with 'Truffle Farm flower bed': geranium-scented icecream, lavender meringue, rosewater lokum, blueberry marshmallow and freesia jelly – all sprinkled with bee pollen. The queues down the stairs in high season are testimony to the quality here.

Open Mon–Fri 8.30am–3pm; Sat–Sun 8am–3pm; Mon–Thurs 5.30–9pm; Fri–Sun 5.30–9.30pm (closed Tues in low season)
Typical prices E $18 **M** $37 **D** $15
Cards MC V Eftpos
Wine Menu-driven list of local, regional and the occasional Spanish interloper; 16 by the glass; BYO (corkage $10 a bottle)
Owners Mikhiala Slade & Steven Earl
Chef Steven Earl
Seats 56

And ... Don't forget breakfast and lunch, with a more casual cafe set-up.

Marks

124 Mountjoy Parade, Lorne **5289 2787**

CONTEMPORARY **14.5/20**

Lorne is chef Mark Purdie's home town, and his colourful restaurant's been a Mountjoy Parade mainstay for around two decades. Purdie knows where to find the area's best ingredients and how to treat them, and the wines to do them justice. Raw broadbeans from his ample vegie garden make a welcoming nibble with spicy salt. Flathead tails may be given a dusting of spices, baked, and perched atop quinoa tabbouleh. Local calamari in a whisper of batter might come with Japanese-style spinach and sesame salad. Pork belly could be paired with gingery wombok. Purdie has a way with pasta too – usually house-made, perhaps tumbled with an ossobuco-style sauce of beef shin. Chocolate mousse is a menu fixture, steaming banana and walnut pudding with house-churned icecream and caramel sauce another regulars' favourite. The mood's relaxed but attentive (think bare tables, linen napkins, wicker chairs and a mini bathing box as waiter station) and service usually copes well with the coming and going of the tourist tide.

Open Daily 6–9pm; Sat–Sun noon–3pm (Melbourne Cup–Easter); Tues–Sat 6–9pm (rest of year); closed mid-July–mid-Sept
Typical prices E $16 **M** $34 **D** $13
Cards AE MC V Eftpos
Wine A smart selection, including the region's best; BYO (corkage $9 a bottle)
Owners Mark & Caroline Purdie
Chefs Mark Purdie & Jo Yates
Seats 80; outdoor seating; bar
www.marksrestaurant.com.au

And ... Many tables offer glimpses of the sea.

Royal Mail Hotel

Parker Street (Glenelg Highway), Dunkeld **5577 2241**

CONTEMPORARY **18/20**

The Royal Mail is a magnificent restaurant built around pleasant obsessions, interwoven and shared. There's the owner's incredible cellar and nearby farms, the chef's passion for great produce coaxed into edible art, and the diners who have made the roads to Dunkeld well-travelled routes of culinary pilgrimage. These hungry wanderers receive decorous service in an understated dining room, though there's no doubting the sense of occasion on the plate – and even the crockery itself can be breathtaking. Some dishes are gorgeous paeans to produce, such as a plate of many-hued carrots with soy cream or opalescent flathead fillet with jewel-like pea halves. Other dishes are playful, as with a glossy sheet of chicken skin that shatters like ice and tastes like naughty fun. The menu mirrors the seasons though cult favourites tend to stick around: the lovely yet unlikely combination of eel nougatine, pickled beets, bone marrow and burnt eggplant is but one Royal Mail calling card to Australia's fine-dining pantheon.

Open Wed–Sun 6.30pm–late
Typical prices Tasting menu $170; vegetarian menu $140
Cards AE MC V Eftpos
Wine An outstanding wine list of great depth and dynamism with impressive Old World back vintages
Owner Dunkeld Pastoral Company
Chef Dan Hunter
Seats 40; bar
www.royalmail.com.au

And ... The degustation dinner requires a good lie down; luckily there's on-site accommodation.

The Stag

22 Sackville Street, Port Fairy **5568 3229**

CONTEMPORARY **14/20**

The corner dining room of this historic portside building has witnessed many incarnations in its 160-year history. Since mid-2011, energetic new young owners have breathed real life into the old Stag. The decor is stylish, the staff are switched-on and owner-chef Matthew Murphy is working some real magic with local produce. His skill is evident in vibrant starters like a special of rare tuna rolls with blue swimmer crabmeat, avocado puree and mango-mint salsa. Whole quail with gnocchi, fried sage leaves and burnt butter is both beautifully composed and utterly moreish. Mains might feature top-quality local lamb cooked sous-vide, wrapped with sage and jamon and served with parsnip skordalia. You'll find local pork and seafood too, and desserts like baked chocolate mousse, strawberry salad, mint icecream and chocolate soil, as well as some quality Henty region wines. The menu and prices don't over-reach, which means that the locals are loving it, too.

Open Tues–Sat 6pm–late
Typical prices E $19.50 **M** $36 **D** $16
Cards AE MC V Eftpos
Wine Well-priced list with nice representation of regional wines; great by-the-glass selection
Owners Matthew Murphy & Lisa Bayliss
Chef Matthew Murphy
Seats 38; private room
www.seacombehouse.com.au

And ... Coordinate your visit with an event from Port Fairy's impressive calendar of festivals and events.

Sunnybrae

4285 Cape Otway Road, Birregurra **5236 2276**

CONTEMPORARY **15.5/20**

The industry is catching up with Sunnybrae. Now every serious chef is concerned with food provenance and seasonal, sustainable produce, but 'slow' food has obsessed George Biron for three decades, and his weekend lunches here in the Otway hinterland barely travel a food mile. The olive oil is his, the honeycomb served with the passionfruit tart is from his hives, the lemony succulent aptenia just picked from his garden. A platter of home-made cheese, local prosciutto, celeriac remoulade and heritage tomatoes allows ingredients to speak for themselves. Biron's skill shines through in a perfect wood-fire roasted veal shoulder and the delicate braising of baby carrots. The 'tongue-in-cheek' sandwich of tongue in beef cheek is simply masterful. Lunch in Sunnybrae's convivial light-filled room, presided over by Biron's partner Diane Garrett, of five courses (with a traditional 'savoury dessert' such as turkey livers in duck fat), interspersed with a garden stroll, is one of Victoria's great dining experiences.

Open Sat–Sun 12.30–2.30pm
Typical prices Set menu $75 (5 courses)
Cards AE MC V Eftpos
Wine Carefully selected list of mainly local and Victorian wines with some European interlopers; a wide choice by the glass; BYO (corkage $10 for first bottle, $15 second, $20 thereafter)
Owners George Biron & Diane Garrett
Chefs George Biron & Richard Hooper
Seats 58; private room
www.georgebiron.com

And ... Hang around until Monday for one of George's cooking classes.

Aireys Inlet Foodstore & Cafe

new

89 Great Ocean Road, Aireys Inlet **5289 6641**

CAFE

With baskets of produce for sale, menus printed on brown-paper bags, bare designer bulbs, concrete floors and a communal table, this foodstore/cafe/icecreamery delivers farm-stand chic by the creek. There's Allpress coffee and house-made fare, like rustic egg and bacon tarts (using Babka pastry), rice and quinoa salad, or pork and eggplant lasagne, warmed or dished up to enjoy indoors or out.

Open Daily 7am–4pm **Typical prices** Breakfasts $6.50; lunches $9.50 **Unlicensed** aifsc.com.au

Avanti at Witchmount

Witchmount Estate, 557 Leakes Road, Plumpton **9747 1177**

ITALIAN

Artworks adorn the walls of this large modern restaurant in a rural setting overlooking the estate's vineyard. With white linen and captain's chair settings, Avanti serves traditional Italian fare like home-made penne with zucchini and garlic, char-grilled quail on crisp-fried polenta and ever-popular tiramisu. The bluestone function centre is a popular wedding venue.

Open Wed–Sun noon–3pm, 6–10pm (daily in summer) **Typical prices E** $16.95 **M** $36.95 **D** $13.95 **Licensed** witchmount.com.au

Christopher Grace Restaurant

Basalt Vineyard, 1131 Princes Highway, Killarney **5568 7424**

CONTEMPORARY

A country house with verandah and kitchen garden is the charming setting for excellent food. Brunches range from Malaysian noodles to grills. Lazy lunches might feature carrot risotto with just-snipped herbs, perfectly rendered pork belly and exemplary creme brulee. Interesting ideas, cooking that is spot-on, and pure, distinct flavours make this a worthwhile stop.

Open Wed–Sun 9am–4pm **Typical prices E** $18 **M** $23 **D** $12 **Licensed & BYO** christophergrace.com.au

Darriwill Farm

169 Gray Street, Hamilton **5571 2088**

CONTEMPORARY

A pleasing stop for country squires and roadtrippers, Darriwill Farm comprises a provedore, gift emporium and wine store as well as attractive dining rooms. Swoop in for coffee and cake (buttery pear frangipane tart) or settle in for proper meals. Beyond sandwiches, there may be pan-fried sardines with lemon and caper mayo or baked semolina gnocchi with walnut, fig and rocket salad. A one-stop shop for hungry gourmets.

Open Mon–Wed 10am–5pm; Thurs–Sat 10am–late **Typical prices E** $14 **M** $30 **D** $11 **Licensed** darriwillfarm.com.au

Forrest Brewing Company

Forrest-Apollo Bay Road, Forrest **5236 6170**

CONTEMPORARY

This satisfying pitstop makes roadside dining a revelation. All things to all people, there are rowdy long tables inside and rustic hunks of local gum favoured by international tourists outside. There's BLT at brekkie and, to take away, burgers and a classy Asian crisp pork and prawn salad. And then there are the beautiful beers – try a straw-coloured Silvertop ale.

Open Thurs 10am–5pm; Fri–Sat 9am–late; Sun 9am–5pm (daily during hols) **Typical prices M** $20 **D** $5 **Licensed** forrestbrewing.com.au

Kosta's

48 Mountjoy Parade, Lorne **5289 1883**

GREEK

The whitewashed Kosta's has been here for 35-plus years and is a place where many will remember spending glorious summers past. Under new management, a few highlights recall glory days: grilled scallops with grapefruit, avocado and an orange and poppyseed dressing; or char-grilled pork fillets in a deep prune and port sauce, served with bacon and skordalia.

Open Tues–Sun 6–9.30pm (extended hours in summer) **Typical prices E** $18 **M** $35 **D** $11 **Licensed & BYO**

Lorne Beach Pavilion

new

81 Mountjoy Parade, Lorne **5289 2882**

CONTEMPORARY

Make your sunset booking for this fresh dining room with widescreen beach views. The food is straight-up seafood-oriented, without any technical trickery from the kitchen: plump scallops on cauliflower puree, pan-roasted blue-eye with cherry tomatoes, or a simple bouillabaisse swimming with seafood. There's a low-key cafe by day serving eggs at breakfast and fish and chips or steak sandwich at lunch.

Open Daily 9am–9pm **Typical prices E** $18 **M** $36 **D** $16 **Licensed** lornebeachpavilion.com.au

Maple Tree

116 Mountjoy Parade, Lorne **5289 1004**

CONTEMPORARY

Owner-chef Josh Harrison acknowledges that admirers of his former wee backstreet restaurant are at sea in these glossy new dress-circle digs. Doting staff deliver dishes categorised as small, medium or large – where you might find succulent dukkah-crusted lamb backstrap. Specials may include linguine with prawns, mussels and scallops, and dessert may be old favourite, coconut panna cotta.

Open Daily 6pm–late; Sun noon–3pm **Typical prices E** $12 **M** $38 **D** $14 **Licensed** mapletreelorne.com

The Meating Place Cafe

new

Birregurra Farm Foods, 43 Main Street, Birregurra **5236 2611**

CONTEMPORARY

Local? It's never more so than at this one-stop provedore, butcher, wine shop and cafe, a catch-all for the region's top produce. Local meats (lamb cutlets, porterhouse) are cooked on the grill, thin-crust pizzas are fired in the wood oven, and handmade Alligator Brand ravioli might be sauced with Otway mushrooms and black garlic. Sit by the fire in winter or on the shady verandah in summer.

Open Fri 6–9pm; Sun noon–3pm (provedore open daily, closed Tues in winter) **Typical prices E** $16.50 **M** $26.50 **D** $13 **Licensed** birregurrafarmfoods.com.au

Merrijig Kitchen

1 Campbell Street, Port Fairy **5568 2324**

CONTEMPORARY

Country inns don't come cosier than this historic wharf-side tavern. The wine list promotes a stay-a-while vibe and the food is generous and hearty, with the simpler dishes often the best. Spinach soup may be poured at the table over a lightly spiced dhal, rabbit braised with black-eyed beans to create a comforting stew, and chilli churros make a simple finish.

Open Thurs–Mon 6pm–late **Typical prices E** $18 **M** $36 **D** $16 **Licensed** merrijiginn.com

Nonna Casalinga

69 Liebig Street, Warrnambool **5562 2051**

ITALIAN

The warm, minimalist interior of Nonna Casalinga ('grandmother's house') means the focus stays on the gratifying food. The fortnightly changing menu might bring classics such as pumpkin and parmesan ravioli with crisp sage leaves, or charred chicken breast served with chorizo potatoes. Impeccable service and a broad wine list make Nonna's a go-to destination.

Open Tues–Sat 6–9.30pm; Fri noon–2pm **Typical prices E** $18 **M** $31 **D** $13 **Licensed**

Old Lorne Road Olives

45 Old Lorne Road, Deans Marsh **5236 3479**

MEDITERRANEAN

More a lazy-day lunch destination than a quick pitstop, Old Lorne Road is as laid-back as its name suggests. Savour a shared plate of jamon, prawns, cheese and pickled vegies, or try mussels in Pernod and cream, prawns with fregola and chorizo, or snapping fresh blue-eye with salsa verde, fennel, apple and radish. Browse the oils, gaze over the groves.

Open Fri–Mon 10am–5pm (Sept–June) **Typical prices E** $13.50 **M** $26.50 **D** $10 **Licensed** oldlorneroadolives.com.au

Ovenhouse

46a Mountjoy Parade, Lorne **5289 2544**

CONTEMPORARY

The buzzy, smart-casual Ovenhouse keeps kids and kids-at-heart happy with its wood-fired pizzas: maybe margherita or smoked salmon, capers, dill and sour cream. But there are other points of appeal: mussels from Portarlington, with white wine, garlic, basil and a palpable chilli kick; and the slow-roasted lamb shoulder, brightened by mint yoghurt.

Open Daily 9am–10pm (Dec–Feb); daily 10am–3pm, 6–9.30pm (Feb–Easter); Thurs–Mon 10am–3pm, 6–9.30pm (Easter–Nov) **Typical prices E** $15.50 **M** $30 (pizzas $20.50) **D** $14.50 **Licensed** ovenhouse.com.au

Royal Mail Hotel Bistro

Parker Street (Glenelg Highway), Dunkeld **5577 2241**

CONTEMPORARY

Same soaring Mount Sturgeon views, same culinary creativity and produce as next door's world-class restaurant, but on a bistro budget. Entrees impress: roasted bone marrow with white miso and pickled vegetables. Some mains can seem overly complicated, such as flathead littered with crumbs of coconut and hazelnut, and leaves and petals, but desserts simply rock: discs of burnt plum topped with creamy pumpkin icecream.

Open Daily noon–2.30pm, 6–8.30pm **Typical prices E** $22 **M** $37 **D** $16 **Licensed** royalmail.com.au

Timboon Railway Shed Distillery

Railway Yard, Bailey Street, Timboon **5598 3555**

REGIONAL

A cafe that distils malt whisky knows people need to be warmed from the inside. In pretty, shady Timboon, the Railway Shed also crisps wood-fired pizzas for dinner and bakes a mean hummingbird cake to get you through the day. Fish and chips, steak sandwiches and salads are pretty standard, but there's a commitment to local produce and heritage here.

Open Sun–Thurs 10am–5pm; Fri–Sat 10am–late (reduced hours in winter) **Typical prices E** $5 **M** $19 **D** $5 **Licensed** timboondistillery.com

Wickens Provedore & Deli

Shop 1, 137 Great Ocean Road, Apollo Bay **5237 1045**

CAFE

When the sun beats down on an overcrowded holiday town, it's good to know that an artisan coffee, a 29-degree poached egg and a lemon balm and eucalypt cupcake are in reach. Top city chef Robin Wickens escaped to this glamour pie shop (slow-cooked pork belly and Bramley apple anyone?), with local wine on sale alongside fresh seeded sourdough.

Open Wed–Mon 7am–6pm (closed Aug); no bookings **Typical prices M** $8 **D** $4.50 **Licensed** wickensprovedore.com.au

The Wye General

35 Great Ocean Road, Wye River **5289 0247**

CONTEMPORARY

The Wye is a social hub, cafe, store, bakery, and funky yet stylish beachside diner rolled into one. In summer, the coffee queue is out the door. Daily baked goods range from Danish pastries and Polish doughnuts to sourdough bread. The menu changes weekly and caters for every palate – from gourmet pizzas to beef burgers to roast veg salad.

Open Daily 7am–9pm (Dec–Feb); Mon–Thurs 7.30am–4pm; Fri–Sat 7.30am–9pm (Feb–mid-Apr); daily 8am–4pm (mid-Apr–Dec) **Typical prices E** $19 **M** $26 **D** $5 **Licensed** wyerivergeneralstore.com.au

Wyton Cellars

new

127 Kepler Street, Warrnambool **5562 7533**

CONTEMPORARY

Wooden floorboards give this cosy local hub a lived-in feel. Food is made here, like the roast pumpkin tart strewn with pinenuts, goat's cheese and rocket (as homely and satisfying as the pot-belly stove) and to-die-for raspberry and white-choc muffins. Or try a scallop risotto, with just-cooked orbs of seafood, roasted fennel and cherry tomatoes. The coffee's good, and Friday night is tapas night.

Open Mon–Thurs 7.30am–5pm; Fri 7.30am–11pm; Sat 8am–2.30pm; Sun 9am–2.30pm **Typical prices M** $15.90 **D** $12 **Licensed**

NORTH-WEST VICTORIA

Spoons Riverside

Oscar W's Wharfside

101 Murray Esplanade, Echuca **5482 5133**

CONTEMPORARY **14.5/20**

Don't be surprised if Oscar W's transports you back to the days of Echuca's rollicking Murray River inns. From the rustic dining room's riverside windows you can see steam-driven paddle-steamers moored below or tootling past. New chef Ludovic Baulacky (ex-Sam Miranda winery) was still rolling out his menu as we went to press, with a list of dishes drawing on produce from within a 200-kilometre radius, and running from small to big plates. That means Echuca feta with beetroot 'carpaccio', local beef, or Milawa chicken, perhaps cooked sous-vide and finished on the massive red gum charcoal grill, fired by wood from the owners' property. Lamb rump is braised for 15 hours, and served with figs and cous cous. Murray cod might be the day's fish, or yabbies could feature, perhaps poached and paired with gnocchetti. Service, distracted on a first visit, improved on a second. And Valrhona chocolate fondant, with banana cream and house-made vanilla icecream, ensures a finish as stunning as the setting.

Open Daily 11am–11pm
Typical prices E $18 **M** $38 **D** $16
Cards DC AE MC V Eftpos
Wine More than 500 wines from Australia and Europe; 21 by the glass
Owners Dean Oberin & Renee Oberin
Chef Ludovic Baulacky
Seats 120; outdoor seating; private room; bar
www.oscarws.com.au

And ... Wines come not only by the glass but by the taste (75ml), carafe (300ml) and with food-matching suggestions.

Spanish Bar & Grill

Grand Hotel, corner Langtree Avenue & Seventh Street, Mildura **5021 2377**

STEAKHOUSE **14/20**

Alfresco, beneath a vine-leaf canopy, with an aged grass-fed Mallee T-bone, there's not a lot wrong with the world. But then, the subdued elegance of the dining room, with views of the massive red gum charcoal pit, is not bad either. The Grill and its co-tenant, Seasons, share a stellar wine list and a predilection for local, seasonal produce. Despite chef changes, both restaurants have matured well (like aged beef) and are consistent purveyors of high-quality modern food. A case in point: a starter of spiced baby calamari with tahini yoghurt. The Grill's close relationship with two local butchers ensures superb grass- and grain-fed cuts, a good selection of which comes on the platter for two with grain-fed Mallee lamb backstrap, grain-fed eye fillet medallions, grass-fed aged Mallee sirloin, fried potatoes and seasonal vegetables. And there's a choice of sauces, including red-wine jus and bearnaise. The menu is augmented with South Australian seafood, and there are chocolates by local maker Trudie Chant.

Open Tues–Sun 6pm–late
Typical prices E $14 **M** $34 **D** $12
Cards DC AE MC V Eftpos
Wine Extensive selection of local and regional wines, plus interesting drops from Oz and abroad; good by-the-glass options
Owners Andy & Mandy Williams
Chefs Marco Paladini & Ali Ashgar
Seats 60; outdoor seating; bar
www.seasonsmildura.com.au

And ... Seasonal lunch happens periodically, so call ahead to see if it's on.

Stefano's

Cellar, Grand Hotel, Langtree Avenue, Mildura **5023 0511**

ITALIAN **17/20**

Respected, revered, even deified, Stefano's is one restaurant that deserves the hyperbole. Its reputation as a crucible of edgily rustic Italian food with a produce-driven sensibility is as relevant today as when Stefano de Pieri established his restaurant in the dim and moody cellar of the Grand Hotel 20 years ago. Make the effort – booking ahead, naturally – and be rewarded with honest, spot-on Italian cooking with the occasional modern flourish. Campari and salt-cured salmon holding air-light goat's milk 'panna cotta' dusted with a powder of beetroot and lime is as tricky as Stefano's gets. Otherwise, there's the perfect sweetness of roasted yabby tails with dehydrated corn polenta and a vibrant sauce of stinging nettles; or the simplicity of tagliolini with a soulfully earthy mushroom sauce, aged grana and black truffles grated at the table. The lengthy wine list is a great opportunity to explore some lesser-known Italian byways, and the feeling of abundance extends to desserts, with a concoction of figs, almonds and honey icecream a grand finale.

Open Tues–Sat 7–11pm
Typical prices Set menus $110 (6 courses), $135 (8 courses)
Cards AE MC V Eftpos
Wine A lovely, lengthy and comprehensive list with plenty of interest on the Italian side
Owners Stefano de Pieri & Donata Carrazza
Chefs Stefano de Pieri & Jim McDougall
Seats 55; private room
www.stefano.com.au

And ... Wander along the cellar corridor for an arresting collection of hospitality memorabilia.

Teller

55 Fryers Street, Shepparton **5822 4451**

CONTEMPORARY **15/20**

It takes a brave chef to open a degustation-only restaurant in a regional hub best known for its canneries, but Matthew Milsome has the pedigree to pull it off. The crafty chef spent time at Jacques Reymond before opening Teller in Mooroopna, then shifted the whole operation to Shepparton. A refined upstairs space is devoted to seven-course dinners, and it's clear that Milsome flexes his creative muscle here, with a series of standout dishes on a menu that's a steal at $70 a head. The menu doesn't give much away: 'fish, chip, lemon' equals a sandwich of crisps and mullet escabeche; 'fig, prosciutto, ricotta, rocket' is a natty fig tortilla with curls of ham. Thankfully, friendly, familiar staff give each dish a grand introduction. 'Snickers' speaks for itself, however: a hedonistic mix of choc-caramel brownie, nougat and peanut butter icecream. While upstairs is all mood lighting, linen-dressed tables, towering vases and art-adorned walls, downstairs is a more casual all-day affair, but pinstriped banquettes are a common denominator.

Open Thurs–Sun 6.30–9pm
Typical prices Set menu $70 (7 courses)
Cards AE MC V Eftpos
Wine Pocket-friendly selection with an eye to regional wines; BYO Sun night (no corkage)
Owners Matthew Milsome, Daina Winch & John Marsden
Chef Matthew Milsome
Seats 30; private room
www.thetellercollective.com

And ... Standout breakfasts, lunches and dinners are served downstairs at Collective.

The Black Pudding Deli

525a High Street, Echuca **5482 2244**

CONTEMPORARY

Diners spill on to the footpath, into the courtyard overlooking the Campaspe River and fill the upstairs rooms of this cafe-deli. Wherever you end up sitting, the range of breakfasts (eggs are a particular strength), lunches and snacks is always tasty. Chef's specials might include pumpkin soup served with toasted sourdough or creamy fettuccine carbonara. Coffee is good and service is impressive.

Open Daily 8am–2pm **Typical prices E** $6 **M** $16 **D** $5 **Licensed** theblackpuddingdeli.com.au

Bohjass

Level 1, 276b Wyndham Street, Shepparton **5822 0237**

CONTEMPORARY

Friendly staff, cosy groups of couches and a deep verandah lined with fairy lights add to the convivial nature of this first-floor wine bar. A commendable wine list offers little-known drops from boutique producers, bolstered by affordable imported gems. Tapas plates can underperform – calamari perhaps overly seasoned – but pastas are appealing, such as mushroom ravioli with home-made ricotta.

Open Mon–Sat 5pm–late **Typical prices E** $16 **M** $35 **D** $15 **Licensed** bohjass.com.au

Ceres

554 High Street, Echuca **5482 5599**

CONTEMPORARY

Ceres is a large, linen-dressed corner restaurant housed in a former pharmacy – the old signs remain – dispensing an interesting array of tapas and antipasto day and night. Praiseworthy mains might include home-made gnocchi with chicken, roast pumpkin and spinach, or double-roasted duck on creamy mash with sauteed spinach and cherry jus. Ceres is open for brekkie too.

Open Mon–Fri 10am–9pm; Sat–Sun 9am–10pm **Typical prices E** $12.50 **M** $29 **D** $13 **Licensed** ceresechuca.com.au

Collective

new

55 Fryers Street, Shepparton **5822 4660**

CONTEMPORARY

The laid-back sibling to upstairs Teller, Collective charms with its bare tables, pinstriped banquettes and buzzy, welcoming vibe. Breakfast may be smoked trout omelette or French toast with poached quince. Soup, salad and pasta lunches take over at noon. Dinner is a spread of house-made charcuterie and well-crafted comfort food, including prime steaks and gnocchi with beef ragout.

Open Mon–Sat 8am–10pm; Sun 8am–3pm (reduced hours in winter) **Typical prices E** $9 **M** $32 **D** $10 **Licensed** thetellercollective.com

Java Spice

17 Beveridge Street, Swan Hill **5033 0511**

SOUTH-EAST ASIAN

Stumble into this virtual Javanese village and be guided by polished and confident service into tasting some smart and lively food. It's themed and vast, the tucker is Thai and Malaysian rather than Indonesian, and standards are high. Start with dark and chewy goat satays and progress to a curry – perhaps the Thai red duck with lychee and pineapple.

Open Thurs–Fri & Sun noon–2.30pm; Tues–Sun 6pm–late **Typical prices E** $12 **M** $22 **D** $9 **Licensed & BYO** javaspice.com.au

Spoons Riverside

new

Horseshoe Bend, 125 Monash Drive, Swan Hill **5032 2601**

CONTEMPORARY

Grab a table by the Murray and watch fat carp scoff insects from the surface as you consider the stylish menu. Chicken and vegie soup comes with a warm savoury scone. A pumpkin quiche is lightly constructed and a ricotta apple cake is even lighter. The dinner menu is more ambitious with a focus on less familiar local ingredients (emu chipolatas, roo prosciutto). A top spot.

Open Sun–Wed 8am–5pm; Thurs–Sat 8am–11pm **Typical prices E** $12 **M** $32 (lunch mains $15) **D** $12 **Licensed** spoonsriverside.com.au

Stefano's Cafe Bakery

27 Deakin Avenue, Mildura **5021 3627**

CONTEMPORARY/ITALIAN

Stefano de Pieri gets his casual groove on at this cafe, bakery and smart modern art space complete with kerbside dining underneath trailing grapevines. The easygoing menu includes eggs any which way and lunches like beer-battered barramundi and chips, open steak sandwiches and ricotta gnocchi in napoli sauce. Stefano-branded items (bread, preserves and cookbooks) are waiting to be taken home.

Open Mon–Fri 7.30am–4pm; Sat 7.30am–3pm; Sun 8am–2pm **Typical prices M** $17 **D** $8 **Licensed** stefano.com.au

Tahbilk

new

254 O'Neils Road, Tabilk (via Nagambie) **5794 2555**

CONTEMPORARY

Overlooking the eucalypt-lined Goulburn River, this country-chic cafe boasts a deck and comfy dining room with sandstone fireplace. Share a generous antipasto platter of pork terrine, marinated veg and house-baked rye, perfect with a flight of Tahbilk's noteworthy marsannes; then move on to a zesty Vietnamese salad of prawns and pork belly. For dessert, icecream sundaes score smiles all round.

Open Mon & Thurs–Fri 11am–4pm; Sat–Sun 10am–4.30pm **Typical prices E** $10 **M** $24 **D** $10.90 **Licensed** tahbilk.com.au

Trentham Estate Winery

Sturt Highway, Trentham Cliffs **5024 8888**

CONTEMPORARY

That old man Murray rolling by, grassed terraces down to its banks, red gums overhead, the scent of meat on the barbie ... Whether in Trentham Estate's airy formal restaurant feasting from its Italian-leaning modern menu – a yabby souffle or house-made ricotta gnocchi – or cooking for yourself using produce bought here, this is an idyllic location. Sample the estate's range and idle away the afternoon.

Open Tues–Sun noon–3pm **Typical prices E** $16 **M** $28 **D** $9.50 **Licensed** trenthamestate.com.au

Yiche

77 McLennan Street, Mooroopna **5825 1001**

MODERN ASIAN

The Momofuku craze has made it to Mooroopna, with pork-belly buns (steamed bread pockets) popping up on the menu at this stellar little Asian eatery. The no-frills setting may speak of the '70s, but the menu is thoroughly modern. Smoked salmon sashimi with soy 'caviar' and a checkerboard dessert of fried banana and cubes of butterscotch jelly are brilliant.

Open Tues–Sun 5.30–9.30pm; Sun 12.30–2.30pm (yum cha) **Typical prices E** $8 **M** $25 **D** $10 **Licensed & BYO** yicherestaurant.com

Yutaka Sawa

107 Campbell Street, Swan Hill **5032 3515**

JAPANESE

There's a measure of authenticity here, though maybe only one species (salmon) on the sashimi list. Standard dishes – tempura, tonkatsu, even bentos – are adequate. Better is beef tataki, slivers of seared but otherwise raw local eye fillet served with a raw egg to dip. There's a limited wine selection, surpassed by sake and Japanese beers, and good service.

Open Mon & Wed–Fri noon–2.30pm; Wed–Mon 5pm–late **Typical prices E** $10 **M** $17 **D** $6 **Licensed & BYO** yutakasawa.com.au

Gary Mehigan, Celebrity Chef

Wombat Hill House

Annie Smithers' Bistrot

72 Piper Street, Kyneton **5422 2039**

CONTEMPORARY **15.5/20**

Ribbons of melon, shreds of buffalo mozzarella, a splash of zingy salsa verde – combined, they're a simple, superb dish, its success dependent on spanking-fresh produce handled with care, imagination and experience. Sometimes that's all it takes, as with a main of expertly cooked mulloway fillet, rubbed with tapenade and served alongside zesty peperonata, blistered cherry tomatoes and lightly wilted spinach. But there's technique here too, in spades. You might find it in a special of duck tortellini, tender rounds of pasta in rich, light, verjuice-scented sauce. Or in a deceptively straightforward dessert of roasted fig, smooth yoghurt sorbet and trembling panna cotta flavoured with local honey. The restaurant has bare tables and exposed brick walls, good table napkins and heavy cutlery. Framed botanical drawings remind diners of the owner's kitchen vegetable garden in nearby Malmsbury: the bowl of vegetables included in main course prices comes from there. The menu changes almost daily and service is as assured as the cooking.

Open Fri–Sun noon–2.30pm; Thurs–Sun 6–9pm
Typical prices E $19.50 **M** $36 **D** $16.50
Cards AE MC V Eftpos
Wine Predominantly Australian and French; plenty of choice below $80; 10 by the glass
Owner Annie Smithers
Chefs Daniel Whelan & Annie Smithers
Seats 35; bar
www.anniesmithers.com.au

And ... Take home Smithers' garden diary-cum-recipe book, *Annie's Garden to Table.*

The Dispensary Enoteca

9 Chancery Lane, Bendigo **5444 5885**

CONTEMPORARY **14.5/20**

This hip little eating house and bar (think '70s LPs, massed beer bottles, and a laneway locale) has spunk. It also has new chef Hugh Maxwell (former sous at Daylesford's Perfect Drop), an ambitious owner, good staff and a drinks lists with five pages on gin alone. Much of the sassy menu features produce from Central Victoria: Tooborac Berkshire pork, Erindale Farm rump steak. Time is another prime ingredient, used liberally in soft, sweet lamb neck cooked for 18 hours, which might come on a base of eggplant puree and with pea-sized cous cous, with currants and harissa. Vegetarian dishes are approached with care; a pretty triplet of cooked, raw and pickled baby vegies with a dainty quail's egg, silky pumpkin custard and Middle Eastern-spiced almond soil for earthy depth of flavour. Desserts run from a ruinous chocolate tart, biscuit, fudge and icecream line-up to the delicate flavours of green-tea lamington with elderflower and lychee jelly.

Open Mon 11am–4pm; Tues–Sat 11am–11pm; Sun 8am–4pm
Typical prices E $16.50 **M** $28.50 **D** $12
Cards DC AE MC V Eftpos
Wine A thoughtful selection of local and international wines in a huge, fun and informative drinks list big on beer and spirits; BYO Tues–Thurs nights (corkage $10 a bottle)
Owner Tim Baxter
Chef Hugh Maxwell
Seats 24; outdoor seating; bar
www.thedispensaryenoteca.com

And ... There's a full calendar of beer master classes and winemakers' dinners.

TOP 10 DATE NIGHT

Cafe Di Stasio
31 Fitzroy Street, St Kilda **9525 3999**
A restaurant that really gets the drama and romance of dining.

Circa
2 Acland Street, St Kilda **9536 1122**
An elegant room with secluded corners, food to share and beautiful wine.

The Commoner
122 Johnston Street, Fitzroy **9415 6876**
Quirky cuteness brings its own unique intimacy.

Cumulus Inc
45 Flinders Lane, City **9650 1445**
Score a couple of stools at the bar to get some positive frisson going.

Il Bacaro
168–170 Little Collins Street, City **9654 6778**
Small, dark, intimate, stylish, Italian – the rest is up to you.

Izakaya Den
Basement, 114 Russell Street, City **9654 2977**
Order sake and snuggle up on a bar seat built for two.

MoVida
1 Hosier Lane, City **9663 3038**
Securing a table for two here immediately demonstrates seriousness of intent.

The Point Albert Park
Aquatic Drive, Albert Park **9682 5566**
Watching sunset and then lights sparkling across the water – pure romance.

Spice Temple
Riverside, Crown Complex, Southbank **8679 1888**
Dark and sexy with fiery flavours, powerful cocktails and intimate nooks.

Vue de Monde
Level 55, Rialto, 525 Collins Street, City **9691 3888**
Proves the innate romantic power of a vast sea of sparkling lights.

Empyre Hotel
68 Mostyn Street, Castlemaine **5472 5166**

CONTEMPORARY **14.5/20**

Queen Victoria reigned over an empire and gold was king in Castlemaine when this beautifully restored boutique hotel with iron-lacework balcony was built. There's an imperial feel too, dining under glittering chandeliers in the ornately opulent Gwynedd Room. On busy evenings, the restaurant spills over into the former front bar that at other times, together with the former carriageway room and rear garden, serves as a more casual (and lower-priced) bistro. Butler-like service and chef Michael Nam's inspired contemporary take on classic dishes are in keeping with the grandeur of the surroundings, as are such extras as an amuse-gueule and pre-dessert. Choose, perhaps, a marvellously varied charcuterie platter, followed by sliced rump of lamb with a braised lamb croquette and a tarragon-flavoured hollandaise. Kyneton Angus eye fillet usually features, perhaps with a pithiviers of braised beef cheek, and there's always something for non-carnivores. For dessert, try a trio of chocolate (fondant, delice, sorbet) or a speciality cheese, like Holy Goat Black Silk.

Open Wed–Sun noon–3pm; Wed–Sat 6–9pm; Sat–Sun 9–11.30am
Typical prices E $19 **M** $36 **D** $16
Cards MC V Eftpos
Wine Serious list dominated by Australian and NZ wines, with plenty of locals
Owners John Ganci & Tony O'Mahoney
Chef Michael Nam
Seats 45; outdoor seating; private room
www.empyre.com.au

And ... Come for breakfast at weekends.

Flouch's

12-14 Piper Street, Kyneton **5422 3683**

CONTEMPORARY **14/20**

Roast duck and Roederer? A burger and glass of red? Croque-monsieur or poached eggs? Being all things to all people isn't easy, but long-time chef Michael Flouch aims to cover the bases in this cavernous and somewhat characterless carpeted space with mustard walls and bentwood chairs. Good cutlery adorns bare tables and pleasant, professional staff pour wine into Riedel glasses. Breakfast is served all day, while the lunch menu ranges from a club sandwich to fish and chips (which comes as three battered strips of barramundi with fries, green salad, house-made tartare and chutney); plus there's a couple of dishes from the concise, more formal dinner menu. Flouch's classical training is evident in an entree of French-style potato gnocchi with roast pear in a peppery, creamy blue-cheese sauce, while a herby, Thai-inspired salad showcases his deft way with duck. For dessert, revisit one of the greatest hits of the '90s with a fluffy, saucy sticky date pudding.

Open Wed–Fri 11am–3pm, 6pm–late; Sat 10am–late; Sun 10am–3pm
Typical prices E $17.50 **M** $36 **D** $14
Cards AE MC V Eftpos
Wine Strong examples from Australia's leading wine regions, plus a handful of Europeans, modestly priced
Owners Michael & Karen Flouch
Chef Michael Flouch
Seats 60; outdoor seating; bar
www.flouchs.com.au

And ... You can call in at any time just for a glass of wine.

Kazuki's at the Raglan

1 Camp Street, Daylesford **5348 1218**

JAPANESE/EUROPEAN **14.5/20**

Japanese maples by the door, oriental paper lanterns dangling from high ceilings and an evocative logo etched on the windows set the warmly welcoming scene for this charming rising star. Kazuki Tsuya draws on his Japanese heritage and French culinary experience to offer a menu that, based largely on local produce, displays a sometimes playful fusion of Japanese aesthetics and inspiration with European ingredients and techniques. Dishes in three sizes ('nibbles', entrees and mains) invite sharing and discovery. A mushroom risotto may be crowned with an onsen (slow-poached) egg poured from a glass filled with wood smoke. Pork belly is garnished with shiitake, konbu (dried kelp) and umeboshi (pickled red plum) salad. Braised goat is wrapped in filo on creamed celeriac with truffle pecorino and sweetly spiced daigaku imo (sweet potato). For the less adventurous, there's eye fillet with pepper sauce or tarragon mayonnaise. The apple pie with elderberry and milk gelato is a taste delight. Do try the Japanese tea.

Open Fri–Mon noon–2.30pm; Thurs–Tues 6–10pm
Typical prices E $22 **M** $30 **D** $12
Cards DC AE MC V Eftpos
Wine Discerning selection of predominantly Central Victorian wines, plus examples of Japanese beer and sake
Owners Kazuki & Saori Tsuya
Chef Kazuki Tsuya
Seats 36; outdoor seating
www.kazukis.com.au

And ... Try the Japanese banquet lunch, with sake, on the last Sunday of each month.

Lake House

4 King Street, Daylesford **5348 3329**

CONTEMPORARY 16.5/20

Everything that Daylesford is famous for is here in one luxurious location. Lake House's spa, hotel and restaurant all celebrate the picturesque region and its verdant produce. In the restaurant, glassware twinkles on crisp double-dressed tables. Cushions are propped along the window banquette – behind which sit giant bunches of flowers and pretty Lake Daylesford. The kitchen turns boutique ingredients into exquisite-looking, highly worked dishes. Three discs of smoky Skipton eel, skirted with pancetta, on individual beds of beetroot remoulade come on a long white plate scattered with petals, daubed with mustard creme fraiche, dotted with basil oil and painted with a streak of beetroot glaze. Every plate is picture-perfect, whether a main of delicately sweet Dory fillets with sheer 'scales' of locally grown baby zucchini, or a wild 'textures of chocolate' dessert. With eight-course tasting menu options (including vegetarian), besuited service and a thick wine list, Lake House is so much more than a meal; it's an occasion.

Open Daily noon–3pm, 6pm–late
Typical prices Fixed-price menus $76 (2 courses), $94 (3 courses), $112 (4 courses), $135 (8 courses)
Cards DC AE MC V Eftpos
Wine Award-winning tome with local and Euro drops
Owners Alla, Allan & Larissa Wolf-Tasker
Chefs Alla Wolf-Tasker & David Green
Seats 100; outdoor seating; private room; bar
www.lakehouse.com.au

And ... You may dine with kookaburras who visit the balcony for their daily meat fix.

Masons of Bendigo

25 Queen Street, Bendigo **5443 3877**

CONTEMPORARY 14.5/20

Nick and Sonia Anthony have returned to Bendigo and delivered just what it needed. Drawing on years of cooking internationally and locally, they've created a stylishly casual all-day operation offering up a great range of tasty snacks through to larger dishes and knockout steaks. They've developed a strong network of Central Victorian producers: 95 per cent of Masons' produce is local. Maybe start with fried chicken spare ribs zingy with chilli salt and lime, silky duck-liver parfait on brioche or roast pork bun with Japanese mayonnaise. From the larger dishes perhaps opt for juicy char-grilled jumbo quail with fresh figs and fregola or what might be the best steak for the money in the state – whole and dry-aged from nearby Inglewood – arriving with green peppercorn butter, perfect chips and a lovely little salad. A not-too-sweet trifle incorporating botrytis jelly and mascarpone rounds things out very nicely.

Open Tues–Sat 8.30am–9.30pm
Typical prices E $10 **M** $25 **D** $14
Cards AE MC V Eftpos
Wine A smart list with a good selection of Central Victorian wines; 16 by the glass
Owners & chefs Nick & Sonia Anthony
Seats 64; outdoor seating; private room; bar
www.masonsofbendigo.com.au

And ... A good range of produce is available for purchase, including Chef Sonia's range of baking kits aimed at budding junior chefs.

Mercato @ Daylesford

32 Raglan Street, Daylesford **5348 4488**

CONTEMPORARY **14.5/20**

The evocative pictures of European market scenes are clues to the restaurant's name, Italian for market. It's apt, too, as the reborn weatherboard cottage is just down the road from Daylesford's popular Sunday market, and owner-chef Richard Mee takes pride in selecting the best seasonal produce of the region. The candlelit interior is more spacious than it first appears, with crisp white table linen, upholstered chairs and deft, well-groomed staff adding a touch of formality without stuffiness. To begin, a tempura of zucchini flowers with Meredith goat's cheese, or maybe carpaccio of Romsey emu with shaved percorino. Creatively conceived, finely crafted mains follow. Kangaroo fillet may come on truffled polenta; there might be aged Kyneton Angus eye fillet; rare-breed lamb, and Western Plains pork, perhaps with pickled rhubarb and sweet potato. All dishes are imaginatively garnished, and there are sides for the really ravenous. A dessert plate is sure to include luscious house-made icecreams. This is fine dining with commendable class.

Open Thurs–Tues 6pm–late; Sat–Sun noon–3pm
Typical prices E $18 **M** $38 **D** $16
Cards DC AE MC V Eftpos
Wine Fine choice of wines, many from surrounding regions; a dozen-plus by the glass
Owners Richard Mee & Maree Britt
Chef Richard Mee
Seats 65; outdoor seating
www.mercatorestaurant.com.au

And ... A main and glass of wine costs $25 on Monday nights.

Mr Carsisi

37c Piper Street, Kyneton **5422 3769**

MIDDLE EASTERN **14.5/20**

This versatile gent rocks around the clock and the Bosphorus, with smart young staff dishing up Turkish-tinged breakfasts, nightcaps at the bar and mezze-style meals in between. Inside, beneath a corrugated iron roof, there's a cafe area plus a big dining room cleverly broken up by a bar and a retro-industrial cabinet of wine. Outside, a shady verandah looks on to a park. Begin with small dishes – perhaps football-shaped zucchini fritters, cheesy and salty, or crisp, lightly floured curls of baby calamari dressed with green olives, lemon and cinnamon – you may decide to make a meal of them. A main of Persian-spiced lamb shoulder comes with three rounds of meat, aromatic and cooked to slightly dry but moistened by a pile of tabbouleh with Victorian-grown pearl barley and pomegranate, plus bright yellow chickpea puree. The dessert taster for two includes sugar-plum-sized Egyptian doughnuts, dreamy pistachio-crusted Turkish delight semifreddo and smooth-meets-crunchy vanilla halva icecream.

Open Fri–Tues 8am–late
Typical prices E $10 **M** $34 **D** $14
Cards AE MC V Eftpos
Wine Lots of local choice plus nods to Spain, Greece and Lebanon; modestly priced; 10 by the glass
Owners Matthew & Clare Fegan
Chef Matthew Fegan
Seats 45; outdoor seating; bar
www.mrcarsisi.com

And ... Aperitifs include arak, raki and Levantine-themed cocktails – orange blossom martini, anyone?

Perfect Drop Wine & Food Lounge

5 Howe Street, Daylesford **5348 3373**

CONTEMPORARY **14/20**

Behind the cottagey facade is this busy, boisterous bistro-cum-wine-bar with Scrabble-board-sized dining tables. Swanky it's not, but the food is fine – think share-plates of fresh, clean, in-season ingredients and skilful cooking with Middle Eastern flair and Mediterranean zest. Blessed with an abundant local bounty, much of it organic, free-range and heirloom, grown by small producers and plucked from the chef's own kitchen garden, the clipboard menu can change daily. Look for things like light, golden cauliflower and oregano fritters, fried haloumi and refreshing kasoundi yoghurt, or soft piquillo peppers plump with herbed ricotta and salmoriglio. Next, try sweet, tender, cinnamon-spiced duck breast and caramelised nectarine on a finely shredded zingy tangle of cabbage, kohlrabi and walnut, and a perfect drop – a Ballarat-region pinot noir. Sadly, service was patchy on one visit. Finish with baked figs spun in kataifi pastry, burnt honey icecream and raspberries. Sweet.

Open Mon–Thurs 5–9.30pm; Fri 5–10.30pm; Sat noon–10.30pm; Sun noon–9.30pm
Typical prices E $16 **M** $35 **D** $16
Cards MC V Eftpos
Wine Nicely priced, concise list of boutique Central Victorians, plus a few imports; 10 by the glass
Owner Devon Taylor
Chef Andrew Dennis
Seats 40; outdoor seating; private room; bar
www.aperfectdrop.com

And ... Look out for live music, alfresco.

Public Inn

Criterion Corner, 165 Barker Street, Castlemaine
5472 3568

CONTEMPORARY **14.5/20**

Filmmaker Alfred Hitchcock liked to slip into his thrillers what he called a MacGuffin: something quirky or unexpected. Here the MacGuffin is an inverted pyramid of barrels protruding from a stone wall. Each has a tap from which wines of the region can be dispensed in old-fashioned glass-stoppered medicine bottles. Hospitality virtuoso Hayden Winch, who created the Dispensary Enoteca in a Bendigo laneway with pharmaceutical history, has now has taken Castlemaine's Criterion Hotel from goldrush origins to vibrant bistro and bar. The restaurant-style food, drawn from top-notch regional ingredients, is as contemporary-chic as the whole creative concept. Expect the likes of Tuki trout ballotine with oyster puree, Spa venison on poached rhubarb and wagyu rump cooked sous-vide with an oxtail and cognac consomme. A vegetarian menu offers dishes just as imaginatively composed. And if your server extols the delights of a chocolate brioche and butter pudding with fig icecream, they're not kidding.

Open Fri–Sun noon–late; Mon–Thurs 4pm–late
Typical prices E $18.50 **M** $32 **D** $17
Cards DC AE MC V Eftpos
Wine Top drops of the neighbouring regions, and some worthy but lesser-known global selections
Owners Hayden Winch, Peter McMahon, Greg Dedman & Gavin Smith
Chef Ryan Crossley
Seats 60; outdoor seating; private room; bar
www.publicinn.com.au

And ... There's an impressive range of boutique beers – some are on tap at the bar.

Sault

2349 Ballan-Daylesford Road, Sailors Falls **5348 6555**

CONTEMPORARY **14.5/20**

Flanked by fields of lavender, fronted by a formal rose garden and fountain and overlooking a lake from the rear picture windows, the sandstone villa and grounds could be a nostalgic transplant from Provence were it not for the backdrop of Australian eucalypt forest. The cosy fireside lounge and spacious dining room deliver a sense of occasion, enhanced by the gently attentive service. A new Spanish-born chef with impressive credentials (including as head chef at a Michelin two-star restaurant on Mallorca) has lifted the seasonally adjusted, regionally sourced produce-driven menu up a notch or two. A wild hare and venison terrine with streaks of pumpkin puree, dots of bitter chocolate and a baton of tokay jelly is a visual and taste sensation. Pink-roasted duck breast sits atop braised witlof with a Guinness-reduction sauce and autumnal garnish of chestnut puree and quince. And for Spanish-style dessert, try a pile of churros with chocolate dipping sauce, creme Catalan and caramel icecream.

Open Wed–Sun 6pm–late; Fri–Sun 11am–3pm
Typical prices E $18.50 **M** $35 **D** $16.50
Cards AE MC V Eftpos
Wine Well-chosen list with a commendable focus on typical and top vintages from surrounding regions
Owners Jodi Flockhart & Damien Aylward
Chef Santiago Nine-Fernandez
Seats 60; outdoor seating
www.sault.com.au

And ... There's a changing lower-priced 'locals night' menu on Wednesdays, as well as weekend brunch.

Whirrakee Restaurant

17 View Point, Bendigo **5441 5557**

CONTEMPORARY/FRENCH **14/20**

Opposite Bendigo's central landmark, Alexandra Fountain, an Edwardian-era bank building has bloomed into Whirrakee Restaurant – named after a local wattle. Chandeliers on high ceilings over white-clad tables add an air of special-occasion formality to the dining room. Owner-chef Brent Slade's enthusiasm for fine food is indicated by three pages of culinary descriptions with the menu, and by his creatively crafted dishes. The bill can add up, especially with side dishes, though complimentary extras help compensate: an appetiser here, a little pre-dessert there, and petits fours. A tasting plate of pâté, terrine, smoked duck and rillettes may precede Erindale lamb with stuffed eggplant. A small beet salad with goat's cheese, and a watery pea and fennel risotto might underwhelm; better is smoked ocean trout with a beetroot puree and touch of wasabi, followed by a trio of duck – roasted breast, leg confit braise and sausage – on savoy cabbage with a fragrant tarragon jus. The quartet of Valrhona chocolate delicacies is a masterpiece.

Open Tues–Sun noon–3pm, 6.30–9.30pm
Typical prices E $18 **M** $36 **D** $18
Cards AE MC V Eftpos
Wine Impressive international list, with an admirable breadth and depth of Central Victorian vintages
Owner & chef Brent Slade
Seats 55; outdoor seating; private room
www.whirrakeerestaurant.com.au

And . . . Lunch is good value: two courses for $30, two for $45.

Apple Annie's Bakery Cafe

31 Templeton Street, Castlemaine **5472 5311**

BAKERY/CAFE

Aromas of freshly baked pastries and coffee welcome you to this working bakery's homely-as-apple-pie cafe with courtyard – just the place to tuck into a buttery, flaky croissant, a soft deep-dish quiche, or a simple lunch of grilled salmon and asparagus. The voluptuous Paris Brest, choux pastry filled with praline and brandy cream, could be the pick of the gorgeous pastries.

Open Wed–Sat 8am–5pm; Sun 8am–3pm **Typical prices E** $7.50 **M** $14 **D** $8 **Licensed** appleannie.com.au

Bouchon

61 High Street, Bendigo **5444 5272**

FRENCH

Chef Travis Rodwell honed his skills at Circa and Dispensary Enoteca. In a tiny kitchen out back of his friendly, unpretentious, well-priced bistro he char-grills quail as an entree that's served with zingy bois boudran sauce and palate-freshening shallot, tomato and parsley salad. Bendigo also loves him for excellent charcuterie, confit duck and other French classics given a fresh, local twist.

Open Tues–Sat 10am–4pm, 6–11pm **Typical prices E** $16 **M** $28 **D** $12 **Licensed** bouchonbendigo.com.au

Breakfast & Beer

117 Vincent Street, Daylesford **5348 1778**

REGIONAL

Over brunch, dinner or a graze-and-guzzle, produce sings in this pint-sized Euro-style beer cafe. A considered, cross-continental menu draws on A-list local, organic, heirloom and free-range ingredients to complement a fridge full of international beers. Try Blanche de Namur (Belgian wheat beer) and fresh, clean caprese; dunkelweizen (dark ale) with spiced venison rissoles, and coffee stout to cut through toffee pud.

Open Wed–Sun 8am–11pm **Typical prices E** $15 **M** $28 **D** $12 **Licensed** breakfastandbeer.com.au

Bress

3894 Calder Highway, Harcourt **5474 2262**

REGIONAL

Settle at one of the granite-topped refectory tables, take in the view of Mount Alexander and enjoy the communal three-course lunch of the day, drawing on the vineyard's biodynamic gardens. Expect an antipasto platter (perhaps bruschetta, chicken and chorizo terrine, parmesan-crusted zucchini wedges and pretty little salads), fresh-baked rolls, a casserole dish baked in the wood-fired oven, and a fruity dessert.

Open Sat–Sun 12.30–3pm (Oct–May); bookings required **Typical prices** Set menu $45 (3 courses) **Licensed** bress.com.au

Cafe Re-public

new

26 Templeton Street, Castlemaine **5472 1582**

CONTEMPORARY

This funky little offshoot of the Public Inn occupies Castlemaine's old fire station. Its dishes are simpler than the Inn's, but just as imaginative, as in a 'Chinese water bun' with blue swimmer crab and lemon caper mayo, or smoked duck salad with marinated kipflers and hazelnuts. Cakes are from a local patisserie, and coffee, roasted daily, is expertly prepared.

Open Daily 8am–3pm; no bookings **Typical prices M** $14 **D** $7 **Licensed** re-public.com.au

Captains Creek Cafe

new

Kangaroo Hills Road, Blampied **5345 7408**

REGIONAL

Lamb, wines and freshly picked vegetables from the May brothers' organic farm, plus ingredients from local producers, form the basis for lunch. Share a generous tasting or cheese platter, or enjoy a Moroccan-spiced lamb burger; asparagus and goat's cheese tart; and coffee and cake with cream. It's all served with charm and finesse by the fire, or on the cellar-door verandah overlooking vines and vegies. Marvellous value.

Open Sat–Sun noon–3pm; Fri 6–9pm **Typical prices E** $10 **M** $20 **D** $5 **Licensed** captainscreek.com

Colenso

42d Anslow Street, Woodend **5427 2007**

CONTEMPORARY

This quaint old bakery building shares its site with an art gallery and native plant nursery. It's long been popular for fulfilling breakfasts, coffee and cake, all-day snacks and lunch dishes from diverse salads to a daily braise (perhaps duck-leg, celeriac mash and cabbage sauteed with apple). Saturday night features a fixed-price ($48), three-course dinner with a theme, say, French provincial or regional Italian.

Open Mon–Sat 8.30am–3pm; Fri 6–8.30pm; Sat 6.30pm–late **Typical prices E** $12 **M** $18 **D** $6 **Licensed** colenso.com.au

Darmagi

new

97 Main Road, Hepburn Springs **5348 2221**

ITALIAN

Darmagi is a reborn wine bar and diner with an expansion in the offing. It's a restaurant to watch, with its discriminating list of local and Italian wines, a 'happy hour' serving $1 apiece oysters, six Italian-style charcuterie platters, a trio of pastas, and three mains including ultra-tender wagyu rump cooked sous-vide.

Open Thurs–Mon noon–9.30pm **Typical prices E** $13 **M** $28 **D** $13 **Licensed** darmagi.com.au

Dhaba at the Mill

18 Piper Street, Kyneton **5422 6225**

INDIAN

In Kyneton's atmospheric old mill, this Punjabi-style curry house dishes up authentic daily offerings using top ingredients. Try samosas plump with Trentham potatoes or fragrant curries such as lamb roghan josh and free-range butter chicken. Sundays bring a curry buffet ($20 a head). Check online to find Dhaba's road-side food trucks.

Open Thurs–Sat 6–9pm; Sun noon–2.30pm, 5–9pm; no bookings except for 8 or more **Typical prices E** $8 **M** $14 **D** $5 **Licensed & BYO** dhaba.com.au

Du Fermier

new

42 High Street, Trentham **5424 1634**

FRENCH PROVINCIAL

Annie Smithers' Trentham outpost is a foodstore and cafe, though 'foodstore' is a loose term for a place that sells axes (nice ones) and cheeseboards, along with Annie's signature comestibles. And 'French provincial' is a tag that loosely describes food that incorporates ingredients from Annie's garden: maybe a coarse ham-hock terrine, a main of braised lamb, and brûlée for dessert.

Open Thurs–Sat 10am–4pm; Fri–Sat 6–9pm; Sun 10am–5pm; no bookings at lunch **Typical prices** Breakfasts $14; Lunches $18.50; Sweets $4.50 **Licensed** dufermier.com.au

Ego's Culinaria

new

10 Howe Street, Daylesford **5348 4001**

CONTEMPORARY

Everything on the menu in this finessed cafe, with its fresh whitewashed interior, is made from scratch using ingredients sourced within the 'hood. Cakes are a speciality, while all-day brekkies may include cumin-and-mint-topped fried eggs on Ego's own Turkish bread, and blackboard lunch specials might offer slow-roasted lamb shoulder. High teas and lunch boxes, too.

Open Thurs–Mon 8am–4pm **Typical prices** Breakfasts $18; Lunches $26; Sweets $6 **Unlicensed** egosculinaria.com.au

Ellender Estate L'Osteria

new

260 Green Gully Road, Glenlyon **5348 7785**

PIZZERIA/REGIONAL

Two loveable labradors may welcome you to this picturesque spot where Graham Ellender bakes wonderful, ultra-thin-crust pizzas in the wood-fired oven. Zigzag down the path to tables on the terrace or lawns. Toppings include taleggio and mushroom; buffalo mozzarella and herbed potato; or fromage frais and Tuki smoked trout. Or try a platter of regional delicacies. Estate wine by the glass or bottle.

Open Sat–Sun & pub hols 12.30–3.30pm (closed Sept) **Typical prices E** $8 **M** $19 **D** $8 **Licensed** ellenderwines.com.au

Farmers Arms Hotel

1 East Street, Daylesford **5348 2091**

PUB DINING

This charming 150-year-old pub has a no-fuss, no-bookings approach to match its warm hospitality and fresh, honest food with a world view. So, come when it suits, sit anywhere and order at the bar. Think smoked eel salad, fall-apart beef cheek with aromatic herbs or sweet, spicy Tunisian goat stew. To finish? Meringue-topped mascarpone, pistachio and raspberry cassata.

Open Daily noon–3pm, 6–9pm **Typical prices E** $16 **M** $29 **D** $16 **Licensed** farmersarmsdaylesford.com.au

Frangos Restaurant & Jimmy's Bar

82 Vincent Street, Daylesford **5348 2363**

MEDITERRANEAN

You can shop, eat, drink, spa, caffeinate and stay over at Jim and Dianne Frangos's cool and stylish corner building. Jimmy's Bar and fine-diner Frangos share a split-level room: the former might offer baccala croquettes, pig's cheek and peach chutney, while the lights are turned down and the charm up in terrace-windowed Frangos. Expect, perhaps, grilled lamb backstrap with lentils, and roast duck with pistachio and confit rhubarb.

Open Fri–Sun 6pm–late (bar daily 10am–late) **Typical prices E** $16 **M** $34 **D** $14 **Licensed** frangosandfrangos.com

Gallery Bistro

10 Lydiard Street South, Ballarat **5331 1377**

CONTEMPORARY

Previous guests include British royals and Don Bradman, so it's not surprising 19th-century Craig's Royal Hotel feels like a special-occasion spot. An airy atrium houses the bistro, a classy setting for an ambitious modern menu. Golden-crusted goat pithiviers is a fine fit, as is calamari with cucumber and Chinese sausage, dressed with soy and ginger. Though service can be patchy, a silky orange creme caramel makes a fine finale.

Open Daily 7am–2.30pm, 6–9pm **Typical prices E** $18 **M** $31 **D** $12 **Licensed & BYO** craigsroyal.com.au

The Good Table

233 Barker Street (corner Templeton Street), Castlemaine **5472 4400**

EUROPEAN

Owner-chef Alexander Perry takes inspiration from Spain and Italy for a menu that celebrates the seasons and honours local small growers and wineries. Shareable dishes run from jamon croquettes and smoked eel terrine to heartier confit duck on semolina gnocchi. Good-value 'austerity measures' set menus operate Monday to Wednesday.

Open Thurs–Sun noon–4pm, 6pm–late; Mon–Wed 5.30pm–late **Typical prices E** $12 **M** $26 **D** $12; Mon–Wed set menus $25 (2 courses), $30 (3 courses) **Licensed** thegoodtable.com.au

GPO Bar & Grill

60–64 Pall Mall, Bendigo **5443 4343**

CONTEMPORARY

With a prime position opposite the Bendigo GPO and an easy-pleasy menu, this big cafe bustles along. The lengthy list moves from share-plates of grilled fish tacos through to good thin-crust pizzas – maybe topped with local Istra pancetta, sliced Harcourt pear and blue cheese – or perhaps a whopping T-bone from the grill. A solid drinks list features a range of excellent local reds.

Open Daily 10am–late **Typical prices E** $10 **M** $27 **D** $12 **Licensed** gpobendigo.com.au

Lavandula La Trattoria

Lavandula Swiss Italian Farm, 350 Hepburn-Newstead Road, Shepherds Flat **5476 4393**

ITALIAN

Lavandula's lush grounds, complete with farm animals, lavender fields and buildings of Swiss-Italian heritage, are worth the $3.50 entrance fee. Relax in the ash grove or in the stone loggia for lavender scones and tea, or rustic lunches of regional antipasti, osso buco on tagliatelle or salad with local blueberries and prosciutto. Lovely little cakes are a plus.

Open Fri–Tues 10.30am–5.30pm Sept–May (daily school hols; Sat–Sun only Jun–Aug) **Typical prices E** $17.50 **M** $27 **D** $8.50 **Licensed** lavandula.com.au

L'espresso

417 Sturt Street, Ballarat **5333 1789**

ITALIAN/CONTEMPORARY

You'd happily come to cosy Euro-style L'espresso every day – and some do – for the expertly espressed Vittoria coffee, enticing cakes, fab breakfasts, Italian-themed lunches and mood music. For lunch, enjoy a sumptuous risotto with mushrooms, caramelised onion and sage, or confit duck-leg with pear and walnut salad and truffled pecorino. It's an example of cafe culture at its best.

Open Fri 7am-late; Sat–Thurs 7am–6pm **Typical prices E** $16.50 **M** $28 **D** $12 **Licensed** ballarat.com/lespresso.htm

Lydiard Wine Bar

15 Lydiard Street North, Ballarat **5327 2787**

CONTEMPORARY

This modern metro-chic rendezvous is tucked inside an 1862 bank building, where owner-chef Damien Jones prepares tempting share-plates that reflect his French training and Asian experience. You'll find exotic appetisers (ground fish on watermelon and betel leaf), light dishes (zucchini flowers filled with spicy pork and crab) and a handful of more substantial meals such as aged steaks. The dessert sample plate is a winner.

Open Tues–Sat 5pm–late **Typical prices E** $12 **M** $34 **D** $15 **Licensed** lydiardwinebar.com.au

Naam Pla Thai Kitchen

217 Barker Street, Castlemaine **(no phone)** new

THAI

Such a hit is this petite food dispensary in an old pharmacy that the owners are too busy to take phone calls – no number is given. Eat in or take out fragrant dishes from spicy Thai fishcakes and larb gai to pan-Asian creations like Chinese-style roast duck in red coconut curry with lychees. Tom yum? That too. All yum, in fact.

Open Wed–Sun noon–2.30pm, 4–8.30pm; no bookings **Typical prices E** $7.50 **M** $15.50 **D** $6.50 **Licensed**

Phoenix Brewery

10 Camp Street, Ballarat **5333 2686**

CONTEMPORARY

Phoenix is not – and never has been – a brewery. Located in the arts precinct, it's a cosy restaurant and tapas bar with a rustic fitout of exposed brick and warm timbers. Cheese souffle could be the opener on the set menu, then maybe a crisp-skinned snapper fillet in a subtle lavender-infused broth, and apricot creme caramel to finish. And there are 19 beers to 'Cheers!' with.

Open Mon 5pm–late; Tues–Sat 11am–late **Typical prices** Set menus $68 (2 courses), $88 (3 courses) **Licensed** ballarat.com/phoenix

Pizza Verde

62 Piper Street, Kyneton **5422 7400**

PIZZERIA

Look first to the specials board for starters like chicken liver pâté or beetroot-and-pistachio dip. Then move on to thin-based pizzas with toppings like leek, blue cheese and prosciutto, or mint, zucchini and ricotta. Fruity boutique beers are a good match in the retro-styled room with laminate tables. Kids like the toys and sundaes using Jock's Ice Cream.

Open Thurs–Mon 5–9pm; Sun noon–3pm **Typical prices E** $9 **M** $18 **D** $8 **Licensed & BYO** pizzaverde.com

Royal George Hotel

24 Piper Street, Kyneton **5422 1390**

CONTEMPORARY

Drinkers from a century ago might recognise the verandah and high ceilings but today's mushroom-coloured walls and double-clothed tables could surprise. On the short seasonal menu might be cured salmon with shaved fennel, duck breast with sour cherries, and a 'trifle' of blood-orange curd, jelly and citrus. Service is warm and friendly. A new chef joined as the *Guide* went to press; a change of ownership was possible longer term.

Open Wed–Sat 6pm–late; Thurs–Sun noon–3pm **Typical prices E** $18 **M** $38 **D** $17 **Licensed** royalgeorge.com.au

Tuki

Tuki Trout Farm, 60 Stoney Rises Road, Smeaton
5345 6233

REGIONAL

At this idyllic trout farm, catch your own lunch or order it. Either way, adore the tumbling valley views (now through bigger windows in the converted stable restaurant) and sample Tuki's smoked trout, part of a sharing platter with house-made tuna pâté, antipasti and smoked sausage. For main, try moist fresh baked trout, or thick eye fillet, from Tuki's own herd.

Open Daily 11am–6pm; dinner by arrangment **Typical prices E** $20 **M** $33.50 **D** $10.50 **Licensed** tuki.com.au

The Village Larder

Shop 3b, 81 High Street, Woodend **5427 3399**

CONTEMPORARY

Country produce and former Melbourne Wine Room chef Marika Oost team to great effect at this retro cafe. Western Plains pork piled on ciabatta, with rhubarb-date relish and apple matchsticks, is a deserving bestseller. Minty lamb shoulder may come with brik pastry and herbed yoghurt. Comfort desserts include golden-syrup dumplings. Serves are generous, the wines local and the coffee good.

Open Daily 8am–4pm; Fri–Sat 6pm–late **Typical prices M** $19 **D** $10 **Licensed** thevillagelarder.com.au

Warrenmang Vineyard Resort

188 Mountain Creek Road, Moonambel **5467 2233**

CONTEMPORARY

High on a ridge amid vines and bushland, Warrenmang is the complete package: a tranquil retreat with fine wines and onsite timber cottages. Veteran restaurateur and vigneron Luigi Bazzani ensures a high standard of European-style hospitality. Dry-aged cuts may feature a Cape Grim sirloin drizzled with bitey olive oil, a sprinkle of salt and lemon. Order the sides, like '50/50 mash' – half butter, half potato with a well of gravy in the middle.

Open Tues–Sun noon–2.30pm; Tues–Sat 6–9pm **Typical prices E** $22.90 **M** $39.50 **D** $16.50 **Licensed** warrenmang.com.au

Whistler Cafe

Shelmerdine Vineyard, Lancefield Road, Tooborac
5433 5188

REGIONAL

Cradled amid conical hills and granite outcrops, this rustic cellar-door cafe is the centrepiece of Merindoc, one of Stephen Shelmerdine's three vineyards. A generous platter of charcuterie, farmhouse cheeses, dips and grilled vegetables is offered midweek. The menu expands Thursday to Monday, with dishes like tender estate-grown lamb and organic salad, well matched with Shelmerdine's superb Heathcote shiraz.

Open Daily 10am–4pm **Typical prices E** $15 **M** $22 **D** $12.50 **Licensed** shelmerdine.com.au

Wine Bank on View

45 View Street, Bendigo **5444 4655**

CONTEMPORARY

This bank was the biz in 1876. Its now-awkward spaces create intimate corners treasured by regulars: sidle up to the hearth, step into the manager's office or secure a front-steps pozzie with a glass from one of the 1000 or so well-priced bottles. Exercise fiscal responsibility with sausage rolls or one of six big-flavoured bruschettas, or go global with paella or the chef's Sri Lankan chicken curry.

Open Mon–Fri 7.30am–9.30pm; Sat 8.30am–9.30pm; Sun 8.30am–4pm **Typical prices E** $12 **M** $27 **D** $13 **Licensed** winebankonview.com

Wombat Hill House

new

Wombat Hill Botanic Gardens, Central Springs Road, Daylesford **4373 0099**

CONTEMPORARY

Lake House's Wolf-Taskers have transformed a former caretaker's cottage in the Botanic Gardens into a breezy cafe. The menu is stamped with local produce and covers breakfast (ricotta hotcakes with maple butter flecked with figs), grazing (local salumi, beetroot remoulade), pies and pizzas. As well as the main 'house', there's seating on the terrace and among the raised vegie plots out the back.

Open Thurs–Mon 9am–4pm; no bookings **Typical prices** Breakfasts & lunches $16; sweets $5 **Licensed** wombathillhouse.com.au

NORTH-EAST VICTORIA

Tea Rooms of Yarck

The Epicurean Centre

Brown Brothers Vineyard, 239 Bobinawarrah Road, Milawa **5720 5540**

CONTEMPORARY **14.5/20**

Buildings dot the tree-shaded grounds of this sprawling vineyard, including the old barn (the original 19th-century winery) and the modern Epicurean Centre with its indoor-outdoor restaurant. Each dish is matched to a Brown Brothers wine (included in the price), and on-trend food favours local ingredients. A multicoloured heirloom tomato salad with confit tomato and tomato jelly, goat's cheese and toasted brioche makes a good marriage with an estate pinot grigio. The wonderful Patricia chardonnay, named to honour the family's matriarch, accompanies chickpea gnocchi with mushrooms, zucchini and pinenut crumble, a dish as satisfyingly complex as the wine. And lamb loin may be teamed with an earthy tempranillo. There are appetisers as well, including locally made charcuterie and Milawa cheeses, and inventive desserts, like a chocolate fondant pudding, the accompanying icecream studded with toasted marshmallow. The menu changes seasonally, and the wines with it. All up, an impressive package, offering everything an epicurean could want: great setting, service, food and wine.

Open Daily noon–3pm
Typical prices E $22 **M** $37 **D** $16
Cards DC AE MC V Eftpos
Wine Brown Brothers wines only, with a wide range of varieties, styles and prices
Owner Brown family
Chef Douglas Elder
Seats 80; outdoor seating
www.brownbrothers.com.au

And ... Try the cellar door for limited releases.

Gigi's of Beechworth

69 Ford Street, Beechworth **5728 2575**

EUROPEAN **14/20**

Gigi's is Beechworth's Miss Congeniality. Full, happy, sometimes leaning towards loud as a result of both, this appealing little bistro with pressed metal ceilings, timber floors, bare tables, warm coffee tones and leather banquettes epitomises a happy local. Well-made food will warm the cockles of your heart – big ricotta ravioli with prawns, burnt butter and sage; risotto lush with taleggio and thyme; little fish 'n' chip shop-style paper cones of fried calamari. Local produce stars, whether in chestnut soup, Harrietville salmon tartare, or Beechworth rabbit pithiviers. Menu favourites include a regional tasting plate to start, and to finish, its dessert counterpart, big enough to serve four if you're friendly enough to not squabble over bitter choc mousse, lemony creme brulee, coffee semifreddo, chocolate parfait, marshmallow and strawberries. Though busy times can challenge service, it's little wonder Gigi's is the popular girl in town (even if actually named after Luigi, the founder).

Open Fri–Tues 9am–2.30pm; Mon–Tues & Fri–Sat 6pm–late
Typical prices E $19 **M** $35 **D** $15
Cards AE MC V Eftpos
Wine A list for enthusiasts or Saturday-night tipplers. Won Tattslotto? Give the cellar's vintage Giacondas a workout, including magnums; BYO Fri night (corkage $10 a bottle)
Owner Allan Parker
Chef Sean Ford
Seats 40; outdoor seating; private room
www.gigisofbeechworth.com

And ... A children's menu runs from pizza and pasta to $13 fillet steak.

Provenance

86 Ford Street, Beechworth **5728 1786**

CONTEMPORARY 16.5/20

Someone should nab Michael Ryan, throw him and his wine-savvy wife in a bag, and smuggle them to town – because Ryan's food, quite simply, rocks. Not that the gorgeous north-east doesn't deserve a restaurant of this calibre. Degustation or a la carte, beautifully balanced dishes show rare mastery of flavour. Perhaps it comes from Ryan's chemistry background, or his adoring immersion in things Japanese, or perhaps just because he's very, very good. Chestnut fettuccine tossed through burnt butter with local hazelnuts and crisp sage; snapper marinated in sake lees, with steamed clams and house-made udon noodles in snapper dashi; crisp-fried smoked potatoes with chilli and Kewpie mayo. 'You have to like licorice,' says the quietly professional waitress of the dauntingly grey semifreddo – like a gorgeous licorice allsort Mother Nature might make, with rhubarb and fennel. In an old bank, Provenance has style, not glamour, but it's home to some of Victoria's best eating and drinking.

Open Wed–Sun 6.30–9pm
Typical prices E $25 **M** $37 **D** $15
Cards AE MC V Eftpos
Wine You need not stray more than 40km from Beechworth for great drinking here, unless it's to France, or Japan for fine sake
Owners Jeanette Henderson & Michael Ryan
Chef Michael Ryan
Seats 45
www.theprovenance.com.au

And ... They've got some of Beechworth's most elegant accommodation out the back.

Range

258 Great Alpine Road, Myrtleford **5752 2885**

MODERN EUROPEAN 14/20

At the foothills of the alps, Range restaurant's decor is simple and bold, with bare black tables, grey walls, and red accents in sculptural art glass. The menu might feature Myrtleford butter and ricotta, Murray Valley pork, Wangaratta lamb, beef and ocean trout from Tasmania, and West Australian Cone Bay barramundi – evidence of a chef who supports regional but thinks Australia-wide. The cooking is adventurous – ocean trout tartare served on a smear of dijon mustard with microherbs and a quail egg is a satisfying entree with punchy flavours; while the filled zucchini flower with preserved lemon, beetroot and hazelnuts may be an enthusiastic but less successful mix. A lamb dish that combines rack and braised shoulder with a haricot-bean puree might provide succulent cutlets but a rectangle of braised shoulder was a little dry. Desserts appeal, especially Stanley apples between fine leaves of pastry, salted caramel and spice icecream. Floor staff are friendly.

Open Tues–Sat 6–10pm
Typical prices E $19 **M** $38 **D** $16
Cards DC AE MC V Eftpos
Wine Varietally listed; good representation of local wines among the mainly Australian choices
Owners Andrew & Heather Dale
Chef Paul Mounsey
Seats 50; outdoor seating; private room
www.range.net.au

And ... The restaurant is in a motel: stay overnight and explore the area.

Simone's Restaurant

98 Gavan Street, Bright **5755 2266**

ITALIAN **14.5/20**

Patrizia Simone is the north-east's culinary champion – her homely Victorian cottage restaurant celebrates local, seasonal produce, and it's been making pilgrims happy for 26 years. Pine mushrooms are plucked from nearby forests to pair with polenta; emu, goat and pig are farmed locally. There's much ambition here, and plaudits deserved for offering this kind of linen-dressed hospitality far from the capital's crowds. That it doesn't always match city experiences will not trouble those who don't mind napkins not unfurled into laps, nor wine by the glass not poured at table – warm hospitality compensates. Dishes can feel too fussy – seafood, steamed in a jar with spaghetti, is frustratingly tricky to eat, while fruity 'minestrone' dessert is a busy, confusing mix, despite a lovely custard at its heart. A dish of porchetta, capers and pickled shallots, with moreish lightly battered broccolini, and a fabulous disc of house-made cotechino plays to Simone's strengths. A six-course degustation showcases the talents of Bright's own celebrity chef.

Open Tues–Sat 6.30pm–late
Typical prices E $25 **M** $39 **D** $18
Cards DC AE MC V Eftpos
Wine From special-occasion vintage Italians, to local stars; 17 by the glass
Owners George Simone & Patrizia Simone
Chefs Patrizia Simone & Anthony Simone
Seats 55; outdoor seating; private room
www.simonesrestaurant.com.au

And ... Children's and vegetarian menus too.

The Stanley

6-12 Myrtleford-Stanley Road, Stanley **5728 6502**

CONTEMPORARY **14.5/20**

This lovely 19th-century building has everything a great country pub needs – stylish dining rooms, open fires, a cosy bar and a rambling beer garden – plus two charming hosts who know the meaning of hospitality. Classic comfort food – think burgers and fish and chips – is on offer in the bar but the dining room is where chef Shauna Stockwell really gets to show off. A compact menu, five dishes per course, is full of tempting choices. An artfully plated heirloom tomato confit bursts with sweetness, while dabs of Milawa goat's cheese and tiny croutons provide balance and crunch. A superbly tender poussin is matched with soft artichokes, creamy fromage frais and crunchy cos, an exercise in perfect textural balance, and a special of lamb with a wet chickpea braise has a smoky spiciness that does justice to this North African classic. Desserts, such as the elegant pot of thick caramel cream with crunchy hazelnut biscotti, are pure indulgence.

Open Thurs–Sun noon–3pm; Wed–Sat 6–9pm
Typical prices E $19 **M** $34 **D** $15
Cards AE MC V Eftpos
Wine Locals dominate with north-eastern Victorian wine, sherry, beer and cider well represented; plus, a small selection of French and NZ wines
Owners Shane & Annemarie Harris
Chef Shauna Stockwell
Seats 30; outdoor seating; private room; bar
www.thestanley.com.au

And ... Stay overnight and enjoy a breakfast of house-made bread, local nuts, fruit and juices, and organic muesli and yoghurt.

Tea Rooms of Yarck

6585 Maroondah Highway, Yarck **5773 4233**

ITALIAN **16/20**

Forget about making the weekend drive from Melbourne: this kind of restaurant inspires moves to the country. Filled with folksy antiques, platters of antipasti and jars of preserves, the sun-drenched dining rooms of this weatherboard cottage are made for lingering in. A good thing, too, as the Tea Rooms' fabulous weekend lunch is no hurried affair. You could go a la carte, selecting pasta or braises from the blackboard menu, but by handing over the reins to the chef, you're assured a procession of dishes, generous both in flavour and size. The meal kicks off with small tastes from the sideboard, perhaps rockmelon and pancetta salad, or tiny pork meatballs, all delivered swiftly by a team of switched-on staff. Part of the joy of dining here is that you never know what's coming next. Scampi with ricotta tortellone may follow, or you could spy a duck version being ferried to the next table. Cross your fingers that dessert features a fine apple and quince tart.

Open Thurs 5–9pm; Fri–Sat noon–10pm; Sun noon–4pm
Typical prices E $26 **M** $39 **D** $16; chefs' four-course menu $89
Cards DC AE MC V Eftpos
Wine From local gems to Italian heavyweights, with a few intriguing Sardinians in the mix
Owners Van Nguyen, Bianca Stephenson & Pietro Porcu
Chefs Luca Flammia & Francesco Rota
Seats 75; outdoor seating
www.thetearoomsofyarck.com.au

And ... They fire up the wood-fired oven for pizzas on Thursday nights.

The Terrace Restaurant

All Saints Estate, All Saints Road, Wahgunyah
(02) 6035 2209

CONTEMPORARY **14.5/20**

It's a fairytale location – 1880s castle, sweeping lawns, tree-lined driveway – so unsurprisingly Eliza Brown chose to marry at the family vineyard last year – and enlisted her husband, restaurateur Denis Lucey (Bottega) to help revamp the Terrace. A permanent marquee forms the dining space, offering bucolic views of the All Saints Estate vineyard. The contemporary menu makes a feature of local produce. You might start with a minty salad of broad beans, asparagus, fennel and ricotta, or gnocchi rich with four cheeses and herbs. Follow with fork-tender slow-braised Rutherglen suckling lamb with almond and olive salsa, or twice-roasted half duck with estate-grown oranges. Dessert might be variations on a rhubarb theme – including brulee, semifreddo and souffle – or a Myrtleford buttermilk panna cotta with muscat-poached cherries. And for those with a soft spot for cheese, a wide-ranging plate could include Scottish and French imports as well as a less-travelled Milawa blue. It's elegant fare in stately surrounds.

Open Wed–Sun noon–3pm; Sat 6–11pm
Typical prices E $21 **M** $36 **D** $16
Cards DC AE MC V Eftpos
Wine All Saints and St Leonards wines, 14 by the glass, plus imports
Owners Eliza, Angela & Nicholas Brown
Chef Matthew Wright
Seats 100; private room
www.allsaintswine.com.au

And ... Take a post-prandial wander to heritage-listed dormitories that housed Chinese immigrant labourers from the 1860s.

Villa Gusto

630 Buckland Valley Road (south of Bright), Buckland
5756 2000

ITALIAN 15/20

An evening at Villa Gusto invites you to surrender to the charm of a secluded Italianate villa nestled in the shadow of Mount Buffalo. Ornate waterfalls and manicured gardens lie below a sun-drenched balcony, and in the dining room, right on 7pm, a leisurely, rustic five-course meal unfolds. Calabrian and Sicilian influences of chilli, fennel and white anchovy create a powerfully delicious bruschetta. A sublime cannelloni of delicate smoked Harrietville trout comes in a luxe, creamy sauce of dill and vermentino; then a mound of slow-cooked, shredded duck with cherries and red wine is the quintessential match. On a daily-changing menu, quibbles are few; an Amalfi-style tumble of perfectly cooked prawns and bugs might be accompanied by less tender pipis and mussels. Classic cannoli of whipped Myrtleford ricotta restores faith. Homely knowledgeable service is passionate about all things Italian. With produce from the gardens and orchards, and a sip of chilled falanghina, this is indeed la dolce vita.

Open Thurs–Sun 6–11pm; Sun noon–3pm
Typical prices Set menu $75 (5 courses)
Cards MC V Eftpos
Wine A passionately selected range of 30 interesting Italian wines; daily glasses and bottles chosen to match the food
Owner Colin McLaren
Chef Emma Handley
Seats 30; outdoor seating
www.villagusto.com.au

And ... Lavish low-impact accommodation makes for a gorgeous weekend getaway.

Alfresco Dining

Boynton's Feathertop Winery, 6619 Great Alpine Road, Porepunkah **5756 2356**

CONTEMPORARY

On a clear day you can eat forever here – perched high above the valleys, matching Japanese-leaning dishes with bold, market-leading wines. Beef tataki with tempranillo? Perfect. Set three-course meals are terrific, and may include a crisply pan-fried duck breast. Wrap things up, perhaps with a honey panna cotta. There's deli food to go, too.

Open Thurs–Mon noon–3pm Sept–June (daily Dec–Jan) **Typical prices E** $16 **M** $34 **D** $14; set menu $45 **Licensed** boynton.com.au

Bank Street

new

5 Bank Street, Avenel **5796 2522**

PIZZERIA

This old bank's lush backyard garden is a lovely surprise, inviting languid lunching on pizza by the pond, with well-priced local wines. Funky front rooms house a wood-fired oven turning out charry, chewy, crisp-crusted pizzas, perhaps topped with pork sausage made by the local butcher, or hot sopressa and roasted peppers. It's casual and chilled – let them know if you're rushed.

Open Fri 6–10.30pm; Sat noon–10.30pm; Sun noon–9pm **Typical prices E** $12 **M** $18 **D** $8 **Licensed**

Black Bull Rutherglen

new

121b-c Main Street, Rutherglen **(02) 6032 8899**

CONTEMPORARY

Formerly a fromagerie with tapas, Black Bull has moved and expanded into an attractive black-and-red themed restaurant. Freshly made wontons and spring rolls rate highly among the entrees. Generous mains feature fish (Atlantic salmon, garlic and chilli prawns) and locally reared meat (Murray River pork rib, King River sirloin). And there's still a range of premium cheeses to take home.

Open Mon–Sat 9am–4pm; Wed–Sat 6–11pm; Sun 9am–6pm (reduced hours in winter) **Typical prices E** $16 **M** $30 **D** $7.90 **Licensed**

Border Wine Room

Level 1, 492 Dean Street, Albury **(02) 6021 0900**

CONTEMPORARY

Albury's best restaurant is a welcoming spot, with clock-tower views; olive, sage and pinot-toned decor; bare timber tables; and walls lined with empty bottles of memorable wines, plenty of which are on the broad list. The globetrotting menu might offer house-made terrine, swordfish with a mountain of Asian slaw, good steak, and glossy pappardelle with almond pesto, all with interesting by-the-glass matches.

Open Tues–Sun 4pm–midnight **Typical prices E** $13 **M** $33 **D** $11.50 **Licensed** borderwineroom.com.au

Bridge Road Brewers

Old Coach House, rear Tanswell Hotel, Ford Street, Beechworth **5728 2703**

PIZZERIA

Behind Beechworth's main strip is this temple to great beer and good food. Think soft and salty giant pretzels, or a fabulous thin-crust pizza (apple and blue cheese; roasted duck). A ploughman's plate includes beer bread, pork terrine, ham and pickles, or try mussels poached in beer with herbs and local butter. Order inside, where friendly staff will happily guide your beer choices.

Open Mon–Tues 11am–4pm; Wed–Thurs 11am–5pm; Fri-Sat 11am–6pm; Sun 11am–9pm **Typical prices E** $15 **M** $19.50 **D** $8.50 **Licensed** bridgeroadbrewers.com.au

The Butter Factory

15 Myrtle Street (Great Alpine Road), Myrtleford **5752 2300**

CONTEMPORARY

Butter – smooth, delicious, made in the artisinal European tradition – stars at this functioning factory-cafe, where the hospitality's honest and keen to please. Breakfast on baked eggs with spinach and parmesan, brunch on BLT with smoky bacon and semi-dried tomatoes, lunch on herbed buttermilk ricotta gnocchi. The coffee is good and there are take-home logs of fine butter – a worthy high-country pitstop.

Open Thurs–Mon 8.30am–5pm; **Typical prices E** $14.50 **M** $18.50 **D** $8.50 **Licensed** thebutterfactory.com.au

Cafe Fez

145 Great Alpine Road, Myrtleford **5751 1155**

MIDDLE EASTERN

A trip to Cafe Fez, in the middle of a homewares bazaar, is worth the effort even if you don't feel like shopping. Cosy under the tent-like interior hung with Moroccan lanterns, the casual Middle Eastern menu includes a breakfast tagine with baked eggs and spicy sausage, classic minced lamb or cheese pastries and lamb kibbeh with flatbreads.

Open Mon–Thurs 8.30am–5pm; Fri 8.30am–11pm; Sat 8.30am–3pm; Sun 10am–3pm **Typical prices E** $12 **M** $17 **D** $4 **Licensed** redramia.com.au

Fowles Wine

Corner Hume Freeway & Lambing Gully Road, Avenel **5796 2150**

CONTEMPORARY

Pause here for a stylish lunch – or something lighter – to break the drive north. A bright dining room opens into an airy courtyard, and the menu has a focus on game dishes in line with the winery's acclaimed 'Ladies Who Shoot Their Lunch' vintages. Tastes include smoked eel, rabbit rillettes, venison on polenta and fine desserts: lemon tart or spiced apple and pinenut torte.

Open Daily 9am–3.30pm **Typical prices E** $8 **M** $26 **D** $10 **Licensed** fowleswine.com

Ginger Baker

new

124 Gavan Street (Great Alpine Road), Bright **5755 2300**

TAPAS/CAFE

Rough-hewn timber tables dot the Ovens River bank at this funky, sprawling all-day cafe, with its preserving-jar lights and warming wood stove. Breakfast could be house-toasted muesli or silky scrambled eggs with magnificent bacon. Then tapas takes over till late – maybe chunky pork and fennel meatballs in a rich, winey sauce; unctuous cubes of pork belly; or a farm-fresh salad of baby cos and toasted local hazelnuts.

Open Tues–Sun 8am–3pm; Thurs–Sat 6–10pm **Typical prices** Breakfasts $14; tapas dishes $12 **D** $11.50 **Licensed** gingerbakerwinebarcafe.com

Graze

Rundells Alpine Lodge, 12 Big Muster Drive, Dinner Plain **5159 6422**

CONTEMPORARY

Disperse the last of those urban cobwebs with a swift drive up the Great Alpine Road to this enchanting hideaway with its many comforts – among them fine food and a lively bar with an open fire. Dine on Kiewa Valley red peppers with Milawa goat's cheese, perhaps a whole rainbow trout (Harrietville) with sage butter (Myrtleford) before addressing an array of local cheeses, all with smart local wines.

Open Daily noon–2.30pm, 6–9pm (June–Sept); Mon–Sat 6–9pm (Nov–May); closed Oct **Typical prices E** $18 **M** $35 **D** $16 **Licensed** rundells.com.au

The Green Shed Bistro

37 Camp Street, Beechworth **5728 2360**

CONTEMPORARY

Built in 1891, this quirky former printery, with its original green paint-daubed brick walls and soaring ceilings, turns out pleasant contemporary fare. The tight menu is playful (aloe vera jelly here, shiitake foam there) and Asian-influenced: tempura soft-shell crab with avocado mousse and kaffir lime mayo followed by five-spice Murray Valley pork cutlet, gingered sweet potato and fuji apple puree.

Open Wed–Sun 11am–2.30pm, 6–9pm **Typical prices E** $18 **M** $35 **D** $16 **Licensed** thegreenshed.com.au

Jones Winery Vineyard Cafe

new

Jones Winery, Jones Road, Rutherglen **(02) 6032 8496**

FRENCH

Elegant period tables and antique chairs set the scene at this excellent winery-cafe, run by brother-sister team Arthur and Mandy Jones. Perhaps try a summery tomato tart, roast duck on home-made rye bread with fennel salad, or cured ham with melon chunks marinated in white port. The citrus tart, made with fruit from the winery's garden, is close to perfection. And check out the on-site gallery, with work by local artists.

Open Thurs–Sun noon–3pm **Typical prices E** $14 **M** $22 **D** $9 **Licensed** joneswinery.com

The Kitchen at the Courthouse Hotel

new

46 Hawkins Street, Howlong **0419 700 619**

CONTEMPORARY

Jodie Jones (chef) and Steve Carne (front-of-house) were behind Albury's former Sourcedining. Now they've opened the Kitchen in an old Howlong pub, creating a smart dining room, with historic town photos and an antler chandelier. Expect glorified pub favourites, such as top-grade steaks or seared duck breast with mushroom stew and polenta and, maybe, spiced crumble for dessert.

Open Thurs–Sun noon–2pm; Wed–Sat 6–8pm **Typical prices E** $15 **M** $28 **D** $12 **Licensed**

Mountain View Hotel

new

4 King Valley Road, Whitfield **5729 8270**

CONTEMPORARY

City slickers deprived of wagyu burgers need look no further than this pub, positioned on the best route back to Melbourne from the north-east. In a return to form, the Mountain View, back under Pizzini management after years in the culinary wilderness, offers more than the posh burgers. Try chicken-liver parfait with house-made lavosh, cassoulet, local (Harrietville) salmon, fine puds and a Pizzini-powered wine list.

Open Wed–Sat noon–9pm; Sun noon–3pm **Typical prices E** $10 **M** $30 **D** $14 **Licensed** mvhotel.com.au

North Eastern Hotel

1 Nunn Street, Benalla **5762 7333**

CONTEMPORARY

Hands-on owners Helen and Tony Ashton add small-town charm to their big pub. It's in the fitout (a bowl of apples on the bar; wee windmills on each table) and the friendly service. Contemporary, well-crafted fare may include house-made flatbread topped with slow-braised lamb and tabbouleh, and a roast of the day, perhaps confit pork loin with apple sauce and a mountain of veg.

Open Wed–Sat noon–2.30pm; Tues–Sat 6–8.30pm **Typical prices E** $16.50 **M** $28 **D** $10 **Licensed**

The Ox & Hound Bistro

52 Ford Street, Beechworth **5728 2123**

MODERN EUROPEAN

Loaded with charm, from pressed-metal ceilings to wicker chairs and classic vintage posters, this is an intimate bistro with attentive service. The menu may be small but its inspiration is diverse. Start with a delicate tomato consomme with poached Balmain bug, or rustic baked polenta with rich chorizo. Main might be a gravy-rich chicken pot pie and dessert a French-style chocolate pot with hazelnut praline and caramel icecream.

Open Thurs–Mon 6pm–late **Typical prices E** $16 **M** $28 **D** $13 **Licensed**

The Pickled Sisters Cafe

Cofield Wines, Distillery Road, Wahgunyah **(02) 6033 2377**

CONTEMPORARY

In the grounds of the winery, this is a lovely airy space to relax and enjoy brunch, coffee and cake, a vineyard platter or lunch from the comprehensive locally sourced menu. There might be chicken liver and Rutherglen muscat pâté, sticky braised pork cheeks, or honey-glazed confit duck. Take home a jar of Pickled Sisters chutney, relish or jam from the well-stocked shelves.

Open Wed–Mon 10am–4pm **Typical prices E** $14.50 **M** $32 **D** $11 **Licensed** pickledsisters.com.au

The Plough Inn

Beechworth Road, Tarrawingee **5725 1609**

CONTEMPORARY/PUB DINING

Country Victoria is full of dining surprises; one such is the grand dining room and wisteria-shrouded rear patio of Tarrawingee's Plough Inn. Expect the unexpected: to begin, plump, translucent scallops with jamon crumbs, then a perfectly judged wild barramundi fillet. An artistic deconstructed lemon meringue pie eaten under the keen gaze of the pub peacocks is a neat, sweet ending.

Open Fri–Sun noon–2pm; Thurs–Sat 6–8pm **Typical prices E** $12.50 **M** $27.50 **D** $12.50 **Licensed** theploughinn.com.au

Poplars

Shop 8, Star Road, Bright **5755 1655**

FRENCH

Velvet drapes, starched white linen and a classic kitchen reveal a proud Gallic heart. Sugar-cured local trout with chive-flecked creme fraiche and a chilled soup of sweetcorn and crab are elegant starters. Simple mains like confit chicken with herbed lentils satisfy, and if the gorgeous chocolate souffle is on, don't miss it. Service may sometimes be stretched but it's unfailingly friendly.

Open Tues–Sat 6–9.30pm **Typical prices E** $17 **M** $28 **D** $14 **Licensed & BYO** poplars.com.au

Restaurant Merlot

Lindenwarrah, Milawa-Bobinawarrah Road, Milawa **5720 5777**

CONTEMPORARY

The restaurant – named for the varietal vineyard it overlooks – has the level of comfort you'd expect in a country-house hotel of restrained elegance. The food combines the familiar (coq au vin) with the less expected, such as quail saltimbocca, or local trout fillets with bok choy and spiced rice timbale. The wine list supports regional producers, and the service is attentive.

Open Daily 7.30–9.30am; Fri–Sun noon–3pm; Thurs–Sun 6.30–9.30pm **Typical prices E** $18 **M** $31 **D** $14 **Licensed** lancemore.com.au/lindenwarrah

Rinaldo's Casa Cucina

8 Tone Road, Wangaratta **5721 8800**

ITALIAN

The handsomely constructed galvanised iron shed with its timber floor can be noisy, but don't be deterred. Regional and seasonal dishes star – prosciutto-wrapped baked figs with blue cheese, heirloom tomato salad, tender gnocchi with a robust beef ragu, and perhaps something less local, such as king salmon with crisp salty skin and a tomato salsa. Drinks include local beers and many regional wines.

Open Fri–Sat 11.30am–2.30pm; Tues–Sat 5.30–10pm **Typical prices E** $16 **M** $28 **D** $12 **Licensed** rinaldos.com.au

Roi's Restaurant

177 Kiewa Valley Highway, Tawonga **5754 4495**

ITALIAN

This quirky local legend continues with the inimitable Roi Rigoni at the stoves. Thursday is $15 pasta night (and often packed); otherwise the modern Italian menu includes an incomparable roasted pork loin chop – impossibly moist and tender with blistered crackling – under caramelised apples on sauerkraut and mash. It's an eclectic establishment cluttered with rare books, phones and picnic sets, with great desserts.

Open Thurs–Sun 6.30–9.30pm **Typical prices E** $16 **M** $30 **D** $16 **Licensed**

Tanswell's Hotel

50 Ford Street, Beechworth **5728 1480**

PUB DINING/CONTEMPORARY

It's a classic, grand old country pub: the dining room has boldly patterned red carpet, and there's DIY service at the busy bar. But the menu offers some surprises among the pub classics (fish and chips, steak and chips). A caramelised onion and goat's cheese tart comes with a perfect green salad, or spicy goat is served with polenta. There's a wide-ranging and affordable wine list.

Open Daily noon–3pm, 6–9pm **Typical prices E** $15 **M** $26 **D** $12 **Licensed**

Tuileries

new

13-35 Drummond Street, Rutherglen **(02) 6032 9033**

CONTEMPORARY

Tuileries elegantly showcases regional produce in its equally smart dining space. Entrees could be risotto featuring Harrietville smoked trout, or smoked veal tongue with sauce gribiche; and mains: Myrtleford buttermilk fried chicken or braised Murray Valley pork cheek with beetroot gel and an apple and olive salsa. Vegetarians can enjoy options like mushroom ravioli with baby spinach and porcini cream reduction.

Open Daily 6.30–9pm **Typical prices E** $19.50 **M** $33.50 **D** $13.50 **Licensed** tuileriesrutherglen.com.au

The 2 Cooks Cafe

new

577 Whorouly Road, Whorouly **5783 6110**

CAFE

Cute 2 Cooks Cafe has such spirit that eating there nourishes the soul. Kay Menzies and Nora Spitzer lost everything in the 2009 Buxton bushfires and they've started afresh here. The justly famous 'Rouly burger' features a 160g beef patty with the lot. Spicy lamb kofta comes with tabbouleh and yoghurt sauce. And the old-fashioned made-here cakes include lumberjack and gooey lemon custard teacake.

Open Fri–Sun 9am–5pm; Sat 6–9pm; bookings essential Sat night **Typical prices E** $7 **M** $15.50 **D** $6.50 **Licensed** the2cookscafe.com.au

Waddington's at Kergunyah

2688 Kiewa Valley Highway, Kergunyah
(02) 6027 5393

REGIONAL

Expect country cuisine with flair at this rustic restaurant, once a barn on this historic cattle property. Chef Jan Waddington takes inspiration from her cottage garden, plucking herbs and flowers to adorn dishes such as pan-seared scallops on cauliflower puree. Lamb, beef and duck feature (and there are always vegetarian options). Desserts reflect the season in dishes such as chestnut honey panna cotta with quince soup.

Open Thurs–Sun noon–4pm **Typical prices E** $15 **M** $30 **D** $14 **Licensed**

Watermarc

56-58 Faithfull Street, Wangaratta **5722 4000**

CONTEMPORARY

This bistro's terrace overlooks the Ovens River and great old gum trees. It's a prime spot to watch the sunset while sharing antipasti – maybe cured salmon, arancini, bresaola with a miniature salad. Follow with thin-crusted pizza or perhaps house-made spaghettini with prawns, or more conventional mains, such as steak. There's a good drinks list, including local beer and affordable, mainly local wines.

Open Tues–Sat 11am–3pm, 5pm–late **Typical prices E** $14 **M** $28 **D** $12 **Licensed** watermarc.com.au

GIPPSLAND

Raeshaws at Fulham

The Boathouse

201 The Esplanade, Lakes Entrance **5155 3055**

SEAFOOD **14/20**

The Boathouse fronts a busy holiday complex, but is sufficiently removed from the resort hubbub to be an appealing eatery in its own right. It's bright and modern with expansive windows overlooking the adjacent harbour. Quality linen and tableware, together with attentive service, make this a popular special-occasion restaurant. The fare is mostly seafood; expect ocean trout from Tasmania, mussels from Eden, flathead tails from Bass Strait. Oysters from Coffin Bay are served at least five ways, including as a rich concoction of grilled oysters wrapped in prosciutto, topped with tomato salsa. Lakes Entrance scallops deftly combined with citrus butter sauce make for zesty tortellini, while seafood mains include a hefty fillet of blue-eye poached in butter and fillet of John Dory on a creamy prawn risotto. For those eschewing seafood there are a few 'land' options, one of which might be a tender duck breast in a rich jus matched with foie gras and sauteed mushrooms.

Open Tues–Sat 6–9pm
Typical prices E $18 **M** $37 **D** $15
Cards DC AE MC V Eftpos
Wine A short list with a focus on Gippsland wines
Owner Chris Banson
Chef Erik Monteith
Seats 40; private room; bar
www.bellevuelakes.com

And ... The lakeside boardwalk out front is perfect for an after-dinner stroll.

The Chambers

3a Smith Street, Warragul **5623 3090**

CONTEMPORARY **14/20**

The Chambers is housed in one of the town's prominent heritage buildings: an impressive 1880s former bank. But, for a fine diner, the atmosphere is casual, with undressed tables and spare wall furnishings, which leaves room for some of the original decorative features to charm almost by stealth. Similarly, dishes aren't technically overcomplicated, but the consistency of the kitchen's offerings is impressive. Entrees like quail with green grapes and shredded red cabbage, and goat's cheese ravioli with burnt butter and sage set the tone. Nicely browned lemon and oregano chicken quarter with warm potato salad is a contemporary evocation of the Sunday roast; equally gratifying is confit duck leg with white bean and smoky bacon cassoulet. A steamed orange pudding may lack intensity, but a baked fondant with oozing chocolate filling proves richly satisfying. Smart service is a feature, making for a smooth operation that caters equally well for a relaxed meal or special night out.

Open Mon–Fri 11am–late; Sat 4pm–late
Typical prices E $15 **M** $28 **D** $13.50
Cards MC V Eftpos
Wine Favours mid-range Australian wines, with forays into NZ, Italy and France; 12 by the glass
Owners Peter Milne & Robert Milne
Chefs Peter Milne, Jamie Lee Goodger & Daniel Martin
Seats 70; outdoor seating; private room; bar

And ... Look up, up, up at the decorative mile-high ceiling – one of the building's original 1880s features.

Neilsons

13 Seymour Street, Traralgon **5175 0100**

CONTEMPORARY **15.5/20**

The improbable location – a cosy bungalow amid fast-food outlets and garish shopfronts – adds to the magic chef Lewis Prince manages to weave here. He delivers enlightened food to entranced locals and astonished travellers alike. Order four tastes of the sea, be diverted with a shot glass of corn velouté while your entree takes shape, and you may suspect you have stumbled into somewhere special. Your 'tastes' will confirm these suspicions: a nugget of cured ocean trout with finger-lime cells, a prawn dumpling fired with XO sauce, a tempura scallop with candied chilli, and laksa laced with blue swimmer fragments. Lamb rump is no less extraordinary: cooked to tender perfection, it is accompanied by crisply finished rib meat, tempura polenta chips, a goat's cheese salad and a sumac foam. Yep. Desserts, also, indicate a confident chef at the top of his game: try passionfruit curd with toasted meringue, poached rhubarb, red velvet sponge and custardy vanilla spheres. Hang on: where are we again?

Open Tues–Sat noon–2.30pm, 6pm–late
Typical prices E $19 **M** $38 **D** $17
Cards DC AE MC V Eftpos
Wine Thoughtful, well-priced list with keen Gippsland focus
Owners Lewis & Rebecca Prince
Chef Lewis Prince
Seats 50; outdoor seating; private room
www.neilsons.com.au

And ... Neilsons has a little gallery displaying paintings and photos by local artists; most works are for sale.

The River Grill

2 Wood Street, Bairnsdale **5153 1421**

CONTEMPORARY **15/20**

Originally built as horse stables, the River Grill's grey barn-like facade belies its chic interior. Bright, white and airy, flowers and artwork add a splash of colour, while comfy chairs, well-spaced tables and quality napery and tableware add a touch of style, enhanced by efficient service. Chef John Forrest fuses the flavours of Asia and the Mediterranean in a skillfully executed menu that changes almost daily. Mains are generous, as is the choice of steaks. Small plates are a popular alternative, such as a delicate spanner crab and smoked chicken salad; house-made prawn ravioli in roasted tomato sauce; and kingfish sashimi with wasabi and pickled ginger. Typical bigger plates are a rich Thai duck curry; classic-style navarin of lamb shoulder served with turnip, peas and creamed potato; and chef's own grilled duck sausages with confit of duck and roasted garlic. Sweet seasonal desserts may include frangipane raspberry tart, and a summery peach and blackberry salad.

Open Mon–Sat noon–3pm, 6–10.30pm
Typical prices E $24 **M** $38 **D** $18
Cards MC V Eftpos
Wine Five whites and four reds by the glass on a modest well-priced list that includes some of Gippsland's better-known labels
Owners John Forrest & Yvonne Williams
Chef John Forrest
Seats 50; outdoor seating; private room; bar

And ... The enclosed garden courtyard is perfect for intimate alfresco dining.

Tinamba Hotel

4-6 Tinamba-Seaton Road, Tinamba **5145 1484**

CONTEMPORARY **14.5/20**

More people dine in the Tinamba Hotel, most days, than live in Tinamba, which is as it should be. Word travels fast out here, and the word's out on operators Damien Gannon and Brad Neilson (ex-Neilsons), and the fine food turned out by their ace chef, Paul van Ruiten. A hotel in name only, this handsome restaurant, with luxe chocolate-toned dining room, has style and substance. The full menu offers a spread of expertly handled top-notch ingredients, and the fixed-price lunches are also well worth a look. Kick off, perhaps, with a silky sweet potato and corn soup that's rich and excellent. Mains can be adventurous, but simply handled dishes are just as good, as in a flawless, fresh herb-coated fillet of blue grenadier served on lemon mash and flanked by a spinach salad sporting a warm prawn vinaigrette. For dessert, crushed meringue with watermelon, strawberry, whipped cream and a passionfruit sauce. Tinamba mess?
Not at all.

Open Wed-Sun noon-2.30pm; Wed-Sat 6pm-late
Typical prices E $17 **M** $35 **D** $15
Cards AE MC V Eftpos
Wine Good domestic selection, strong on Gippsland wines, some gems; 15 by the glass
Owners Brad Neilson & Damien Gannon
Chef Paul van Ruiten
Seats 120; outdoor seating; private room; bar
www.tinambahotel.com.au

And ... There are outstanding local wines by the glass.

Wild Dog Winery

6 Farrington Close (Warragul-Korumburra Road), Warragul **5623 2211**

CONTEMPORARY **14/20**

The name throws you off the scent; Wild Dog is actually the most polished restaurant in the district. In rolling hills just south of Warragul, the spacious pavilion with expansive, timber decks is graced with idyllic views over gum-fringed pastures. The menu showcases Ed McDowell's palette of soils, foams, gels and other textural effects. While an entree like kingfish sashimi with freshly grated wasabi is necessarily spare in its presentation, the mushroom salad is a complex arrangement of shiitake caps, set porcini consomme and gently boiled eggs drizzled with truffle oil. Mains adopt a slightly more traditional stance as in lamb loin on nutty green lentils with sweet pea mash, and poussin ballotine stuffed with ham hock and pistachios. Desserts bring experimentation back to centre stage with a curious but compelling plate of lurid licorice and pineapple jellies and curds of varying intensity and sweetness. Attentive black-clad waitstaff befit the refined sensibility; this is one dog with plenty of tricks.

Open Wed-Fri 11.30am-2.30pm; Sat-Sun 10am-3pm; Fri-Sat 6-9pm (extended hours in summer)
Typical prices E $18 **M** $34.90 **D** $17.90
Cards MC V Eftpos
Wine About 20 estate wines by the glass, plus a small selection of premium Australian wines
Owners Gary & Judy Surman
Chefs Ed McDowell & Justin Sommerville
Seats 120; outdoor seating; bar
www.wilddogwinery.com

And ... The cellar door is open daily, selling Jindi cheese, local produce and estate wines.

Wildfish

40 Wharf Street, Port Albert **5183 2002**

SEAFOOD **14/20**

Such is the commitment to freshness at Wildfish that owner Michael Hobson personally takes out the restaurant's own boat and casts a line or two. This fifth-generation fisherman has created a dazzling restaurant. With its striking location on the water and a chic Scandinavian fitout, you'd be forgiven for wondering how a restaurant like this was born in sleepy Port Albert (population 251). But as Victoria's oldest port, it makes complete sense. Diners get to reap the benefits of the freshly caught bounty with dishes like flake and prawn pie, and crisp-skinned kingfish on peppery rocket with delicate slices of poached pear and shaved parmesan. Tapas can be a hit-or-miss affair: while fish fritters may be a tad chewy, the salmon gravlax is a knockout. The service is warm and efficient, and those stunning harbour views may almost manage to distract you from dessert, perhaps a chocolate and macadamia tart with a swirl of coulis courtesy of some local berries.

Open Thurs–Sun noon–3pm, 6–8pm
Typical prices E $15 **M** $28.50 **D** $12
Cards AE MC V Eftpos
Wine A tight list with many boutique Gippsland wines; nine by the glass; BYO (corkage $10 a bottle)
Owner Michael Hobson
Chef Sarah Groombridge
Seats 65; outdoor seating; bar
www.wildfish-restaurant.com.au

And ... If the sun is shining, enjoy the tranquil water views with alfresco dining on the wharf.

Bancroft Bites

57 Metung Road, Metung **5156 2854**

CONTEMPORARY

This stylish bite-sized diner is big on appeal, dishing up top-notch tucker in a bright convivial space right around the clock. The often-changing, globetrotting menu might include tempura-battered oysters with mild wasabi mayo, or a comforting pork loin chop with horseradish and parsley cream. House-made cakes are a big hit, from a homely hummingbird to indulgent choc mud.

Open Thurs–Tues 8am–9pm (daily in school hols)
Typical prices E $14.50 **M** $27 **D** $6.50 **Licensed & BYO** bancroftbites.com.au

Big Fat Greek Bar & Grill

Shop 2, 9 Beach Road, Rhyll **5956 9511**

GREEK

Proprietors the Gabriels hail from a long line of food-loving Greeks staunchly averse to small servings. Expect to eat lots – whether it's a super-sized starter of house-made spanakopita or a generous main of char-grilled snapper on a plump bed of garlicky skordalia. Chris's lamb mince and eggplant moussaka is a feat – enough for two. Rhyll beach opposite beckons for a post-prandial stroll.

Open Thurs–Mon 6–9pm (extended hours in summer)
Typical prices E $14 **M** $30 **D** $7 **Licensed**
bigfatgreek.com.au

Bullant Brewery

46 Main Street (Great Alpine Road), Bruthen **5157 5307**

CONTEMPORARY

A striking copper-clad brewhouse beckons visitors to this modern micro-brewery restaurant at the confluence of the Great Alpine Road and the East Gippsland Rail Trail. The emphasis is on casual dining, and beer-tasting paddles are popular segues into a menu that ranges across generous share-plates (dips, antipasti), seafood crepes, pizza, chicken caesar salad and grilled bluefin tuna steak.

Open Wed–Sun 11am–5pm; Fri–Sat 6–10pm
Typical prices E $17.80 **M** $26 **D** $10 **Licensed**
bullantbrewery.com

Cafe Aura

Shop 3, 19-25 Seymour Street, Traralgon **5174 1517**

CONTEMPORARY

This sleek and shiny cafe in downtown Traralgon offers a seasonal dinner menu that manages to tick most boxes. Expect unfussy food done well: Gippsland sirloin simply paired with hand-cut potatoes; chilli-spiked seafood linguine. At breakfast, house-made bullboar (pork, beef and fennel) sausages come with a fried free-range egg, while lunch baguettes may come stuffed with crisp hoisin-smothered pork belly.

Open Mon 7.30am–3pm; Tues–Sat 7.30am–9pm; Sun 9am–3pm **Typical prices E** $16.50 **M** $30 **D** $10.50 **Licensed** cafeauratraralgon.com.au

Ferryman's Seafood Cafe

Middle Boat Harbour, Princes Highway, Lakes Entrance **5155 3000**

SEAFOOD

At this colourful floating cafe-cum-fishmonger, blackboards line the gangway spruiking the day's catch. You might try a platter of Bass Strait shovelnose lobsters or some petite but flavoursome grilled local scallops. Or order from the small menu: retro-style prawn and lobster cocktail; classic fish and chips in a crisp golden batter; free-range chicken skewers on black rice.

Open Daily 10am–late **Typical prices E** $15 **M** $30 **D** $12 **Licensed & BYO** ferrymans.com.au

Kalimna Hotel

1 Hotel Road, Kalimna **5155 1202**

GREEK

Perched on a high cliff overlooking the sand dunes and estuarine waters of Lakes Entrance, this hotel is worthy of recommendation for its view alone. But the restaurant's quality Greek food is also a winner – fresh local fish and calamari charred on the grill and flavoured with oregano, lemon, parsley and olive oil; succulent lamb cutlets and tangy saganaki. Hospitable staff too.

Open Daily 11.30am–3pm, 5.30–9pm (reduced hours in winter) **Typical prices E** $15 **M** $32 **D** $12 **Licensed**

Kilcunda General Store

3535 Bass Highway, Kilcunda **5678 7390** new

CAFE

The locals got lucky when sisters Suellen Wilkie and Delyse Graham took over this gastro hub three years ago. Hot pots (spicy chicken tagine on couscous); winter soups (hearty ham hock with Puy lentils); frittatas (local organic zucchini and artichoke with chorizo); house-made cakes and decadent desserts (smashed meringue, raspberry coulis and fairy floss) feature. The vibe is laid-back – '60s op-shop meets '70s country soul – with an ocean view.

Open Daily 8am–5pm **Typical prices M** $17 **D** $8 **Licensed** kilcundageneralstore.com

Koonwarra Store

South Gippsland Highway, Koonwarra **5664 2285**

REGIONAL

Relax in the comfy, timber-furnished cafe or courtyard with food proudly made from scratch using local produce. Free-range eggs (served all day) might come with buttery mushrooms or fat pork sausages. At lunch there's a platter with regional goods: wagyu chorizo, goat's feta and frittata. Find vanilla slice in the chock-full cake cabinet and house-made comestibles on the shelves.

Open Daily 8.30am–5.30pm **Typical prices E** $12.50 **M** $18.50 **D** $8 **Licensed**

Main Hotel

270 Main Street, Bairnsdale **5152 3787**

CONTEMPORARY

The century-old Main is a comfortable blend of old-style local boozer and country gastropub. There's something on the menu to please everyone and servings are generous: perhaps penne in a rich tomato sugo with olives, basil and chorizo; grilled Atlantic salmon fillet with prawns and roasted vegetables; or sous-vide pork fillet with crisp fried kipfler potatoes, chorizo and tomato jam.

Open Mon–Fri noon–2pm; Mon–Sat 6–8.30pm **Typical prices E** $14.50 **M** $25 **D** $8 **Licensed** mainhotel.com.au

The Metung Galley

50 Metung Road, Metung **5156 2330**

CONTEMPORARY

Adjoining the village green in the heart of town, Metung Galley is a relaxed, chic and welcoming spot, popular with coffee diehards. There's a tapas bar (arancini, marinated octopus) and a stylish, airy dining room with a menu that takes in toasted pides, classic beer-battered local flathead tails and a grazing plate of pork rillettes and duck terrine.

Open Mon 8am–4pm; Tues–Sun 8am–9.30pm **Typical prices E** $16 **M** $29 **D** $12 **Licensed & BYO** themetunggalley.com.au

The Outpost Retreat

38 Loch Valley Road, Noojee **5628 9669**

PUB DINING

The Outpost is an old timber homestead partially hidden by rows of lush ferns. Inside, the settler bric-a-brac is laid on thick but the hospitality is genuine. Larger groups gravitate to the Tool Shed bistro out the back; however, all areas enjoy the same robust pub grub featuring eight sorts of platter-sized parmas and whole, local, pink-fleshed rainbow or golden trout.

Open Fri–Sat 6–9pm; Sat–Sun noon–4pm **Typical prices E** $12 **M** $25 **D** $10 **Licensed** theoutpostretreat.com

Raeshaws at Fulham

10 Williams Drive, Fulham **5144 1672**

REGIONAL

In true paddock-to-plate spirit, almost everything used in the kitchen is grown here, including the beef, pork and lamb. Free-range eggs and Raeshaws bacon make for a hearty home-grown breakfast. A bountiful ploughman's platter heads the lunchtime offerings, while roast beef and vegetables with gravy make an appearance at dinner. Rustic Raeshaws is the country family you never had.

Open Thurs–Sun 8am–11.30pm **Typical prices E** $12 **M** $26 **D** $12 **Licensed** raeshawsatfulham.com.au

Tomo's Japanese Inverloch

Shop 1, 23 A'Beckett Street, Inverloch **5674 3444**

JAPANESE

Tomo hums with locals tucking into immaculately prepared Japanese food – perhaps moreish fried prawn dumplings, delicate squares of tuna carpaccio in a soy-spiked sauce or nori-wrapped parcels of lightly battered deep-fried blue swimmer crab. The service is quiet and considered. And if the neat, sparse dining room is full, you might try the atmospheric bamboo-fringed courtyard.

Open Wed–Sun noon–2pm, 6–9pm (daily in summer) **Typical prices E** $15 **M** $30 **D** $11 **Licensed & BYO** tomos-japanese.com

Vela 9

9 A'Beckett Street, Inverloch **5674 1188**

MEDITERRANEAN

This sophisticated space, a stone's throw from the foreshore, works as both an intimate tapas bar and a restaurant. There's plenty of attention to detail in the hardworking kitchen. Share a charcuterie board over a glass of red, or try a main of hand-rolled tagliatelle tangled with enoki and slippery jacks. Home-made icecream comes in excellent flavours such as creamy pecan praline.

Open Thurs–Mon 6–9.30pm **Typical prices E** $17 **M** $36 **D** $16 **Licensed** velanine.com.au

INTERSTATE

Esquire, Brisbane

Sydney

By Terry Durack

The Apollo

44 Macleay Street, Potts Point **(02) 8354 0888** theapollo.com.au

Owner Sam Christie (of Longrain) and chef Jonathan Barthelmess draw on their Greek heritage to fuse ancient and modern Greek flavours and a contemporary dining ethic that's just so Sydney. The 'full Greek' (pita, taramasalata, roast lamb, Greek salad, pastries) pulls the crowd into the spartan-but-chic dining space.

Bar H

80 Campbell Street, Surry Hills **(02) 9280 1980** barhsurryhills.com

After starting life as a contemporary bistro, Bar H has returned to chef Hamish Ingham's Billy Kwong Asian roots. So the streetwise little corner restaurant gets a new lease of life, as well as a legion of new fans, for its braised beef short ribs on sesame leaves.

The Bridge Room

44 Bridge Street, Sydney **(02) 9247 7000** thebridgeroom.com.au

Chef Ross Lusted has settled nicely into this sleek parquetry-floored space in a striking 1938 office building. The appealing modern menu runs from raw wagyu shoulder with robata-scorched enoki mushrooms to delicate white-cut chicken.

Cafe Sopra

Fratelli Fresh, 11 Bridge Street, Sydney **(02) 8298 2701** fratellifresh.com.au

Barry McDonald's fourth Fratelli Fresh occupies a vast basement under the city's historic Burns Philp building, again combining a well-stocked provedore with a thriving trattoria. There's a mozzarella bar, a pizza oven, even a hidden Campari bar.

Chiswick

65 Ocean Street, Woollahra **(02) 8388 8688** chiswickrestaurant.com.au

The latest venture from Aria's Matt Moran and Peter Sullivan comes with its own herb and vegetable garden. The one-time Pruniers site is again packed with the cream of the eastern suburbs, tucking into garden salads and share-plates of wood-roasted lamb from the Moran family farm.

Gastro Park

5-9 Roslyn Street, Kings Cross **(02) 8068 1017** gastropark.com.au

Chef Grant King calls his restaurant a playground of good food. It's hard to tell who's having the most fun – the kitchen, or the diners happily tucking into soy and mustard-glazed swordfish belly and crisply scaled snapper with real, edible scales.

The Grounds of Alexandria

Building 7a, 2 Huntley Street, Alexandria **(02) 9699 2225** groundsroasters.com

You might call this a cafe with the lot. This vast warehouse cafe comes with two separate espresso stations, two Probat coffee roasters, a baker, a pizzeria, and its own herb and vegetable garden, complete with happy chickens. Food runs from breakfast porridge to silky ocean trout salads to crowd-pleasing Groundsburgers.

Marque

Shop 4-5, 355 Crown Street, Surry Hills **(02) 9332 2225** marquerestaurant.com.au

Think Dutch cream potato with bone marrow, sea urchin and coffee, and bonito with foie gras, potato and olive truffle. Not only does Mark Best push out some of Sydney's edgiest degustation dishes, he does it in a serenely civilised space of charm and comfort.

Momofuku Seiobo

Level G, The Star, 80 Pyrmont Street, Pyrmont **(no phone)** momofuku.com

Kick-arse chef Dave Chang brings New York savvy to the Star complex. A gleaming, spot-lit, sexy kitchen dominates the room, bordered by counters of diners happily devouring 15 courses of a tasting menu that might finish on caramelised pork shoulder for petits fours. Bookings online only.

Neild Avenue

10 Neild Avenue, Rushcutters Bay **(02) 8353 4400** idrb.com

Maurice Terzini of Bondi's Icebergs Dining Room moves inland with his boldest venture yet. This 200-seat restaurant/bar/art installation serves up a fast and furious Mediterranean mix of sizzling grills, whole coal-grilled John Dory, hummus and smoky Afghani flatbread, with a groovy soundtrack.

Porteno

358 Cleveland Street, Surry Hills **(02) 8399 1440**
porteno.com.au

If you've been waiting for the popularity of this loud, hip Argentinean grill to die down, forget it. It's as hard to get into as ever. Book for six people, or join the queue when doors open, and hope for the best as you dream of that smoky, juicy lamb or pork cooked over hot coals.

Quay

Upper level, Overseas Passenger Terminal, The Rocks
(02) 9251 5600 quay.com.au

Quay is almost unfairly blessed. There are stunning views of the Bridge and Opera House, one of Sydney's most awesome wine lists, and finally, Peter Gilmore's superbly nature-driven cooking, which has the restaurant at number 29 on the World's Fifty Best Restaurants list.

Rockpool

107 George Street, The Rocks **(02) 9252 1888**
rockpool.com

Since 1989 Neil Perry's groundbreaking restaurant has neatly defined modern Australian cuisine with its clever use of seafood and intuitive handling of both Mediterranean and Asian flavours. Talented chef Phil Wood continues the tradition with a brilliant tuna chirashi zushi ('scattered sushi'), and glazed Chinese roast pigeon with smoked eggplant.

Sepia

Darling Park, 201 Sussex Street, Sydney
(02) 9283 1990 sepiarestaurant.com.au

This warm, welcoming, darkly seductive restaurant just seems to keep getting better. Chef Martin Benn turns out some of the city's finest food, including smoky scampi tails cooked over Japanese charcoal teamed with miso hiramisa kingfish and shellfish custard. Desserts are just as dazzling.

Sixpenny

83 Percival Road, Stanmore **(02) 9572 6666**
sixpenny.com.au

Two former young chefs of the year, James Parry and Daniel Puskas, personally bring an array of dazzling small dishes to the table in this minimalist Nordic-influenced dining room. Everything thrills, from little toasted knuckle sandwiches to an inspired combo of mud crab, macadamia and chamomile.

Three Blue Ducks

141–143 McPherson Street, Bronte **(02) 9389 0010**
threeblueducks.com

What began as a cafe started by surfing mates is now one of Sydney's hottest dining destinations, with three former Tetsuya's chefs in the kitchen. Breakfasts and lunches are laid-back, but the multi-course dinners (bookings online) from Thursday to Saturday nail modern Sydney cooking to the plate.

Out of town

Biota

18 Kangaloon Road, Bowral **(02) 4862 2005**
biotadining.com

James Viles' Scandi-chic restaurant delivers modern, progressive cooking using vegetables from the kitchen garden and local meat and fish. The menu free-ranges across boundaries, with the likes of spatchcock with hazelnut crumbs, spiced pear, chestnut porridge and speck.

No. 2 Oak Street

2 Oak Street, Bellingen **(02) 6655 9000**
no2oakst.com.au

Family restaurants don't get more family-run than Ray and Toni Urquhart's Bellingen gem. Daughter Shani and her service team treat everyone as part of the family, while Ray and son Michael share kitchen duties, serving divine seafood stew, silky oxtail ravioli and duck sausage with borlotti beans.

Restaurant Mason

Shop 3, 35 Hunter Street, Newcastle **(02) 4926 1014**
restaurantmason.com

Owner-chef Chris Thornton trained with fellow Novacastrian Brett Graham of London's acclaimed Ledbury, then came home to wow Newcastle with beautifully crafted food such as quail boudin with figs and almonds, in a sweet, casual bistro space.

Town

33 Byron Street, Bangalow **(02) 6687 1010**
townbangalow.com.au

What was Satiate is now a downstairs cafe ('downtown') and upstairs restaurant ('uptown'). Former Chef of the Year Katrina Kanetani and husband Karl send out six-course degustation dinners of great style. Desserts are playfully seasonal, perhaps layered finger-lime icecream, mango granita and sauterne custard with mango 'egg'.

Canberra

By Barbara Sweeney

Aubergine

18 Barker Street, Griffith **(02) 6260 8666**
aubergine.com.au

Ben Willis is Canberra's chef to watch. His imaginative menu travels from classy sand whiting buckwheat risotto to duck (sausage and breast) with red cabbage and blackberries, and parsley icecream with peach, toasted almond cream, financier and blueberries. The two-tiered room is elegant, but the experience pleasantly relaxed.

Courgette

54 Marcus Clarke Street, Canberra **(02) 6247 4042**
courgette.com.au

James Mussillon's food pleases the senses. Its basis is in France, and seafood shines: from seared scallops and sugar-cured ocean trout with hummus and white beans to John Dory on saffron mash with baby leek, cream sauce and avruga caviar. The room is carpeted and comfortable.

Dieci e Mezzo

Corner Bunda & Mort streets, Canberra
(02) 6248 3142 dieciemezzo.com.au

The focus on top produce at this refined Italian continues, despite the founding chef's departure. The menu is small - from a salad of pig's head and trotter with soft-cooked quail eggs to polenta with mushrooms. The space feels a bit like a gallery foyer, but gorgeous lighting adds splashes of colour.

Italian & Sons

7 Lonsdale Street, Braddon **(02) 6162 4888**
italianandsons.com.au

This inner-city trattoria is classy, ebullient and modern, with a wood-fired oven, blackboard wall, and curtain of cured meats over the bar. Slow-roasted meats feature (try lamb shoulder in white wine), as does pizza, but don't miss daily specials - or the tiramisu.

Lanterne Rooms

3 Blamey Place, Campbell **(02) 6249 6889**
lanternerooms.com.au

An unremarkable exterior belies an evocative interior of dark wood, bamboo shutters and filmy curtains. Quietly efficient service delivers South-East Asian dishes to share, such as ling with pickled pineapple and chilli.

Malamay

Burbury Hotel, 1 Burbury Close, Barton
(02) 6162 1220 malamay.chairmangroup.com.au

New to Josiah Li's Eastern empire (Chairman and Yip and Lanterne Rooms), Malamay spotlights Sichuan food. It's striking in black and red, with a clubby 1930s Shanghai feel. Food is smoking hot, literally, with house-smoked seafood and meat a feature. Traditional flavours star in dishes such as braised pork ribs with preserved plum.

Ottoman Cuisine

Corner Broughton & Blackall streets, Barton
(02) 6273 6111 ottomancuisine.com.au

Opulent, with fine service and beautifully unfussy food, Ottoman is possibly Australia's best Turkish restaurant. Dishes may sound familiar - dips, kofta, kebabs - but all are luxe renderings by chef Serif Kaya. Feast on perfumed pilau, smoky charred kebabs or banquet menus, which embrace many of Kaya's hallmark dishes.

Silo Bakery

36 Giles Street, Kingston **(02) 6260 6060**
silobakery.com.au

If the aroma doesn't get you, the line-up of shiny tarts, flaky croissants and pastries on the long marble counter will. There's bread, dark and light, round and rectangle, while the food is modern yet simple takes on European classics. Don't miss the cheese room.

Thirst

Melbourne Building, 20 West Row, Canberra
(02) 6257 0700 thirstwinebar.com.au

Thai street food inspires the all-day-and-all-night snack menu; diners are encouraged to finish dishes to their liking, using house-made sauces, or kruang prung (chilli, sugar, fish sauce and rice vinegar) condiments on the table. Casual, cheerful, cool.

Out of town

Le Tres Bon

40 Malbon Street, Bungendore **(02) 6238 0662**
letresbon.com.au

At this idyllic French provincial restaurant in a cute village a short drive from the capital, Christophe Gregoire makes his own terrine, bread and even olive oil. Food is rustic: spice bread with foie gras, rabbit stew, and cassoulet with duck and pork sausage. Crepes suzette are sweet and lovely with cider.

Hobart

By Rodney Dunn

Chado - The Way of Tea

134 Elizabeth Street, Hobart **(03) 6231 6411**

Essentially a tea shop it is also a lunch destination serving sublime Japanese bento boxes with grilled local eel or spanking fresh sashimi using line-caught ikijime spiked fish. Look out for former Violent Femmes star Brian Ritchie's weekly afternoon music performances.

Garagistes

103 Murray Street, Hobart **(03) 6231 0558**
garagistes.com.au

Luke Burgess and team take the best ingredients in the state and transform them into some of the most innovative and exciting food in the country. Stunning, handmade plates from potter Ben Richardson add to the experience. No bookings.

Piccolo Restaurant & Wine Bar

323a Elizabeth Street, Hobart **(03) 6234 4844**

Piccolo by name and nature, this small nook of a restaurant serves up Italian food with heart. The pasta is always excellent, and the small bar is just the spot for sipping sangiovese or indulging a penchant for prosecco.

Pigeon Hole

93 Goulburn Street, West Hobart **(03) 6236 9306**

This tiny, hugely popular cafe punches well above its weight, producing a small but constantly changing list of soups and panini, dainty house-baked treats and good coffee. It's hard to go past the baked eggs for breakfast.

Remi de Provence

252 Macquarie Street, Hobart **(03) 6223 3933**
remideprovence.com.au

Larger-than-life restaurateur Remi Bancal combines his love of fine wine and the fare of his native France to create a warm dining experience suited to the chilliest Hobart evening. Think bubbling cassoulets and long-cooked daubes of beef.

The Stackings Restaurant

Peppermint Bay, 3435 Channel Highway, Woodbridge
(03) 6267 4088 peppermintbay.com.au

The mesmerising D'Entrecasteaux channel plays second fiddle only to the food here. Chef David Moyle's set-course, seasonally driven menu includes delights such as roasted pigeon with beetroot, and angelica and almond cake.

Sweet Envy

341 Elizabeth Street, North Hobart **(03) 6234 8805**
sweetenvy.com

Let the wonderful, whimsical minds of pastry chefs Alistair Wise and Teena Kearney take you into a sugar-induced coma of macarons, cupcakes and icecream. Look out for their pimped 1964 Commer Mr Whippy Van.

Written on Tea

Shop 6, 236 Sandy Bay Road, Hobart
(03) 6223 3298 writtenontea.com

This local favourite serves up northern-influenced Mandarin Chinese cuisine. It's hard not to over-order, but dumplings such as xiao long bao are a must, as are crisp spring-onion pancakes and dry-fried green beans with pork.

Launceston

Black Cow Bistro

70 George Street, Launceston **(03) 6331 9333**
blackcowbistro.com.au

There is no better location for an ode to Tasmanian beef than an old butcher's shop. At Black Cow it's all about the beef - grass-fed, dry-aged, cooked perfectly and served with simple sides and a bottle of good red.

Stillwater

Ritchie's Mill, 2 Bridge Road, Launceston
(03) 6331 4153 stillwater.net.au

Housed in the old Ritchies flour-mill building, Stillwater runs the gamut of breakfast, lunch and dinner seven days a week and admirably uses and promotes local ingredients such as Cape Grim beef, lobster, quail and rabbit.

Brisbane

By Natascha Mirosch

Aria

Eagle Street Pier, 1 Eagle Street, Brisbane
(07) 3233 2555 ariarestaurant.com.au

For deal brokers, date nights and big birthdays, Aria hits the right note. Service is smooth, the Story Bridge views iconic and the menu contemporary and sophisticated. The highly regarded wine list has some well-priced top-end bottles.

Bucci

15 James Street, Fortitude Valley **(07) 3852 3323**
buccirestaurant.com.au

Brisbane immediately fell for Bucci's lunch-at-nonna's vibe, and it feeds the love with a menu drawing inspiration from both sides of the butter/oil north/south Italian divide. Twice-cooked pig's trotter with salsa verde from the assaggini (share-plate) menu is becoming legendary among regulars.

1889 Enoteca

10–12 Logan Road, Woolloongabba **(07) 3392 4315**
1889enoteca.com.au

The patina of age in this wine store/restaurant may be a careful construct, but the remarkable Italian wine list is real. Whether wine or food is the star depends on you, but the signature dish of spaghetti with pecorino and pepper, and a glass of vermentino should help make up your mind.

Esquire

145 Eagle Street, Brisbane **(07) 3220 2123**
esquire.net.au

Scandinavian design sensibilities and river views pair with the choice of a speedier express char-grill section or a degustation option. Staff are well versed in a menu that changes with the seasons, chefs' whims and the tides. Expect highly innovative, precision-plated cuisine.

Ortiga

446 Brunswick Street, Fortitude Valley
(07) 3852 1155 ortiga.com.au

Beautiful, moody Ortiga does double duty – wine and tapas at street level or descend to the rustic beamed cellar and open kitchen where chef Pablo Tordesillas's modern Spanish menu delivers big on flavour and originality.

Public

Level 1, 400 George Street, Brisbane **(07) 3210 2288**
lovepublic.com.au

Public is an island of laissez-faire hipness in the laced-up legal district, but no one seems to care. Barristers and off-duty hospitality folk rub shoulders at the bar, happily perusing one of the city's kookiest cocktail lists. Flexible share-plates are cheekily frivolous and seriously sophisticated.

Spring

26 Felix Street, Brisbane **(07) 3229 0460**
spring.com.au

Spring brings a warmth rarely seen to Brisbane's corporate heartland. Take classes in a state-of-the-art cooking school; buy an expertly made coffee and sweetly packaged cake; or sample chef Kym Machin's produce-focused, seasonal menu in the stylish bistro.

Stokehouse

Sidon Street, South Bank **(07) 3013 0333**
stokehousebrisbane.com.au

The Stokehouse brand may have been transplanted from Melbourne but it's taken root very happily on the Brisbane riverside. Inside is all dark wood and soaring ceilings, with crisp white-clothed tables offering views of the water and the city skyline. Service is prescient, and chef Tony Kelly's food is urbane.

The Survey Co

32 Burnett Lane, Brisbane **(07) 3012 8725**
surveyco.com.au

Owner Simon Livingstone has his finger on Brisbane's pulse and recently diagnosed it in need of a laneway wine bar/bistro. An architect-designed fitout of urban edginess, softened by a courtyard garden, is the result. The well-priced European bistro menu is matched with a wine list where each is generously offered by the glass.

Tartufo

Emporium, 1000 Ann Street, Fortitude Valley
(07) 3852 1500 tartufo.com.au

Modern mixes it up with southern Italian classics at this exemplar of warm hospitality and fine food. Owner-chef Tony Percuoco keeps his eye on everything, frequently leaving the kitchen to check on diners' happiness levels. The menu changes with season and market availability but Kingaroy pork belly with mustard fruits is a fixture by popular demand.

Queensland resorts

Chill on Tedder

Shop 10, 26 Tedder Avenue, Main Beach
(07) 5528 0388 chillontedder.com.au

Refreshingly down-to-earth, this popular little bistro has a strong following. Owner-chef Daran Glasgow's ethos is produce-driven dishes with a European accent. Inside is understated and contemporary, but for people-watching the leafy courtyard's the spot.

Coast Restaurant & Bar

469 The Esplanade, Hervey Bay **(07) 4125 5454**
coastherveybay.com.au

Ex-e'cco young gun Nick Street-Brown and partner (pastry cook extraordinaire) Krista Graham's sea change to this quiet coastal village had locals toasting their luck. The casual ambience and laid-back service belie the quality of the contemporary menu starring local produce like sweet Hervey Bay scallops.

Harrison's

22 Wharf Street, Port Douglas **(07) 4099 4011**

Tables with proper starched cloths set around a verandah and tree-filled courtyard offer a cool green retreat from the tropical heat during the day, and a romantic setting for loved-up couples at night. The modern European food sets the bar high but never falters, and service is assured and knowledgeable.

The Long Apron

Spicer's Clovelly, 68 Balmoral Road, Montville
(07) 5452 1111 spicersgroup.com.au

The posh country-house surrounds give no clue to the cutting edge cuisine on the menu at this boutique hotel in the verdant Sunshine Coast hinterland. Chef Cameron Matthews' training is traditional but he takes the classic principles of cuisine and turns them on their head to create Heston-like dishes that will have you exclaiming like a delighted child.

Nu Nu

123 Williams Esplanade, Palm Cove **(07) 4059 1880**
nunu.com.au

With its billion-dollar view over a palm-fringed beach and turquoise Coral Sea, Nu Nu could serve up WWII ration packs and diners wouldn't give a toss. Which is why it deserves big plaudits for its amazing showcasing of beautiful north Queensland produce on a menu that is always fresh and inventive.

Seaduction

Sea Temple, Level 2, 8 The Esplanade, Surfers Paradise
(07) 5635 5700 seaduction.com.au

It can be difficult to stand out in the sea of neon and lame that is the Gold Coast, but Surfer's Paradise's Seaduction shines brightly. Chef Steve Szabo is ex-Vanitas at Palazzo Versace, so expect a bit of culinary bling on your plate. Polished service and tables with surf and sand views give extra sparkle.

Spicebar

Shop 4, 19 First Avenue, Mooloolaba **(07) 5444 2022**
spicebar.com.au

Fnd your way to this cool little backstreet pan-Asian eatery. From the elegant restraint of Japanese flavours to tastebud-shimmying Sichuan spice, eccentric plateware and a blackboard of globally roaming boutique wines it's a crazy mix that shouldn't work but does. Great food, great fun.

The Spirit House

20 Ninderry Road, Yandina **(07) 5446 8977**
spirithouse.com.au

Follow the scent of kaffir lime and lemongrass through lush tropical gardens to open-air pavilions around a lily pond. The Spirit House is a long-time temple of modern Thai – order two of everything, loosen your belt and take in the serenity. There are cooking classes, too.

Thomas Corner Eatery

Shop 1, 201 Gympie Terrace, Noosaville
(07) 5470 2224 thomascorner.com.au

Though a more casual venture than his previous restaurant (The River House), David Rayner hasn't compromised his ethos of using the highest quality produce with the lowest possible air miles. Thus the local bounty, from fresh herbs to spanner crab, is exploited to fine effect with an appealing menu of pared back cuisine promising 'no frills, froths or fancy garnishes'.

Wasabi

2 Quamby Place, Noosa Sound **(07) 5449 2443**
wasabisb.com

Suspended over the Noosa River, Wasabi is renowned for its inventive modern Japanese menu. Tuck yourself into a table in the tatami room or take a riverside seat, where shutters open to the breeze, and sample chef Hajime Horiguchi's pure flavours, precision knife techniques and the freshest local seafood.

Adelaide

By Nigel Hopkins

Celsius

95–97 Gouger Street, Adelaide **(08) 8231 6023**
celsiusrestaurant.com.au

Noma-trained chef Ayhan Erkoc scours the city's parklands for garden snails, chickweed, soursob (wood sorrel) and wild herbs for the most innovative cooking in town. We love his roast quail with foie gras wrapped in prosciutto, with licorice foam. Colourful, clever and delicious.

Chloe's

36 College Road, Kent Town **(08) 8362 2574**
chloes.com.au

When it comes to fine dining, Adelaide comes to Chloe's: a gorgeous 130-year-old bluestone mansion loaded with antiques, a cellar filled with well-aged treasures, and expertly executed contemporary dishes from chef Johnny Triscari, often with produce from the surrounding gardens and orchard.

Giallo

39a Rundle Street, Kent Town **(08) 8362 9006**
giallowinebar.com.au

Although Giallo can be cramped and noisy inside, its sheltered street-front courtyard is well protected from both elements and traffic, making it perfect for a summery lunch or dinner. Both the mod-Med menu and wine list are as cool as an Aperol spritzer.

Jasmin

31 Hindmarsh Square, Adelaide **(08) 8223 7837**
jasmin.com.au

Now in its 31st year, Jasmin is famed for its fiery chicken tindaloo and beef vindaloo, served in the quiet luxury of its basement dining room. It's a tribute to the elegance and subtlety of northern Indian cooking, with a wine list that disproves every theory about spices and matches.

Kenji

Shop 5, 242 Hutt Street, Adelaide **(08) 8232 0944**

Kenji Ito is a fully trained kaiseki chef whose masterly and often challenging approach delights Japanese culinary purists and adventurers alike. Dishes range from classic puffer fish to a more contemporary slow-cooked pork belly with steamed gyoza and green apple.

Press Food & Wine

40 Waymouth Street, Adelaide **(08) 8211 8048**
pressfoodandwine.com.au

Clever industrial chic rules downstairs, while the quieter upstairs dining room is for more leisurely grazing on Andrew Davies' tapas-style menu, marked into raw, offal, small plates, wood-grilled and more. The butcher's block just inside the front door sends a message about the no-nonsense approach.

Vincenzo's Cucina Vera

77 Unley Road, Parkside **(08) 8271 1000**
vincenzoscucinavera.com.au

They say they do things differently here. And chef Vincenzo LaMontagna certainly does, preparing individual degustation menus for each table. At its best, his creative take on Italian traditions is marvellous – think porcini 'steak' with gremolata and mozzarella foam – with almost everything made in-house, including stunning salumi.

Out of town

Appellation

The Louise, Seppeltsfield Road, Marananga
(08) 8562 4144 appellation.com.au

Passionate about Barossa produce, chef Mark McNamara pulls out all his culinary stops at the uber-luxurious Louise retreat in the Barossa. It's backed by a terrific wine list and a clientele that is prepared to wait up to a month for a booking.

Ferment Asian

90 Murray Street, Tanunda **(08) 8563 0765**
fermentasian.com.au

In a region steeped in old-fashioned German tradition, Ferment Asian is a breath of fresh Vietnamese air. Located in a handsome Tanunda bluestone villa, self-taught chef Tuoi Do draws on organic, locally grown produce for a modern take on traditional Vietnamese dishes.

Fino

8 Hill Street, Willunga **(08) 8556 4488** fino.net.au

If small is beautiful, then Fino's co-owner/sommelier Sharon Romeo has created a tight wine list that is close to perfection. Chef David Swain's regional menu is similarly brief and brilliant with dishes such as tommy ruff fillets with Willunga almonds.

Perth

By Megan Anderson

Barque

125 George Street, East Fremantle **(08) 9339 5524**
barquerestaurant.com.au

There's a warm welcome at this East Freo cottage, where a share-plate ethos adds celebratory atmosphere. Dishes have an Asian hint, like chilli salt squid, duck spring rolls and satay ribs, and a neat line in cocktails adds frisson to afternoons on the verandah.

Bivouac

198 William Street, Northbridge **(08) 9227 0883**
bivouac.com.au

This bar-cum-eatery doesn't shout – both signage and service are tastefully understated – but it is loud. So try for a table out front, and you won't miss out on exquisite chermoula-crusted goat chops, haloumi and watermelon salad or gnocchi with oxtail ragu.

Clarke's of North Beach

97 Flora Terrace, North Beach **(08) 9246 7621**
clarkesofnorthbeach.com.au

A classy yet comforting fine diner with spellbinding food. The degustation option solves the tussle between suckling pig and honey-roasted duck, and a BYO booze clause means if you bring something fancy, attentive waitstaff will decant it.

El Publico

511 Beaufort Street, Highgate **0418 187 708**
elpublico.com.au

Among the newest of Perth's authentic Mexican joints, El Publico blends urban-cool bar with punchy street food. Enamel plates bear dishes designed to share, like spiced quail, salmon and salsa tacos, and braised chicken. Add Sam's hot sauce to taste – there's plenty of tequila and mescal too.

Greenhouse

100 St Georges Terrace, Perth **(08) 9481 8333**
greenhouseperth.com

This city bistro has survived the hype of its sustainability premise – from roof-grown food to recycled bar stools – to become a reliable provider of well-imagined and executed meals. From Welsh rarebit at brekkie to barramundi wings at night, it has 'wholesome' and 'inventive' in sync.

Il Lido

88 Marine Parade, Cottesloe **(08) 9286 1111**

From beachside breakfast to mood-lit dinner, Il Lido defies the Aussie coastal stereotype and instead offers rustic flavours with a European groove. Think share tables, famed house-made pasta, ragu, risotto and slow-braised meats, friendly service, buzzy vibe.

Jackson's

483 Beaufort Street, Highgate **(08) 9328 1177**
jacksonsrestaurant.com.au

An oldie but a goodie. For classic, sophisticated dining with loved-up service, Neal Jackson's establishment keeps the bar high. Reliable for a special occasion, its impeccably presented dishes include Stilton bread-and-butter pudding with braised oxtail and beef cheek, Baldivis rabbit, and a famous Turkish delight souffle.

Petite Mort

225 Onslow Road, Shenton Park **(08) 9388 0331**
petitemort.com.au

The air is still rarefied at the site of the late, great Star Anise restaurant. This new kid is more hip – the dishes are entree-sized; the wine list comes on an iPad – but technique and flair in the kitchen keep it classic. Small, beautiful-to-behold plates like goat's cheese pithiviers and seared scallop with pig's head allow multiple dips into the modern French menu.

P'tite Ardoise Bistro

283 Beaufort Street, Highgate **(08) 9228 2008**
ptiteardoisebistro.com.au

Cheerful and serious at once, this is the go-to spot for great bistro fare with real live French bits: waiters have accents; snails are imported from the motherland; pastry is shaped like the Eiffel Tower. It's no gimmick though. Slate-plated meals are imbued with the flavours of Normandy, and the service is friendly.

Out of town

Margaret River Farm Shop

5962 Caves Road, Margaret River **(08) 9757 9684**

There are fancy winery restaurants, and then there's this low-key cafe where the simple fare – soup, tart, rillettes, gorgeous cakes – is the perfect antidote to a busy day of vineyard touring. Taste the wine, stock up on wild olives and lentils, and leave with a cut of property-grown lamb or pork.

SUBURB

CUISINE

CROATIAN

DALMATIAN

EASTERN EUROPEAN

EUROPEAN

FRENCH

GREEK

HISPANIC

IBERIAN

INDIAN

ITALIAN

ACCOMMODATION

BARS

BREAKFAST AVAILABLE

BYOs

FAMILY FRIENDLY

GOOD WINE LISTS

GOURMET CAFES

NEW ENTRIES

OPEN LATE

PRIVATE ROOMS

VEGETARIAN MENUS

VIEWS

WHEELCHAIR FRIENDLY

WINERIES

YUM CHA AVAILABLE

ALPHABETICAL

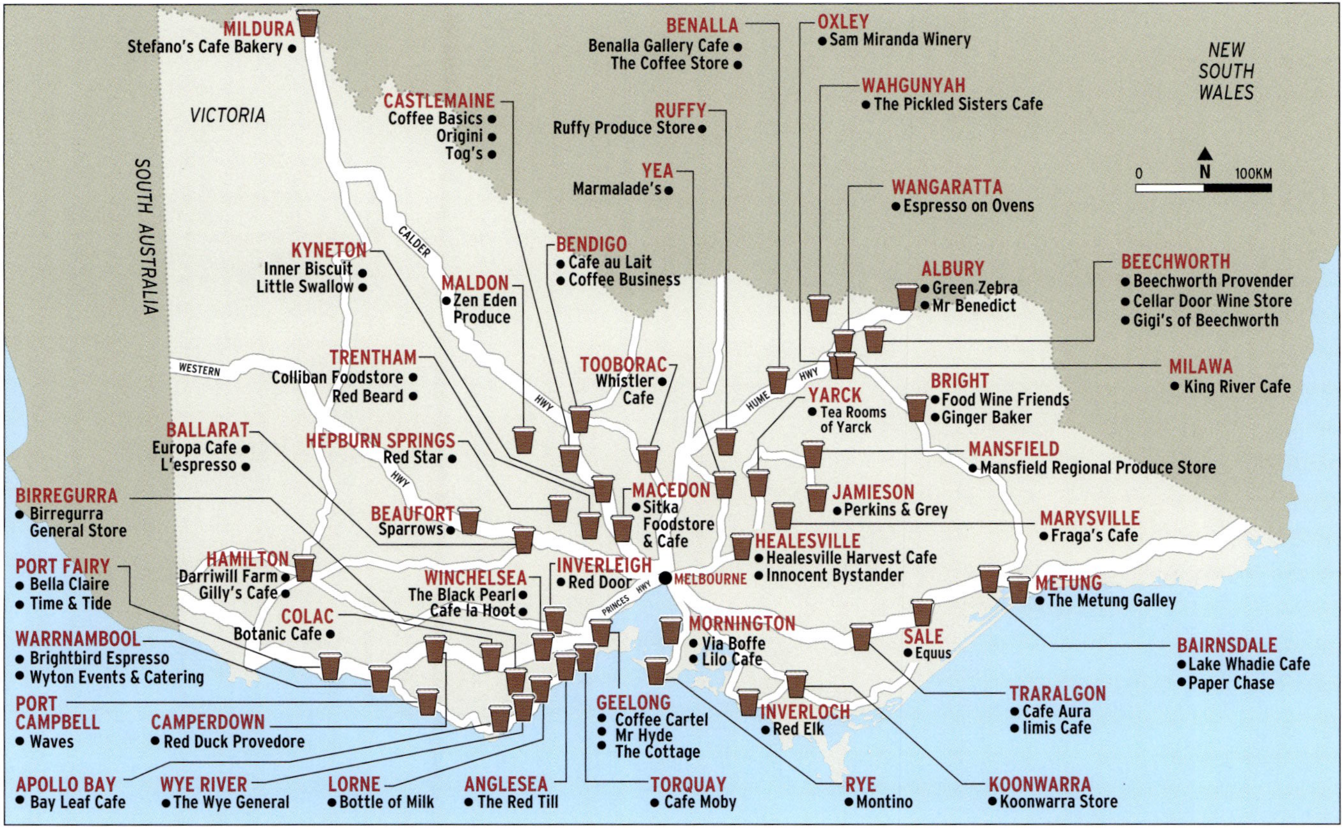
NEW SOUTH WALES
VICTORIA
SOUTH AUSTRALIA
0 N 100KM
MILDURA
Stefano's Cafe Bakery
CASTLEMAINE
Coffee Basics
Origini
Tog's
BENALLA
Benalla Gallery Cafe
The Coffee Store
RUFFY
Ruffy Produce Store
YEA
Marmalade's
OXLEY
Sam Miranda Winery
WAHGUNYAH
The Pickled Sisters Cafe
WANGARATTA
Espresso on Ovens
KYNETON
Inner Biscuit
Little Swallow
MALDON
Zen Eden Produce
BENDIGO
Cafe au Lait
Coffee Business
ALBURY
Green Zebra
Mr Benedict
BEECHWORTH
Beechworth Provender
Cellar Door Wine Store
Gigi's of Beechworth
TRENTHAM
Colliban Foodstore
Red Beard
TOOBORAC
Whistler Cafe
MILAWA
King River Cafe
YARCK
Tea Rooms of Yarck
BRIGHT
Food Wine Friends
Ginger Baker
BALLARAT
Europa Cafe
L'espresso
HEPBURN SPRINGS
Red Star
MANSFIELD
Mansfield Regional Produce Store
MACEDON
Sitka Foodstore & Cafe
JAMIESON
Perkins & Grey
BIRREGURRA
Birregurra General Store
BEAUFORT
Sparrows
MARYSVILLE
Fraga's Cafe
HEALESVILLE
Healesville Harvest Cafe
Innocent Bystander
PORT FAIRY
Bella Claire
Time & Tide
HAMILTON
Darriwill Farm
Gilly's Cafe
WINCHELSEA
The Black Pearl
Cafe la Hoot
INVERLEIGH
Red Door
MELBOURNE
METUNG
The Metung Galley
COLAC
Botanic Cafe
MORNINGTON
Via Boffe
Lilo Cafe
SALE
Equus
BAIRNSDALE
Lake Whadie Cafe
Paper Chase
WARRNAMBOOL
Brightbird Espresso
Wyton Events & Catering
PORT CAMPBELL
Waves
CAMPERDOWN
Red Duck Provedore
GEELONG
Coffee Cartel
Mr Hyde
The Cottage
INVERLOCH
Red Elk
TRARALGON
Cafe Aura
Iimis Cafe
APOLLO BAY
Bay Leaf Cafe
WYE RIVER
The Wye General
LORNE
Bottle of Milk
ANGLESEA
The Red Till
TORQUAY
Cafe Moby
RYE
Montino
KOONWARRA
Koonwarra Store
CALDER HWY
WESTERN HWY
HUME HWY
PRINCES HWY

COUNTRY COFFEE TRAIL

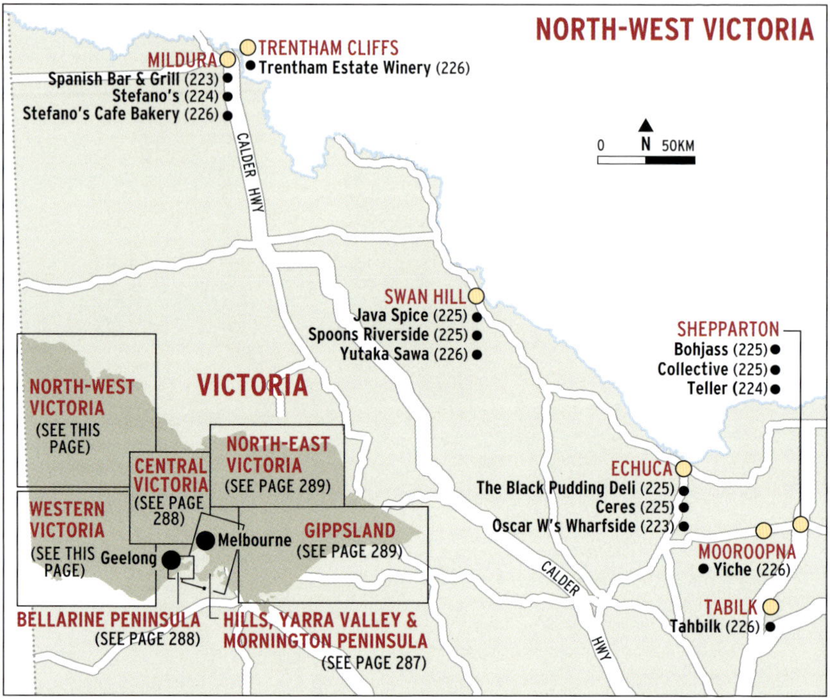
NORTH-WEST VICTORIA
TRENTHAM CLIFFS
Trentham Estate Winery (226)
MILDURA
Spanish Bar & Grill (223)
Stefano's (224)
Stefano's Cafe Bakery (226)
CALDER HWY
0 N 50KM
SWAN HILL
Java Spice (225)
Spoons Riverside (225)
Yutaka Sawa (226)
SHEPPARTON
Bohjass (225)
Collective (225)
Teller (224)
VICTORIA
NORTH-WEST VICTORIA (SEE THIS PAGE)
CENTRAL VICTORIA (SEE PAGE 288)
NORTH-EAST VICTORIA (SEE PAGE 289)
WESTERN VICTORIA (SEE THIS PAGE)
Melbourne
Geelong
GIPPSLAND (SEE PAGE 289)
BELLARINE PENINSULA (SEE PAGE 288)
HILLS, YARRA VALLEY & MORNINGTON PENINSULA (SEE PAGE 287)
ECHUCA
The Black Pudding Deli (225)
Ceres (225)
Oscar W's Wharfside (223)
MOOROOPNA
Yiche (226)
TABILK
Tahbilk (226)
CALDER HWY

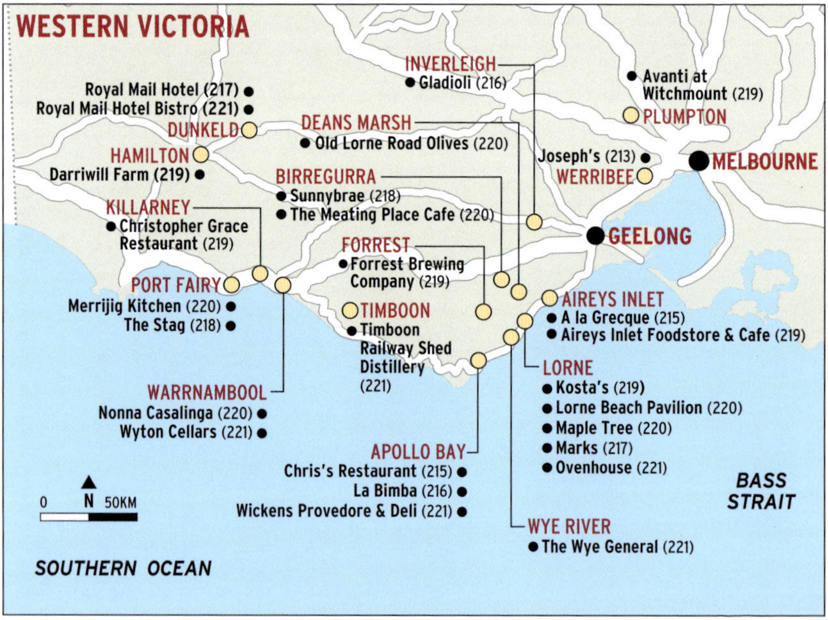
WESTERN VICTORIA
INVERLEIGH
Gladioli (216)
Avanti at Witchmount (219)
PLUMPTON
Royal Mail Hotel (217)
Royal Mail Hotel Bistro (221)
DUNKELD
DEANS MARSH
Old Lorne Road Olives (220)
HAMILTON
Darriwill Farm (219)
Joseph's (213)
WERRIBEE
MELBOURNE
BIRREGURRA
Sunnybrae (218)
The Meating Place Cafe (220)
KILLARNEY
Christopher Grace Restaurant (219)
GEELONG
FORREST
Forrest Brewing Company (219)
PORT FAIRY
Merrijig Kitchen (220)
The Stag (218)
TIMBOON
Timboon Railway Shed Distillery (221)
AIREYS INLET
A la Grecque (215)
Aireys Inlet Foodstore & Cafe (219)
LORNE
Kosta's (219)
Lorne Beach Pavilion (220)
Maple Tree (220)
Marks (217)
Ovenhouse (221)
WARRNAMBOOL
Nonna Casalinga (220)
Wyton Cellars (221)
APOLLO BAY
Chris's Restaurant (215)
La Bimba (216)
Wickens Provedore & Deli (221)
BASS STRAIT
0 N 50KM
WYE RIVER
The Wye General (221)
SOUTHERN OCEAN

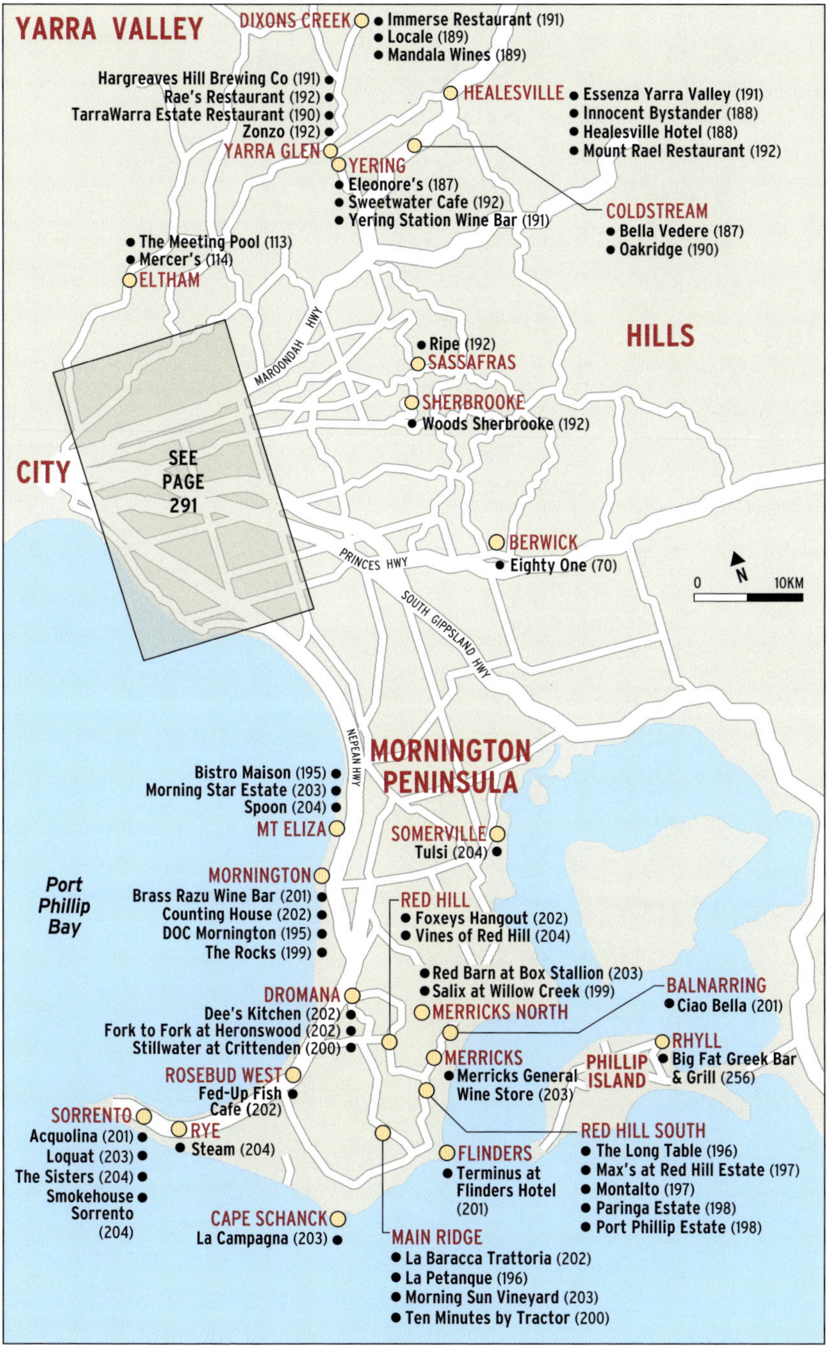

YARRA VALLEY
DIXONS CREEK
Immerse Restaurant (191)
Locale (189)
Mandala Wines (189)
Hargreaves Hill Brewing Co (191)
Rae's Restaurant (192)
TarraWarra Estate Restaurant (190)
Zonzo (192)
YARRA GLEN
HEALESVILLE
Essenza Yarra Valley (191)
Innocent Bystander (188)
Healesville Hotel (188)
Mount Rael Restaurant (192)
YERING
Eleonore's (187)
Sweetwater Cafe (192)
Yering Station Wine Bar (191)
COLDSTREAM
Bella Vedere (187)
Oakridge (190)
The Meeting Pool (113)
Mercer's (114)
ELTHAM
MAROONDAH HWY
HILLS
Ripe (192)
SASSAFRAS
SHERBROOKE
Woods Sherbrooke (192)
CITY
SEE PAGE 291
BERWICK
Eighty One (70)
PRINCES HWY
SOUTH GIPPSLAND HWY
N
0
10KM
NEPEAN HWY
MORNINGTON PENINSULA
Bistro Maison (195)
Morning Star Estate (203)
Spoon (204)
MT ELIZA
SOMERVILLE
Tulsi (204)
MORNINGTON
Brass Razu Wine Bar (201)
Counting House (202)
DOC Mornington (195)
The Rocks (199)
Port Phillip Bay
RED HILL
Foxeys Hangout (202)
Vines of Red Hill (204)
Red Barn at Box Stallion (203)
Salix at Willow Creek (199)
BALNARRING
Ciao Bella (201)
DROMANA
Dee's Kitchen (202)
Fork to Fork at Heronswood (202)
Stillwater at Crittenden (200)
MERRICKS NORTH
RHYLL
Big Fat Greek Bar & Grill (256)
MERRICKS
Merricks General Wine Store (203)
PHILLIP ISLAND
ROSEBUD WEST
Fed-Up Fish Cafe (202)
SORRENTO
Acquolina (201)
Loquat (203)
The Sisters (204)
Smokehouse Sorrento (204)
RYE
Steam (204)
RED HILL SOUTH
The Long Table (196)
Max's at Red Hill Estate (197)
Montalto (197)
Paringa Estate (198)
Port Phillip Estate (198)
FLINDERS
Terminus at Flinders Hotel (201)
CAPE SCHANCK
La Campagna (203)
MAIN RIDGE
La Baracca Trattoria (202)
La Petanque (196)
Morning Sun Vineyard (203)
Ten Minutes by Tractor (200)

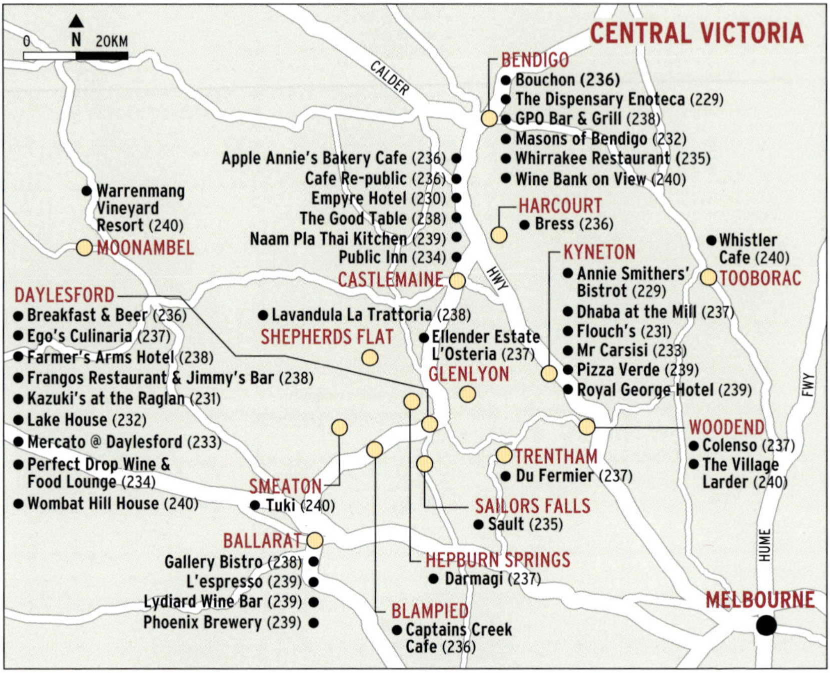
CENTRAL VICTORIA
0 N 20KM
CALDER
HWY
FWY
HUME
BENDIGO
Bouchon (236)
The Dispensary Enoteca (229)
GPO Bar & Grill (238)
Masons of Bendigo (232)
Whirrakee Restaurant (235)
Wine Bank on View (240)
Apple Annie's Bakery Cafe (236)
Cafe Re-public (236)
Empyre Hotel (230)
The Good Table (238)
Naam Pla Thai Kitchen (239)
Public Inn (234)
CASTLEMAINE
HARCOURT
Bress (236)
Warrenmang Vineyard Resort (240)
MOONAMBEL
KYNETON
Annie Smithers' Bistrot (229)
Dhaba at the Mill (237)
Flouch's (231)
Mr Carsisi (233)
Pizza Verde (239)
Royal George Hotel (239)
Whistler Cafe (240)
TOOBORAC
DAYLESFORD
Breakfast & Beer (236)
Ego's Culinaria (237)
Farmer's Arms Hotel (238)
Frangos Restaurant & Jimmy's Bar (238)
Kazuki's at the Raglan (231)
Lake House (232)
Mercato @ Daylesford (233)
Perfect Drop Wine & Food Lounge (234)
Wombat Hill House (240)
Lavandula La Trattoria (238)
SHEPHERDS FLAT
Ellender Estate L'Osteria (237)
GLENLYON
WOODEND
Colenso (237)
The Village Larder (240)
TRENTHAM
Du Fermier (237)
SMEATON
Tuki (240)
SAILORS FALLS
Sault (235)
BALLARAT
Gallery Bistro (238)
L'espresso (239)
Lydiard Wine Bar (239)
Phoenix Brewery (239)
HEPBURN SPRINGS
Darmagi (237)
BLAMPIED
Captains Creek Cafe (236)
MELBOURNE

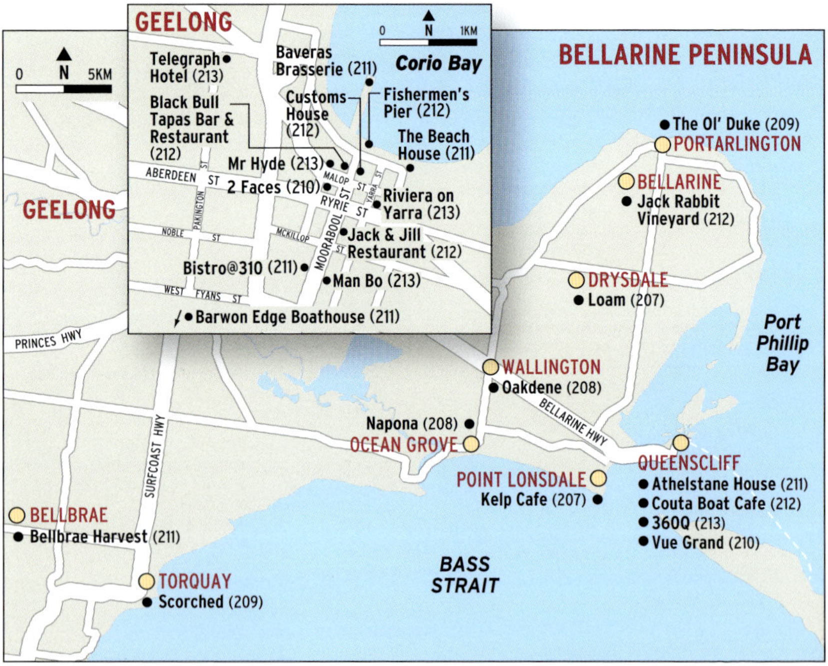
GEELONG
0 N 1KM
Corio Bay
Telegraph Hotel (213)
Baveras Brasserie (211)
Customs House (212)
Fishermen's Pier (212)
Black Bull Tapas Bar & Restaurant (212)
The Beach House (211)
Mr Hyde (213)
ABERDEEN ST
2 Faces (210)
MALOP ST
YARRA ST
RYRIE ST
Riviera on Yarra (213)
PAKINGTON ST
NOBLE ST
MCKILLOP ST
MOORABOOL ST
Jack & Jill Restaurant (212)
Bistro@310 (211)
Man Bo (213)
WEST FYANS ST
Barwon Edge Boathouse (211)
BELLARINE PENINSULA
0 N 5KM
GEELONG
PRINCES HWY
SURFCOAST HWY
BELLARINE HWY
The Ol' Duke (209)
PORTARLINGTON
BELLARINE
Jack Rabbit Vineyard (212)
DRYSDALE
Loam (207)
Port Phillip Bay
WALLINGTON
Oakdene (208)
Napona (208)
OCEAN GROVE
QUEENSCLIFF
Athelstane House (211)
Couta Boat Cafe (212)
360Q (213)
Vue Grand (210)
POINT LONSDALE
Kelp Cafe (207)
BELLBRAE
Bellbrae Harvest (211)
TORQUAY
Scorched (209)
BASS STRAIT

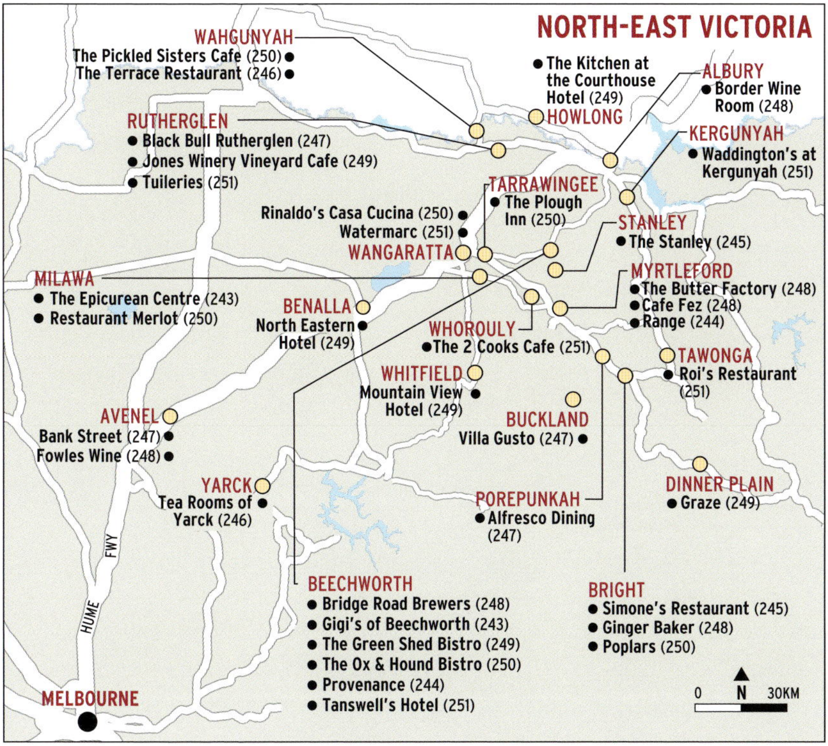
NORTH-EAST VICTORIA
WAHGUNYAH
The Pickled Sisters Cafe (250)
The Terrace Restaurant (246)
The Kitchen at the Courthouse Hotel (249)
HOWLONG
ALBURY
Border Wine Room (248)
RUTHERGLEN
Black Bull Rutherglen (247)
Jones Winery Vineyard Cafe (249)
Tuileries (251)
KERGUNYAH
Waddington's at Kergunyah (251)
TARRAWINGEE
The Plough Inn (250)
Rinaldo's Casa Cucina (250)
Watermarc (251)
WANGARATTA
STANLEY
The Stanley (245)
MILAWA
The Epicurean Centre (243)
Restaurant Merlot (250)
MYRTLEFORD
The Butter Factory (248)
Cafe Fez (248)
Range (244)
BENALLA
North Eastern Hotel (249)
WHOROULY
The 2 Cooks Cafe (251)
TAWONGA
Roi's Restaurant (251)
WHITFIELD
Mountain View Hotel (249)
AVENEL
Bank Street (247)
Fowles Wine (248)
BUCKLAND
Villa Gusto (247)
DINNER PLAIN
Graze (249)
YARCK
Tea Rooms of Yarck (246)
POREPUNKAH
Alfresco Dining (247)
HUME FWY
BEECHWORTH
Bridge Road Brewers (248)
Gigi's of Beechworth (243)
The Green Shed Bistro (249)
The Ox & Hound Bistro (250)
Provenance (244)
Tanswell's Hotel (251)
BRIGHT
Simone's Restaurant (245)
Ginger Baker (248)
Poplars (250)
MELBOURNE
0 N 30KM

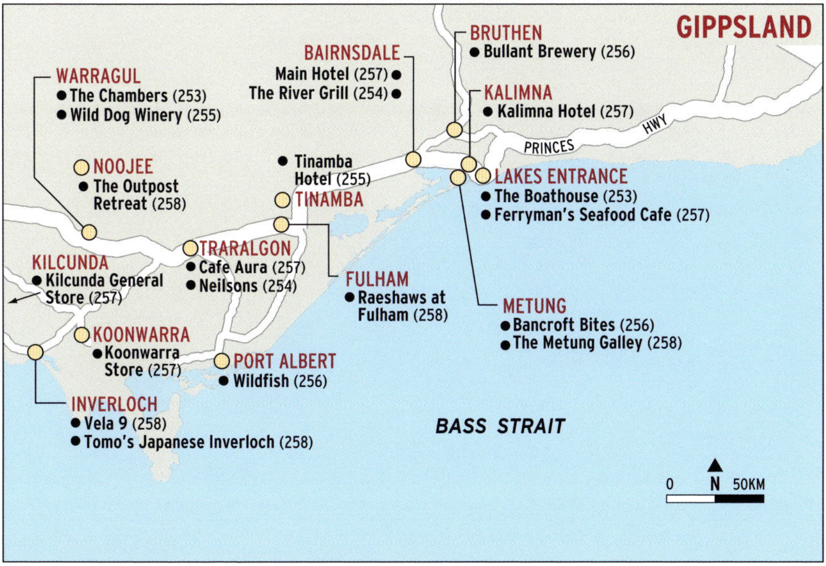
GIPPSLAND
BRUTHEN
Bullant Brewery (256)
BAIRNSDALE
Main Hotel (257)
The River Grill (254)
WARRAGUL
The Chambers (253)
Wild Dog Winery (255)
KALIMNA
Kalimna Hotel (257)
PRINCES HWY
NOOJEE
The Outpost Retreat (258)
Tinamba Hotel (255)
TINAMBA
LAKES ENTRANCE
The Boathouse (253)
Ferryman's Seafood Cafe (257)
TRARALGON
Cafe Aura (257)
Neilsons (254)
KILCUNDA
Kilcunda General Store (257)
FULHAM
Raeshaws at Fulham (258)
METUNG
Bancroft Bites (256)
The Metung Galley (258)
KOONWARRA
Koonwarra Store (257)
PORT ALBERT
Wildfish (256)
INVERLOCH
Vela 9 (258)
Tomo's Japanese Inverloch (258)
BASS STRAIT
0 N 50KM

INNER SOUTH-EASTERN SUBURBS

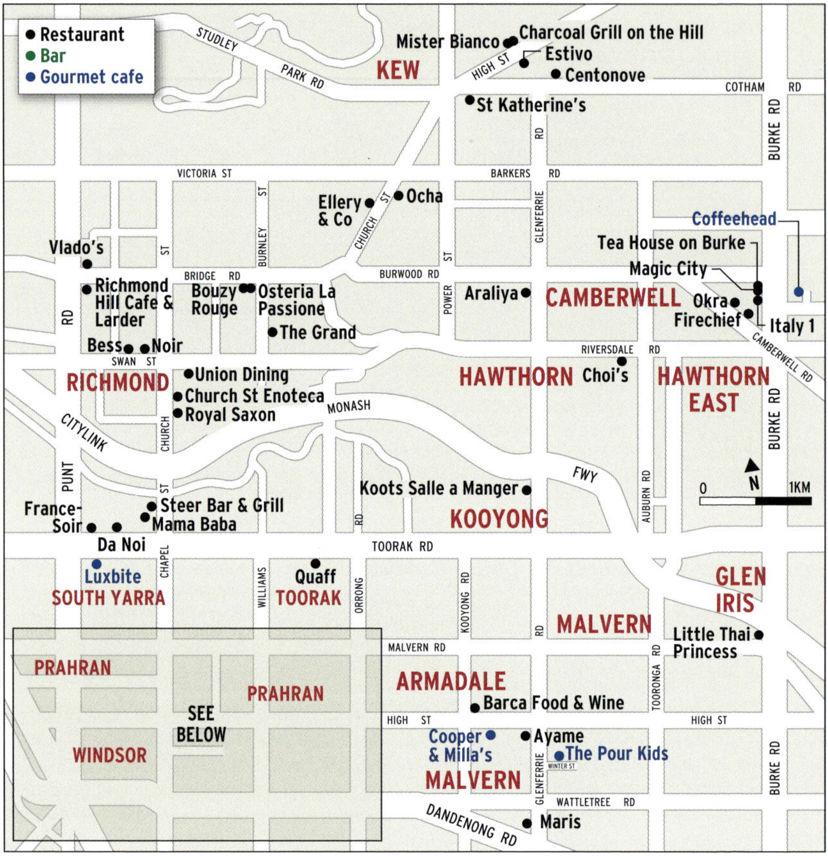
Restaurant
Bar
Gourmet cafe
KEW
Mister Bianco
Charcoal Grill on the Hill
Estivo
Centonove
St Katherine's
STUDLEY PARK RD
HIGH ST
COTHAM RD
BURKE RD
VICTORIA ST
BARKERS RD
GLENFERRIE RD
Ellery & Co
Ocha
CHURCH ST
BURNLEY ST
Vlado's
Richmond Hill Cafe & Larder
BRIDGE RD
Bouzy Rouge
Osteria La Passione
The Grand
BURWOOD RD
POWER ST
Araliya
CAMBERWELL
Coffeehead
Tea House on Burke
Magic City
Okra
Firechief
Italy 1
CAMBERWELL RD
Bess
Noir
SWAN ST
RICHMOND
Union Dining
Church St Enoteca
Royal Saxon
MONASH FWY
RIVERSDALE RD
HAWTHORN
Choi's
HAWTHORN EAST
CITYLINK
PUNT RD
CHURCH ST
Koots Salle a Manger
AUBURN RD
0
1KM
N
France-Soir
Steer Bar & Grill
Mama Baba
Da Noi
KOOYONG
TOORAK RD
Luxbite
SOUTH YARRA
CHAPEL ST
WILLIAMS RD
Quaff
TOORAK
ORRONG RD
KOOYONG RD
GLEN IRIS
MALVERN
Little Thai Princess
TOORONGA RD
MALVERN RD
PRAHRAN
ARMADALE
SEE BELOW
Barca Food & Wine
HIGH ST
WINDSOR
Cooper & Milla's
Ayame
The Pour Kids
WINTER ST
MALVERN
GLENFERRIE RD
WATTLETREE RD
DANDENONG RD
Maris

PRAHRAN & WINDSOR

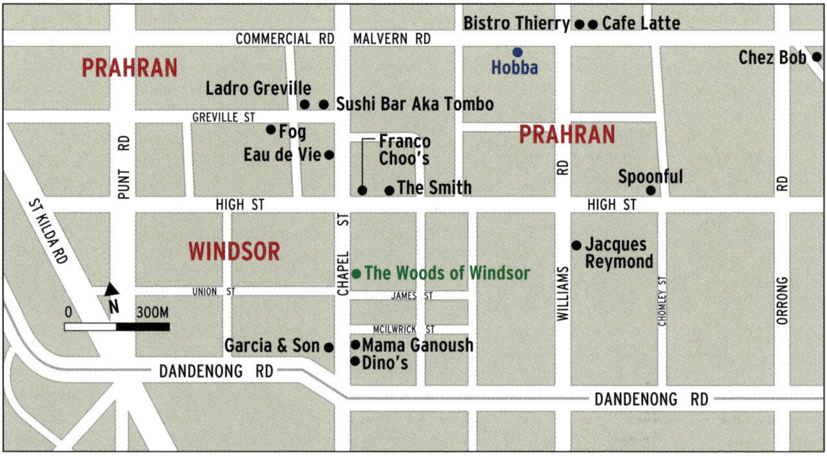
COMMERCIAL RD
MALVERN RD
Bistro Thierry
Cafe Latte
PRAHRAN
Hobba
Chez Bob
Ladro Greville
Sushi Bar Aka Tombo
GREVILLE ST
Fog
Eau de Vie
Franco Choo's
PRAHRAN
PUNT RD
The Smith
Spoonful
RD
HIGH ST
HIGH ST
ST KILDA RD
WINDSOR
CHAPEL ST
Jacques Reymond
The Woods of Windsor
UNION ST
JAMES ST
WILLIAMS
CHOMLEY ST
ORRONG
0
N
300M
MCILWRICK ST
Garcia & Son
Mama Ganoush
Dino's
DANDENONG RD
DANDENONG RD

Restaurant
Bar
Gourmet cafe
Miss Marie
THORNBURY
BELL ST
ST GEORGES RD
ROSANNA RD
BANKSIA ST
The Moor's Head
MANSFIELD ST
Kitschen Pantry
Otsumami
Vasko
Estelle Bar & Kitchen
Barrio
Va Tutto
Cafe Bedda
Merricote
STATION ST
Paladarr
Fifteen Pounds
IVANHOE
BULLEEN
TEMPLESTOWE
DONCASTER EAST
Tender Trap
BLACKBURN RD
HEIDELBERG
HIGH
FAIRFIELD
EASTERN FWY
BALWYN NORTH
DONCASTER RD
DONCASTER
The Firehouse
The Scented Garden Cafe
Ora
KEW
BURKE RD
BELMORE RD
BALWYN RD
Pure Italian
BOX HILL
MAROONDAH HWY
SEE PAGE 293
SEE PAGE 290
SEE PAGE 294
WHITEHORSE RD
Triple King
MONT ALBERT
SURREY HILLS
CANTERBURY RD
Wildflower
FOREST HILL
CANTERBURY
ELGAR RD
STATION ST
The Treasure Restaurant
PUNT RD
CAMBERWELL
WARRIGAL RD
BURWOOD HWY
TOORAK RD
BURWOOD EAST
SPRINGVALE RD
GLEN IRIS
HIGH ST
Preserve Kitchen
Livingroom
MALVERN EAST
MOUNT WAVERLEY
Shira Nui
Potsticker
BALACLAVA RD
Le Petit Bourgeois
CHADSTONE
GLEN WAVERLEY
Spout
RIPPONLEA
Attica
MONASH FWY
Siam 1
Sette Bello
GLEN HUNTLY RD
ELSTERNWICK
CARNEGIE
FERNTREE GULLY RD
Sails on the Bay
Arabesque
Bombay by Night
Oasis Bakery
PRINCES
NORTH RD
NORTH RD
WHEELERS HILL
Vivace
ST
BAY ST
NEW
Fabulous Fine Food
MCKINNON RD
Bok Choy Brighton
The Baths
McKINNON
CLAYTON
The Pantry
CLAYTON RD
HWY
CHURCH ST
Indian Palace
CENTRE RD
River Kwai
BENTLEIGH
Olie & Ari
BRIGHTON
WERE ST
JASPER RD
SOUTH RD
SOUTH RD
Os Kitchen & Wine Bar
HAMPTON
NEPEAN
SPRINGVALE
WARRIGAL RD
HIGHETT
BAY RD
Port Phillip Bay
BLUFF RD
BLACK ROCK
HWY
Cafeteria
BOUNDARY RD
SPRINGVALE RD
BALCOMBE RD
True South
BEAUMARIS
MENTONE
N
0
2KM

WEST MELBOURNE TO CARLTON NORTH

Restaurant
Bar
Gourmet cafe
0
N
500M
Albert St Food & Wine
Kumo Izakaya
Bar Idda
Rumi
Bishop of Ostia
BRUNSWICK
BRUNSWICK EAST
EDWARD ST
WESTON ST
BARKLY ST
SYDNEY RD
BRUNSWICK RD
FITZROY NORTH
PIGDON ST
SCOTCHMER ST
RICHARDSON ST
MACPHERSON ST
CARLTON NORTH
LYGON ST
Bistro Flor
Crafternoon
FENWICK ST
Gerald's Bar
The Kent Hotel
CURTAIN ST
STATION ST
NICHOLSON ST
ROYAL PDE
La Luna Bistro
PRINCES ST
RATHDOWNE ST
Scopri
GATEHOUSE ST
Markov Place
ELGIN ST
Abla's
Masani
Carlton Wine Room
Embrasse
FARADAY ST
DOC
CARLTON
FLEMINGTON RD
GRATTAN ST
GRATTAN ST
NORTH MELBOURNE
The Metropolitan Hotel
PELHAM ST
BERKELEY ST
Middle Fish
PEEL ST
CURZON ST
ERROL ST
The Courthouse
Hotel Lincoln
QUEENSBERRY ST
QUEENSBERRY ST
The Crimean
ELIZABETH ST
SWANSTON ST
CARDIGAN ST
LYGON ST
DRUMMOND ST
RATHDOWNE ST
NICHOLSON ST
Roller Door Cafe
Sosta Cucina
Libertine
VICTORIA ST
VICTORIA ST
WEST MELBOURNE
KING ST
SPENCER ST
SEE PAGE 296
CITY

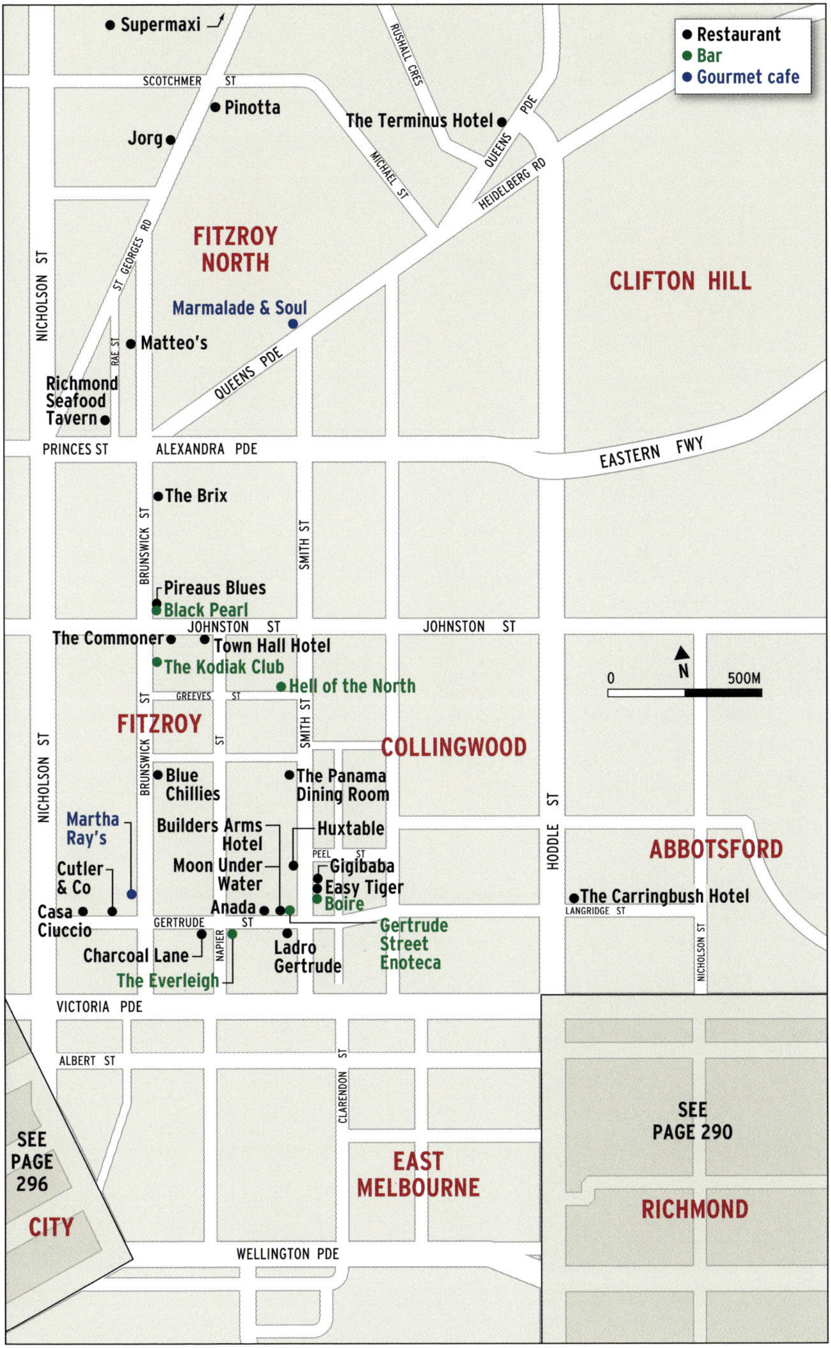

Restaurant
Bar
Gourmet cafe
Supermaxi
SCOTCHMER ST
Pinotta
Jorg
The Terminus Hotel
RUSHALL CRES
MICHAEL ST
QUEENS PDE
HEIDELBERG RD
FITZROY NORTH
ST GEORGES RD
NICHOLSON ST
CLIFTON HILL
Marmalade & Soul
Matteo's
RAE ST
QUEENS PDE
Richmond Seafood Tavern
PRINCES ST
ALEXANDRA PDE
EASTERN FWY
The Brix
BRUNSWICK ST
SMITH ST
Pireaus Blues
Black Pearl
JOHNSTON ST
JOHNSTON ST
The Commoner
Town Hall Hotel
The Kodiak Club
Hell of the North
0
N
500M
GREEVES ST
FITZROY
COLLINGWOOD
Blue Chillies
The Panama Dining Room
Martha Ray's
Builders Arms Hotel
Huxtable
HODDLE ST
ABBOTSFORD
PEEL ST
Cutler & Co
Moon Under Water
Gigibaba
Easy Tiger
Boire
The Carringbush Hotel
LANGRIDGE ST
Casa Ciuccio
Anada
GERTRUDE ST
Gertrude Street Enoteca
NAPIER ST
Charcoal Lane
Ladro Gertrude
NICHOLSON ST
The Everleigh
VICTORIA PDE
ALBERT ST
CLARENDON ST
SEE PAGE 290
SEE PAGE 296
EAST MELBOURNE
RICHMOND
CITY
WELLINGTON PDE

ST KILDA TO ELWOOD

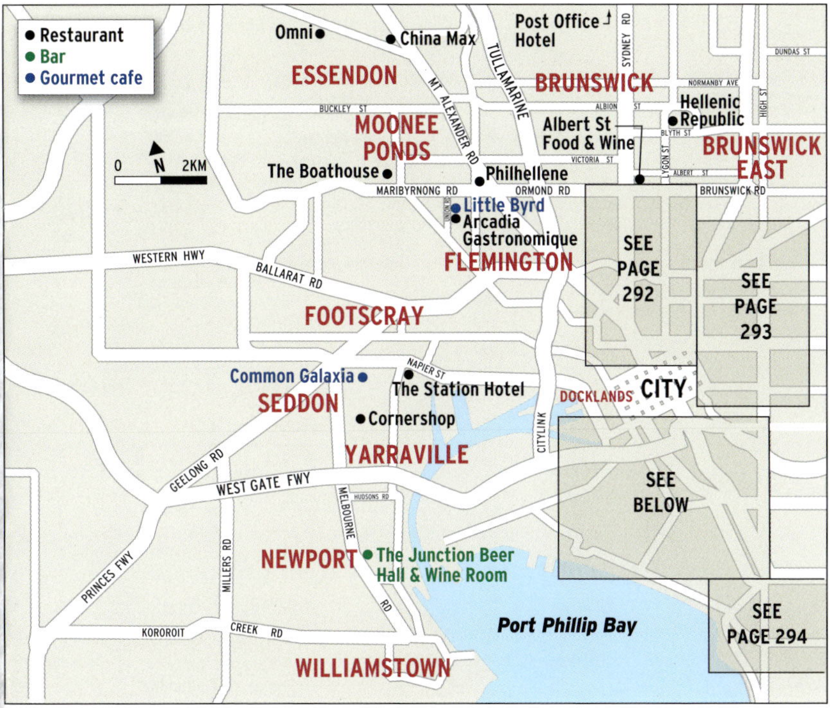

● Restaurant
● Bar
● Gourmet cafe
0 N 2KM
Omni
China Max
Post Office Hotel
ESSENDON
BRUNSWICK
MOONEE PONDS
Hellenic Republic
Albert St Food & Wine
BRUNSWICK EAST
The Boathouse
Philhellene
Little Byrd
Arcadia Gastronomique
FLEMINGTON
SEE PAGE 292
SEE PAGE 293
FOOTSCRAY
Common Galaxia
SEDDON
The Station Hotel
DOCKLANDS
CITY
Cornershop
YARRAVILLE
SEE BELOW
NEWPORT
The Junction Beer Hall & Wine Room
Port Phillip Bay
SEE PAGE 294
WILLIAMSTOWN
TULLAMARINE
MT ALEXANDER RD
SYDNEY RD
DUNDAS ST
NORMANBY AVE
ALBION ST
BUCKLEY ST
BLYTH ST
HIGH ST
LYGON ST
VICTORIA ST
ALBERT ST
MARIBYRNONG RD
ORMOND RD
BRUNSWICK RD
UNION RD
WESTERN HWY
BALLARAT RD
NAPIER ST
CITYLINK
GEELONG RD
WEST GATE FWY
HUDSONS RD
MELBOURNE RD
PRINCES FWY
MILLERS RD
KOROROIT CREEK RD

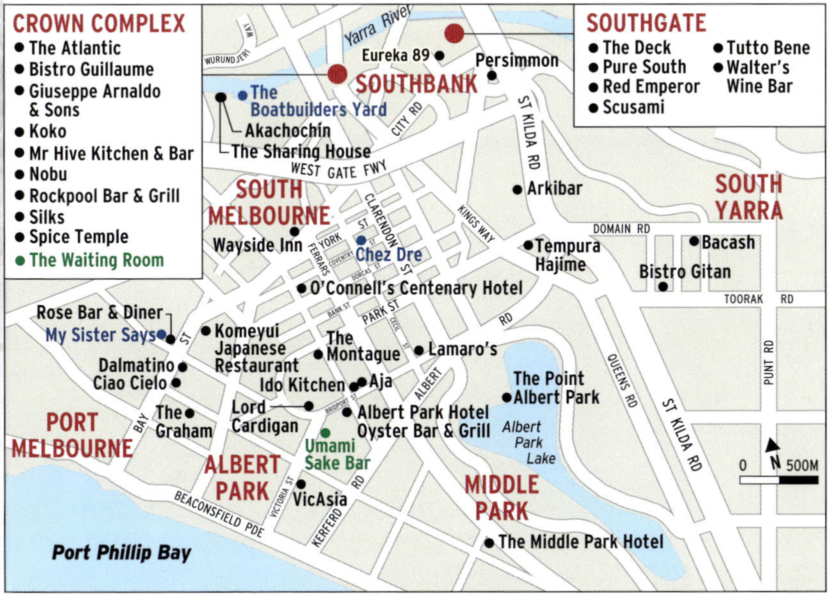

CROWN COMPLEX
The Atlantic
Bistro Guillaume
Giuseppe Arnaldo & Sons
Koko
Mr Hive Kitchen & Bar
Nobu
Rockpool Bar & Grill
Silks
Spice Temple
The Waiting Room
SOUTHGATE
The Deck
Pure South
Red Emperor
Scusami
Tutto Bene
Walter's Wine Bar
Yarra River
Eureka 89
Persimmon
SOUTHBANK
The Boatbuilders Yard
Akachochin
The Sharing House
WEST GATE FWY
CITY RD
ST KILDA RD
Arkibar
SOUTH YARRA
SOUTH MELBOURNE
Wayside Inn
Chez Dre
Tempura Hajime
Bacash
Bistro Gitan
O'Connell's Centenary Hotel
DOMAIN RD
TOORAK RD
Rose Bar & Diner
My Sister Says
Komeyui Japanese Restaurant
The Montague
Lamaro's
Dalmatino
Ciao Cielo
Ido Kitchen
Aja
The Point Albert Park
The Graham
Lord Cardigan
Albert Park Hotel Oyster Bar & Grill
Albert Park Lake
PORT MELBOURNE
Umami Sake Bar
ALBERT PARK
VicAsia
MIDDLE PARK
The Middle Park Hotel
Port Phillip Bay
0 N 500M
WURUNDJERI WAY
CLARENDON ST
KINGS WAY
YORK ST
FERRARS ST
COVENTRY ST
DORCAS ST
BANK ST
PARK ST
CECIL ST
ALBERT RD
BAY ST
BRIDPORT ST
VICTORIA ST
KERFERD RD
BEACONSFIELD PDE
QUEENS RD
ST KILDA RD
PUNT RD

MELBOURNE CITY

Restaurant
Bar
Gourmet cafe
SPRING ST
EXHIBITION ST
RUSSELL ST
SWANSTON ST
ELIZABETH ST
QUEEN ST
WILLIAM ST
KING ST
SPENCER ST
LA TROBE ST
LITTLE LONSDALE ST
LONSDALE ST
LITTLE BOURKE ST
BOURKE ST
BOURKE ST MALL
LITTLE COLLINS ST
COLLINS ST
FLINDERS LA
FLINDERS ST
PUNCH LA
LIVERPOOL ST
CROSSLEY ST
MEYERS PL
MARKET LA
ALFRED PL
MALTHOUSE LA
GEORGE PDE
MELB. PL
WARATAH PL
ARTEMIS LA
HEFFERNAN LA
CELESTIAL AVE
TATTERSALLS LA
RUSSELL PL
HOSIER LA
DREWERY LA
DEGRAVES ST
RANKINS LA
GILLS LA
BLIGH
HARDWARE LA
MCKILLOP ST
BOND ST
BANK PL
MARKET ST
Siglo
City Wine Shop
European
Takumi
Mezzo
Punch Lane
Longrain
Bamboo House
Kuni's
Becco
Gingerboy
Wallis & Ed
Society
San Telmo
Senoritas
Lupino
Bar Lourinha
Kenzan
Mamasita
No35
Pei Modern
Cumulus Inc
Bottega
Grossi Florentino
Grossi Florentino Grill
Cecconi's Cantina
The Press Club
The French Brasserie
EDV Melbourne
The Aylesbury
The Aylesbury Rooftop
Seamstress
Nihonbashi Zen
Mahjong Black
Collins Quarter
Papa Goose
The Italian
Il Solito Posto
Chin Chin
Shoya
Flower Drum
Mask of China
Comme
Oli & Levi
Saint Peter's
Yu-u
Coda
Izakaya Den
PM24
Il Bacaro
Sarti
Bar Ampere
Yak Bar
Pasta Artigianale
MoVida
Ezard
Bistrot d'Orsay
CITY
FEDERATION SQUARE
Bokchoy Tang
Chocolate Buddha
Taxi Dining Room
Cookie
The Toff in Town
Money Order Office
Bar Americano
Journal Canteen
Manchester Press
The Deanery
Hako
Gills Diner
Red Spice Road
Maha
Bluestone Restaurant
Quanjude
Caterina's Cucina e Bar
Bistro Vue
Threefold
Syracuse
Benito's
MoVida Aqui
Henry & the Fox
Merchant Osteria Veneta
The Lui Bar
Vue de Monde
Hare & Grace
Sud
Hanabishi
0
200M
N